INTELLIGENCE POLICY AND NATIONAL SECURITY

INSTITUTE FOR FOREIGN POLICY ANALYSIS, INC.
675 MASSACHUSETTS AVE.
CENTRAL PLAZA BLDG.
10th FLOOR
CAMBRIDGE, MASSACHUSETTS 02139

INTELLIGENCE POLICY AND NATIONAL SECURITY

Edited by

Robert L. Pfaltzgraff, Jr

Uri Ra'anan

and

Warren Milberg

ARCHON BOOKS
HAMDEN, CONNECTICUT

First published 1981 in the UK by
THE MACMILLAN PRESS LTD
London and Basingstoke
and in the USA as an Archon Book,
an imprint of
THE SHOESTRING PRESS INC.
995 Sherman Avenue
Hamden, Connecticut 06514

Printed in Hong Kong

Library of Congress Cataloging in Publication Data

Main entry under title:

Intelligence policy and national security.
  Expanded and updated papers from a conference held
during Apr. 1979, sponsored by the International Security
Studies Program of the Fletcher School of Law and Diplo-
macy, together with additional material.
  Includes bibliographical references and index.
  1. Military intelligence.   2. National security.
I. Ra'anan, Uri, 1926-   . II. Pfaltzgraff, Robert L.
III. Milberg, Warren. IV. Fletcher School of Law and
Diplomacy, Medford, Mass.   International Security Studies
Program.
UB250.I57   1981   355.3'432   80-28577
ISBN 0-208-01918-9

Table of Contents

v

Notes on the Editors and the Contributors

THE EDITORS

Robert L. Pfaltzgraff, Jr, is Professor of International Politics and a Member of the International Security Studies Program, the Fletcher School of Law and Diplomacy. He is also Director of the Institute for Foreign Policy Analysis, Cambridge, Massachusetts.

Uri Ra'anan is Professor of International Politics and Chairman of the International Security Studies Program at The Fletcher School of Law and Diplomacy.

Lt Col. Warren Milberg, USAF, is a member of the Issues Team, Office of the Air Force Vice Chief of Staff.

THE CONTRIBUTORS

Richard K. Betts is a Research Associate in the Foreign Policy Studies Program of The Brookings Institution, Washington, DC.

Ladislav Bittman spent fourteen years with the Czechoslovak intelligence service; following the Soviet invasion of Czechoslovakia, in August 1968, he was granted political asylum in the United States. At present, he is Associate Professor of Journalism at the School of Public Communication, Boston University.

Albert Carnesale is Professor of Public Policy at the John F. Kennedy School of Government and also Associate Director of the Center for Science and International Affairs, Harvard University.

William E. Colby is former Director of the Central Intelligence Agency and, at present, is a member of the law firm of Colby, Miller and Haynes, Washington, DC.

John Erickson is the Director of Defence Studies at the University of Edinburgh, Scotland.

Patrick J. Friel is President of the consulting firm, Friel and Company, Inc., Lincoln, Massachusetts.

Michael I. Handel is Research Associate at the Center for International Affairs, Harvard University, Cambridge, Massachusetts.

Reginald V. Jones, author and former Director of British Scientific Intelligence during the Second World War, is now Professor in the Department of Natural Philosophy, University of Aberdeen, Scotland.

Amrom Katz, formerly Assistant Director for Verification and Analysis, of the US Arms Control and Disarmament Agency, is now a consultant.

Thomas K. Latimer is Staff Director, House Permanent Select Committee on Intelligence, US House of Representatives.

Richard Mancke is Associate Professor of International Economic Relations and a Member of the International Security Studies Program at The Fletcher School of Law and Diplomacy.

Richard Perle is Assistant Secretary of Defence (for National Security Affairs).

Richard Pipes is a member of the staff of the United States National Security Council.

Ithiel de Sola Pool is the Arthur and Ruth Sloan Professor of Political Science at the Massachusetts Institute of Technology.

Clarence A. Robinson, Jr, is Senior Military Editor of *Aviation Week and Space Technology*, Washington, DC.

John P. Roche is a former Special Consultant to President Lyndon Johnson (1966–68), and is now a syndicated columnist and Henry R. Luce Professor of Civilization and Foreign Affairs at the Fletcher School of Law and Diplomacy.

Edgar Ulsamer is Senior Editor of *Air Force Magazine*, Washington, DC.

Major General Jasper A. Welch, Jr, USAF, is Special Assistant to the Chief of Staff, US Air Force.

Roberta Wohlstetter is an eminent author, historian and scholar.

Introduction

The seeds of this volume were planted at the Eighth Annual Conference of the International Security Studies Program of The Fletcher School of Law and Diplomacy, during April 1979, in Cambridge, Massachusetts. That gathering brought together, within the parameters of a working symposium practitioners, former officials, and theorists, drawn from the governmental, private, and academic policy 'communities'. Several of the approximately 70 participants pointed out that this seemed to be the only forum for creative interaction between the various sectors.

Meeting under the formal heading of 'Intelligence: Deception and Surprise', the Conference furnished an unusual opportunity for examining issues, such as: the adequacy of existing, and former, organisational structures to cope with increasing demands by decision makers for adequate intelligence; the closely related issues of command and control; the problem of political and strategic warning; and the numerous political and psychological–perceptual–cultural factors impinging upon intelligence gathering and evaluation. Moreover, special sessions were devoted to specific, including technological, problems affecting assessments of the correlation of forces between the Soviet Union and the United States, within SALT II and beyond, as well as such purely American issues as the roles, respectively, of the Executive and of Congress in intelligence gathering and evaluation.

However, helpful as this gathering was in establishing a broad conceptual framework and in providing the insight offered by the eye-witness accounts of former practitioners (from our own 'community', as well as refugees from 'the other side'), the editors of this volume felt that much more was attainable. Consequently, the contributions of participants (both discussants and those who presented papers) were expanded and updated, while additional chapters were commissioned to deal with aspects inadequately covered at the Conference.

The final product, assembled in these pages, addresses itself to the examples of history, as analysed by Professor Reginald V. Jones and Dr Roberta Wohlstetter; to the contributions of the social sciences, reviewed by Professor Ithiel de Sola Pool; to the conceptual and technological problems besetting our assessments of adversaries, especially the USSR, as presented by Professors John Erickson, Richard Pipes, and Uri Ra'anan, as well as by Mr William Colby and

Dr Patrick J. Friel; to the complexities of verification relating to SALT II, as viewed by Major-General Jasper A. Welch, Mr Richard Perle, Professor Albert Carnesale and Dr Amrom Katz; to the technological ingredients of surprise, as discussed by Mr Clarence Robinson, Mr Edgar Ulsamer, and Dr Patrick J. Friel; to the political and psychological factors involved, as interpreted by Dr Michael Handel and Professor Ladislav Bittman; to the economic aspects of intelligence, as seen by Professor Richard B. Mancke; and to the issue of intelligence management, with contributions by Professor John P. Roche, Mr Richard K. Betts, Mr Thomas K. Latimer, and Lieutenant-Colonel Warren H. Milberg. Finally, the implications for United States policy in the 1980s are set out by Professor Robert L. Pfaltzgraff.

It is the belief of the editors that, despite the attempt to focus this study upon the relatively confined topic of 'Deception and Surprise', rather than 'Intelligence', as a whole, not one, but several, volumes could be devoted to this aspect alone, without exhausting the material available. Consequently, there is no pretence that the present book, in any sense, can be *the* 'definitive work'.

Nevertheless, it is our hope that this compendium may prove to be a useful base for further studies in depth of such a fascinating subject (with all its complexities) as the focus of the present work.

The editors would like to take this opportunity to express their deep appreciation to the Scaife Family Charitable Trusts and the Sarah Mellon Scaife Foundation for their generous support to The Fletcher School in general, its International Security Studies Program in particular, and to the Conference which proved to be the catalyst for this book. Gratitude is also due to the new Dean of the Fletcher School, Theodore L. Eliot, Jr, whose support and understanding make possible the continued momentum of the Program.

ROBERT L. PFALTZGRAFF, JR
URI RA'ANAN
WARREN H. MILBERG
Medford, MA

Part One

Overview: What has been Learned?

1 Intelligence and Deception

Reginald V. Jones

DECEPTION IN THE NATURAL WORLD

If we accept that good intelligence is essential to successful action, it follows that intelligence will tend to invoke deception on the part of an ingenious adversary, with the object of leading up to a surprise which he can turn to advantage. And before we consider the problem in the military and political spheres it may be illuminating to look at some manifestations in the natural world. 'Illuminating' is indeed a suitable term for our first example, because it concerns fireflies; these have been discovered to flash their lights as sexual recognition signals, each species having its own characteristic sequence of flashes. It has further been established[1] that female flies of the species *photuris versicolor* lure the males of other species by mimicking the recognition signals emitted by the females of those species. The unfortunate males, duped into thinking that they are homing on females of their own kind, are then caught and devoured.

Sex is exploited, too, by Bolas spiders which, instead of spinning a web, let down a single thread at the end of which is a sticky ball. As a moth of the fall armyworm, *spodoptera frugiperda* flies past, the spider swings the ball at it, and depending on the accuracy of the aim the ball sticks to the moth and the spider then climbs down the thread and eats it. But how is the moth tempted to fly near enough to be caught? The answer appears to be that the spider can manufacture a volatile substance which mimics the female attractant scent of the armyworm moth, which the male uses as its major source of information that there is a female somewhere upwind, and so homes on the decoy.[2]

Many other examples can be found in the natural world where the victim is deceived into a trap set by the predator, in the belief that it is about to satisfy its sexual or gastronomic appetite. The angler fish of the *antennarius genus*, for example, camouflages itself as a rock or sponge and waggles in front of its mouth a lure that looks very like a small fish which even simulates the undulations of a swimming fish, and thus

3

successfully attracts would-be predators which are themselves devoured.[3]

These three examples illustrate how deception exploits the means of intelligence used by the victim. The first two depend on the fact that the victim is using one channel of information only – light flashes in the case of the firefly, which cannot see the actual form of the mating female until too late, and scent in the armyworm moth which might be able to recognise visually that it had homed in on a false target if the latter were fixed, but is then caught because at the last moment the spider has turned the target into a missile. With the angler fish the main channel of information is visual, but it is possible that the undulations produced in the lure then generate pressure waves simulating a genuine fish in the hydrodynamic as well as in the visual medium, so consistent symptoms are given in the two different channels.

HOAXES

Deception becomes more complicated as the number of channels of information available to the victim increases, since consistent symptoms should ideally be given in all available channels. This is why it is relatively easy to hoax victims over the telephone. If all the information that the victim has available are the sounds he hears over the telephone, and if he can be persuaded to depend on them, he can with little difficulty be led into such ridiculous actions as putting his telephone into a bucket of water in the belief that he is cooperating with the distant telephone engineer in an effort to establish the location of a leak to earth.

One of the most exquisite of telephone hoaxes known to me was one contrived by Dr Carl Bosch when he was a research student in Germany. He happened to work in a laboratory situated several floors up, where from his window he found that he could survey a block of flats across the road. Having discovered that the occupant of one of the flats was a newspaper correspondent, Bosch telephoned him pretending to be his own professor. Excitedly he explained to the correspondent that he had just invented a marvellous system of television (the date was 1933) which you could clip on to an ordinary telephone set, look into it and see the man that you were speaking to at the other end. Of course, the newspaper man was incredulous. The 'professor' then offered to demonstrate the system to him, inviting him to point the telephone towards the middle of his room, then stand in front of it and do anything that he liked, such as standing on one leg, after which the 'professor' would tell him what he had done. The result was a rave article in the local newspaper, an embarrassed newspaperman, and an astonished 'professor'.

TECHNICAL DECEPTION IN WAR

The very situation conjured up by the foregoing example illustrates my point: if television were available alongside a telephone, the hoaxer would not only have to simulate the vocal character of the being he aims to impersonate, but the visual character as well, which would make his task much more difficult. Let us extend this to two examples of technical deceit in warfare. The first (and older) example is the development of countermeasures to the naval mine, which was originally a contact device depending on the differences of inertia between a ship and the water in which it moves. When the magnetic mine was introduced, depending on the modification to the earth's magnetic field produced by the presence of the ship, it had to be countered either by producing changes of magnetic field simulating the presence of a ship and thereby causing the mine to explode when no ship was present, or by so neutralising the magnetic field of a genuine ship that the mine failed to operate. When the pressure-wave mine was developed, depending on the reduction of local pressure when a moving body passed nearby, it was not enough to take magnetic countermeasures, so some form of pressure-simulating device had to be employed. Similarly, further triggering devices could be made to function on the light obscured or the sound emitted by a ship overhead, and assuming that a mine could be made that would only explode if appropriate systems appeared in all channels – magnetic, acoustic, optical, and hydrodynamic – then it could only be deceived by a device which had many of the characteristics of a genuine ship, and which would take a comparable effort to construct.

The second example is the development of countermeasures in the Second World War to prevent a controller of fighter defences from detecting the approach of incoming bombers. Apart from the tactic of flying the bombers low enough to avoid giving signals to the defending radar system, it was virtually impossible in the Second World War to avoid signals appearing on the defending cathode-ray screens and thus indicating that bombers were present. In that case, an obvious countermeasure was to give so many spurious signals that the defending controller would not be able to recognise the genuine bomber among the many signals which his radar system was showing. This followed the precept that the best way of hiding a pebble is to place it on a beach. So what we had to do was to create a radar 'beach' on which all the pebbles looked more or less alike; and owing to the particular properties of radar it was possible to simulate the echo from an aircraft simply by ejecting a relatively small packet of metal foil strips, window 'or chaff'. We could thus saturate the German radar screens so that the bombers were in effect obscured.

This device, however, could be defeated by a thoughtful enemy. The efficiency of the metal strips depended on resonance, which would occur only on a narrow band of frequencies. If the defences could change their frequencies, the difference between the packets of foil and an aircraft would be apparent, for the former would now be far less reflective. As the defences multiplied their frequencies, the strips had to be cut to many different lengths, and the defences in turn had to seek for a further difference. This was not difficult to find, for the strips would drift with the speed of the wind, whereas aircraft would move much faster. The echoes from the aircraft would therefore be changed in frequency (by the Doppler effect) appreciably more than those from the strips, and again receivers could be built which would detect the difference.

So now, in principle, the strips would have to be given up, and modified to something that would move through the air with the speed of an aircraft, and reflect radio waves over a wide range of frequencies exactly as an aircraft would. Theoretically, this could be done by towing gliders of the same size as the aircraft, and letting them go at suitable intervals. But gliders are silent, and aircraft are not; if the defences then bring back their sound detectors, they can tell the difference and will not be fooled. So a device has to be put into the glider that will make the sound of aero engines. Even so, the defences can resort to physics once again, and exploit the fact that aero engines emit more energy in heat than they develop for actual propulsion. So by using infrared detectors they can differentiate between a noisy glider and a genuine aircraft, unless a powerful source of heat is put into the glider as well. At the end of this process, however, one is left with such an expensive decoy that it may be almost as cheap as to build another aircraft.

Consideration of examples like the above leads to the conclusion that no deception can be perfect without being an exact copy of the real thing, and then it automatically changes the situation because now there are *two* real things instead of one. But while no deception can be perfect against an omniscient adversary this should not inhibit us from further thought, because no adversary can be omniscient. All observations leading to the establishment of fact take time, and even an able adversary may not gather enough evidence to distinguish true from false within the time available to him; and it is surprising what can be achieved by well-contrived deceptions, especially in the heat of war.

MILITARY DECEPTION

Deception as a branch of the military art is so ancient that an historical survey would be a book in itself, with quotations and examples ranging from Gideon in the Bible, Sun Tzu in China and Kautilya in India (three to four centuries BC), to Clausewitz[4] and Goldhamer.[5] Throughout that vast period of history the practice and the principles of deception have barely changed. Much the same is true of warfare as a whole; allowing for the invention of artillery and firearms, Wellington would have had little difficulty explaining his methods of warfare to Hannibal. And until the communications revolution of this century, the deception techniques available to commanders and governments were much the same as those practised in the ancient world: the planting of verbal or written information on spies known to be working for the enemy, double agents, and feints.

Marlborough, for example, was a master of deception, which he had on occasion to employ, not only against his enemies but also his allies, notably in his march to Blenheim in 1704. Of it, his descendant Winston Churchill wrote 'The annals of the British army contain no more heroic episode than this march from the North Sea to the Danube. The strategy which conceived, the secrecy and skill which performed, and the superb victory which crowned the enterprise have always ranked among the finest examples of the art of war.' First Marlborough had to secure the agreement of the Dutch to moving his army from Holland. He put it about that he was only going as far as the Moselle, in order to turn up that river and attack France, and so he would not be too far away if Holland had to be defended. When he reached the Moselle, however, instead of turning right he crossed it, turned left, and proceeded to cross the Rhine at Coblenz. He then marched up the right bank of the Rhine, and led the French to believe that this was an outflanking movement from which he would recross the Rhine again, some 190 km (120 miles) on from Coblenz at Philippsburg, to attack Alsace. He ordered a bridge of boats to be built at Philippsburg, apparently in anticipation of his crossing; the French commander, Tallard, poised himself with his army in Alsace to withstand the impending attack. But instead of turning westwards some 16 km (10 miles) east of Philippsburg, Marlborough continued on south to the Danube, leaving Tallard behind, and giving himself the chance to join Prince Eugen.

The bridge of boats at Philippsburg is an example in classical warfare where a Commander resorted to technical as well as verbal spoof in advance of an operation. Many commanders, of course, used technical spoof in the sense of mounting token attacks to get their opponents to concentrate their forces in wrong places, but not many went to the trouble of having bridges built so as to cause whole armies to be misplaced.

An even greater stratagem was employed by Marlborough in his forcing of the Ne Plus Ultra Line in 1711. This had been constructed by his French opponents, and his problem was how to penetrate it with minimum loss. It appears that he had decided that the most suitable point was at Arleux, about some 24 km (15 miles) east of Vimy Ridge; this fort commanded a vital causeway through marshy terrain, and Marlborough wanted to destroy it well in advance of his attack. On the other hand, if he destroyed it he would give the French a clue to his plan. He therefore contrived to get them to destroy it themselves. For this, he first captured it; and proceeded to fortify it further; he then sacrificed the garrison, allowing it to be taken by the French who, thinking that it must be essential to Marlborough's plan, destroyed it. Feigning vexation at the news of its destruction, which he hoped would be reported by the spies in his camp, he then did little but draw up his forces before the French army, commanded by Villars, to the west of Vimy Ridge, apparently for a frontal assault; this the French confidently awaited. At sunset, they saw light cavalry moving still further to the west; but after nightfall Marlborough struck camp, marched 32 km (20 miles) to the east, took Arleux (now no hindrance) and the causeway it formerly covered; he thus completely penetrated the Ne Plus Ultra line without opposition while his opponents were still awaiting an attack 32 km (20 miles) away.

MILITARY DECEPTION IN THE FIRST WORLD WAR

The development of both photography and radio communication profoundly influenced the practices of deception, even though its principles remained the same, because they multiplied the channels by which information could be obtained. Moreover photographs taken by spies, and later by aircraft and satellites, could be examined with deliberation far from the dangerous places in which visual observations had to be made, with the observer under stress and lacking time for his observation. Messages from spies, hitherto subjected to delays of manual transmission, could now be sent by radio. At the same time, though, the radio communications of the enemy could be examined; and in the knowledge that he would in turn be examining yours, counterfeit messages might offer the chance of misleading him. The First World War therefore afforded far greater scope both for intelligence and for deception than any previous conflict; and in Admiral Sir Reginald Hall, the Director of Naval Intelligence of the British Admiralty, it found a man to take full advantage of both.

In addition to the traditional methods of espionage, Hall had at his disposal the talent of the service which had been set up by Alfred Ewing in the famous Room 40 OB for the interception and decrypting of radio messages between units of the German fleet and their shore stations. The same decrypting techniques could also be applied to German diplomatic messages sent by commercial cable. Typical of Hall's ingenuity was his deception of the Germans regarding the damage to Beatty's flagship *Lion* after the Dogger Bank action in January 1915, where she had to be berthed in the Tyne for repair, away from the battle cruiser Squadron. The fact was known to the Germans, who could be expected to keep U-boats lying in wait for her coming out after repair. Hall secured some photographs of a Russian battleship damaged in the Russo-Japanese war of 1904, which was much more badly damaged than *Lion*, and arranged for them to be transmitted to Germany by one of the top German agents who was believed by his masters to be operating freely in England but who had in fact been caught. The Germans paid their supposed agent highly for the information, and accepted his assessment that *Lion* was so badly damaged that she could not put to sea for several months. They therefore decided to use their U-boats on other duties until nearer the time that she was expected to be ready. In fact, she was repaired in a fortnight and rejoined her squadron unmolested.[6]

Hall regularly arranged, through apparently talkative friends, to let hints fall about the movement of British ships; and he had a bogus Secret Emergency War Code printed, bound and weighted so as to sink if the ship carrying it were sunk. He arranged from time to time to have radio messages sent in this code, so that they would be intercepted by the Germans; in May 1915, having found that they watched a particular hotel in Rotterdam for British visitors, he arranged for a diplomatic courier to stay there, with a copy of the bogus code book in his luggage. A German agent searched his room in his contrived absence, removed the book, copied it, and returned it, watched by Hall's agent from a vantage point outside the hotel. Hall then built up German faith in the book by arranging for apparently special signals to be sent in the code, taking care to provide truthful but unimportant information.

Hall was twice asked to make the German High Command think that British forces intended to invade behind the German lines. The first was in April 1915, where the supposed target was the island of Sylt, with the idea of diverting German troops from the front line in Belgium when the British forces had been weakened by the Gallipoli operation. The second was in August 1916, with the object of relieving pressure on the British front line by diverting German troops to prepare for a British invasion of north Belgium. Hall built up the intelligence picture for the Germans by providing clues that would lead them step by step to the desired conclusion. Besides carefully spread rumours, Hall arranged for signals to be sent to ships in the bogus code instructing them for their tasks in conveying the invasion fleet in the groups starting from Harwich, Dover, and the mouth of the Thames, where a fleet of monitors and tugs was being concentrated. As the final touch, he arranged for a bogus edition of the *Daily Mail* to be printed and withdrawn, allowing a few copies to be sent to Holland; some of these appeared to be of a later censored edition, the others uncensored. The censored copies had one item missing, of which the headline ran 'East Coast Ready. Great Military Preparations. Flat Bottom Boats', and the article reported large concentrations of troops in the eastern and south-eastern counties. Surely we see here the ancestor of the deception plan for D-Day in 1944?

The ruse was successful, and the Germans moved a large number of troops to the Belgian coast; but it had an awkward consequence. British agents began to report the German troop movements, and over authorities, who were unaware of Hall's efforts, concluded that the Germans must be intending an invasion of England, giving rise to the worst scare in Britain in the First World War. Hall could not be absolutely certain that his efforts were the only cause of the German movements, so he had to watch in silence. There is the element of a lesson here that may be reinforced by consideration of the U-boat crisis in 1917: deception has its dangers.

Before we leave Hall, we ought to recall the masterly manner in which he handled the vital affair of the Zimmermann telegram in 1917; here he succeeded in conveying its contents to the American Government, inevitably leading to their publication, while at the same time providing the Germans with clues which convinced them that espionage or treachery, and not cryptography, had been the cause of their exposure.

SELF-DECEPTION IN WAR

Returning to the U-boats, their threat was ultimately contained by the adoption of the convoy system; but there was strong resistance from the British Admiralty before the decision was forced upon them by Lloyd George. Part of the reason was that, as Churchill pointed out,[7] the Admirals were the victims of the hierarchical attenuation of front-line experience as this was reported upwards through the chain of command. Although Clausewitz said 'Everyone is inclined to magnify the bad in some measure. Firm in reliance on his own better convictions, the Chief must stand like a rock against which the sea breaks its fury in vain',[8] Churchill's experience was 'The temptation to tell a chief in a great position the things he most likes to hear is the commonest explanation of mistaken action. Thus the outlook of the leader on whose decisions fitful events depend is usually far more sanguine than the brutal facts admit'.[9]

So we have here a seed of self-deception which should properly be included in any discussion of deception. As regards hierarchical attenuation, Churchill pointed out that 'The firmly inculcated doctrine that an Admiral's opinion was more likely to be right than a Captain's, and a Captain's than a Commander's, did not hold good when questions entirely novel in character, requiring keen and bold minds unhampered by long routine, were under debate'. In this instance, the more junior officers were in favour of adopting convoys, and ultimately the Admirals were overruled.

Their resistance had been stronger because they were in addition the victims of a deception that they themselves had started. Its effects were two-fold: first, they thought that there would be so many ships requiring to be convoyed that they could not provide sufficient escorts, and second, they tended to believe that their percentage of casualties was not, after all, so serious as to bring Britain to her knees. How did they reach these conclusions? The Admiralty statistics showed that some 5000 vessels entered or left the United Kingdom ports each week. Against this figure, the weekly sinkings by U-boats did not look particularly serious, but the figure of 5000 had originally been deliberate propaganda by the Admiralty to reassure neutrals that there was no great risk in using British ports. The figure was in a sense correct, but it included not only oceangoing ships on which British survival depended, but also the much smaller ships of 100 tonnes or more; so a cross-channel steamer, for example, might notch up five or more entries in a single week. If only oceangoing ships had been taken into account, the weekly total was around 260 instead of 5000. While in one sense the Admiralty figures were true, they were deliberately intended to mislead both the neutrals and the Germans regarding the success of the U-boat campaign.[10] As the war developed, the fact that these figures were propaganda was forgotten, and the Admirals took them as gospel, thereby providing an almost unique exception to the definition of propaganda given by F. M. Cornford[11] as 'That branch of the art of lying which consists in very nearly deceiving your friends without quite deceiving your enemies'.

Along the same theme of self-deception, we should allow Amrom Katz[12] to remind us of the comment of Admiral Godfrey, Director of Naval Intelligence at the Admiralty in the Second World War, regarding why the British failed to appreciate that the *Bismarck* and the *Tirpitz* were much larger than they thought had been negotiated by the Anglo-German Naval Agreement of 1935: 'the tendency of naval officers and others who have taken part in negotiations to become advocates of the integrity of the persons with whom they have secured agreement, and to lose the skepticism which is part of vigilance'.

Alongside Hall's bogus landings in Belgium, another First World War precedent for British deception operations in the Second World War was the work of Richard Meinertzhagen who spent the early part of the war in East Africa. On one occasion he deceived the Germans into eliminating one of their own best agents who was providing information about train movements on the Uganda railway which had led to an effective programme of sabotage. Meinertzhagen arranged for a payment to be sent on British behalf to the agent, thanking him for information and giving sufficient detail of the information about the Germans which was in fact correct, but which Meinertzhagen had obtained not from the agent but from German radio messages.

The episode for which he has gone into the annals of deception was the misleading of the Turks and the Germans during Allenby's offensive in Palestine. Allenby was intending to advance northwards, with his left flank approaching Gaza and his right Beersheba. Both these were strongly held, with difficult country in between. Meinertzhagen adopted the device of providing information through the loss of his dispatch case which contained plans for Allenby's advance, along with a number of personal documents including a letter from the wife of the officer whose case it purported to be, telling him of the arrival of their first baby. The counterfeit plan indicated that the main attack would come at Gaza, while there would be merely a reconnaissance towards Beersheba. Meinertzhagen himself rode out on the counterfeit reconnaissance until he encountered some Turkish opposition, and allowed himself to be shot at. Feigning a hit, he dropped his dispatch case, now sprinkled with blood that he had taken with him, and escaped. Though Turks were not entirely convinced, the Germans were. To add to the seeming reliability of the information provided by the dispatch case, Allenby opened a heavy barrage on Gaza. The Germans knew that this had been his practice in France and anticipated that it would go on for several days; while they were thus standing ready at Gaza a sudden assault was made at Beersheba, which fell, and Allenby was then able to concentrate on Gaza and carry it.[13]

It may be worth remarking in passing that after the First World War Meinertzhagen and T. E. Lawrence (of Arabia) worked out a scheme for unifying all British intelligence services under one aegis, and were on the point of putting the scheme to the Treasury when Lawrence was killed in 1935.[14]

MILITARY DECEPTION IN THE SECOND WORLD WAR

If I appear to have been labouring examples of British deceptions in the First World War, it is at least partly to offset giving the impression that elaborate deception was invented by those of us who were concerned with it in the Second World War. Moreover, I have given British examples because these are the ones I know best. Certainly, the Germans and others (Stonewall Jackson, for example) showed much skill in deception, and I would refer to Whaley[15] for an analysis of the complex plan of deception to cover the German invasion of Russia in 1941. Hitler himself took an interest in deception, for example in keeping constructional work going at Mimoyecques, the emplacement for the multibar-relled guns intended for the bombardment of London, after the project had been abandoned on technical grounds, because the site was diverting so much of the allied bombing effort.

On the German side, Oberstleutnant H. J. Giskes must be specially mentioned. He was responsible for *Operation Nordpol*, in which, as a security officer in Holland, he hoodwinked the British Special Oper-ations Executive (SOE) Organisation. Having captured a Dutch agent, Giskes forced him to transmit bogus messages back to London, making it appear that the agent had arranged the dropping point for the next man who was to come out from England. This second man was then captured by Giskes, who repeated the process until he had caught about 30 men. It was only when two of his captives succeeded in escaping and getting information back to Britain that the deception was unmasked. In the meantime, Giskes had not only paralysed SOE operations in Holland, but had in addition played a private joke. On one flight he persuaded SOE to drop, instead of the customary load of sabotage equipment, a supply of tennis balls, on the plausible grounds that the Dutch agents were now in touch with the King of the Belgians, and saw a way of enlisting his support if they could keep him supplied with tennis balls, of which – owing to the exigencies of war – he was now running short.

British deception in the Second World War depended on a feat essentially similar to that accomplished by Giskes and his security service. MI5, its British counterpart, had effectively caught all the German agents in Britain, including both those who were already present in 1939, and those who were sent into the country later. Some of them were sent into the country later. Some of them were persuaded to cooperate by way of sending bogus information by radio or by letter, and they were organised by a special committee of MI5 whose activities have been described by J. C. Masterman[16]. Its greatest exploit was 'Operation Bodyguard', the elaborate deception plan to persuade the Germans that we had a whole army assembled in East Anglia intended to undertake the main invasion operation across the Straits of Dover, while the genuine landing in Normandy was only a feint. This thoroughly executed plan succeeded in keeping very substantial German forces east of the Seine until it was too late for them to intervene in Normandy.

If the 'Bodyguard' plan was a descendant of Hall's effort in 1917, 'The Man Who Never Was' owed its ancestry to Meinertzhagen. Once again it was a deception centred on allowing the Germans to acquire a briefcase, this time on a drowned body dressed in the uniform of a Royal Marines Officer, washed up on the shores of Spain; this briefcase contained bogus secret instructions for General Alexander from

London regarding his next operations, which were to be landings in Sardinia and Greece in July 1943, when in fact Sicily was the target. The deception was so successful that the Germans diverted an armoured division to Greece, not realising until it was too late the importance of the major operation in Sicily. Such a deception is easy to conceive, but much more difficult to execute successfully. The man who masterminded it told me that he himself wore the uniform of the supposed Marine major to age it suitably; the only trouble was that he was about 6 foot 3 inches in height, and one of the minor difficulties was to get a sufficiently tall corpse to fit the uniform as well as he did. He also carried the various incidental papers such as theatre tickets in his pockets to get them worn to a state consistent with their dates; and it was these touches of detail that helped to convince the Germans that they were not being hoaxed.

SOME TECHNICAL DECEPTION IN THE SECOND WORLD WAR

I myself collaborated with this same officer in several deceptions, more in the technical field. A description of one of them will serve to show the increase in the range of deception techniques that had to be exploited owing to the increasingly technical nature of warfare. A crisis had occurred because our bomber command in August 1941, contrary to orders, had risked flying three of our prototype Gee receivers over Germany, and one of the aircraft had been shot down. Gee was to be the first of our radio bombing aids, which we now knew to be essential if the bombing campaign was to have any hope of success, and yet the production models could not be brought into service until March 1942. So, by losing the prototype, Bomber Command had quite possibly given the Germans seven months' notice of the countermeasures that they had to prepare. An emergency meeting was called by the Air Staff with Tizard as chairman, and I was asked to assess what the Germans would be able to find out; Tizard then asked me whether I could mislead them.

First, I had to consider the channels through which they could have already obtained, or could obtain within the next seven months, information regarding the nature of Gee. These channels included the examination of crashed aircraft, the interrogation of shotdown air crew, listening to the transmissions from our Gee ground stations in England, and photographic reconnaissance of those stations. In addition, the Germans could hope to obtain information from their agents who were supposed to be operating freely in Britain. And they could draw on their own experience of radio bombing methods in assessing what we might do, as well as on their knowledge of the radio and radar developments that we ourselves had so far employed. As regards deception, the issue at stake – the success of our bombing campaign – was so great that I could have anything I wanted within reason.

My plan involved two aspects: first the masking of any clues that the Germans might have already gathered or would gather in the future regarding the true nature of Gee, and second the planting of other clues to make them think that we were adopting an entirely different technique, since we could not avoid providing clues that *some* new kind of equipment was to be installed in our bombers. The first step was to abolish the name 'Gee'. The next was to get the type number changed from one in the R3000 series, which indicated its true nature as a receiver of pulse-type transmissions, and which the Germans could have known from the airborne radar equipment that they had already captured. The new type number should be one in the ordinary communications series, and TR1335 was chosen, since this would suggest a new transmitter/receiver system for radio telegraphy or telephony such as might be part of any ordinary bomber's equipment. This solved two problems: for some months before Gee was installed on a large scale, all aircraft coming off the production line would have to be fitted with the necessary hooks and so forth to accept the Gee receiver, and our production people insisted that it was necessary that these fittings should be labelled from the start. The Germans would therefore have more advanced warning that something new was coming along, if they did not know already, and an R3000 number would have given them a vital clue. As it was, by changing the type number to one that was thoroughly misleading, an awkward situation was turned to our advantage.

One obvious characteristic of the Gee transmissions that would enable the Germans to distinguish them from normal radar was that they were synchronised, so we arranged that the synchronisation should be removed until operations were intended. A further clue that the Germans might obtain, if they had located the stations and photographed them from the air, was that the Gee stations did not have as many masts as normal radar stations, so false masts were added.

The next step was to provide something on which the Germans could focus their attention. Since it was likely they would get wind that we were introducing some new system, what better than to flatter them into thinking that we were going to copy them and use beams? I found that we had already made some beam transmissions to give our bombers a line when they were attacking the German naval units in Brest, so these beams were commandeered and re-erected on the east coast of England; I gave them the title of 'Jay beams'; the new bombing system was now to be called Jay, and I hoped that if the Germans had previously overheard British prisoners of war talking about 'Gee' they would be misled into thinking they had heard 'Jay' instead. And to give the Jay beams a further touch of authenticity, bomber crews were to be encouraged to use them as a directional aid when returning to base in England, and possibly on the way out too.

There was also the chance of providing false information via the German agents in Britain who were under MI5 control. I therefore suggested that one of these agents should purport to have overheard a conversation on the evening of New Year's Day 1942 between two RAF officers chatting in the Savoy Hotel. One who was rather disgruntled said 'Why did Sir Frank Smith get his GCB? All he has done is to copy the German beams – and a year late at that. In any case it was not him alone but the chaps under him.' 'But', said his companion, 'you must admit that at any rate we now have the Jay beams to get us to our target: they worked OK on Brest and we shall soon have them over Germany.' The second officer demonstrated the Jay system by having the salt cellar as one beam station and the pepper pot as the other and impressing the lines of the beams on the tablecloth with the end of a fork.

Another agent who was supposed to have met RAF personnel reported that he had been told that a 'Professor Ekkerly' (whom I hoped the Germans would identify as Ekkersley, our leading propagation expert) had been giving special lectures to RAF units in which he described the new 'Jerry' radio navigational system using Lorentz-type beams. I left it to my German opposite number to evaluate whether 'Jerry' stood for 'Jay' or for 'German' or any other object with which his knowledge of English may have acquainted him. The agents were enthusiastically thanked by their German masters for their valuable information.

In the event the deception was so successful that we experienced no jamming of Gee until August 1942, and so had nearly five months' clear run with it, even though we had lost the equipment seven months before it could be brought into service.

One of the aspects of the Jay hoax that I found satisfying was the turning of a difficulty into an advantage when we devised the new type number and labels for the hooks in the new aircraft that might otherwise have alerted the Germans to the kind of equipment to be installed. There was a similar and greater satisfaction in another episode in which the same MI5 officer and I worked together. This occurred a few days after the opening of the V1 bombardment of London in June 1944. MI5 was in a dilemma because the Germans had asked their supposed agents in London to report the points of impact of their missiles. If MI5 told the Germans the truth, thereby safeguarding the apparent reliability of the agents, this would be aiding the enemy. If MI5 provided false information, this could be checked by photographic reconnaissance, and the entire deception organisation unmasked.

My colleague asked me what could be done. Having seen many agents' reports of our own, I had found that they could usually be relied upon to describe the site of an activity correctly, although they might be widely wrong as to what the activity itself was, or even the time of its occurrence. The trials which we had been able to follow of the V1 in the Baltic had indicated a tendency of the missiles to fall short, and there was a similar tendency in operations. Instead of falling on the centre of London, the main point of impact was $6\frac{1}{2}$ to 8 km (4 to 5 miles) to the south, in Dulwich. I saw the chance not only to keep this point of impact where it was, but also perhaps to cause the Germans to aim even shorter, if they could be convinced of their tendency to fire over the centre of London. I therefore suggested to MI5 that they should indeed report points of impact correctly, but bias these in favour of impacts which had tended to go beyond Central London, coupling them with the times of missiles which we knew to have fallen short. If the Germans had any reason to think that these missiles had fallen short, and then found that they had apparently fallen beyond Central London, making any corrections at all would tend to shorten the range still further. The detailed story of this deception is not without its entertaining side, but it may be simply summarised as successful. What I did not know was that the Germans had put transmitters into a number of their missiles, which they were able to follow by normal direction finding, and this evidence indicated correctly that the bombs were falling short; but by that time the Germans had so much faith in their agents that they thought that there must be something wrong with the radio method, so the deception survived.

THE PRINCIPLES OF SECURITY

I hope that, without being historically comprehensive, the examples that I have given above will illustrate the principles of deception as far as I know them. As a first step, what has to be done is to prevent the enemy from deducing at least one of the following:

(1) Where you are, and/or where he is.
(2) What weapons and forces you have at your disposal.
(3) What you intend to do.
(4) Where you intend to do it.
(5) When you intend to do it.
(6) How you intend to do it.
(7) Your knowledge of the enemy's intentions and techniques.
(8) How successful the enemy's operations are.

All these objectives are in a sense negative, but they may be sufficient to achieve surprise. Basically they involve security rather than deception. Wolfe, for example, surprised Montcalm at Quebec because Montcalm had not thought that the Heights of Abraham could be scaled;[17] and the introduction of centimetric radar helped to change the balance in the battle of the Atlantic because the Germans were unaware that we had developed this new technique.

THE PRINCIPLES OF DECEPTION

These negative objectives are the function of the *security* organisation: each objective has a positive counterpart, which properly constitutes *deception*. The corresponding objectives of deception therefore are that the enemy must be persuaded to deduce:

(1) You are somewhere else, and/or he is somewhere else.
(2) Your weapons and forces are different from what they are.
(3) You intend to do something else.
(4) You intend to do it elsewhere.
(5) You intend to do it at a different time.
(6) You intend to do it in a different manner.
(7) Your knowledge of the enemy is either greater or less than actually is.
(8) His operations are either more or less successful than they actually are.

In short, you are seeking to provide your adversary with clues in his several channels of observation which are consistent with one another, but from which he will build up a false picture of reality. You hope then that, basing his own actions on this picture, he will at some crucial time either act incorrectly and so make himself vulnerable,[18] or he will fail to take advantage of a situation which is in fact favourable to him but which he assesses as unfavourable.

There is scope for artistry in the devising and presentation of clues. While these should be consistent in every channel by which the victim can derive evidence, they should not be too obvious. For example, if bogus espionage reports are to be fabricated, they should include the kinds of error and misinterpretation a genuine spy is likely to make, so that the analytical officer on the other side will be led to feel that he is getting at the truth by eliminating the errors introduced by faulty observation or interpretation on the part of the spy. The picture that the analyst builds up will then be all the more convincing. As a member of the 'Double Cross' operation said: 'An item of information that the analyst has worked out for himself is worth ten that he has been told'. Or the supposed spy may report an item faithfully and correctly, but add that he himself does not believe it. I call this the 'Herodotus touch' because of the statement in his *History* that he could scarcely credit what the Phoenicians had reported when they sailed round Southern Africa, 'The sun rose on the other side', which subsequent scholars have taken as twin testimony to the *bona fides* of Herodotus and to the feat of seamanship on the part of the Phoenicians.

A further touch of artistry in deception is to provide an alternative to your true intentions so valid that if your adversary detects it as a hoax, you can then switch to it as your major plan and exploit the fact that he has discounted it as a serious operation.

UNMASKING DECEPTION

The important questions of how to deceive and how to detect deception are simple to answer in principle. To deceive, you have first to find what channels of information your adversary has at his disposal, then to make sure that you provide appropriate clues in as many of these channels as possible, and either block or discredit those channels where you cannot provide positive clues.

To unmask a deception, your adversary must either open up new channels unknown to you, or work down to a greater depth in some of the existing channels than the depth to which you have provided clues (or detect an inconsistency in the clues with which you have provided him). One reason why 'The Man Who Never Was' operation succeeded was that the consistency of the clues on the corpse was maintained down to the greatest depth that the Germans could check: the corpse had died from pneumonia, so the condition of the lungs was consistent with drowning, and the dog-eared tickets were consistent with the supposed officer being in London at the right time, and so forth.

The 'Jay' deception worked for the same reason; consistent clues were provided in every channel where we believed the Germans might obtain information: the aircraft themselves, the agents reporting from England, the 'Jay' beam transmitters and so on, while we removed clues from the other channels – photographic and electronic reconnaissance – which could have shown that there was something different about the 'Gee' transmitting stations.

As to how the opening up of a new channel can unmask a deception, I need only point to the transmitters fitted to some of the V1 missiles. I had not known of these, or that they correctly gave evidence that the bombardment was falling short; if the Germans had believed the evidence from this new channel, the deception would have been unmasked.

As regards both the depth of consistency of clues in any one channel, and the opening of new channels of observation, the intended victim of deception should – as soon as he has formed a picture of his adversary's intentions – work out all the consequences that he might expect to find if his diagnosis is correct, and seek to confirm them. It is then a battle of wits and imagination between deceiver and unmasker, and the battle will go, as Haig said in 1918, 'to the side which can hold out the longest' in thinking of verifiable consequences, which the deceiver may have overlooked.

If checks of the above type may be termed 'microscopic' because they are largely seeking for overlooked detail, there is also a macroscopic check. In this, the intended victim should seek the motive by asking what would be the consequences of his own subsequent actions if he believes the picture built up from the evidence that has come into his hands. It was, for example, possible to dispose of Lord Cherwell's theory in 1943 that the German rocket story was a hoax by asking what would be the consequences if we believed it. The obvious answer was that we would bomb Peenemünde, evident from air photographs that it was a major establishment and the testing site for German jet developments; and if we needed further confirmation of its importance, there was the 'microscopic' confirmation that Peenemünde was listed second only to Rechlin in a circular to Luftwaffe research establishments sent out by a minor clerk in the German Air Ministry, and it was very improbable that a hoax would have been so thorough as to provide this small clue, especially as it occurred in an Enigma decode. A successful attack on Peenemünde would therefore wreck a major research establishment, which the Germans would hardly be prepared to sacrifice.

In principle, it should always be possible to unmask a deception, but it is surprising how effective deception can be in the stress and speed of operations. It is a well-known principle of observation in science that to increase accuracy it is necessary to observe for a longer time, and successful deception does not allow the victim a long enough time to establish the truth.

DANGERS OF DECEPTION

As with all problems involving security, deception can itself be dangerous if it is performed so ineptly that it provides the enemy with clues as to what are the real intentions. In the deployment of the V2 sites in France for the bombardment of London, for example, I was able to deduce the intended rate of firing because of the decoy sites which the Germans had erected in the hope that we would bomb them instead of the actual storage sites. To make sure that we spotted them, the

Germans made the decoys quite obvious, but they forgot to maintain any activity and so there were no paths or wearing of the grass as there would have been if the sites were being worked. There were twenty decoys, deployed roughly from Calais to Cherbourg, with fourteen east and six west of the Seine. When we landed in Normandy we, of course, captured not only the decoys west of the Seine, but also the real storage sites, and could easily establish their total storage. Then, assuming that there was the same proportion of genuine storage sites to decoys east of the Seine, this gave the total storage sites as about 400; since it appeared to be German practice to keep two weeks' supplies forward, this suggested an intended monthly rate of fire of 800, which was a fairly close estimate to the actual rate of fire intended, 900 per month. I could not have made such a close estimate had the Germans not tried to deceive us.

CONCLUSION

While it is easy to outline the principles both of deception and its unmasking, it is no easier to instruct would-be deceivers or unmaskers on the grand scale than it would be to tell an artist how to paint a great picture or a playwright how to write a great play – indeed the simile may run quite deep, since there is genuine artistry involved. Both for deception and unmasking, one of the personal qualities required is that of being able to imagine yourself in the position of your adversary, and to look at reality down to the smallest detail from his point of view; this includes not only being able to sense the world through his eyes and ears, and their modern analogies such as photographic and electronic reconnaissance, but also to absorb the background of his experience and hopes, for it is against these that he will interpret the clues collected by his intelligence system. Thus, it was not too difficult to convince the Germans that the 'Jay' system was going to depend on beams because they would naturally be gratified by the 'knowledge' that we had copied from their techniques. To guard against this weakness when one is in danger of being deceived, I can only recommend Crow's Law, formulated by my late friend John Crow: 'Do not think what you want to think until you know what you ought to know'. And if a good guide to successful intelligence is Occam's razor – hypotheses are not to be multiplied without necessity – then an equally relevant guide to avoid being deceived is to multiply your channels of observation as far as possible.

NOTES

1. Lloyd, J. E., *Science*, 187, pp. 452–3 (1975).
2. Eberhard, W. G., *Science*, 198, pp. 1173–4 (1977).
3. Pietsch, G. W. and Geobecker, D. B., *Science*, 201, pp. 369–70 (1978).
4. Despite many examples to the contrary, Clausewitz wrote that craft and cunning 'do not figure prominently in the history of war' (*On War*, edited and translated by M. Howryd and P. Paret, (Princeton, U. P. 1976), p. 202), although he attached great importance to surprise.
5. I am indebted to Andrew W. Marshall for Herbert Goldhamer's report *Reality and Belief in Military Affairs* published after his death by the Rand Corporation (1979). It contains a valuable historical chapter on deception.
6. James, W., *The Eyes of the Navy* (London, Methuen, 1955), pp. 66–7.
7. Churchill, Winston, S., 'The U-Boat War', in *Thoughts and Adventures* (London, T. Butterworth, Ltd. 1932).
8. Greene, J. I., *The Living Thoughts of Clausewitz* (London, Cassell, 1945), p. 15.
9. Churchill, Winston S., *The World Crisis*, (New York, C. Scribner's Sons, 1923–30).
10. Marder, A. J., *From the Dreadnought to Scapa Flow* (London, Oxford University Press, 1969), pp. 150–2.
11. Cornford, F. M., *Microcosmographica Academica*, 2nd edition (1922).
12. Katz Amrom H., *Verification and Salt: The State of the Art and the Art of the State* (Washington, The Heritage Foundation, 1979).
13. Lord, John, *Duty, Honour, Empire* (London, Hutchinson, 1971).
14. Ibid., p. 387.
15. Whaley, Barton, *Codeword Barbarossa* (Cambridge, Mass., MIT Press, 1974).
16. Masterman, J. C., *The Double Cross System* (   ).
17. Similarly, the Japanese surprised the British at Singapore, but there was an element also of self-deception in the British command. See Dixon, N. F., *On the Psychology of Military Incompetence* (London, Jonathan Cape, 1976).
18. Consider the classic exchange between Pompaedrius Silo and Marius:
    Silo: If you are a great general, come down and fight.
    Marius: If you are a great general, make me fight against my will.

2 Slow Pearl Harbours and the Pleasures of Deception

Roberta Wohlstetter

Quite a few years ago, prodded by Andy Marshall and some other friends with a close and long-term interest in intelligence, I looked into the question of why we were surprised at Pearl Harbour. I examined the signals available to us that pointed to an attack on Pearl Harbour and the background of ambiguities in which they were embedded. I looked at what we wanted to believe Japanese intentions to be, as well as what these intentions actually turned out to be. I found it useful to use some distinctions familiar to practitioners of the mathematical theory of information, although I did not and do not pretend to travel in the rarefied atmosphere even of the somewhat lower reaches of this theory. I have been, rather, a fellow traveller, with lots of friends.

In particular, I found it useful to make a distinction between signals and noise–signals pointing to Pearl Harbour that actually might have changed our expectations of the likelihood of an imminent attack (what the theorists grandly call a change in the *a priori* probabilities, or even more mysterious, the negative logarithm of the probability) – and the noise or huge clutter of signs pointing in other directions, for example, to an attack on the Soviet Union or to no attack at all. While this distinction has an obvious commonsense meaning, it also is related to the notion of signal-to-noise ratio that plays a role in the more sophisticated theory of information. Moreover, as in applications of information theory applied to electronic countermeasures, it is clear that one has to distinguish between deliberately created or amplified noise and the noisy background generated by random events, by 'line noise', by the operation of one's own equipment and procedures, or by 'normal' traffic. Of course, there is a relationship between the deliberate and the 'undeliberated'. An adversary, for example, must design his attack so as not to be heard against the normal or random background. Even the suppression of his signals, for instance by going into radio silence, must not arouse suspicions. As an alternative to skirting a warning system, as the Japanese did in coming at Pearl Harbour from the north, an adversary may deliberately conceal radar returns from his low-flying aircraft in the normal ground clutter. Or he may accept radar detection of his aircraft as he penetrates but time it in a way that fits the normal traffic patterns of unknowns and does not therefore alter the prior probabilities. Or the adversary may *create* a normal pattern by a sequence of exercises or penetrations of the warning system before the attack. He may, in short, *condition* his opponent, in the way that R. V. Jones has both theorised and expertly practised (chapter 1 of this volume), to prepare his unlucky victims to be hoaxed.

However, all such conditioning or other forms of deception have to be based on a shrewd appreciation of the normal background, or what the victim considers normal, and how far that background can be altered. It will come as no great revelation that most surprise attacks involve deception by an adversary. They are generally launched with malice aforethought.

What has interested me from the beginning, but more so in recent times, is the role the victim often plays in deceiving himself. This seems especially important in cases that occur between wars, where the critical time to recognise an adversary's intentions may be protracted over years, and where perceptions may be shaped by extended negotiations, past, present and future, based upon the presumed common interests of the opposing sides. These are the slow Pearl Harbours, so to speak.

To mention a few examples:

(1) The reluctant recognition by the British, in the 1930s, that Hitler really was less interested in avoiding an 'unlimited arms race', as he put it, than he was in speeding his own rearmament, and slowing down Britain's. That is to say, he was interested in winning the arms race.

(2) A second example derives from the even slower and more reluctant recognition by American Intelligence that the Russians were not interested merely in having a minimum deterrent force of 200 ICBMs, nor even satisfied with the same numbers as our own, but thought it would be rather nice to have 50 per cent (or half again) more; in short, that they were not simply being dragged along reluctantly by the mad momentum of an arms race (which, allegedly, we were running with ourselves), but were continuing to run along quite smartly long after we had stopped.

Russian intentions on these matters clearly have some significance for various SALT treaties. SALT I and II and, especially, hopes for future SALTs, tend to affect our willingness–or reluctance–to recognise the signals of Russian intentions.

(3) A third example is presented by the refusal of our government to recognise India's military preparations in the nuclear arena. The Indians, in a succession of regimes – Nehru, Shastri, Mrs Gandhi and

Desai – have been able to use as a cover for their military programme the peaceful atom and the desires of the Americans and the Canadians to propagate civilian nuclear electricity (and to sell reactors) and, more recently, to conclude a comprehensive Test Ban Treaty. The noise of these civilian arrangements confused otherwise plain signals of India's accumulation of separated fissile material directly usable in weapons, its capacity to separate more, the manufacture and detonation of a nuclear explosive, and current bland statements that New Delhi may make more nuclear explosives, if these should seem to be economic for mining or other purposes. India has managed to maintain this position while being held up as a prime example of the utility of a comprehensive test ban in slowing the spread of nuclear explosives.

In all of these instances of error persisting over a long period of time, in the face of increasing and sometimes rather bald contrary evidence, a very significant role is played by cherished beliefs and comforting assumptions about the good faith of a potential adversary and the common interests supposedly shared by that antagonist. The victims, in such cases, may be the principal (self-) deceivers. An adversary only may have to help the victim along somewhat; the latter will tend to explain away what might otherwise look like a rather menacing move.

Thus, the British, who had other priorities after the Second World War which entailed keeping down their defence budget, started to assume in 1919 that no major war was likely to occur in the following ten years and continued to base their planning on this increasingly less tenable assumption, well into the decade before the outbreak of the Second World War. This 'prediction' always had a component of wish and fiat in it, and it came to be called appropriately 'The Ten Year Rule'. British estimates, beginning in 1933, as to the number of firstline aircraft the Germans would be able to field, seem to have been much lower than reality, mainly because admitting them to be higher would have dictated a course of action that politically would have been extremely difficult to undertake. One also may invoke the example of the Anglo-German Naval Agreement of 1936. British officials resisted recognising Germany's intention to develop a fleet that might be used against Britain, and delayed in acknowledging strong evidence that the Germans were violating the Agreement. This had something to do with the discomfort of acknowledging the truth. It was difficult, first of all, to do anything about the violations of the Versailles Treaty, which the Anglo-German Naval Agreement legitimised, and, later, to take action against the violations of the 1936 Agreement itself. Not to be deceived was uncomfortable. Self-deception, if not actually pleasurable, at least helps to avoid such discomforts.

The Germans, in the Anglo-German Naval Treaty of June 1936, had agreed to limit battleships to a 35,000 tonnes displacement. However, Admiral Raeder ordered the building of the *Bismarck* and *Tirpitz* to a 45,000 tonne displacement. The particulars of the *Bismarck's* design, confided by the German Embassy to the British Foreign Office, revealed a beam 4.5 m (15 feet) wider than Britain's battleship, *King George V* (which did have a displacement of 35,000 tonnes) and other dimensions which were apparently incompatible with the 35,000 tonne limitation. The British Director of Naval Construction suggested that the large beam went with the shallow draft necessary for navigation through the Kiel Canal and in the Baltic. The Plans Division in London, which had been involved in the limitation agreement, and therefore had a stake in believing it would be observed faithfully, seized on this anomaly and the 'shallow draft' explanation to provide an even cheerier evaluation: the Germans were looking toward the Baltic, rather than toward the British – they were aiming at the Russians.

In Donald McLachlan's excellent account (on which I have relied),[2] there is no indication that the explanation that Germany was aiming at the Russians emanated from the Germans or that they expected the British to elaborate that cover story for them. Admiral Raeder simply lied to the British Naval Attaché in Berlin about the displacement of the *Bismarck*, and the head of the British Plans Division worked out an explanation for some of the troubling inconsistencies. As McLachlan says, the Plans Division in London had been 'closely involved in – and therefore believed in – the various treaties limiting naval armaments'.[3] The Director of Plans had 'allowed himself to write, "Our principal safeguard against such an infraction of treaty obligations lies in the good faith of the signatories"'. Yet he was by nature 'a sceptical and aggressive man'.[4]

In fact, the *Bismarck's* draft differed little from that of British capital ships; and statements about the shallow draft were a cover by the Germans, gratefully accepted by the British, to save their belief in the fidelity of their German opposite numbers, and to rescue London's trust in the safety of the agreement. Britain's Director of Naval Construction, according to Donald McLachlan, did not push the questions about the *Bismarck* specifications even though he was building battleships to oppose that German vessel, because he was 'hard pressed with the new programme and deeper probing of the German design would almost certainly not have led . . . to a change in our own designs which would mean breaking treaty limitations'.[5] As a further nice twist, it appears that the Plans Division in Germany, which knew that the *Bismarck's* true displacement was about one-fifth greater than allowed and announced by the British, argued against revealing the violation on the delicate ground that 'we shall be accused of starting an armament race'.[6]

It appears, then, that both the cheater and the side cheated in an arms agreement may have a stake in allowing the error to persist. They both need to preserve the illusion that the agreement has not been violated. The British fear of an arms race, manipulated so skilfully by Hitler, led to a Naval Agreement, in which the British (without consulting the French or the Italians) tacitly revised the Versailles Treaty; and London's fear of an arms race prevented it from recognising or acknowledging violations of the new agreement.

The second example deals with the American error in underestimating the numbers of ICBMs, SLBMs, and bombers that the Russians would have in their strategic force. This error persisted for about a decade – a very much longer time than did Britain's underestimation of Hitler's aircraft programme. Moreover, it persisted in the face of precise evidence gathered, year after year, with all the marvels of high altitude reconnaissance, using satellites, high resolution cameras and other optical and non-optical sensors which told us exactly what silos and submarines the Russians had completed, what they had under construction, and what bombers were still part of their operational force.

My colleagues at PAN Heuristics have made careful studies of forecasts of the Soviet strategic force made by the Services and by the intelligence community, in consensus, as well as of those consensus forecasts which the various Secretaries of Defence used in their annual Defence Reports as the basis for their budget requests.[7] I will cite only one example of their results.

The United States' long-term projections of Soviet ICBM silos not only were systematically below the mark from 1962 to the end of the 1960s but, in the face of gathering evidence that the forecasts were underestimations, they drifted further below the mark. In 1962, we predicted that the increase in the Soviet force would be about 85 per cent of the amount that actually materialised. In 1969, we predicted an increase that turned out to be less than 20 per cent of the amount the Soviet Union actually fielded. Moreover, the ratio of our predicted increases to the actual increases deteriorated at the rate of about 8 percentage points annually. For all our improved means of collecting information, compared to the primitive devices available to the British in the 1930s, we did even worse than they did in anticipating an adversary's military buildup. Like the British, our interpretation of the data was affected strongly by our strategic doctrines and political predispositions. Moreover, while qualitative forecasts are harder to confirm or refute, it would be quite wrong to suppose that our forecasts of Russian improvements in unit performance erred on the other side, or even produced much less underestimation than American predictions concerning numbers of vehicles in the Soviet strategic force. Nor is it clear that we are doing any better now with such qualitative forecasts. I observe each year that our Secretaries of Defence, like children opening their perennial Christmas stockings, give vent to increasingly familiar expressions of surprise; it seems that the Russians once again have improved their circular-error-probability (CEPs) more than we had expected in the preceding year.

The third example concerns the Indian nuclear programme. In its negotiations with the Indians concerning nuclear energy, the United States, it seems to me, has been amazingly cooperative in going along with some of the Indian fictions. This is partly explained, of course, by the fact that American nuclear officials had entertained some of the same fictions, most notably a belief in the plutonium breeder and the Plowshare programme to further the peaceful use of nuclear explosions in mining or digging canals. The Plowshare programme came to an end in the late 1960s. The plutonium breeder, however, is still on the scene and provides the ultimate justification in most non-weapon states for accumulating stockpiles of weapons material.

This is not the place to go into the pros and cons of the breeder, whether it is necessary or whether one must make a commitment to it now. My purpose here is to explore the effects on the intelligence process of continuing negotiations on what is or is not contained in our agreement with India for nuclear cooperation, and which country is or not in violation of that agreement.

The Indian military nuclear programme has been under way – in what Norman Gibbs, in another context, described as a state of 'open secrecy' – since the early 1970s. Actually, it had its beginnings much earlier – in the mid-1960s, when relations with the People's Republic of China became openly hostile, after the Sino-Indian War of 1962 and the first Chinese nuclear tests of 1964. Nevertheless, the Indians continue to protest that they do not have a military nuclear programme.

The Indians used heavy water of American origin, in a research reactor obtained from Canada, to produce plutonium that they separated in a plant of United States design and made into a nuclear explosive which they detonated. Since the mid-sixties, the Canadians and Americans have both made explicit many times that a nuclear explosive, even if it were said to be contemplated for eventual use in engineering, in digging a canal, had a more obvious and patent military use. That canal could always be dug suddenly in the middle of an adversary's city. We made clear that the use of equipment or material or services of American or Canadian origin for the manufacture of a nuclear explosive, however labelled, would violate the obvious commonsense meaning of our agreements with the Indians (namely, that they would limit their use of what we had provided to 'peaceful', that is, civilian, purposes *only*).

When the Indians detonated their nuclear explosive, the Canadians cut off further aid. The United States, on the other hand, went through a series of contortions, first ignoring the whole affair, but reiterating our general belief that spreading nuclear explosives to more countries would be unfortunate. Then, in defiance of what we had been saying for many years, we allowed that, if the Indians said their nuclear explosive was peaceful, we could hardly doubt them. Moreover, in any case, it was a problem for the Canadians, since it was their reactor, and we had nothing directly to do with it. Then, when nasty questions were raised about our heavy water, we pointed to India's contention that all the materials, equipment and personnel were 100 per cent Indian and stated that we believed them. Subsequently, when it was clear that our heavy water had been used in the CIRUS reactor, we maintained that, by the time of the manufacture of the bomb, our heavy water must have been replaced by 100 per cent Indian heavy water. When it appeared that the last statement defied some well-established laws of physics and arithmetic, we agreed that there was some heavy water. On the other hand, the Indians were telling the truth – there was none.

It might appear to be troubling – in accordance with some of the familiar standards of western logic – that the CIRUS should have been both empty and non-empty of our heavy water. However, by that time, some of our officials, through long dealings with the Indians, appear to have gone native. In some Indian writings, such as those of the Madhyamika school of Buddhist philosophy, founded by Nagarjuna, a rather more relaxed view is taken of such matters: There are other possibilities than simply being empty or non-empty. For, as Nagarjuna says, 'If something non-empty existed, then there might be something termed empty; there is not something non-empty, and so nowhere does there exist a non-empty something'.[8] In some cases, one can say that something or someone is 'not to be called empty, nor non-empty, nor both, nor both-not . . . . Everything is either true or not true, or both true and not true, or neither true nor not true; that is the Buddha's teaching.'[9] That may explain why the Buddha was smiling on the occasion of the Indian nuclear explosion.

Whatever suspicions Westerners might harbour about the validity of the logic involved, one can hardly doubt the diplomatic utility of an attitude of mind that can contemplate with equanimity a statement being simultaneously true and false. In fact, this approach seems to have penetrated our own officialdom.

The story of how our preferences and predispositions affected the writing of the various agreements and our estimates of what the Indians were doing up to May 1974, the date of their nuclear explosion, would take a good deal of time to state adequately. However, the developments of American policy and the estimates of Indian nuclear activity since that time are related to the negotiations on the Comprehensive Test Ban

Treaty, and form an interesting parallel to the other cases discussed here: Britain during the 1930s and the United States strategic force predictions. The American position on the Comprehensive Test Ban Treaty is based in part on the argument that countries like India are driven to acquire nuclear weapons by the fact that it is inequitable to have a distinction between nuclear have and have-not states. Any move, therefore, by the two superpowers to restrict their nuclear might is a step towards greater equity.

In fact, however, the Indians developed their nuclear explosive programme with an eye to the People's Republic of China. They have little active interest in the armament of the two superpowers. The original motivation for the Non-Proliferation Treaty, as expressed by the Irish resolution, was based on the interests of the non-weapon states in seeing to it that potentially hostile neighbours did not obtain nuclear weapons. The treaty naturally also contains a good deal about encouraging peaceful nuclear developments, steps toward general nuclear disarmament and, in fact, general and comprehensive disarmament. However, these are rhetorical flourishes that have little to do with actual concerns. They can, however, as in the case of the Treaty of Versailles, serve as a justification for the acquisition of arms, in this case nuclear arms.

In fact, the Indians have produced a welter of statements about the circumstances in which they would explicitly give up nuclear explosives. Our foreign service officers, and the State Department as a whole, have selected those quotations that sound hopeful, in as far as they suggest that, if only the United States and the Soviet Union took a long stride towards nuclear disarmament, the Indians would follow suit. However, an examination of the full range of signals and noise emerging from the official declarations and policies, press statements and debates in the Lok Sabha, demonstrates that this selection is as wishful as our prior perceptions of Indian policy. In viewing the Comprehensive Test Ban Treaty as a stride, it is useful to see what India's Prime Minister has in mind. In his address to the United Nations General Assembly on 9 June 1978, Mr Desai made clear that, *inter alia*, there was no point in considering a complete ban on testing that extended to some countries and not all. It would have to include the entire globe. 'It is idle,' he said, 'to talk of regional nuclear free zones . . . the whole world should be declared a nuclear free zone.' In short, Mr Desai leaves no doubt in this context that any Comprehensive Test Ban Treaty that is less than universal, that fails to include China and France among its signatories, will not fulfil the conditions that he is stipulating for Indian cooperation.

Mr Desai went on to say that we should take decisive steps towards the general acceptance of the philosophy and practice of non-violence and Satyagraha. However, conceding that this will take time, he calls only for 'one step': that step, however, involves quite a leap. The 'first step' he outlines includes:

(a) a declaration outlawing the use of nuclear technology or research on nuclear technology for military purposes;

(b) 'qualitative and quantitative limitations on nuclear armament and immediate freezing of present stockpiles under international inspection';

(c) the reduction of stocks of nuclear weapons and their total elimination in no more than ten years;

(d) a comprehensive test ban treaty 'with provision for safeguards to prevent breach of the Treaty, which in my view can only be through independent inspection'; the ban must be 'universal and non-discriminatory';

(e) a programme of drastic reductions in conventional arms should be initiated before the end of the decade: 'in fact, we should visualize a time when the use of armed forces would not be necessary even for internal security'.

In the past, members of the Ministry of External Affairs in India who advocated the acquisition and testing of nuclear bombs have referred to nuclear and conventional disarmament as an 'adorable dream'. As a dream we should all cherish it. However, we should be aware that stipulating it as a condition for non-proliferation is simply a justification for the spread of nuclear weapons.

One of the points to be made in reviewing this history is that, when Hitler talked about his sincere desire to avoid an unlimited arms race, he referred to the outbreak of the First World War as the result of such an arms race. In this way, he was drawing on a body of beliefs about the causes of the First World War which were very much in the centre of British pacifist writings of the interwar period. Lord Grey, who had been Foreign Secretary at the outbreak of the First World War, and Lewis Fry Richardson, the Quaker physicist and meteorologist, were outstanding exponents of this cluster of beliefs. The revival of an interest in Richardson, at the beginning of the 1960s, has accompanied the growth, down to the present time, of the belief that the process of negotiation with the Russians on strategic weapons constitutes the only way to stave off an unlimited 'arms race' and the inevitable nuclear holocaust that would follow. As in the 1930s, the facts about what was happening to the force levels of both sides have had to be stretched and pushed entirely out of shape to preserve the doctrine. Revisionist history of the 'cold war' today, and the related notion that the United States has been forcing the reluctant Russians to spend money on weapons that they would rather spend otherwise – all of this resembles the British belief that it was the Allied failure to disarm after Versailles that compelled the Germans reluctantly to rearm. After all, did not Hitler reiterate many times that he would much prefer to forego armament altogether, if only the Allies would disarm completely?

Other beliefs that have been popular since the early 1960s have it that, just as our unilateral military buildup forced the arms race, so a unilateral act of self-restraint would induce reciprocity. *Inter alia*, this view is likely to make us rather relaxed about the bargains we strike. If they seem a little onesided against us, our concern may be regarded either as a quibble or as a useful indicator of our restraint. The belief in reciprocity, moreover, is likely to make us indifferent about the precise interpretation of the bargain, and about intelligence that seems to suggest our adversary may be violating the agreement or, at any rate, interpreting it very differently from the meaning we had claimed it to have.

One of the disabilities of the current mind-set and the optimistic forecasts about adversary behaviour which it encourages is that the adversary may be tempted to exploit our trust. This sort of optimistic forecast has a way of undermining itself.

For those who want to believe – in the face of a plethora of evidence – that the world is really not a very dangerous place, the sociologists' category of self-confirming beliefs offers some reassurance. According to this view, the adversary, who becomes a threat because we distrust him and arm to meet his threat in a 'threatening way', can become once again no threat at all, if only we trust him. The proposition 'he is trustworthy' is as potent in making itself come true as the proposition 'he is not to be trusted'. At least, so the theory goes.

Alas, however, in the hard world not everyone can be trusted to act peacefully, even when not actually threatened himself. Some may make war because they believe that it is 'easy pickings'. 'I am in no danger whatsoever' is an example of a self-annihilating proposition. According to the sociologist, Robert Merton,

> This mechanism, picturesquely termed the
> 'suicidal prophecy' by the nineteenth-century
> logician John Venn, involves beliefs which
> prevent fulfillment of the very circumstance
> which would otherwise come to pass. Examples
> of this are plentiful and familiar. Confident
> that they will win a game or a war or a cherished
> prize, groups become complacent, their complacency
> leads to lethargy, and lethargy to eventual
> defeat.[10]

The British Ten Year Rule, predicting that, 'there will be no war in the next ten years', when uttered in the early 1930s, justified a lack of preparation for defence and vain hopes of the goals held out by disarmament negotiations. These beliefs, in turn, encouraged the Germans to believe they could rearm without calling forth sanctions or rival rearmament until it was too late. In this way, the prediction that there would be no war in 1942, helped to lead to war three years earlier and so to its own refutation. Such self-destroying prophecies, then, can be suicidal in two senses: They endanger not only the prophecy, but also the prophet.[11]

In the interwar period, as in the 1960s and 1970s, the perverse kind of prophecies that it was fashionable to study were those which converted innocent men deserving of trust into something untrustworthy. (Merton himself became known for his work on self-fulfilling predictions.) The bank run started by false rumours of insolvency was a favourite example in the 1930s, as was also the minister of defence or prime minister of 'Anycountry' or 'Jedesland' who wanted only to defend his country, but was misinterpreted as being interested in aggression, and so frightened his neighbour, and was himself in turn frightened into an arms buildup leading to war. That was Lewis Fry Richardson's concern.

In fact, in the 1930s Hitler was busy talking like the Minister of Jedesland in Richardson's theory, making exactly the noises that the British wanted to hear, while his behaviour was signalling the opposite – that the governments of *some* countries at any rate had something in mind other than self-defence. While the fashionable political and sociological theories concentrated on *self-fulfilling* prophecies, the actual practice (reinforced perhaps by the sociological theories) illustrated the use of what John Venn called 'suicidal prophecies'. Hitler, when trusted, did not become trustworthy. He took advantage of British trust, complacency and guilt.

Similarly, recent history suggests that the unilateral restraints embodied in our informal practices in advance of an agreement, in our lax agreements themselves in SALT, and in our lax interpretation of these agreements, encourage the Russians to believe that they can gain an advantage through the continued expansion of their defence effort.

A basic underlying characteristic of such prophecies which are perverse or have perverse effects is that there are genuine ambiguities in the evidence supporting them. The unanticipated consequences upset the initial assumption. However, policy predispositions, desires and prejudices may lengthen the time it takes to recognise that the prophecies are false or have perverse effects.

Nothing I have said should be interpreted as meaning that we will inevitably persist in holding on to such self-destroying prophecies. The instinct for self-preservation, after all, is strong. Our political birdwatchers often wrongly identify an ostrich as a dove. However, the habit of sticking one's head in the sand does not appear to be a survival trait. We have survived so far. The British finally pulled their heads out of the sand. So, I hope, can we.

NOTES

1. Webster, Sir Charles and Frankland, Noble, *History of the Second World War. The Strategic Air Offensive against Germany: 1939–1945*, Vol. I: *Preparation* (London, Her Majesty's Stationery Office, 1961), p. 57.
2. McLachlan, Donald, *Room 39: Naval Intelligence in Action. 1939–45*, (London, Weidenfeld & Nicolson, 1968), pp. 135–48.
3. Ibid., p. 136.
4. Ibid., p. 137.
5. Ibid., p. 127.
6. Ibid., p. 193.
7. Wohlstetter, Albert, 'Racing Forward? Or Ambling Back?', *Defending America* (Basic Books, Inc., 1977).
8. Robinson, Richard H., 'Some Logical Aspects of Nagarjuna's System', *Philosophy East and West*, Vol. VI, No. 4 (January 1957), p. 297.
9. Ibid., p. 302.
10. Merton, Robert K., *Social Theory and Social Structure* (Glencoe, Ill., The Free Press, 1949), p. 121.
11. There is, of course, a more attractive class of self-destroying predictions. For example, the prediction that 'The enemy is mobilising for an attack on you' can lead to your mobilisation, and cancellation of the attack.

Part Two

Intelligence: Conceptual Approaches

3 Approaches to Intelligence and Social Science

Ithiel de Sola Pool

It takes two to disinform. To be fooled is not the fault of one party, but of an interaction. The interpretation of what someone means is very largely conditioned by an inclination to accept what we want to hear. Disinformation consists mainly of the art of telling others something that they will accept because they want to hear it.

This may be viewed as a platitude that experienced intelligence operatives know well and that can be documented also by means of the social sciences. However, the frequency with which such a simple truth is disregarded suggests that it is worth reaffirming. The lore among journalists, intelligence operatives, or social scientists concerning information processes is fairly straightforward. Each of these professions has identified certain practices of its particular art, designed to avoid obvious but common mistakes. This chapter is intended to spell out a few of these simple rules, as they have been stated by social scientists.

The magic of the social scientist, I suggest, is not more profound or very different from that of the government official or the newsman. On the contrary, I would argue that there are several prominent professions, perhaps four, with a basically similar task, consisting essentially of intelligence. Some of the practitioners do not like to be told that they are engaged in intelligence activities because such work does not enjoy a very good reputation. However, social scientists, newsmen, diplomats, and intelligence personnel all are, to a large extent, doing the same kind of work. They are all 'deciphering' a world in which information is deliberately concealed, in which there are problems of interpretation, in which prediction is difficult, and concerning which they are supposed to be more knowledgeable than the persons to whom they report. There are, of course, some differences in the lifestyles of members of these four professions. There are differences, for example, concerning the institutions and personalities for whom they work, and also the manner in which they report. To take only a few categories: some report in journals, others in private documents; some report to decision-makers, others to the general public. However, many of the research methods employed are identical; moreover, the problems that they face – of ambiguity, of incomplete information, and of deception – are very much the same.

An excellent description of day-to-day problems in securing information is found in the autobiography of Lincoln Steffens. He describes the manner in which he, as a newsman, operated in corrupt cities ruled by political machines at the turn of the century. He noted that there was a close transactional relationship between the crusading reporter and the persons he was exposing. While his image was that of a reformer unmasking the 'bad guys', he still had to retain his relations with the 'machine', or he could not obtain news. The crooks had to regard him, in some respects, as a friend and a person they could trust. True, they also had to fear him. Consequently, part of his art was never to write everything he knew. The gangster or corrupt 'boss' had to realise that Steffens was deliberately holding back on a few of the juiciest tidbits he knew. Thus, the subject would be kept both worried, yet also feeling that Steffens was not entirely hostile, since he was keeping a confidence. In such a 'double bind', a politician might believe that, if he continued to cooperate, Steffens might continue to refrain from 'lowering the boom'.

Thus, there was a kind of buddy relationship, together with an adversary relationship. Of course, the press likes to claim that it has an adversary relationship with persons in power, but that is only a half-truth. There is much literature lauding this alleged inbuilt antagonism, but it is partly fantasy. A buddy relationship is the essential condition for maintaining contact and continuing to obtain information.

Protection of access to such buddies is precisely the reason why newsmen are so concerned about the confidentiality of sources. That is also a prime issue for the intelligence community, as well as for social scientists. Issues regarding both the press and intelligence agencies have recently attracted wide attention in Congress and the Courts. If you follow social science in-house discussions, it is apparent that there is also a great deal of concern in universities, these days, about the relationship of the researcher to the human subjects with whom he deals and about the confidentiality of their data. In all these professions there exists a complex code of integrity in the pursuit of knowledge and, at the same time, a very ambiguous and complex relationship that limits disclosure of some aspects of material being investigated. The claim to be pursuing both knowledge and openness again is an ideological half-truth. The person pursuing knowledge needs to protect confidentiality of his sources, so as to obtain the particular data he may wish to publish or reveal. The same basic moral and loyalty issues arise in all the professions mentioned.

In all these instances, but particularly, perhaps, in the case of the (governmental) intelligence profession, there is a tendency (especially under autocratic regimes) for knowledge to become corrupted and to be abused as a kind of police instrument. It is not unknown, in some countries, for social scientists or newsmen also to be used by governments in this manner. When the search for information becomes identified with police activity, it tells us more about the nature of the government and the power of the police in that country than it does about intelligence as such. Basically, intelligence is not a police function. Policemen are not very good researchers.

Still, it is common for the intelligence function to become confounded with police tasks. For historical reasons, there has been a tendency for these two kinds of activities to be organisationally merged (even though, conceptually, they have little to do with each other): the police do require intelligence to function effectively. Military services also need intelligence. So do all sorts of instrumentalities. Historically, all powerful organisations, including police, have created or adopted intelligence agencies. However, the police activities of a SAVAC or of a GPU in running a *Gulag* have nothing at all to do with the basic function of trying to help statesmen understand the processes that are going on around them. In fact, it is documentable that of the various Soviet intelligence agencies, those that have done the best job on the analytical side are the ones that have been most free of the police operational responsibility that has so severely corrupted Soviet intelligence in general. It is the merger of intelligence with repressive police functions that has given it a popular image derogatory to its genuine functions.

The only protection that any organisation or society can have against surprise in a conflict-ridden world is to support the professional integrity of analysts. If they, as a group, are to produce answers that are honest — not determined by what Irving Janis[1] calls 'Groupthink' – their conclusions will be varied and contradictory, because the chances of any one conclusion being right are very small in a complex world. The deformation which is most likely to underlie the occurrence of surprise is that of the existence of a canonical view. In all the kinds of research organisations that we have discussed, there is considerable pressure to conform. To offset that tendency, protections for diversity have to be created deliberately. In this respect, the social sciences represent a somewhat better model to be followed than the one we see in government. Government practice tends to put much more emphasis upon conformity.

An ambassador, for example, is supposed to sign off on all cables from his team. In fact, in a large embassy he cannot do it; he cannot control all the flow. In the modern world of telecommunications, all sorts of unrecorded communications occur. Nonetheless, the tradition remains that it is the individual ambassador whose views are being expressed and who has to sign off on whatever analyses come out of the embassy.

The same sort of emphasis upon an official view can be found operating throughout the processes of governmental organisations. Agreed estimates are made; sometimes footnotes may be permitted, with divergent views, but these are often limited to official views of different agencies.

All of this has a history. It concerns the thin channel of communication that used to be all there was between an individual diplomat, who performed the basic intelligence function abroad, and the ruler to whom he reported. However, as that individual diplomat turned into a large and organised bureaucracy, the system began to produce results that were quite different from those that emerged when the reporting was simply done by one man.

Technology is working against the possibility of producing genuine conformity, or of having single, agreed, or sincere consensus views. The flood of information spreading across the world started with the telegraph and then the overseas cable. This first breakthrough still constituted a thin channel. It did not move much information, although it moved quickly. For the first time in history, decision-makers knew immediately what was happening around the world. Before that, decisions had to be taken on the basis of information that was, in part, weeks old. To President Andrew Jackson and to the British on the spot, the battle of New Orleans seemed to be the decisive battle of the War of 1812. However, this major battle of the conflict occurred when the war was over and after the treaty of peace had been signed. After the telegraph, a short, crucial message would have prevented that.

Shortwave broadcasting diffuses information *en masse*; so does the jet aeroplane. Twentieth-century technology has changed the thin stream of important, tightly controllable, telegraphic information into a flood.

The effects of satellites are extremely interesting. In one sense, they are nothing new. A satellite is simply a microwave antenna in the sky. What is significant about satellites, however, is that they make the costs of both long-distance and short-distance transmission essentially the same. Once you send a message 35,880 km (22,300 miles) up to the satellite and 35,880 km (22,300 miles) down, it makes no difference at all whether the two points between which that message flows are 800 or 8000 km (500 or 5000 miles) apart. The cost is identical as long as the two points are within the same beam. And the message capacity of satellites is enormous. The significance of this fact is that now there can be a tremendous flow of information over global distances.

The most advanced communications network with which we are all familiar is the airline reservation network. You walk up to a counter anywhere and immediately consult a computer on the other side of the world about your reservation, or have it changed. The cost of that action, within the United States, is a couple of pence. Around the world, where the system is a little less efficient, it costs somewhat more, but it need not do so. Many businesses are setting up similar private communications networks. I know of one enterprise, for example, that has a very common kind of communications network with its computer switch in the United States, a high-grade line between Europe and the United States and a network of private lines on each continent. It happens to own two factories in a city in Germany, and these are a couple of blocks apart, but the messages between the two plants flow by way of the computer switch in the United States. The cost of the long haul no longer makes a difference.

We saw another example of the impact of changing communications technology when the Ayatollah Khomeini started dictating his messages of the day from Paris onto tapes. One of his assistants would then dial direct to Teheran, play the tape, and it would be retaped at the other end in Teheran. These tapes would then be copied and sold in the bazaar shortly thereafter.

Thus, an enormous and rapidly growing global flow of international communications makes it increasingly difficult to concentrate information into certain channels with an official view imposed. Technology is creating an increasingly diverse flow. One important aspect of the technology, making it impossible to channel information into single, simple, canonical views, is the power of the computer as an information retrieval device. 'Hard copy' printed reports are beginning to be replaced by dynamic retrieval systems. Those not only bring up more information faster, but also in combinations and formats created *ad hoc* by the enquirer. The retrieved data otherwise would constitute a veritable flood in which one would be lost, but in a good computer system the user controls the winnowing, taking over some of the tasks of an editor. That has important implications. For example, it can extend the concept of footnotes a great deal further.

In ordinary writing, when something has to be explained, or a source cited, it is placed in a footnote. The job of following up on the footnote, and looking up the references, is vast. One has to go down to the library and search. A branched information retrieval system places the footnoted references online, ready to be called up if the note is intriguing.

Such developments do not create joy on the part of those persons who, in the past, have organised intelligence systems in traditional bureaucratic ways. Alarm is stirred by the notion that every evaluated intelligence report could be challenged by the reader, who can ask, 'Who said that; let me see his underlying evidence'. The notion that a report could be followed back in a trail to its source is not welcomed by the intelligence analyst whose evaluation is thus questioned.

There is a strong defence to be made for evaluated conclusions. There is a case for protecting unsophisticated and unitiated users from details and misleading information which they may not be able to understand. There is a case for providing unsophisticated decision-makers, such as a president, only with evaluated, carefully analysed conclusions; there is no reason to assume that he knows how to analyse raw data as well as his specialised advisors. Yet that is the root of surprise. As Roberta Wohlstetter and Barton Whaley have taught us, in most instances of surprise the information has been there if one chose to look. Almost always one can recognise with hindsight that there were lots of people calling the shots right, but the filters worked to bring one canonical interpretation to the fore and not others.

I could sustain exactly the same points from social science studies. Much psychological research has dealt with problems of group decision-making. Groups fool themselves. It is hard to produce an environment in which a multiplicity of possibilities and ideas are discussed.

Robert Axelrod has published an article on the discussions, right after the Second World War, in a British cabinet-level committee, on the Persian problem.[2] The discussions in this committee were secret but, contrary to normal practice, they were completely transcribed, so a total record of the discussions exist. By detailed content analysis, Axelrod plotted and graphed the discussions, argument by argument and step by step. From these elaborate statistical and graphic representations there emerges the interesting conclusion that the committee split into simpleminded coherent factions. There were those who said that what was going on in Persia was serious and that it would not be very hard to do something about it, and that it would not cost much to do so. On the other side, there were those who said that the problem was really not very important, and to do anything about it would be very difficult and very expensive. Completely absent from these candid, internal, secret discussions is anyone saying that the problem is very important, but awfully hard to do anything about, or stating that the problem is really not very important, but would be pretty easy to do something about. It is as if, by some magic, all the considerations point the same way. There is, in short, no cost-effectiveness balancing. Nowhere in the discussions does anybody say – on the one hand, this, and, on the other hand, that. Each person has simplified his perceptions to the point where they make a coherent, persuasive, self-contained argument, all points of which lead in the same direction.

The simplification of reality into a one-sided picture is one of the common characteristics of public discussions. Recall, for instance, the American debates on Vietnam. Doves said that the United States had no important interests in the area, victory was impossible, the war was immoral and expensive, and a Vietcong victory would be a reasonably benign outcome. Hawks said major American interests were at stake, victory could be had at reasonable cost, morality required American action, and a Vietcong victory would lead to a bloodbath and further war in South East Asia. It would be hard to find a quotation from a decade ago affirming the strong American interest in Vietnam, the moral legitimacy of the military effort, forecasting a bloodbath and continued war in South East Asia if the communists won, but asserting that the United States was bound to lose if it tried to do anything about it. However reasonable such an assessment may seem in hindsight, it was not the sort of dissonant statement that could be heard in public debates *at the time.*

The interesting aspect of the Persian problem discussions is that the same absence of admitted dilemmas was to be found in very private discussions also. It is hard for many to accept the fact that real-life considerations may conflict with one another. And the more the tension, the greater the controversy, the more discussions tend to fall into an oversimplified polarised mould. Only the encouragement of a variety of views can offer some challenge to a misleading but easy consistency.

The vigour with which individuals resist facts at variance with their theories is illustrated in Leon Festinger's book, *When Prophecy Fails:*[3] a Mrs Keech, in a suburb of Chicago, predicted the end of the world, on a certain date. Spacemen would descend first to rescue the true believers, notably Mrs Keech and her followers. The rest of the world would be destroyed. Festinger and his colleagues seized this opportunity for research and joined the sect. They assembled with the believers waiting for the end of the world, taking mental notes and preparing to write it up in a journal article afterward.

Well, what happened? The world, as far as is known, did not come to an end, so the prophecy was not fulfilled; but what about the true believers? That is more complicated. Not all of them were gathered in the one room in Chicago. Some of them, for various personal reasons, were scattered in other places. Those were not heard from again; when the world failed to end, they abandoned the faith. However, those who were together in the group, when the prophecy failed, became even more fervent than they had been before. The attitude of the sect toward the press had been uncooperative, before the deadline at which the world was to end. There were reporters who sensed a good story and knocked at the door, trying to obtain interviews with those who were waiting for the cataclysm. The reply was that of any sensible person awaiting the end of the world. They asked to be left alone. There were more important matters to be attended to than providing a headline for tomorrow which would never come. The sect had no use for the press.

When the deadline passed, and Mrs Keech announced that the world had been given a reprieve because the group had prayed so hard and been so faithful, the members opened the door to the press; news conferences were held to explain that events really confirmed Mrs Keech's previous beliefs and proved them right. Some started proselytising around the country, recruiting for the sect. Festinger's hypothesis had been that this was exactly what would happen. His historical study had shown that a large number of proselytising groups had begun with a prophecy that failed.

Here again, we see a set of problems all too familiar in the intelligence process. Those who have been pilloried for an incorrect forecast must explain even more vehemently why they were right. The creation of an environment in which persons are willing to accept a fair batting average, in which errors are viewed as normal, in which correction is part of the process, in which change of opinion is somehow respectable, is difficult to achieve. It is a situation that the sciences have had to institutionalise with great effort, not that science is free of the strain towards doctrinal orthodoxy. In the hard sciences, too, there are schools that become ideologies. However, a major effort is made in science to institutionalise the process of testing established theories. The scientist is rewarded for disproving what had been believed before. That is called 'discovery' and is praised. The acceptance of new evidence is a normal, reputable process. There is a notion, perhaps even a fashion, which makes it acceptable that the assumptions of the past may not necessarily be binding for the future; and the evidence for any view is always made a matter of record.

Other professions engaged in intelligence would do well to copy some of these characteristics. Journalism has many desirable characteristics that the social sciences lack; for example, journalists generally write good English and usually meet their deadlines. Journalism, however, does not have the same willingness to operate under exposure and documentation of evidence. The same must be said also of government intelligence analysis.

There are many features of government intelligence operations that could well be emulated by journalists and social scientists. Intelligence organisations, for example, compile massive documentation, and have shown a willingness to use modern technologies of information. This is partly because they have more money, but it is also because so much more is at stake in their being correct than there is in the speculations of their social science or journalistic colleagues. However, in other respects, the intelligence tradition has much to learn from the tradition of science. Intelligence operations too often lack the detachment and willingness to engage in debates that have been built into science as ways of offsetting the inclination to hear what one wants to hear. Often it turns out that the discipline of a governmental intelligence organisation serves to aid those on the other side, whose job it is to disinform.

NOTES

1. Janis, Irving, *Victims of Groupthink: A Psychological Study of Foreign-Policy Decisions and Fiascos*, (Boston, Houghton Mifflin Co. 1973).
2. *Psycho-Algebra: A Mathematical Theory of Cognition and Choice with an Application to the British Eastern Committee in 1918*, Peace Research Society, Papers, XVIII (1972), pp. 113–31.
3. Festinger, Leon, *When Prophecy Fails* (Philadelphia, Peace Research Society, 1972).

Part Three

Problems of Evaluation: The Soviet Union and the United States

4 The Soviet Military Potential for Surprise Attack: Surprise, Superiority and Time

John Erickson

Irreverent though it may seem, perhaps the most purposeful way to embark upon this investigation is through a conundrum all too reminiscent of juvenile party games: when is a surprise not a surprise?[1] Such whimsy, however, speedily gives way to a reality which is surpassing grim, precisely because this is a matter of life and death for the Soviet Union (and ourselves, for that matter). Indeed, it is no exaggeration to say that the spectre of 'surprise attack' haunts the Soviet mind, having dominated Soviet thinking for more than three decades, and shows little sign of abating with the passage of time. Much, though not all, can be explained by the massive trauma brought on by the devastating German surprise attack loosed upon the Soviet Union on 22 June 1941, an attack which brought the Soviet system to the brink of catastrophe and from which recovery was agonising almost beyond belief; delineating this brush with extinction, apportioning blame and lauding recovery, furnishing alibis – even to the point of insisting that this 'surprise' was no 'surprise' – has occupied many years and produced some involved commentaries, as we shall see shortly. Meanwhile, by way of recent elaboration on this theme, Army General (now Marshal) V. Kulikov, writing at the time in his capacity as Chief of the General Staff of the Soviet Armed Forces, insisted that 'the most important consideration' in relation to any future conflict was to 'oppose an attempted enemy surprise attack' not merely by defensive mechanisms but by utilising the combat readiness of the Soviet forces to parry an attack *under any conditions* and to encompass the decisive defeat of the enemy. New methods must comprise not only advanced military technology but also incisive and perceptive appreciation of the entire strategic environment and the problem of surprise.[2]

In any examination of the Soviet approach to surprise attack it would be grotesque to ignore the implications of the experience of June 1941, though this is not to give undue place to historical analysis and exposition – rather to see to what use the Soviet command has put these data. Here we must have recourse to three studies by Colonel V. A. Anfilov, expressly devoted to the 'surprise attack' of 1941.[3] Three features stand out at once with respect to this work: first, the period of 'surprise attack' is steadily extended throughout the span of these three versions (the first version stopping in mid-July); second, much greater consideration is given to Soviet military doctrine and Soviet facility in forecasting the form of a future war (in the second and third versions); and, third, the latest version of the 'surprise attack' saga covers not only the impact of the initial blow itself, but also the Soviet 'recovery stage' and its attendant politicoeconomic aspects.[4]

Though avowedly a historical excursus, the Anfilov volumes can serve as an introduction to what might well be called an expansive Soviet theory of 'surprise' at all levels of operations, strategic, within operational art,[5] and in tactical terms. By the same token, we must also account for a vocabulary which is at once complex and sophisticated, employed within Soviet circles, terminology designed not merely to discuss 'surprise' in a narrow operational context but also to comprehend what might best be described as the 'surprise environment' with all its ramifications – political, military, technical, economic, psychological and so on. Using this assembly of terms and their associated contexts it is possible to group the Soviet 'theory of surprise' into five main elements – evaluation of the 'threat situation' (including 'rational timing'),[6] the exploitation of 'manoeuvre' (including deception, disinformation, concealment and diversion), planning under severe time constraints (military operations), technical means (extending also to 'technological ambush', or unexpected impact upon tactical performance of new weaponry) and, finally, the *time factor* in relation to performance (Soviet performance, enemy performance, both anticipated and realised).

Compressed into a formula, this might be expressed as the relationship between *surprise, superiority and time* (all of which terms require the most careful qualification). For proper elucidation, however, the whole proposition about 'surprise attack' must be inverted and pride of place given to the Soviet preoccupation with *how not to be surprised*, what Lieutenant Colonel A. L. Elliott has nimbly described as 'counter-surprise'.[7] To put this in rather awkward fashion, the Soviet view seems to be that the essential prerequisite for a successful 'surprise attack' procedure is provision for counter-surprise. It would be unwise to impute too much prescience to the Soviet command – and Soviet writers themselves are cautious in proclaiming the infallibility of any 'calculus of surprise' – but it should be noted that the 'counter-surprise' basis can itself maximise resources for surprise and, perhaps more important, allow *standard operating procedures* to be used as a vital resource for surprise attack. Above all, as Dr Axelrod has pointed out, this recourse to standard operating procedures – deliberately made available for inspection and observation[8] – instils in the opposing side confidence about its ability to predict. (Even some specific aberration from SOPs could be fitted into this perception pattern by arguing that it was only one 'abnormal' action, thus shoring up the notion that all is 'normal' and demonstrably routine.) Facility to observe, in paradoxical fashion, is *not* a guarantee that 'resources for surprise' will be detected, least of all the mobilisation and co-ordination of these same resources. Grand though some of these concepts may seem, and for all the imposing language, there is more than a hint of plain ambush (*zasada*) in such circumstances and I am tempted to introduce the term 'strategic ambush' to explain some elements of Soviet planning.

Crucial to the whole problem is the *time factor*, not merely in the attack/operational phase but in defining what the Soviet military press recites as the 'threat of attack situation' (*pri ugroze napadeniya protivaika*), though this might be called the whole 'threat environment', a distinct and definable timespan which precedes the actual initiation of military operations introducing the 'initial stage' (*nachal'ayi period*). This 'threat environment' is marked by particular governmental decisions, prompted in the first instance by change in the international situation at large or some particular focus of tension – local conflict – as well as by the activation of civil defence measures on the part of a potential enemy, an increase of a potential opponent's combat readiness, in all a phase which might be circumscribed within *one week* (though the 'threat environment' can prevail over several weeks or, yet again, be compressed into a matter of hours). Within this period of threat, the 'more immediate threat' must be identified and 'counter-surprise' initiated, for, at this point preparation for war moves into a *concealed mode*, followed in turn by overt measures which come into their own once more – all within hours of the actual launching of an attack.

The prevalent Soviet view seems to be that 'warning' cannot be discounted and cannot be wholly eliminated under present or fore-seeable circumstances, but this by no means nullifies the factor of 'surprise'. The doctrinal underpinning insists on a condition of deployed readiness, consistent both with 'counter-surprise' and the launching of a 'surprise attack' (both sets of preparations being interconnected), the emphasis on a high degree of security and 'concealment' (*skrynost'*) and, at the very root of the matter, further 'counter-surprise' provision. Embedded in this whole concept is the application of *maskirovka*,[9] easily rendered as 'camouflage' but embracing a whole gamut of measures designed to deceive, conceal, disorientate and unnerve. *Maskirovka* is more than concealment in the passive sense (and *skrytnost'* in the Soviet context has also a sense of tight security as well as technical camouflage). *Maskirovka* is a manipulative technique, directed as much against friend as well as foe, designed not merely to deceive (in the narrowest tactical sense) but to bring about a total restructuring of perceptions and either by disinformation or distortion inhibit effective decision-making.

The attainment of surprise is still possible, for all the prevalence of modern electronic gadgetry. Decision-making capabilities, whether collective or individual means, can be interrupted by the application of 'manoeuvre' – the repetition of actions designed to make the opposing system decreasingly sensitive to the actual possibility of military attack. The essence of this method lies in avoiding *stereotypes*: as Colonel Savkin points out, there must be 'a continuous search for newer techniques and methods of achieving surprise'.[10] In short, there must be intensive training for surprise attack operations and greater reliance on effective and efficient staff work – and even 'old' methods of achieving surprise can be given a new lease of life if employed intelligently,[11] but the problem of *attacker and defender* must be studied simultaneously.

Probably the one great advantage which the Soviet Union can exploit is its facility to pursue contradictory (and even inconsistent) policies at one and the same time without reference to public opinion (or any other kind of organized opinion, such as Congress or Parliament), thus maximising its opportunity for the implementation of *maskirovka* – deception even in a crude sense, disinformation in any number of subtle guises, 'diplomatic noise', the creation of images and the manipulation of perceptions shared by friend and foe alike. This would be 'manoeuvre' in its broadest sense, supplemented by special intelligence activities and selective propaganda offensives, not to mention economic strategems. The covert measures associated with this phase not merely are passive (concealing Soviet deployments and military preparations) but are also active, or operational in the sense that they include widespread use of decoys and deception designed to confuse, if not actually to inhibit hostile reconnaissance; the operational attack phase involves the physical destruction of reconnaissance elements, enemy command and control centres and communications.

The other element of Soviet preoccupation with surprise attack is the emphasis on limiting, even eradicating, the opportunity for an enemy to recover while developing the 'sustainability' of the Soviet system, hence the balance between substantial forces-in-being and the provision for strategic reserves on an ever-expanding scale: that same balance can also promote Soviet 'counter-surprise' programmes, a hedge also against any American resort to 'first-strike'[12] as a worst-case contingency (extending also into a more overt move on the part of the United States to counter-force capabilities).[13] Inevitably Soviet discussions about surprise attack assume the worst, that is, possible US/NATO surprise attacks directed against the USSR and its allies, 'though much of this is clearly designed to meet a propaganda requirement and to rationalise Soviet insistence on 'combat readiness', 'vigilence' and 'security/secrecy'; on the other hand, 'counter-surprise' is deeply embedded in their system, whether in the form of a genuine increase in combat readiness, levels of weapons, a semi-mobilisation posture, dispersal, concealment, deception and a civil defence programme linked to a form of post-attack recovery (a programme, be it noted, set in train as early as February 1955). At the same time, this preoccupation must be reflected in a concern for the responsiveness of the *Soviet* system as a whole, including effective prior planning, due preparation and timely execution, all to cope with the circumstances of 'surprise': there is something of a paradox here, to project an expected outcome from the unexpected. (Here we come at once across an act of self-deception on our part, namely, the *ingrained*, almost ineradicable assumption that the Soviet *modus operandi* is so 'rigid' that managing the unexpected is quite beyond Soviet capabilities – there is difficulty enough in coping with the expected and the pre-planned, so runs accepted wisdom. The *Wehrmacht*, manned also by 'rigid' Germans, suffered nastily at times through this Soviet-style 'rigidity'.)[14]

To recapitulate briefly, the Soviet command is assured of the vital importance of the surprise factor both for strategic and tactical surprise; if anything, surprise has ever greater value than that demonstrated by historical experience (though that historical record is constantly weighed as in General Ivanov's major work *Nachal'nyi period voiny*).[15] The concept of 'surprise' is linked, quite logically, with considerations of this 'initial period', which is adjudged to be of relatively short duration and involves, therefore, rational calculation of surprise, superiority and time. Maintaining what Dr Axelrod calls 'resource for surprise' thus is critical to Soviet war-planning; here it is worth noting that attainment of surprise might involve withholding 'resources' in order to maximise their exploitation under conditions of rational timing and in relation to 'the stakes' – or *the* stake. While much of this is configured about all-out nuclear war, the Soviet theorists have not ignored conventional operations, even in the 'initial phase'; conventional operations can themselves provide cover under which nuclear forces can be brought to full readiness all with the chance of less detection about the modes of preparation and readiness states. Finally, we must pay much more attention to the whole meaning of *maskirovka*, linking it to other key ideas (such as *predvidenie*–'foresight'),[16] so that we have a rather complex syllogism of 'deception/detection/anticipation' as operational elements; going a little further, it is possible to make more sense of the apparent contradiction between preplanning and flexibility, as well as fitting various modes into particular phases – for example, *maskirovka* and 'threat of attack situation', the covert/overt modulations, 'counter-surprise' and 'surprise' in relation to the 'initial period'. However, the heart of the matter is 'the stake', those conditions and necessities under which the military capability, political dexterity and prior preparation of the Soviet Union could be utilised to maximise 'surprise' and with what ends in mind.

There can be no doubt that the Soviet command has long been interested in an effective war-waging capability; in brief, a war-waging capability is regarded as a deterrent in its own right and a realistic provision for action, if and when deterrence 'fails'. (The fact that 'deterrence' has little common usage in Soviet circles, being displaced rather by *aborona* – defence, though with a tinge of 'deterrence' about it, is not without relevance.) The crux of the matter is the degree to which this concept of war-waging is translated into 'war-winning' capability and nuclear 'armament norms' are built up to meet a specific doctrinal stipulation[17] about 'victory' in nuclear war. In this context, Defence Secretary Harold Brown's statement that all this sounds like 'World War II refought with nuclear weapons' appears as a gross oversimplification; the whole tendency of Soviet investigations of the 'doctrine-armament norms' relationship has been to adjust the Second World War 'norms' and to extend that formula into the area of efficiency in command and control matters, managing and controlling the entire strategic effort. At the same time it should be emphasised from the outset that there is thus far no discernible 'military factor' in Soviet strategy which can be distinguished from political processes and discrimination; on the contrary, the nature of war and its objectives are defined in political terms rather than being subject to particular 'technological' manipulation – for example, a 'limited war' (should that term be admitted into the Soviet vocabulary) is not one circumscribed by the type of military technology but rather by the political process and objective.[18] Nor is it sensible to ignore the fact that the Soviet leadership at large no doubt regards the best strategy as one which achieves its ends without firing a shot – or only a very few.

However, surprise attack has been and continues to be a dominant theme in the context of Soviet military doctrine. On the United States side 'the contingency of a Soviet surprise attack on our/US strategic forces' has become the 'fundamental test of the adequacy of those forces and the main basis for . . . strategic nuclear planning'.[19] Of course, we could fall into the trap of self-deception over 'surprise' by arguing that since doctrine does not make provision for an all-out 'out of the blue', once-and-for-all bid for the military neutralisation of the United States and the NATO alliance – the 'cosmic throw of the dice' – then it should not be expected; however, the essence of surprise is departure from anticipated behaviour patterns, and formal doctrine can be drastically adjusted to fit this circumstance. It is an eventuality which should be considered, but on all careful calculations it must come low on the list; at least it does terrible violence to one doctrinal fundamental that in the process the survival of the USSR would be put at cataclysmic risk. On the other hand, it is conceivable that some wholly unforeseen and quite violent *internal* spasms within the Soviet Union might impel an immediate recourse to a general military solution, 'clearing the decks' for better or for worse. As for any dangerous swing in the strategic balance against the United States, some attack could well be expected and could scarcely come under the rubric of acute 'surprise'; the damage under these circumstances would have been largely self-inflicted, so that 'surprise' would be little more than the *coup de grâce*. There are, therefore, compelling circumstances for the United States to 'take measures to correct . . . impending vulnerabilities'.

Both Soviet and American opinion seems to coincide over the virtual impossibility of a *disarming attack*. Meanwhile there is the problem of attempting to distinguish in Soviet usage between 'pre-emption' and 'preventive attack' (even as the problem of superimposing Western terminology induces some confusion); perhaps the best analogy can be drawn from Soviet Second World War practice and artillery techniques, the *kontrpodgotovka* which was carefully timed fire designed to break up (or 'frustrate') enemy deployments, the operation of command and control and the movement of operational reserves – all with the object of disrupting the momentum of an impending attack, gaining time and winning some relative advantage for the defender. As such, it is neither 'pre-emption' nor a spoiling attack. There is some justification in Defence Secretary Harold Brown's observation about a 're-run of World War II' in that the Soviet view of nuclear operations seems to be akin to the notion of a 'nuclear battle' with all the properties of a 'battle' in the orthodox sense; by the same token, someone has to win. However, in view of comments on United States capabilities, the Soviet command accepts that 'total surprise'–with the elimination of all warning signs and indicators–is virtually out of the question, so that surprise must be given a different emphasis.

Possibly manoeuvre is the answer. Somewhat earlier, 'manoeuvre' – that is, skilful disposition and deployment – was considered to be an answer in itself as a means to offset any relative disadvantage in strength and numbers.[20] Manoeuvre can also be construed as part of the process to debilitate enemy sensitivity to the prospect of attack, to confuse decision-making and to implement covert measures designed to inhibit reconnaissance means, all with the aim of 'muddling' the intelligence picture. Even the full throes of a crisis may not be a proper 'indicator'; it is conceivable that a major crisis could be allowed to 'lapse', to fall below the imminence of mobilisation and war, in order to provide a phase of covert preparation for full-scale military operations. To be crude, this means playing on the gullibility of an opponent. To this would be added a massive political 'whispering campaign' and 'diplomatic noise', manipulated and managed by the KGB (responsible also for assessments of enemy responses and receptivity). There is also every prospect that any period of tension – let us say that it lasts some two weeks – will be accompanied by *overt* drills and some deliberate demonstrative mobilisation, possibly purposefully cancelled in order further to confuse the intelligence picture, but under this same cover *key* mobilisation will have been carried through and select economic mobilisation set in train.[21]

Manoeuvre will also encompass the redeployment of air defence forces (*PVO Strany*), not merely bringing them to war stations but with the intention of altering the 'targeting map', plus the initiation of 'radio-electronic warfare' (with false radio traffic, radio silence, misleading radar returns . . .);camouflage measures will also be introduced in order to hamper enemy choices for air attack. Within this war deployment plan there will be limited movement of strategic missile elements, *PVO Strany* forces and related arms in order to maximise survivability. Inevitably there would also be 'deployment by exercise', particularly with the naval forces whose manoeuvres would well have preceded the onset of the immediate crisis. Speed goes hand in hand with deception (which term signifies nothing invidious, merely the implementation of the operational code of *maskirovka*), the preparation to fight the 'nuclear battle' on the most favourable terms.

The concept of the 'nuclear battle' emerged very early in Soviet military thinking, which worked steadily to develop its 'counter-battery' capability, targetting the United States ICBM force as a matter of commanding priority and thus able to effect some, if not all, of the requirements of *kontrpodgotovka*: this has its nearest equivalent in 'counter-force', or is interpreted as a commitment to 'pre-emption' – yet even that fails to expound the full Soviet requirement, as we shall see.[22] The early generation of Soviet missiles – the SS-4s and SS-5s – provided a bombardment capability to cover European/Eurasian targets, mostly soft targets which did not require major accuracy on the part of the missiles, nor massive warheads. Targets in the continental United States presented a much more variegated problem, being both 'soft' and 'hard', with the hard targets requiring special attention – hence the Soviet 'heavy bombardment' force with its multi-megaton warheads, aimed at

ICBM silos, launch control centres and nuclear storage sites, the very large warheads dictated by lesser accuracy (CEPs). First (and second) generation Soviet ICBMs – SS-7s, SS-8s, SS-9s and SS-11s – reflected this propensity for large warheads, the SS-9 with its 20–25 MT and the SS-11 with 1–2 MT loading. However, it proved to be impossible to build up a sufficiently numerous force of SS-9s to target them on all United States silos – even the 3-RV SS-9s could not compensate and the RV was certainly no substitute for the MIRV – so that the Soviet command turned to targeting 100 United States ICBM launch control complexes (two SS-9s to each complex), only to be thwarted in this design with the advent of United States airborne launch control system. The SS-11s were probably aimed at urban targets, but the SS-9 could not afford a true 'counter-force' capability and the existing Soviet ICBM arsenal did not afford any great degree of flexibility, least of all in total coverage of the mix of 'hard' and 'soft' targets.[23]

In view of the numerical array of targets and their diversity, it is no surprise at all that in SALT I the Soviet Union struck out for high numerical ceilings both for ICBMs and SLBMs, as well as resisting any substantial reduction in the 'heavy bombardment' force (represented at that time by the SS-9s, though four new systems were under development). The attempt to limit the throw-weight of the newer Soviet ICBMs (save for the follow-on missile to the SS-9) to that of the SS-11 failed; the liquid fuelled SS-17 and the SS-19, replacements for the SS-11, were already configured as 'heavy' ICBMs – with the SS-17 carrying at least twice the payload of its predecessor. If there was reluctance on the Soviet side at agreeing to the limitation of 308 silos (326 with training silos) for 'heavy' missiles, this was more than outweighed by seeing the disappearance of any extensive United States ABM deployment (which would have wreaked havoc on the Soviet 'numbers' solution and targeting plans). The Soviet command, however, could anticipate the advent of a very substantial MIRV-ed force, with the SS-18 ICBM (the successor to the SS-9) carrying eight to ten MIRVs – and a reported capability of no less than fourteen – in the van of a genuine counter-force build-up; even more striking, the accuracy of the SS-18 has evidently improved in dramatic fashion with a CEP of 180 m reported from recent tests. In the wake of the SS-18 came the SS-17 (with four MIRVs) and the SS-19 (with six MIRVs), adding to the stock of warheads.

The advances in missile accuracy combined with the growing number of warheads all too obviously enhances the threat to United States ICBMs. The high ceilings for all delivery vehicles clearly meets a basic Soviet requirement – 2250 vehicles all told, with a 'heavy ICBM bombardment' force of 308 and MIRV-ed missiles at 1320. At the present time the targeting map facing Soviet operational planners consists of 'super-hardened' (6890 kN/m² – 1000 lb/in²), hardened (2060 kN/m² – 300 lb/in²) and soft targets, in round figures some 2000 targets.[24] The 'super-hard' targets predominate, being Minuteman silos, launch control complexes and associated C3–1130–followed by 180 hardened targets and a tally of 750 'soft' targets including urban targets, bomber bases and industrial/administrative/communication facilities. The number of existing (and projected) warheads must clearly rule out the notion of a three-on-one (much less a five-on-one) attack on United States ICBM silos, but a two-on-one strike is regarded as quite feasible, given the improved accuracy; attacking 1054 silos (including Titan sites) would mean 2108 warheads for two-on-one strikes, with the SS-18, SS-17 and SS-19 available in several combinations. (The revised estimates of the yield of the SS-18 MIRVs – set now at 600 KT as opposed to 1.2 MT – does not seem to invalidate the missile's utility for these silo attacks, for improved accuracy is more relevant and, in any event, smaller warheads reduce the 'fratricide' effect).

The present Soviet advantage centres on the implication that a 'two-on-one' strike against United States ICBM silos could be launched and still conserve the bulk of Soviet ICBM re-entry vehicles for other targets. General de Gaulle used to speak of the role of the French deterrent as '*arracher le bras*', but if the Soviet command could '*arracher la jambe*', tear off the ICBM 'leg' of the United States triad, then the outcome would be grave indeed. Loss of second-strike target coverage, a reduction in United States capability to attack time-urgent targets and a decrease in flexibility to manage the surviving United States forces would be the inevitable consequence, in Defence Secretary Harold Brown's view; worse, it might well excite the Soviet command to attack other second-strike forces.[25] But all this presupposes the conditions of a well-executed surprise attack, using ICBMs under operational conditions. One assumption is that under war conditions the 'working CEP' will be regarded as in the order of 0.2 nm, to say nothing of overall missile readiness and performance, aborts, trajectory variations – and the possible United States response of *launch under attack*, which would be the most extreme solution to ICBM survivability. The warhead/target ratios, which suggest a more promising outcome for a Soviet counter-force first strike, are also based on high readiness rates and also allow for the firing of multiple rounds; the possibility of error in target positioning must be compounded by the conditions prevailing for re-entry of warheads and the environment of the target area.[26] At the same time, there can be no absolute guarantee that Soviet missiles – ICBM or SLBM – will catch all United States bombers on the ground and that there will be much more than a third of United States SSBNs pinned in port. Even under 'perfect' surprise attack conditions, alert bombers and

SSBNs on partrol cannot be eliminated, assuming even the best possible synchronisation.

The United States bomber forces, which form a considerable part of the United States strategic component, can be tackled by Soviet SLBMs in a depressed trajectory mode, using a low re-entry angle at about 6° to the horizon in order to curtail the ballistic flight path and to reduce radar warning time, but a fully effective SLBM strike against United States bomber bases would mean deploying at least a score of SSBNs off United States coasts and this would hardly go unnoticed. The Soviet command could scarcely ignore one-third of the United States deterrent force and bomber bases would be included within time-sensitive targets. However, the business of hunting down other mobile systems (particularly SSBNs) would consume much time and could not be assured of total success. Meanwhile the Soviet command would be heavily dependent on effective post-strike reconnaissance, if only to facilitate retargeting and the delivery of further nuclear strikes. The involved calculations and the *ex cathedra* statements pertaining to Soviet 'surprise attack' capability differ substantially, save for the general consensus that United States ICBMs are becoming increasingly vulnerable under a threat which grows incrementally and where the number of surviving United States ICBMs could be 'marginal'; to take but one example, it is argued that only half of United States destructive power – compared with the early 1960s – would remain after a Soviet first strike and, by 1985, that the *Soviet* force remaining after such a strike would have twice the destructive power of the surviving United States force.[27]

On the other hand, what can be gleaned from open Soviet military publications tends to be cautiously pragmatic (which could admittedly be construed as *maskirovka*, where the essence of surprise is radical departure from 'received doctrine', or yet again, maintaining a particular doctrinal stance deliberately for external assumption). Whatever the impact of surprise, formal Soviet doctrine does not envisage nuclear war terminating with one cataclysmic exchange – a 'one shot' win (or less) – but rather it will consist of several phases or stages, so that 'survivability' and 'sustainability' (*zhivuchest*) are mandatory requirements; the role of 'surprise' in relation to the 'initial phase' is paradoxically less to achieve total 'knockout' than to ensure that any protracted phase of the war will be conducted on terms of relative force more favourable to the USSR and to facilitate the eventual military ascendancy of the Soviet Union. Equally, Soviet military commentators are forced to recognise that counter-force has its natural limits, hence the deliberate offensive–defensive mix, with the latter designed to cope with the inevitable retaliatory blow – albeit reduced in scale and intensity – which cannot be entirely eliminated or totally deflected. It is reasonable to suppose also that the Soviet military has carefully studied the 'pre-emptive first-strike margin' and investigated the shifting measures of superiority (in terms of the *total force exchange outcome*) attending the launch of first strike; the Soviet SLBM arsenal, currently built up to its SALT limit, can now be admitted into this equation both for use in the 'initial phase' and for retention as a reserve.

We are, thus, not talking about some single 'knockout' blow. The first 'pre-emptive counterforce strike', utilizing surprise to the greatest possible degree, is to be followed by a series of strikes and recourse to the 'political targeting' for each TVD. The contingency of a United States 'first strike' is at least admitted, in which circumstance the Soviet aim will be to allot *maximum firing* to their *first launch* in order to secure the greatest degree of missile survivability. Otherwise the initial strike will probably consist of several salvos, in true artillery fashion, each separated by a few hours so that a full strike will take up to a whole day, though the entire nuclear operation is conceived of some more protracted period – hence the importance of manoeuvre during the initial phase (regrouping and redeploying for the several strikes) and then engaging reserves. It must be assumed that the Soviet command has reload/reserve ICBM rounds; a 1×1 load/reload capability raises the overall salvo strength to some 3500 weapons and the ideal 'norm' for load/reload could well be in the order of two to three rounds per ICBM.[28] Even without silos, missiles could be launched from emergency hardpads previously camouflaged with collapsible concealment structures. If such reloads exist, as assuredly they must, then the problem of maintaining wartime production of ICBMs would be less significant. Finally, SLBM holdings afford a secure reserve force and in the very worst circumstances SS-16s could be deployed for further retaliatory capability.

It appears that the 'nuclear battle' is planned along classic military lines, with first and second echelon forces, with a mandatory requirement to 'conceal' the second echelon. If the nuclear battle is duly conceived in terms of some protracted period, then the time requirement for the second echelon falls into the category of many hours, if not days, and thus concealment can be made more effective; the deployment of new formations at the strategic level (that is using 'formation' in the British sense of armies/divisions) must involve fresh, second-echelon SRF armies. It is *not* assumed that the first echelon will escape loss, hence the application of the classic second-echelon/reserve principle. If the Soviet command places little reliance on a single massed strike but envisages phases within the 'initial period', then it is logical that 'second echelon/reserve/mobilisational' elements of the SRF will be engaged in due sequence, with refire/reload sequences and an ultimate recourse to reserves. It is also worth noting that the Soviet military has shown increasing interest in a greater degree of flexibility for its ICBM force, possibly for rapid retargeting during the course of the 'initial period' itself and also to combine counter-force with counter-value targeting.

But to return to the language and the logic of military orthodoxy – the 'nuclear battle' – it must be assumed that the Soviet attack will be a mass attack, utilising the SS-18s and the SS-19s. Surprise is a factor in Soviet planning, but it must be fitted into a Soviet 'scenario' of protracted war with multiple exchanges; this is no 'bolt-from-the-blue' stuff. On the other hand, Soviet programmes embrace a huge new dimension in terms of space warfare, developing their own manned command and control spacecraft (not dissimilar to the US E-4B National Emergency Airborne Command Post) while directing possible strikes against United States C_3 systems with vulnerable nodes on the ground and in space, designed to inhibit United States decision-making in the initial phase. For their part the Soviet military relies on an ICBM 'heavy bombardment' force which can be controlled and launched with a survivable C_3 system, heavy with redundancy, as opposed to SLBMs where C_3 is problematical. One of the problems with antisatellite weapons is to know when one is being attacked – whether by a non-nuclear ASAT or by a laser weapon; registration of attack and the survivability of satellites is obviously of commanding importance, where groundbased surveillance sensors are not adequate to meet the operational task. United States DSP (Defence Support Programme) satellites – three of them – are useful but vulnerable, dependent as they are on two fixed and unprotected ground sites; the Mosaic Sensor Programme (MSP) could be less vulnerable and still provide reliable early warning.[29]

Both sides are going to have to counter layered defence systems. Ambush in space might be one recourse and here the Soviet military has expended enormous effort and applied much ingenuity. The aim is to win specific advantage in terms of *time* and *relative numbers*, to utilise the 'initial period' to shape further outcomes but most immediately to adjust the 'correlation of forces' in Soviet favour, first to blunt or diminish the weight of an enemy nuclear counter-blow and finally to produce a post-exchange balance in which those *several hundred rounds* still remaining to one side are Soviet. In view of the protracted nature of the exchange and its *multiple phases*, it is sensible to provide for second-echelon SRF forces plus their reserve/mobilisational elements which can bring fresh 'armies' (SRF formations) into the field, even as the whole Soviet system swings into its strategic defensive mode and further afield activates its 'combined-arms' solution (using a mix of nuclear/conventional weapons and forces to achieve related objectives in associated TVDs). A single obliterative 'first strike' does not seem to meet Soviet perceptions – if this were so, then there is something very odd about Soviet efforts to implement 'sustainability' for nuclear war. This is no *blitzkrieg*, for if *vnezapnost* (surprise) is a key factor, so then is *zhivuchest*, 'sustainability'; the *blitzkrieg* concept failed and whatever the mild snickering about the Soviet view of nuclear war looking like a rerun of the Second World War fought with nuclear weapons, at least the Soviet command has no intention of repeating the mistakes of the Second World War, neither the German mistakes nor the Soviet mistakes. Much thought has gone into this, deep Soviet preoccupation and deliberation, to a degree that we can surmise that the Soviet theory of 'surprise/pre-emption' is the most sophisticated in the world.

We must now attend to some calculations, albeit of a very perfunctory nature – *pace* Soviet military operational analysts. We must assume also that there is motivation for a Soviet pre-emptive counterforce strike against United States ICBMs, either to shift the strategic balance hugely in favour of the USSR, to reduce United States options in any limited nuclear conflict and yet again to produce a diminished strike against the USSR in general nuclear war. We might also assume that for operational purposes 0.2 nm CEP is the acceptable 'norm' (360 m – 1200 ft), whatever test runs indicate. This could well be the criterion for attack effectiveness, while the 'two-on-one' attack mode would be an optimum solution with both warheads aimed for ground contact (thus ensuring a nuclear explosion upon a given silo). Given a CEP of 360 m (1200 ft) and a two-on-one attack, the Soviet command could reckon on the destruction of about 60 per cent of the United States ICBM force; given the uncertainties of the operational environment and the operational performance of Soviet ICBMs, then Soviet planners must work on assumptions of destructions ranging from 40 to 60 per cent, relative to the United States ICBM force. Improving accuracy (to 0.1 nm or 180m– 600 ft) the 'two-on-one' attack boils down to a single warhead strike on each silo, with the second warhead aimed to ensure that the silo was actually struck, a seemingly favourable attack outcome but the Soviet command would have to calculate whether the surviving United States ICBM force would be in the order of 100 or 250 missiles and their equivalent megatonnage (*EM*). Meanwhile, in this co-ordinated strike United States bombers would have to be dealt with and even allowing for the use of depressed trajectories (with SLBM flight times of 4 to 7 minutes) alert bombers might just escape, though non-alert bombers would be eliminated; however, as has been pointed out earlier, the concentration of SSBNs to carry out this strike would surely not go unnoticed. (Dispersal of bombers to the deep interior of the continental United States could also unhinge much of this plan.) The Soviet forces would also have to cope with the mobile seaborne platforms, the SSBNs, some of which could be 'caught' – about 30 to 40 per cent – while undergoing overhaul, though the Trident programme promises longer

life to the reactor core and better logistics, so that the 'at-sea' rate of
these SSBNs will be well over 60 per cent. We can thus arrive at a
hypothetical attack picture of 70 per cent of the B-52 bombers
destroyed, about 40 per cent of the Poseidon fleet and about 33 per cent
of the Trident fleet, all under most favourable circumstances.[30]

The 'balance', the attack outcome or the post-attack 'correlation of
forces', assuming that almost 300 SS-18 ICBMs (with an operational
accuracy of 0.2 nm) equipped with eight warheads are used for an attack
on United States ICBM silos, would leave the United States with 6400
warheads (megatonnage equivalent 1400) and the USSR with 6000
warheads and 6000 equivalent megatonnes. Given a condition of overt
tension before the launch of a Soviet strike and thus United States forces
in a generated alert posture, then the survivability of bombers inevitably
increases, as does that of the sea-based missile force. However, increased
accuracy with Soviet ICBMs and contraction in the United States forces
(for example, with withdrawal of Poseidon SSBNs) can contribute to
alerting attack outcomes: with Soviet CEPs down to 0.1 nm the
projection of a 90 per cent destruction of the United States ICBM force
is feasible, which would still leave a residual United States capability of
4500 warheads, though the present range of destruction appears to be *in
the order of 40 to 60 per cent.* Even as the Soviet Union improves missile
accuracy, the United States plans to introduce the MX advanced ICBM
in a 'survivable basing mode', with 200 missiles distributed among 8000
to 9000 launch points – with 25 hard points along the 25 km (15 mile)
trench (200 trenches in all), hard points being protected to 4100–
6900kN/m² (600–1000 psi).[31]

The Soviet military must now ponder the implications of an American
recourse to a form of counterforce – will it be 'slow counterforce' (cruise
missiles) or 'prompt counterforce' (MX and Trident II), weapons
designed to strike reserve Soviet ICBMs and thus smother the Soviet
second salvo? More immediately, the 'window of opportunity', exposing the growing vulnerability of US silo-based ICBMs, open ever wider
between the years 1981–86; assuming no United States improvements,
the use of Soviet ICBMs with 180 m (600 ft) CEPs would produce a
catastrophic imbalance against the United States after a Soviet first-
strike – a post exchange ratio of 11:1 in the USSR's favour (Soviet first-
strike/United States second strike). The real question, however, is
whether this would realistically lower the 'pre-emptive strike margin' in
Soviet eyes and also raise the incentive; that incentive might be
established in fearfully ironical fashion, where the United States search
for a secure counter-force second-strike capability might be construed in
Soviet circles as the implementation of a first-strike facility, particularly
if the United States solution is 'prompt counter-force'. More than that,
recourse to 'hiding' ICBMs in deliberate fashion makes deception a

formal and inescapable element of the strategic scene. Random deployment is the technical answer to the threat of 'surprise attack'; given this and the growing 'deception environment', the Soviet response would probably be to develop (and procure) exotic weaponry, particularly those aimed at space warning/surveillance systems, 'quick fixes' to meet both 'prompt' and 'slow' United States counterforce solutions – there are already signs of that – and, finally, to 'drain off' the production which might have gone into higher ICBM levels (but for SALT II) into reload/reserve rounds. The United States move to 'hardened *horizontal* shelters' may prompt some equivalent Soviet move, but this seems to be the least of the dangers; the most debilitating effect is that deception is fully legitimised and *maskirovka* finally comes into its own.

'Surprise', 'pre-emption' and 'first strike' have perhaps their least ambiguous context in terms of a 'theatre campaign' and most specifically, the European theatre. Of course, in any general crisis leading to (or gravely threatening) general war, the several TVDs – Europe included – would be targeted for a pre-emptive counterforce blow, though some are inclined to argue that we may be seeing the possibility of an 'independent theatre option', an operation designed to 'clear' Europe of dangerous circumstances, and conducted with that speed and selective destruction which would make resort to general war futile. Twice already the Soviet Union has exploited 'surprise' in the European context: in 1956 when the Soviet Army carried out the full-scale military reduction of the Hungarian insurgents to the amazement of many and the consternation of all, and again in 1968 when, much aginst the 'accepted wisdom' to east and west alike, the Soviet Army raced into Czechoslovakia.

The present situation in terms of Soviet capability has now moved further and faster in two major directions, so that the trundling armies of the 1950s and 1960s might be somewhat *passé*: modernised theatre nuclear weapons (such as the dramatic improvements in *conventional aircraft* performance, payload and range) can now accelerate any 'surprise' military effort by an appreciable factor. Not least significant is the disappearance of a number of traditional 'indicators' – for example, the marshalling of aircraft before a strike, now eliminated with increased range, and the reduced flight time (and diminished vulnerability) of modernised ICBMs with multiple warheads and greater accuracy; by the same token, Warsaw Pact 'combat readiness' has come to mean just what it says, greater readiness for full-scale military operations on reduced warning time. The political rationale for a Soviet 'surprise' move against and into Europe is, inevitably, a matter for conjecture, so that any scenario is loaded with implausibilities and must entertain only contingencies. However, let us assume that there is a *prima facie* case for such action, possibly motivated by Soviet concern with 'encirclement' to east and west or activated by the need to shoot through the 'window of opportunity' presented by maximised Soviet strength.

The chances of the Soviet command achieving operational and tactical surprise appear to be good by any reckoning, particularly if this were an in-place unreinforced attack mounted with the aim of attaining major objectives before NATO could react with nuclear weapons and before overseas reinforcement could be brought to bear. The 'decision buildup' to this type of action might occupy no more than four days, while the operational preparations would consume 72 hours at the most and reduce NATO's own warning time to less than 36 hours. The distinction between nuclear and conventional operations could be narrow for the Soviet command and, in both modes, Soviet aims in the first instance would be identical – NATO nuclear delivery means, HQs and C_3, identified defensive positions, and logistics installations and operational reserves. NATO's own maladeployment can only work in favour of the USSR, while the most dangerous consequences of the recent rash of 'spy cases' in NATO may well be that the Soviet command is even better informed of those circumstances and conditions under which some NATO nations would *not* initiate particular courses of action or do so only belatedly – all facilitating Soviet 'selective strikes', even as deeper Soviet knowledge of NATO's crisis management procedures and nuclear release timetables enables more precise calculation for time-to-objective(s). Soviet theatre forces must be able to outpace NATO for time-into-action for all major formations, while NATO's defensive measures can be further inhibited by KGB 'disinformation', KGB 'diversionist groups' (concentrated in the first instance in the Federal Republic) and para-commando groups (25 to 50 men) trained to carry out sabotage and psychological warfare throughout western Europe. The aim is to inhibit and unhinge NATO's response to a full-scale alert.

General Close has already examined much of this in detail and for public scrutiny.[32] Whatever the arguments about particular aspects, most would agree that NATO's warning time has now been drastically reduced, with realistic warning time down to the order of 36 hours though officialdom insists on a 'few days'. In a striking coincidence of argument, recent authoritative Soviet military writing on 'operational planning for offensive operations under severe time constraints' has identified the time span of 48 hours for the 'warning order/operational planning/operational preparation' process (though it is conceded that preparations involving several fronts could take up to 30 days, at the other extreme). By the use of 'parallel planning' (as opposed to 'sequential planning') the Soviet command inclines to the view that the decision-making period can be cut to a few hours (the shorter time expended, the better), thus 'freeing' time for actual operational preparation which *at all levels* (army/division down to battalion) could consume 30 hours, including also the essential 'combined arms' planning and preparation.[33] Not all of this is mere theorising. Warsaw Pact 'combat readiness' has become more of a reality recently (a principle now being applied to the Far Eastern forces); on receipt of alert orders, Soviet and select Warsaw Pact divisions can be moved from their stations to their war deployment areas in about five hours, more or less fully manned and carrying their vehicle stocks, ammunition uploaded. It must be assumed that during any period of tension, or during a time of 'deployment by exercise', Soviet divisions deployed forward in east-central Europe would have been 'topped up' discreetly with specialists, extra tank crews, combat engineers and logistics personnel to bring manning levels to war strength. Indicators such as a change from training to live ammunition would no longer apply, for divisions 'on exercise' and on the move would bring their own ammunition stocks with them; air combat units no longer need protracted and complex marshalling, for strikes can be launched from the depth of Soviet positions.

Soviet surprise movement is also appreciably assisted by the fact that Soviet deployment to war stations in Group of Soviet Forces Germany is not as complicated as that within NATO, which requires much lateral and north–south movement: perhaps the only anomaly in GSFG is the situation of 2nd Guards Tank Army, reinforcement of which would require a 150 km (90 mile) march (assuming that 2nd Tank is committed to a drive along the Baltic coastline, assisted by Polish and some specialist East German units). The twenty divisions of GSFG (plus an artillery division) are generally at full strength, the Soviet formations having practised movement and deployment along presumed axes of advance; 16th Air Army with its immediate strength of 844 aircraft can be similarly 'topped up' with reconnaissance and light bomber elements, as well as being supported by SU-19s to the east, MiG-25s for reconnaissance and 500 medium bombers. Armoured strength needs no advertising, where, for example, 3rd Shock Army deployed near Magdeburg is itself the equivalent of the British Rhine Army (BAOR) – with about 50,000 to 55,000 men, over 1000 tanks, BTR/BMP in strength and a heavy concentration of artillery (which can be supplemented very speedily). The main Soviet attack echelon consists of fifteen tank divisions and MRDs, supported in turn by the Baltic MD, the Carpathian MD and elements of the Belorussian and Kiev MDs.[34] The tactical air component (16th Air Army/GSFG, 37th Air Army/Poland, 57th Air Army/Carpathian MD and what was latterly 10th Air Army in Czechoslovakia) has at least 90 airfields at its disposal for forward deployment and dispersal; well over 2000 tactical aircraft are available, while the non-Soviet Warsaw Pact elements would in the main be charged with defence of their own national air space (though under the overall direction of Soviet *PVO Strany* in the grand air defence design).

'Surprise' must also certainly rule out any protracted and involved mobilisation of the Warsaw Pact (which, in any event, lacks a mobilisational section or administration); under 'surprise' conditions the Soviet command could well elect to utilise only select non-Soviet formations and units, such as the Polish amphibious brigade, a Polish airborne division, Czech air support, East German specialist units. . . . This process can be assisted presently by the concentration on *air mobile* formations within the Warsaw Pact forces (where, for example, three of the eight Polish MRDs each have a fully operational air landing brigade, quite a transformation in order of battle which shows nominally only one Polish airborne division – the 6th). The same process of Soviet with select non-Soviet formations can also be promoted by the recent Soviet practice of carrying out 'regional' exercises involving very specific types of offensive operations; equally important is the extensive employment of airborne brigades landed in the depth of the 'enemy' deployments.

It could also be argued that the United States Army is inadvertently coming to the aid of the Soviet command in Europe, should the latter ever commit itself to full-scale action and under conditions of maximum surprise. United States Army FM 100-5 pays inordinate attention to the problem of coping with Soviet divisions echeloned in depth for a massive breakthrough operation on a narrow front. Clearly this simplifies the problem of identifying the direction of the main Soviet assault and allows for certain tactical handling problems to be solved under these conditions, but even while admitting that the Soviet command has resources to embark on eight to ten breakthrough sectors, this begs the question of a Soviet resort to the meeting engagement. It also presupposes that the second echelon will provide a lucrative target – but since it is Soviet practice to reinforce success rather than support failure, then this 'second echelon' will be committed at unknown times and unknown locations only when this success has been achieved.[35] The Soviet command is probably investing in 'flexible reinforcement' (to quote Dr Canby's judicious phrase) rather than relying on a cumbersome and vulnerable second echelon, just waiting for 'target servicing';[36] 'combined arms reserves' would serve the Soviet command well, with the Baltic MD, for example, able to furnish two such 'combined arms reserves' of tank/MRD elements (with airborne elements) rather than trundling the 11th Guards Army the long and dangerous route from Königsberg to the west. Such a format would also conform to the Soviet stipulation that the 'second echelon' will no longer correspond to a 'field army' (or armies) as such and also that a 'second echelon' can and must be concealed.

The element of Soviet 'surprise' could be augmented if the authors of FM 100-5 are themselves surprised by a Soviet operational method which overturns and overrides the axioms of FM 100-5 – namely, that modern weapons lethality works in favour of the defence, that *sensor technology* is reliable enough to register enemy intentions and that Soviet tactical handling will conform to stereotype and adhere to rigid patterns. In the first instance, relatively large numbers invest the Soviet commanders with a considerable degree of flexibility – deception is built into Soviet doctrine and operational methods *at all levels*; as for the FM 100-5 defence, even allowing for the lethalities of the most modern weapons, a Soviet attacking force could probably work through at least some gaps in the defences, whereupon the defensive forces would be the more speedily enveloped and cut off. All this is based on the very reasonable assumption that Soviet commanders are unlikely to choose an attacking mode which simply flings Soviet divisions against United States firepower. The surprise element could be compounded by our having concluded – all too erroneously – that Soviet departures from 'received doctrine' are not feasible; it is also an assumption which ignores the quite wide repertoire of Soviet battle-drills. There is a great deal of evidence to suggest that the Soviet command is adjusting in *tactical terms* to changes in the situation, not least in recognising that increased lethality of modern weapons will mean higher combat losses and thus demands a greater 'sustainability' in Soviet formations; the same condition places even greater emphasis on surprise and deception.

In a nuclear context, first strike in the European theatre is manifestly improved with the advent of the SS-20 IRBM, which will facilitate accurate coverage of the 1200 or so targets in the European TVD(s), with modernised air elements available for more effective attacks on time-sensitive targets. On the other hand, improved conventional air could conceivably be used in this surprise, first-strike role, committed to an initial strike against NATO nuclear means, NATO air bases, command and control centres and defensive positions. Leaving bases in east-central Europe, within 15 minutes Soviet aircraft could be over NATO territory, with a first attack echelon committed to clearing 'corridors' through NATO air defences and using a wide array of EW. The Soviet strike force would be protected by MiG-23 (FLOGGER Bs), with MiG-25s carrying through post-strike reconnaissance. In addition, the bomber force would also join the attack to even greater range, while through cleared 'corridors' the attack on NATO air fields would be stepped up (though strikes on airfields would have to be balanced against the need to attack nuclear weapons sites and command/control centres). The total elimination of NATO's air forces would seem to be impossible to accomplish in this single fell swoop, but an appreciable reduction of the NATO sortie rate would work substantially to Soviet advantage, not least to inhibit the United States Air Force. The use of *chemical weapons* against airfields could have a major crippling effect in view of the special vulnerabilities of aircraft and air force services and installations.

We must, therefore, understand 'surprise' in a theatre war context under several guises. In conditions of general war, with the use of nuclear weapons, Soviet operations in the European theatre (and in Asia also) would take the form of first-strike pre-emption, all with the aim of eliminating enemy nuclear capabilities and reducing the scale of the threat to the USSR. In Europe itself the 'bolt from the blue' attack seems to be an unlikely contingency; much more likely is the in-place unreinforced attack proceeding from a known condition of tension, where the Soviet aim would be to maximise operational and tactical surprise – and here NATO's own deficiencies would appreciably assist the Soviet design.

In a recent issue of *Voenno-istoricheskii Zhurnal* Major-General V. Matsulenko comments on yet another aspect of surprise capability, 'surprise in local wars', turning to an investigation of the Korean war and the Inchon landings, United States operations in Vietnam and Israeli operations in the Middle East (with a topical insertion on the Chinese incursion into Vietnam). The article is concerned both with the 'surprise factor' as such, being a short disquisition on the essentials of the Soviet theory of surprise and with its relevance to 'local wars'.[37] The surprise factor is assuming greater importance in modern warfare, supported by extensive use of *maskirovka* and with significant diplomatic as well as military preparation (*operativnaya maskirovka* and *dezinformatsiya*). In Vietnam United States forces used not only *maskirovka* on a considerable scale but combined this with new tactical methods and new weapons – airmobile units, revised air tactics to overcome air defence systems, the extensive use of 'special forces', night operations and improved coordination of intelligence. For reconnaissance at night the United States command used VO-3A aircraft with reduced noise, while B-52 bombers proceeded to their targets with complete radio silence. The Israeli examples are geared to the 'operational–strategic' scale, and were both in 1956 and in 1967: the lesson to be derived here emphasises the 'surprise factor' and the massive commitment of *air power*, which utilises new methods and new tactical modes, leading to significant 'operational results' in a very short period of time. The significant conclusion to be drawn here is that friendly air elements must be dispersed, with aircraft and airfields camouflaged and provided with reliable air defence cover: in addition, 'radar reconnaissance' must be so organised that it can uncover the main direction of enemy attacks from the flanks and rear alike, as well as countering low level attacks – here visual watch can be important. The prime lesson to be drawn from the Six-Day War of 1967 is that combat readiness of friendly forces must be realistic and effective and not a mere formality. At the same time, *operativnaya maskirovka* and disinformation (including much 'diplomatic noise') play a major part in achieving surprise.

Among the new weapons which enhance surprise are *chemical agents*; this weapon, combined with the tactical innovations connected with air power, increases the importance of PVO (Air Defence) measures for all towns and potential military targets, the defensive plan making wide provision for protection against enemy use of CW. Fending off the impact of surprise means 'counter-surprise' provision to improve combat readiness, efficient reconnaissance and effective intelligence and the *rapid* activation of both mobilisational and deployment plans for field forces (forces in being) and for *reserves*.

This somewhat generalised survey of Soviet commitment to and capability for 'surprise' nevertheless raises some intriguing points. In the first place, there is undoubtedly a major problem of semantics/linguistics in emplacing and evaluating 'surprise', 'pre-emption', 'first strike' against a complex Soviet vocabulary. It would appear that an important element of Soviet 'surprise' doctrine is provision for 'counter-surprise'; the objective in general war is to utilise 'surprise' to maximise 'counter-surprise' and also to adjust the *initial phase* in terms of relative force levels so that the war can be continued on a 'sustainable' basis – paradoxically, not so much as to 'win' outright but rather to assure that protractedness which will bring an ultimate outcome in Soviet favour. In a theatre war, the Soviet system is designed to utilise 'surprise' to maximise the conditions specifically favoured by the Soviet command – engaging an opponent off balance (or deliberately unbalanced), the rapid envelopment and defeat of forward enemy forces, plus the inhibition of resistance in the 'deep rear'. Though the principle of mass still holds good, only elements of first line formations need to be committed to this 'initial blow', with mass applied more to the consolidation of success. The method relies on seizing and holding the *initiative*, effective strategic concentration, defending ground once seized and reducing the defense to improvised and uncoordinated attacks, while employing those tactical modes which have been standardised and rehearsed to a point which facilitates widespread use of reservists. This, however, is not to imply total rigidity to the Soviet methods. In short, though we speak so frequently of the Soviet *blitzkrieg* – and there are *blitz* elements in Soviet military thinking and planning – we need to know more about it. And there is a blatant irony in that while speaking of this Soviet *blitz*, we are in part preparing to counter the opposite, a slow-moving, cumbersome heavy breakthrough 'slugging match'. Who, then, will be the more surprised?

NOTES

1. The bemusement is reflected equally in the title of Erich Helmdach's monograph on the German attack in 1941, *Überfall? Der sowjetisch-deutsche Aufmarsch 1941* (3rd edn.), (Neckargemünd, 1976). An even more interesting study in ambiguous interpretation is to be found in a recent major British publication, Hinsley, F. H., *et al.*, *British Intelligence in the Second World War*, Vol. 1, (London, HMSO, 1979), Chapter 14, 'Barbarossa', pp. 429–83 (also app. 15, 'M(il) I(nt) Summary of German Troop Movements to the East April–June 1941). See also under the rubric of 'Surprise' (*vnezapnost*), *Sovetskaya Voennaya Entsiklopediya* (Moscow, Voenizdat, 1976, Vol. 2, pp. 161–3 (signed M. M. Kiryan).
2. Kulikov, V., 'Sovetskaya voennaya nauka sevodnya', *Kommunist* (1976), No. 7 (May), pp. 38–47.
3. Anfilov, V. A., *Nachalo Velikoi Otechestvennoi voiny*, Moscow, Voenizdat (1962) (June–mid-July 1941): *Bessmertnyi podvig* (Moscow, Nauka, 1971) (enlarging on the entire 'first phase'): *Proval 'blitskriga'* (Moscow, Nauka, 1974) (to the repulse of the *Wehrmacht* before Moscow).
4. See *Proval 'blitskriga'*.
5. The level of connecting strategy and tactics: see Savkin, V. Ye., *The Basic Principles of Operational Art and Tactics* (Moscow, 1972: USAF translation, Vol. 4 in series *Soviet Military Thought*).
6. See Axelrod, Robert, 'The Rational Timing of Surprise', *World Politics* (1972) No. 2, pp. 227–46 – a most perceptive study.
7. Elliott, A. L., 'The Calculus of Surprise Attack', *Air University Review* (March–April 1979), pp. 56–67. This is a wholly gratuitous comment, but one dictated by the term 'counter-surprise'. The great divide between Soviet and Western strategic notions may well reside in the asymmetry of 'counter-surprise' as opposed to 'counter-offensive'. Soviet 'counter-surprise' as opposed to 'counter-offensive'. Soviet 'counter-surprise' is rooted in the principle of not losing the strategic initiative (for once lost it is exceeding hard to regain), while our 'counter-offensive' outlook–'riding out' a first strike and then retaliating with second-strike – is redolent of wartime experience, the great roll-back in Europe and the Pacific, with the strategic initiative firmly regained. The lesson drawn from 1941 on the Soviet side is not the epic process of wresting the strategic initiative from Germany but rather the imperative need never again to allow an enemy to seize this initiative. See also *The Critical Properties of Sudden Attack: A Study Proposal*, HQ/USAF/Net Assessment Task Force (November 1976) (unclassified).
8. Axelrod, R., 'The Rational Timing of Surprise', loc. cit., P. 246.
9. Ruth M. Anderson has compiled an important study '*Maskirovka: A Weapon for Peace or War*' and I am much indebted to it here; the Soviet literature on *maskirovka* is very extensive (such as Major-General V. A. Matsulenko, *Operativnaya maskirovka voisk* (Moscow, 1975) or N. P. Gordeyev, *Maskirovka v boevykh deistviyakh flota* (Moscow, Voenizdat 1971), with a definition in *SVE*, Vol. 5 (Voenizdat, 1978) pp. 175–7

under *maskirovka*, also *maskirovochnye sredstva*.

10. Savkin, V. Ye., op. cit., (USAF translation), pp. 238–9.
11. I have long advocated (vainly, I should add) a typological study of Soviet wartime operations in order to examine the role of surprise, the techniques involved, 'technological surprise', surprise as a deviation from the 'norms' of doctrine and, not least, the *failure rate*: we can use both German and Soviet records to check the operational catalogue (for instance, the German *Operationskalendar*, the Soviet *Soobshcheniya Sovetskovo Informbyuro* . . .). Much as I admire the investigations of the 'Manchurian case' in 1945 and surprise attack, in particular that by John Despres, Lilita Dzirkals, Barton Whaley in RAND Report R-1825-NA, there is perhaps a case for reviewing the whole gamut of Soviet operations and the reliance on surprise. By way of sample, or example, let me cite one useful Soviet study by Colonel A. Rakitskii, 'Vnezapnost deistvii v nastupatel "nom boyu"', *Voenno-istoricheskii Zhurnal* (1977), No. 9, pp. 96–101, dealing largely with tactical surprise.
12. The United States first-strike capability was explored in Aldredge, Robert C., *The Counterforce Syndrome*, TransNational Institute, Washington, DC; a very crude Soviet version can be found in Listvinov, Yu. N., *Pervyi Udar* (Moscow, 1971) (also JPRS 55622, April 1972, English translation).
13. See the celebrated response in *SShA* (1974), No. (11, Milshtein, M. A. and Semeiko, L. S. 'Problema nedopustimosti yadernovo konflikta (o novykh podkhodakh v SShA)', pp. 3–12.
14. The Soviet command is well aware of this stricture: Soviet military literature is filled with exhortation to implement *tvorchestvo* (creativity), to eschew *primitivizm* and so on. I have translated much of this as the search for 'deftness', which is professional skill combined with insight.
15. Ivanov, S. P., *Nachal'nyi period voiny* (Moscow, Voenizdat. 1974), 357 pp., treating the manner to mobilise and deploy to achieve 'surprise': (a) maintaining a specific number of divisions in peacetime close to wartime establishment, (b) a large number of divisions which can be quickly expanded to war strength, (c) concentration points near the enemy frontier, (d) paramilitary organisations included in the *total* mobilisation preparations, for 'organisational readiness'.
16. Kulikov, (loc. cit), laid much emphasis on *predvidenie*, particularly in 'forecasting' the nature of the strategic environment; for a theoretical study of *predvidenie*, see Konoplev, V. K., *Nauchnoe predvidenie v voennom dele* (Moscow, Voenizdat, 1974), 199 pp.
17. See Ch. V. in Gouré, Leon, *et al.*, *The Role of Nuclear Forces in Current Soviet Strategy*, (Miami, University of Miami 1975), pp. 101–18.
18. See Vigor, Peter, *The Soviet View of War, Peace and Neutrality* (London, RKP, 1975), especially Part 2, pp. 5–159.
19. See Brown, Harold, Secretary of Defence, *DoD Annual Report Fiscal Year 1979* (2 February 1978), p. 53.
20. It is difficult to pin down the exact context of manoeuvre, which seems at times to mean 'types/methods of deployment': for a most cogent and some *excellent* Soviet quotations, see Douglass Jr., J. D. and Hoeber, A. M. *Soviet Military Thought on Global Nuclear War* (1978: typed text, pp. 30–8), now printed as a monograph by the Hoover Institution.
21. See Friedman, Norman, 'The Soviet Mobilization Base', *Air Force Magazine* (Fifth Annual Soviet Aerospace Almanac), Vol. 62, No. 3 (March 1979), pp. 65–71, on present Soviet 'semimobilisation' and types of

economic mobilisation for (and in) war.

22. For a basic examination of this terminology, see 'War Initiation: Surprise, First Strike, Preemptive Strike' in Gouré, Leon, op. cit., pp. 102–12.

23. All admirably and lucidly explained in Lee, William T., 'Soviet Targeting Strategy and SALT', *Air Force Magazine* (September 1978), pp. 119–29.

24. See the figures and analysis supplied by Richardson, Doug, 'Could Russia win an ICBM War?', *Flight International*, (2 September 1978), pp. 797–801.

25. Brown, Harold, Secretary of Defence, *DoD Annual Report Fiscal Year 1980* (25 January 1979), p. 81.

26. These conditions also hinge appreciably on *meteorological factors;* there is also the 'fratricide' effect. Reduced aerodynamic dispersion is designed to cut down atmospheric influences.

27. Stipulated by Hughes, Peter, 'Arms Control and Strategic Stability', *Air Force Magazine* (April 1978), p. 63.

28. See Bradsher, Henry S., on Soviet missile totals, *The Washington Star* (12 April 1979).

29. See the major article by Ulsamer, Edgar, 'Defense Technology: Moving into Space, *Air Force Magazine* (June 1979), pp. 46–51.

30. Many calculations and models are advanced to support a variety of conclusions relating to Soviet 'first strike' and United States ICBM vulnerability, *Counterforce Issues for the US Strategic Nuclear Forces*, US Congress (Congressional Budget Office) Washington (January 1978), assembles under *Appendix A and B* data from the SNAPPER Force Exchange Model. For a recent British discussion of this problem, see Bellamy, Ian, 'More Arithmetic of Deterrence, Throw-Weight, Radio-activity and Limited Nuclear War', *RUSI Journal*, Vol. 124, No. 2 (June 1979), pp. 35–8. It is obviously impossible to ignore Jon M. Lodal's major article, 'SALT II and American Security', *Foreign Affairs*, Vol. 57 (1978) (No. 2), especially pp. 254–7.

31. See 'Acceptable Basing Mode for MX Sought', *Aviation Week and Space Technology* (21 May 1979), pp. 14–15.

32. Close, Robert, *'L'Europe sans defense? 48 heures qui pourraient changer la face du monde* (Brussels Edns. Arts et Voyages 1977). (Readied for English edition).

33. An important example of this interest in planning under severe time constraints in I. Gerasimov's article, 'Iz opyta podgotovki operatsii v korotkie sroki', *Voenno-istoricheskii Zhurnal* (1978), No. 8, pp. 26–32.

34. The Baltic MD comprises ten divisions, the Carpathian MD ten to eleven, Belorussian MD ten divisions, Kiev MD eleven to twelve divisions. There is *one tank army* in the Carpathian MD and *two tank armies* in the Belorussian MD.

35. Dr Steven L. Canby in his paper: *A Comparative Assessment of the NATO Corps Battle* (November 1978) puts this most elegantly: 'If allocation of second echelon reserves depends on exploiting the opportunities created by those regimental columns that succeed in working through NATO's defences, it obviously follows that enemy commanders themselves do not know *a priori* the location of their own major thrusts. Accordingly there is no way sensors and good intelligence can discern the location of the main thrust.'

36. See Canby, Steven L., *A Comparative Assessment*, p. 118.

37. Matsulenko, V., 'O vnezapnosti v lokalnykh voinakh', *Voenno-istoricheskii Zhurnal* (1979), No. 4, pp. 54–65.

5 American Perceptions and Misperceptions of Soviet Military Intentions and Capabilities

Richard Pipes

An intelligence community essentially reflects the way a given society tends to think about human problems and alien societies. Thus, most of the vices and most of the virtues of the American intelligence community's perceptions of Soviet intentions and capabilities can be readily ascertained on the basis of open sources, namely, American academic writings on the Soviet Union – especially those in the fields of political science – and American journalism. My personal experiences on Team B confirm that the CIA in its estimates suffers from similar weaknesses and strengths.

The strengths of the American intelligence community's perceptions of the Soviet Union are the same that are revealed by our journalism and in our academic studies, that is, they reflect a remarkable desire for, and ability to obtain, raw information. The *New York Times*'s and the American television's coverage of news is superior to that of comparable media anywhere in the world. The same applies to academic research. American scholars, junior and senior, conduct studies in all parts of the globe. They carry out field research and they work in remote libraries and archives. We are unequalled source and fact gatherers. We have to drive to acquire information and we have research grants for travel and study in distant regions. We have all the instruments needed to collect the data, and we can hardly be rivalled in that endeavour. As a result, our knowledge of what is happening in other countries, including the Soviet Union, is probably unequalled. We have superb information in our intelligence community, as can be seen from the publications which the CIA now releases to scholars on such subjects as the Soviet leadership: where they are, what they do, what they say, what are their career patterns. The order of battle of the Soviet military establishment is presented in great detail. The studies of the Soviet economy produced by the CIA are of high quality as well.

But our weaknesses and failures, too, are common to the intelligence services, journalism and academia. They have to do with the problem of interpreting the vast amount of information available. For example, the analysis of world events contained in the *New York Times*, with its enormous network of correspondents, is inferior to that furnished by the leading European newspapers. The amount of data provided in the *New York Times* is greater, but the depth of analysis and understanding in the *Neue Zürcher Zeitung* is superior. Anyone interested in understanding events in Poland, Soviet policy in Scandinavia or in Afghanistan, will find in the *Neue Zürcher Zeitung* in-depth accounts far beyond the capabilities of the *New York Times*.

Similarly, studies of the Soviet Union conducted by American political scientists tend to be abstruse and doctrinaire. They tell little about what the Soviet Union is like, or where it is going. And this quality is becoming more true rather than less so. The new edition – revision, if you will – of the Fainsod book, *How Russia Is Ruled*, produced by a student of Fainsod, is illustrative. An examination of the original Fainsod volume, the second edition of which came out in 1964, and the new volume reveals a general decline in understanding. The author of the new volume has read much and he has more up-to-date information than Fainsod had at his disposal, but his approach tends to be doctrinaire and flawed by the same fault common to much of our intelligence, namely, mirror-imaging. One of the purposes of the new version of the Fainsod volume is to get away from the totalitarian model which views the Soviet Union as a society fundamentally different from ours and to depict it, instead, as one which is a kind of mildly distorted version of our own American society, but whose basic functioning is similar. This interpretation, I believe, is fundamentally incorrect, as we have learned from Soviet emigrés, people of high calibre, most of whom will tell you that this is not the way Soviet society works at all.

What are the sources of misperceptions, what are the causes of the faulty analysis which cuts across intelligence, journalism, and academia? They are particularly pernicious in a field like Soviet studies for the following reason: if we deal with West European societies, the problem of approach is not so overwhelming because, even though West European societies are different from ours, they are so in a matter of degree. Hence, many of the analytical methods that we Americans employ are applicable to Western Europe. Certainly, English politics or English economics can be understood in terms which are fundamentally not different from American ones. To some extent, this rule applies also to Germany, France or Spain. On the other hand, when we deal with societies which are visibly different – if only because their people belong to different races – if we are concerned with Japan, China or Africa – the problem is not so keen either because it is quite apparent that in these cases you are dealing with entirely different societies for which other methods are required. So here we tend to have recourse to anthropological methods. Very few intelligent people would try to deal with an African tribal society in terms of Western history and concepts. But the Russians are something in between, something quite peculiar, because racially and culturally they belong to the Western community, they have the same religious background, and yet they are very different. For this reason the temptation to think of them like us is strong.

The methodological (as distinct from the psychological) flaws evident in our study of the Soviet Union stem from two sources. One can be attributed to the dominant philosophy of the scientific community, which is logical positivism. The other has to do with the methods of gathering intelligence, which tend to be increasingly scientific, mechanical, technological, and to rely less and less on human contacts and human understanding.

Logical positivism is a doctrine that dominates scientific thinking in the United States, not only the community of natural scientists, but also that working in the so-called social sciences. Because strategic weapons, which are a primary concern of intelligence estimating about the Soviet Union, have been produced by scientists, much of the modern strategic thought in the United States has emanated from the scientific community. Because scientists play so large a role in designing weapons, they have come to play a major role in designing uses for them. Over the past 30 years, American strategic thinking has been dominated by civilian scientists, with little contribution by the professional military. As a result, the dominant scientific philosophy, that of logical positivism, has penetrated our strategic thinking and our strategic assessments.

Modern positivism, or logical positivism, is a philosophical theory whose primary concern is with the validation of statements. It seeks to accomplish this validation by a rigorous logical and linguistic analysis of both general theories and of specific propositions. Logical positivism rejects any statement that does not meet its tests of linguistic or logical verification. Conversely, logical positivism tends to accept propositions which do meet these criteria regardless of their reality: To the logical positivist reality is, in a sense, irrelevant to his judgement and remains largely outside his conscious purview. The leading Polish philosopher Leszek Kolakowski puts the matter succinctly:

> Logical positivism is an attempt to consolidate science as a self-sufficient activity which exhausts all the possible ways of appropriating the world intellectually. In this positivist view, the realities of the

world, if they are to be encompassed by reflection and expressed in words, must be reduced to their empirical properties. Suffering, death, ideological conflict, social clashes, antithetical values of any kind – all are declared out of bounds, matters we can only be silent about in obedience to the principle of verifiability. Positivism so understood is an act of escape from commitments, an escape masked as a definition of knowledge invalidating all such matter as mere figments of the imagination stemming from intellectual laziness. Positivism, in this sense, is the escapist design for living, a life voluntarily cut off from participation in anything that cannot be correctly formulated.[1]

Acceptance of the principles of logical positivism causes one to eliminate from serious consideration many realms of human experience which have traditionally been regarded as of critical importance for strategy and warfare – history, ideology, tradition, human values, religion, national ethos and mass psychology. Historical experience is seen by the logical positivist as providing no guidance because, in his view, the perception of history, as expressed in historical writing, is, by its very nature, unscientific. Human conflicts are traced by the proponents of this school either to ignorance or to misunderstanding or to both. All human problems are soluble once the proper formulas have been found. The scientist-philosopher and his style of thinking provide a model which all societies must in time adopt. It is not necessary to acquaint oneself with the thinking of others whenever it sharply deviates from that of the scientific community because on every subject there is only one truth that is binding on everyone.

It is this kind of thinking that accounts for the popular theory of 'convergence' because, clearly, once you have what is called a 'modernisation' or 'industrialisation' process going on in one society, all others must fall in step. Hence, in the writings of many American social scientists only a few years ago it appeared indisputable that Iran, in time, would become a microcosm of the United States, it had to be such by the very nature of the inflow of capital and development of industry. Little or no allowance was made for totally different cultural traditions, with the tremendous hold that Shi'ite Islam has on the population, or for the popular revulsion produced by changes wrought by 'modernisation'. Our inability to anticipate the Iranian revolution can be directly traced to this methodology rather than to specific flaws in the intelligence process. Our perception of Iran would have been drastically different if it had been based not on positivist preconceptions but on expert advice of people with long residence in Iran and possession of what the Germans call *Fingerspitzengefühl*, that is, a feeling 'in the tips of your fingers' acquired from long familiarity with the country.

The other flaw inherent in our study of the Soviet Union has to do with the nature of intelligence gathering. Because the Soviet Union is a fairly closed society, we have been inclined to rely increasingly on mechanical ways of obtaining intelligence. These are very expensive and involve an increased proportion of the intelligence community personnel which quite naturally develops a vested interest in acquiring infromation in this manner. This, in turn, means that the traditional ways of gathering intelligence decline in importance. This process has been a relentless one in the American intelligence community; a growing reliance on mechanical (technical) means of obtaining information and a proportionately declining ability to analyse this information because the persons who have long personal experience in a given society are less and less consulted.

The results are, on the whole, discouraging. They include our misperceptions of Soviet thought processes in general and Soviet ways of thinking about strategic matters in particular. There is an illustration: We have been quite incapable of understanding the profound difference between the Aristotelian and the Platonic ways of judging reality. Western society, due to its scholastic tradition, essentially relies on the Aristotelian way; Soviet society, in part because of the influence of the dialectic method of thinking which derives from Plato, thinks platonically. Aristotle suggests that the way to understand reality is to draw distinctions; by distinguishing elements which superficially appear similar you gain understanding of objects. So, black and white are different and you grasp the nature of blackness by considering the difference between it and whiteness, and vice versa. That is how we are conditioned to think and, therefore, all our thinking tends to lead to differentiation. The Platonic way is different; it is a dialectical way in which you assume that every phenomenon (or statement) presumes its opposite. The only way you understand what black means is by its relationship (rather than contrast) to white; the concept 'black', as it were, contains the concept 'white'. Unless the two relate to each other they cannot be grasped.

This issue may appear philosophically esoteric but, in fact, it has profound bearing on the way strategic thinking is pursued. When we deal with Soviet strategic doctrine, we tend to think in terms of contrasts rather than interrelationships. We view, for example, 'deterrence' as the opposite of 'war fighting'. It is not. In Soviet thinking, deterrence is an intrinsic part of war fighting. We view defensive weapons as being different from offensive weapons. The Russians do not: they consider them as one and the same, performing various functions on various occasions. We believe that there is a difference between strategic and theatre, or strategic and peripheral, weapons. The Russians do not. They do not share or concept of 'strategic' as being fundamentally different from 'peripheral' because they look at the whole gamut of weapons – from short-range missiles, to medium-range missiles, to long-range missiles – as forming a continuum. From their point of view, for example, it makes no sense to exclude either the Backfire or the SS-20 from SALT negotiations. There is no qualitative difference between SS-20 and an SS-17, or 18, or 19, for, although the range is different, these weapons still perform similar functions.[2] The same applies to the Backfire. Here, we are victims of our own ways of thinking, which the Russians exploit when it suits their purposes. Using our definitions of strategic weapons, they assert: 'The Backfire is not strategic, and neither is the SS-20, so we should not discuss them at SALT'.

The same manner of thinking prevents us, for example, from seeing that in the Soviet Union there is no such sharp distinction between the military and civilian sectors as the one to which we are accustomed. The civilian and military sectors there are two aspects of the same system. Our methodology prevents us from understanding that the Russians, in marked contrast to American thought, do not see a real antithesis between war and peace. War and peace are both aspects of the phenomenon – which is basic to human nature: you resort to one when it suits you, you resort to the other when that suits you better. You may even have a condition of neither war nor peace if it accords with your strategic objectives. The notion that these two are antithetical concepts is totally alien to the Soviet way of thinking. These examples could be multiplied but they show how profoundly the Soviet way of thinking is misunderstood if one's way of grasping reality is Aristotelian and if one's methodology is positivist.

Logical positivism is anathema in the Soviet Union. Communists are great proponents of the scientific method in general but not of the logical positivist method; theirs is a method that takes into account many intangible historical and social factors. In the vast literature published in the Soviet Union on such things as third world countries, no use is made of such concepts as 'modernisation', 'industrialisation', or 'westernisation'. Soviet specialists tend to conduct detailed analyses of the local milieu, micropolitical rather than macropolitical. They deal characteristically with the historical background, with the development of the local economy, with the growth of productive resources, control of property (who owns what). Soviet writings sometimes present a somewhat schematic picture of a given society but it is generally concrete and rarely do they go to any of the extremes to which our scholars are addicted. If you take Soviet works on the United States and compare them with the bulk of American literature on the Soviet Union, you will find a fundamental difference. Theirs deal, very concretely, with social groupings, with the distribution of wealth, with various political alignments, to determine which groups are for 'peace' and 'amity' with the Soviet Union, which groups want to 'revive the cold war', which are 'aggressive', which are 'imperialistic'. They are, on the whole, not badly done – or, at any rate, they serve their purpose. It would be extremely beneficial if we could export logical positivism and all its related methodology to the Soviet Union. There must be a lot of Soviet scientists who would just love to gobble up this methodology but the Party watches very vigilantly because it knows the inherent dangers.

Our way of thinking influences our assessments of Soviet capabilities. For example, we tend to dismiss the concept of grand, national strategy, in which the military element is part of a total strategy that embraces economics, ideology and politics. In addition to isolating the military from other dimensions of strategy, we tend to seperate the strategic from conventional capabilities and then, within that dichotomy, to deal with each strategic–nuclear forces weapons system on its own merits. Under such circumstances, it is easy to rationalise the defensive quality of each Soviet weapons system. One can evalute each Soviet weapons system and conclude as follows: each represents a reaction to a specific problem which the Russians face because of certain things we have done. But, when you view the totality of the picture, it becomes difficult to rationalise in those terms. A different picture emerges which does not fit the action/reaction model at all.

Clearly, we must maintain the superb machine we have for gathering intelligence by mechanical means. This represents a great asset for the United States. When we are dealing with the capabilities of strategic weapons, there is no other way of finding out the facts. When we are dealing with Russian oil problems, there is no other way either. But, equally clearly, it seems that we must make a very major effort – not only in the intelligence community but also in the fields of political science and journalism – to improve our ability to analyse the information that is available in such great quantities.

In such analysis, the historical approach is indispensable. Yet, history is considered to be by many a soft science. There is a certain hesitation in the American intelligence community, which has impressive technological means at its disposal, to rely on analysis that cannot be quantified and that sometimes appears vague and impressionistic. But, in fact, history and disciplines related to history have a very rigrous methodology. The rules of evidence are very strict. How you analyse evidence, how you tell reliable evidence from bad evidence, how you get at the underlying and implicit assumptions behind statements, how you draw your conclusions, none of this is done impressionistically by the professional historian. The understanding of a national ethos acquired by cultural historians, for example, is not impressionistic even though it cannot be quantified.

Quantification has its uses but quantification does not give you all the answers. Quantification provides a means of verifying statements acquired from non-quantitative analyses. We quantify in order to demonstrate the accuracy of some statements. Quantification is an aid to thinking but it is not reality. Intelligence must be based on human understanding that results from deep knowledge of concrete situations and experience with given societies. Only by such means will we be able to analyse the enormous mass of information which comes in from all of the sources at our disposal – mechanical and human – and which, under our present system of thinking, all too often is misinterpreted.

NOTES

1. Kolakowski, Leszek, *The Alienation of Reason: A History of Positivist Thought* (Garden City, New York, Doubleday and Company, Inc., 1968).
2. In this connection, it may be noted that the Soviet strategic forces dispose of both intercontinental and medium-range missiles.

6 'Static' and 'Dynamic' Intelligence Perceptions: The Soviet Union – Problems of Analysis and Evaluation

Uri Ra'anan

The only reservation concerning the cogent points made by Richard Pipes (Chapter 5 of this volume) stems from a reluctance to share his enthusiasm for the supposed accuracy or complete news coverage provided by *any* of our dailies. Apart from that, there are no real disagreements. However, one can address the issue in somewhat different terms, that may appear, perhaps, to be overly 'conceptual', but relate essentially to *operational* aspects, rather than being purely philosophical.

Intelligence evaluation, in the last resort, boils down to the crystalis-ation of perceptions concerning the fundamental posture and the potential moves of another party (usually an adversary or putative adversary). Now, these perceptions may owe their character to very different origins, to wit – they may be 'spontaneous' or deliberately 'manipulated'. In the latter instance, of course, one is dealing with 'deception' of one type or another, and particularly with its most finely honed form, namely 'disinformation'. (Since we have a contribution (Chapter 17) from a former practitioner of the art and a fine analyst to boot, namely Ladislav Bittman, it is unnecessary to deal with this topic here.) Even the more spontaneous, non-manipulated, perceptions have to be regarded as problematical, however, to the extent that they cannot be defined simply as 'correct' or 'incorrect'.

In fact, it may be more appropriate to categorise intelligence perceptions as 'static' or 'dynamic': they are 'static' in so far as the machinery of evaluation itself (or, rather, its *visible* end product in terms of policy actions and statements) does not impact upon the data that are being 'factored into' the ongoing process of analysis, and 'dynamic' to the degree that this analysis feeds back into and, therefore, *ex post facto* affects the character (that is, the accurate interpretation) of the data themselves. In the latter case, one is encountering, as it were, a 'Heisenberg phenomenon', with the act of observation influencing the behaviour of the object observed.

To concretise: A potential adversary leaves 'footprints' consonant with preparations for an attack; intelligence evaluation on the other side interprets the data accordingly and initiates appropriate counteraction of a primarily deterrent kind. The adversary, deducing from this development that any surprise element has been dissipated, calls off the planned move and redeploys military units in a less 'offensive' mode. The perception of the adversary's posture was 'correct' initially, but seems 'false' *ex post facto*, since an attack was anticipated but did not take place. The 'customers' of the intelligence product (that is, perception of the adversary's presumed posture) are confronted by an almost classical dilemma – *which* interpretation is 'right'? The problem is reduced to more manageable proportions, once the 'dynamic' aspect of such perceptions is taken into consideration, .in other words, the additional dimension provided by the potential 'feedback' effect of intelligence evaluations upon the behaviour of an adversary. Otherwise, a catastrophe may be in the offing the next time the adversary repeats his manoeuvre and the intelligence community, believing it has 'learned the lesson' of 'last time', decides that it is confronting mere bluff and eschews (expensive) counteraction.

It may be superfluous, however, to devote much space here to the gamut of complexities that beset the topic of 'perceptions'; approximately seven years ago, assisted by a colleague and former student, Captain Howard Eldredge, I published the product of my reflections on this subject.[1] About three years later, we noted with wry amusement that someone else apparently had attempted to 'rediscover the wheel'.

At this point, it is necessary to turn from the general to the specific, that is, from generic problems of intelligence evaluation to the peculiar issues that confront the analyst of closed societies – particularly the USSR. As a point of departure, Professor Pipes is quite right in assuming that the craft of the historian provides the most suitable modalities for appraising the Soviet Union. At the risk of stating the obvious: The basic methodology of the discipline of history relates to the interpretation of documents. In dealing with the Soviet Union, when all is said and done, the gentle art of content analysis of (mostly open) sources remains, now as ever, a tested and reasonably reliable instrument for interpreting not only the (strategic) posture – partly reflecting *Weltanschauung* – but also the operational (tactical) directives of the Soviet leadership. This proposition could perhaps be regarded as self-serving, content analysis, after all, providing the approach utilised by our profession, 'Sovietology', toward comprehending the decision-making élite in Moscow and 'decoding' its signals. (Note that we are careful to speak in terms of an art, rather than a 'science'.) One cannot but be puzzled that it should continue to be essential, almost daily, to explain, nay defend, content analysis as a valid method of evaluating Soviet policy, a full four decades or more after 'Sovietology' started to demonstrate its utility and relevance.

The degree of scepticism often brought to bear on this topic in certain Western circles is well-nigh incomprehensible. Just for a moment, let us think through the full implications of such a refusal to accept the obvious. We are to believe, if you please, that, at the very apex of the Soviet (primarily civilian) command structure, a small group of distinctly elderly, often ailing, Party leaders, is wasting literally hundreds of hours annually on composing, vetting, and disputing fiercely over a veritable gamut of (usually lengthy) statements (including *Pravda* 'Observer' articles, May Day and October Revolution slogans covering most aspects of international and domestic affairs, definitive articles in *Kommunist*, ceremonial communiqués, successive editions of standard works on Party and State history, on military strategy, etc.) – presumably because it is merely amusing itself and has nothing better to do! The simple fact of the matter is that evidence available *shows* the leadership of the Soviet Union, and of other communist states and parties, to be spending an inordinate proportion of its attention span, energies, and working hours precisely on such pursuits, sometimes down to what would be regarded as sheer trivia in other societies, including 'problems' such as what kind of opera may be performed, which movies should be produced, and the precise type of novels or poetry that can be viewed as permissible. The documentation at our disposal is massive concerning this peculiar aspect of leadership performance in closed societies, especially where there is a penchant for self-expression in 'ideological' terms; much of the material available emanates from defectors, *émigrés*, and other useful sources – and has proved to be mutually reinforcing.

Is it reasonable, then, to assume that a proverbially soberminded, utilitarian élite would take so much trouble, *unless* most of the literature in question actually performed a very serious role within the Soviet *modus operandi*, that is, conveyed, in one way or another, *operational directives*? Of course, the medium of expression in the Soviet Union tends to be Aesopian and somewhat arcane; however, to the degree that the 'message' is 'encrypted' in such language, it can be (and has been, for years) 'deciphered' with relative ease. Just how seriously other communist leaders take this function of Soviet publications may be gathered from the fact that the Politburo of one East European communist party used to convene in the early morning hours around a ticker transmitting the contents of the day's *Pravda*, so as 'to read between the lines'!

Obviously, therefore, such material serves much more than purely 'propagandistic' purposes (and this is underlined by the fact that some of the publications in question tend to be restricted in circulation, rather than being disseminated for universal readership). It has come to our attention, moreover, that, in recent years, there have been repeated instances of serious deliberations, in the Soviet Union and Romania – to cite just two cases, concerning the ability of some Western analysts to attain accurate results with the aid of 'content analysis'. Consequently, the question arose whether published material in the countries mentioned was 'giving away too much'. As far as we can deduce from subsequent practice, the decision reached was that the function of the media (printed and broadcast) in communist states as an operational transmission belt was too important to be weakened because of concern over relatively successful 'cryptanalysis' by a few persons in the West. Moreover, we are told, the Soviet leadership reached the conclusion some time ago that Western decision-makers pay little attention to the practioners of 'content analysis' and, in any case, Western memories concerning revelations about the Soviet Union, however significant or dramatic, tend to be amazingly short!

Thus, a major defector from the Soviet 'disinformation' branch gave detailed evidence in the United States about newspapers in South and South-East Asia utilised by his service for operational purposes during the late 1950s. This testimony was printed prominently by the United States Congress and appeared subsequently in book form. One might have thought that the heads of Moscow's 'disinformation' activities would regard these newspapers as having been 'burned' hopelessly and would cease utilising them. Nothing of the sort! Within a few months, the publications mentioned were continuing their role in various 'disinformation' ploys and Western news agencies already had forgotten the revelations that had appeared and were citing these journals as authentic sources of information!

In the light of all the considerations enumerated here, one reacts with a feeling of utter frustration to airy Western dismissals of the significance of Soviet literature on doctrinal or strategic matters as material meant 'merely for internal consumption'. It is difficult to decide which of the aspects of such lightheaded judgements is more irritating: The word 'merely,' implying that the domestic power base in a closed society somehow is of secondary importance (!), or the assumption that directives conveyed inside the Soviet Union have little impact upon the international arena? For some reason, we are asked to disbelieve the instructions publicly transmitted by the Soviet leadership to its own cadres and allies, but to accept the words whispered by Soviet visitors into the ears of their Western hosts. Needless to say, our unwillingness to interpret and to believe statements printed (with relative candour) in the Soviet Union is *our* problem. To a considerable degree, the Western tendencies described here are the result of an apparently irresistible urge to indulge in 'mirror-imaging'. Just *why* this tendency is so prevalent requires the analysis of experts in entirely different professions from my own! However, the effect of 'mirror-imaging' is very apparent: it leads to the assumption that a very lucid, coherent, and frequently repeated exposition of strategic doctrine, such as presented, for example, in the Gorshkov series and his subsequent book, constitutes 'just another attempt by some admiral to extract larger appropriations for his particular service'. Anyone who believes that there is that much similarity between Capitol Hill and Supreme Soviet, for instance, really has a problem. Other 'mirror-imagers', equally contemptuously, will say that Gorshkov, to continue with the same example, is 'merely a military hardliner attempting to browbeat civilian supporters of *détente*'. Here, it is essential to point out: (a) There is no reliable evidence to the effect that Soviet military personalities necessarily are 'offensively' oriented, while civilians are meek 'doves'; (b) if there is one aspect concerning which our documentation leaves little doubt, it is the unshakeable conviction of Party leaders that 'Bonapartism' has to be prevented at all costs and that one must insist upon the unconditional supremacy of civilian control over the military apparatus.

All this is not to say that we should deal with the USSR by applying the 'single actor model'. A word of caution may be in place at this point: in order to take seriously the contents of the overt communications traffic in the Soviet Union, it is by no means essential to predicate that the political process in that country has reached a state of complete stasis. That is, after all, the unspoken assumption behind the adoption of the 'single actor model' as a suitable approach for analysis of any state or society. Yet, it is questionable whether the political process can be, or has been, halted by mere fiat or ukase, in any environment, for more than some months at most, unless, perhaps, one is dealing with tribal societies. Even at the high water mark of Stalinism, the inner decision-making circle of the top élite strata did not behave in completely 'monolithic' fashion – as demonstrated by the prolonged 'debate' linked with the name of E. Varga, to cite only one example. In fact, the monolith is not the most appropriate metaphor to employ in the Soviet context; it may be useful to reiterate, by way of explanation, words that I had occasion to use in an earlier forum, when attempting to cope with the problem of élite performance in the Soviet Union:

Although factions and factionalism are formally prohibited, political processes, of course, cannot be outlawed . . . even in the Soviet

Union, and there are kaleidoscopic formations and re-formations of alliances and coalitions within the leadership each time a specific decision has to be reached. These factions are not necessarily stable, since they are not specifically issue-oriented, at least not at the very top (groups with a vested professional bias are to be found slightly lower down the ladder, including, of course, the military services). Rather, the leadership reveals a strangely 'feudal' pattern, with each top personality 'investing' subordinates wherever possible with power and position in return for personal 'fealty' and allegiance. These subordinates similarly distribute whatever privileges they command among their various personal collaborators in return for political support and loyalty, until a veritable 'feudal' pyramid of 'enfeoffments' is created (from one of the top leaders all the way down the ladder to minor local functionaries who may not be in direct touch with him but belong to his 'party' through a chain of personal links of allegiance). Sometimes these links are even reinforced by familial ties, including political marriage to create bonds of blood, in truly 'feudal' style. This system strongly influences the *modus operandi* at the very apex of the Soviet leadership. Given a delicate balance of 'collectivity' at the top, each of the main leaders, conscious of the particular power structure he personally commands and which he attempts to preserve and enhance, will attempt temporary coalitions with his colleagues and competitors (above all to prevent the strongest and, therefore, most dangerous among them at any one moment from gaining the degree of overwhelming power, momentum, and control which would lead to the total subordination and possible elimination of the weaker members). The actual issues over which these conflicts are fought out are not necessarily of overriding importance to the various competitors, nor are they inevitably tied to a consistant line on specific issues. The real battle concerns personal power and influence rather than a particular political question, but the latter can and does serve a useful tactical purpose in gathering recruits and allies for one group and alienating supporters from another. Moreover, the outcome of a conflict over a specific issue can have great symbolic and psychological impact in demonstrating which factional alliance is gaining and which is declining. Thus it is almost axiomatic that the advocacy of a proposal by one group will lead to some measure of opposition by various rivals and adversaries.[2]

Clearly, what is being described here *is* a political process, although, to be sure, it assumes very different forms from those habitual in the open society. Consequently, at certain times, under particular circumstances, some proportion of overt communication in the USSR may reflect a factional 'debate', that is, views and actions advocated by one leadership group or another, for essentially tactical reasons. (Of course, this does not guarantee at all that, once their personal adversaries have been defeated finally, the 'victors' necessarily will implement the 'platform' which had served as a useful 'weapon' during the period of struggle.) Does this factor vitiate our assumptions concerning open Soviet sources as 'a tested and reasonably reliable instrument for interpreting not only the (strategic) posture . . . but also the operational (tactical) directives of the Soviet leadership'? The answer, fortunately, is negative, *provided* great care is taken to differentiate between mutually incompatible variations on a single theme (however subtle may be the nuances distinguishing one approach from another), that appear more or less simultaneously, and, on the other hand, changes in attitude over a prolonged period of time, where practically all publications of one period 'play one melody' while those of a subsequent stage adopt an entirely different 'tune'. In the first instance, it is likely that one is noting evidence of a factional 'debate', whereas, in the second case, it is far more likely that one is encountering changes in the central 'Line', in other words, probably in the posture and doctrine of the régime as a whole. In the majority of publications most relevant to our central theme here, particularly concerning strategic–military affairs, the chances are higher that we may be dealing with the latter rather than the former type of material (that is, that content analysis will help to 'decipher' operational directives of the decisionmakers as an entity). Of course, whenever content analysis reveals traces of a 'debate' within the leadership, such a discovery opens up entirely different vistas, for example, the possibility that we, on our part, may be able to manipulate one Soviet faction against another by means of adroit 'signals' or other modalities. One refers to such an option wistfully, since there is singularly little evidence that Western policymakers have even thought of such a possibility, not to speak of taking action.

It is, or should be, self-evident that content analysis of open (and/or more restricted) publications can and must be 'checked against' the 'hard data' that can be garnered from other sources, including National Technical Means of Verification. In practical terms, this means checking the doctrine, posture and 'thrust' of the régime, as revealed by the printed and spoken word, against its military, technological, and economic capabilities (as well as the further development of these capabilities, in so far as it can be detected in its more embryonic stages).

This consideration brings us to yet another problematical issue and that is the utilisation, by some Western circles, of the 'action/reaction' model in evaluating Soviet policies and intentions. There is a fundamental fallacy involved in this approach, which, for want of a better term, we may call the 'hidden portion of the iceberg' factor. 'Action/reaction' might constitute a viable model, particularly in the arena of security affairs, only if the 'visible parts' (that is production and deployment) alone were of significance. It would make sense to utilise this peculiar metaphor if, upon sighting an adversary's deployment, one could 'react' by counter-deploying instantly. In the real world, however, there is a small item known as 'Research and Development' involving another 'detail' called 'lead time', which may cover a period of anywhere from five to ten years or more between the moment at which a certain technological development first becomes theoretically feasible and the day on which the appropriate item then comes off the assembly line and achieves 'visibility'. A party that would be 'reacting' merely to the *actions* of its adversary, that is, the new developments 'on the other side' that could be *detected*, would ensure simply that it was lagging behind by a significant number of years. A realistic planner, therefore, and there is no reason whatever to deny the Soviet leadership that sobriquet, does not wait to 'react' to deployments that already can be *seen* on someone else's turf, but, rather, is liable to give the 'go ahead' soon after a certain technology first becomes theoretically available. There are two 'inbuilt' factors in the Soviet decisionmaking system that increase markedly the probability of a Soviet move precisely along the lines suggested here:

(a) The Soviet leaders retain a Leninist penchant for seizing and maintaining the *initiative*, as their defence literature points out incessantly, since this leaves the adversary to cope with the dilemma of having 'to sit tight and to take it' or making belated and risky countermoves, and because 'he who is not first is relegated to the rubbish bin of history'.
(b) In the economic, as well as the social and political spheres, the system is geared to sudden spurts in a specific direction, considered vital by the elite, with 'campaigns' being unleashed – *à la* 'Manhattan' project – demanding, in effect, total concentration upon one goal and neglect of almost all other concerns. This *modus operandi* is typical especially of the technological sector.

Under these circumstances, we have reason for thinking that Soviet leaders do some 'mirror-imaging' of their own, that is they assume, apparently, that the logical way of acting is to take it for granted that, if technology renders a certain development feasible, then the appropriate steps are bound to be taken. They believe, it seems, that the adversary will behave in precisely the same manner; consequently, they 'react' *not to actions* 'on the other side', as they become visible, but rather to the *assumption* that 'if it is feasible for us, it is feasible for them, and if it *can* be done, then they *will* do it.'. This is a form of 'action/reaction', if you like, but certainly not the kind to which so much of Western thinking about the Soviet Union has become habituated.

It has been possible here to address only a few of the pitfalls and fallacies that bedevil much of our evaluation and analysis of the intelligence material concerning the Soviet Union. Most of the relevant data, as has been indicated, are available; indeed, there is a veritable flood of material and most of it takes the form of open (if not always equally accessible) sources. The problems, as always, pertain less to the data than to our ways of utilising them.

NOTES

1. See Uri Ra'anan, *The Changing American–Soviet Balance: Some Political Implications*, Subcommittee on National Security and International Operations of the Committee on Government Operations, US Senate (1972); reprinted also as Chapter 31 in *Great Issues of International Politics*, 2nd ed., edited by Morton A. Kaplan (New York, Aldine Publishing Company, 1974).
2. Uri Ra'anan, 'Some Political Perspectives Concerning the US–Soviet Strategic Balance', in *The Superpowers in a Multinuclear World* edited by G. Kemp, R. L. Pfaltzgraff, Jr., and Uri Ra'anan, pp. 18–19, (Lexington Mass., D. C. Heath, 1974).

7 Deception and Surprise: Problems of Analysts and Analysis

William E. Colby

Pearl Harbour is the quintessential example of successful deception and surprise. While Japanese diplomats carried on negotiations for peace, a Japanese fleet secretly went to sea and carried out one of the most successful surprise attacks in history.

But Pearl Harbour was also something else; it marked the opening of a new age of *modern* intelligence. After the débâcle, investigations revealed that information was available which should have better alerted the American forces to ward off the impending attack. In fact, the Japanese admiral was under instructions to reverse course and abandon the operation if the fleet was discovered at sea. In such a case, one American reconnaissance aircraft might have averted the entire disaster. The key lesson of the investigations was not the importance of constant reconnaissance and watchfulness, but rather the demonstrated need for a new concept of 'central intelligence'.

The information which should have alerted our forces sufficiently to launch the reconnaissance aircraft was available – but it was scattered in the Army, in the Navy and in the State Department. It had not been integrated into a single analysis and assessment so that the proper conclusions could be drawn. President Truman later summarised this lesson in the remark that if we had had a CIA, we would not have had a Pearl Harbour disaster. Out of this lesson the concept of central intelligence was initiated during the Second World War under General William J. Donovan, in the Office of Strategic Services.

General Donovan assembled a corps of scholars in Washington to man what became a true intellectual and academic centre devoted to assembling and analysing all the information which could be acquired – available from open as well as secret sources – summarising it, and drawing conclusions about its meaning, for the President and the Joint Chiefs of Staff. And he considered this the true core of American intelligence. After dismantling the OSS with the end of the war, President Truman re-established that same function – with many of the same people – in the new Central Intelligence Agency in 1947.

The popular idea of 'intelligence' concentrates on the spy who steals the secret to give to the general to win the battle. This image has been reinforced through fact as in Mata Hari, and fiction as in James Bond. Intelligence has been seen as a zero sum game – knowledge by one side concealed from the other gives the holder a net advantage, an advantage which can only be countered by the intelligence agent penetrating the secret and giving it to the other side. The popular concepts of deception and surprise are obvious offshoots of this construct.

But behind the secrecy which has enveloped the intelligence discipline, America's 'central intelligence' has revolutionised these traditional concepts. We are all aware of the fantastic contributions technological intelligence gathering has made to our knowledge of the world, from the U-2 on up into space, deep in the ocean, in the fields of electronics, optics, sonar and computers. Together, these methods enable us today to peer over the edge of the earth deep into Asia and to learn facts totally beyond our reach ten or fifteen years ago. To this change in 'intelligence' must be added the arrival of the 'information age' of modern communications, media, transportation and information storage and retrieval techniques. Together these changes have geometrically expanded the information base available about the world in which we live.

Behind these two major developments in the acquisition of information, the analytical component of central intelligence has also been expanding. The role of the analyst at the centre, examining the masses of information now available, has of course become crucial as the selector and interpreter of the flood of facts which would otherwise submerge the decision-maker. But even more importantly, the intellectual scope of the analyst function has expanded to reflect the multiple factors and disciplines which can affect international developments – to examine in a 'central' way *all* the relevant political, strategic, economic, social, psychological, cultural and biographical data.

This concept of central intelligence goes beyond the traditional debate over whether to concentrate on an adversary's capabilities or his intentions. Thanks to modern technology, capabilities today can be identified with far greater precision than in previous years. But the very completeness of this knowledge increases the difficulties of overcommitment if every known capability is to be protected against. And a better knowledge of the habits of men shows that an adversary's intention is not necessarily the key to determining future action. Intentions can change, they may not yet be fully formed, or they may be rather a hope than a commitment to action.

Thus 'central intelligence' has grown to provide another new dimension for intelligence: integrating into a coherent analysis all of the *forces* acting, interacting, and reacting to produce future developments. Weapon systems must be examined with respect to the bureaucratic politics affecting them. Economic resources must be analysed against the sociology of the possessing nation, to determine whether they can be allocated to national aggrandisement, or must be distributed for consumer enjoyment. Cultural and psychological pressures must be included in assessments of how events are perceived in another political framework. As the net of analysis widens to capture more of these elements of faraway decisions, deception becomes more difficult for the opponent, as the smallest contradictions challenge a deceptive scenario.

In this process, the analyst must also step away from his own experience and culture and include the emotional, and the apparently irrational among the forces which might produce the surprise result. Egypt *should not* have launched the October 1973 attack over the Suez; but it did, and forced great power resolution of the issues despite predictable defeat. The analyst must shake off the pressures of his own history and culture to avoid complacency over a Maginot Line's strength and look at its flanks. He must not be satisfied that his analysis could explain a phenomenon and that no hard evidence contradicts it, as in our assessment that Vietnamese communist supplies were not being shipped through neutral Sihanoukville until we saw the bills of lading when the government changed. America's insistence that a Vietnam 'war' should be fought by soldiers reflected the civil–military difference in American society, but it failed to come to grips with the political and social strategy the situation on the ground required. Our focus today on strategic weapons and nuclear power diverts attention from a weapon used with greatest effect by the Soviet Union in recent years – the airlift of Cubans to Africa and other trouble spots.

Central intelligence also benefits from the new techniques of analysis which CIA, private think-tanks, and the academic community have all developed. Better indexing and retrieval of relevant information, better identification of trends, better measurements of the comparative influence of similar factors in different environments, more refined alternative models of likely developments, and more disciplined game scenarios to force attention to the unexpected – all of these can enable the analyst to improve his identification of the play and interplay of all the factors which should be reviewed in an assessment. Data-processing machines and similar techniques will not automatically answer an analyst's questions, but they can illuminate contradictions and anomalies he would never have anticipated and require him to identify their causes.

But deception and surprise are still with us and the improvements in central intelligence to date have not eliminated them. The deceptive

Egyptian Suez manoeuvres prior to October 1973; the surprise of the
Indian nuclear explosion despite an assessment that it was likely; the fall
of the Shah of Iran regardless of a universal belief that he was firmly in
place, all show that the phenomena have not been eliminated and pose
the question as to how such intelligence 'gaps' occur and how to
minimise them.

Intelligence will never provide a perfect crystal ball which absolutely
predicts the future. Better awareness of the multiplicity of factors which
contribute to future events, examination of past developments to track
the switching alternatives that might have led the train of events to a
different destination, and the identification of patterns of probable
reactions in particular cultures, all suggest that our greater knowledge
can press back the veil of ignorance, but that we will then confront even
more refined questions. The great scientific discoveries provide whole
new perspectives into the mysteries of the universe, but open as many
new fields of inquiry as they close, and the apparent infinity of human
variety and decision has seen no limits to date.

Intelligence faces the same future, and, in fact, we would not want that
absolute crystal ball, because the true function of intelligence is to help
make decisions to bring about a better future and avoid the dangers that
an intelligence projection might present – to change rather than merely
to know the future. But we must also insist, as the scientists do, on
constant improvements in the scope and provision of our intelligence
knowledge. Additional steps can be taken to improve our central
intelligence analysis to reduce the danger of deception and surprise.

The first of these would apply the concept of central intelligence, but
expand the number of participants. One of the basic principles of
'central' intelligence is to gather diverse analyses and analysts to
examine a problem from different viewpoints and different
backgrounds. Within the government this is done by gathering the
different intelligence agencies of the military, State and other
departments. But the process must be extended. The many centres of
private analysis need to be included in the process. The academics, the
media analysts and commentators, even the conspiracy theorists, must
be heard out, probed for their evidence and rationale. Because a closed
community of analysts, government or academic, can develop its own
predilections, preconceptions, and even myths which need the small
boy's querulous insistence that 'the emperor has no clothes'.

Some work of this nature has been done through outside panels,
through the Team-B exercise, and through the growth of independent
advocacy groups. But it must become a regular element of the process.
To achieve it, a major effort must be made to distribute publicly as much
of the basic information and assessment as possible, to stimulate outside
analysis. The discipline of journalism must be applied – the information

and the assessments must be exposed while the sources are kept secret. 'Deep Throat' is still not identified, but the whole world knows what he said.

This same approach must be adopted for 'central' intelligence. The evident requirement to protect some secrets of intelligence – human sources contributing secretly at risk of life or livelihood, allied cooperation vulnerable to embarrassment or pressure, technical devices subject to frustration by an adversary attempting deception or surprise – does not mean that intelligence must suffer the handicaps of isolation in total secrecy. The fact that huge quantities of important American information are actually shared with our public, from the details of Soviet weapon systems to appraisals of world grain production, indicates that this process is feasible. To the extent that official release of such information would be undiplomatic or provocative, intermediaries in academia, the media and Congress (or its library) could serve as the channel, insulating the executive from foreign reaction.

A second step must be the final adoption of the advice of one of America's wisest analysts, Sherman Kent. In 1949, he advocated[1] that intelligence analysis be organised geographically rather than functionally. But he was not heeded, and the intelligence economists, the current political analysts, and the military experts were comfortably settled into separate bureaucratic islands, submitting their analyses to wise generalists to integrate into overall assessments.

The effect was almost uniformly bad. The generalists approached the problem in categories, attaching supplemental economic essays to political estimates and compromising force projections after adversary proceedings between hawks and doves. Emphasis rapidly focused on current political event reporting at the expense of deeper integrative research. And the clandestine operators of CIA, who were organised geographically, became the CIA spokesmen in Washington inter-agency meetings discussing what United States policies and programmes should be selected to meet challenges in world regions, displacing 'central' analysts to writing academic treatises offering little contribution to frenetic decisionmaking. Reorganisation of the entire analytical community geographically is impractical, as Defence, State, Treasury and the other departments from Agriculture to Commerce to Energy need their functional analysts, but the 'central' organ, CIA, should organise its functional analysts into the geographical entities in which the real world's problems appear.

The third step must be to improve communication between analyst and decisionmaker. The original theory of analysis was that in an ivory tower, carefully segregated from the hurly-burly of collection or decision, refined judgements could be distilled. We have seen this theory fail in the relationship between the intelligence functions of collection and analysis, as the analysts became divorced from grimy reality and the collectors husbanded their information nuggets to pass them directly to hungry decisionmakers. We have also seen it fail between analyst and decisionmaker, who assembled his own analytical staff in frustration over the difficulty of relating the carefully honed statements of the analysts to the real problems he faced.

I do not suggest that intelligence analysis be integrated with decision analysis, but I believe better techniques of communication are essential between the two. Quantitative probability judgements might well have suggested that the Shah's chances of continued control were in the 90 per cent range, just as the verbal assessments apparently were. But a 90 per cent probable also means a 10 per cent improbable. An importance factor multiplying the 10 per cent, might well have given a push to policy-makers to take early and substantial steps to ensure that the 10 per cent probability did not occur.

Thus the central intelligence function must be extended beyond analysis and assessment to a positive responsibility to relate the assessment to policy options. Intelligence must accept the responsibility not only to deliver an effective analysis to the decisionmaker's desk, but also to ensure that it goes into the heads of the decisionmaking officials, and is used by them to launch policies and programmes. The alert memorandum, ringing an alarm bell about a looming short-term probability, must be supplemented by the equally insistent warning of the need for longer-term, perhaps less dramatic but probably more effective, moves to forestall future crises.

These changes in central intelligence, past and future, reflect another fundamental change in the function of intelligence. The zero-sum contribution of the spy has been supplemented by a mutual gain approach. We have experienced a quantitative revolution in information acquisition already; a qualitative revolution in analysis lies before us. With these, both sides of an international issue can replace ignorance, suspicion and fear by knowledge, confidence and wisdom.

Verification permits arms control agreements, and electronic sensors in the Sinai desert give erstwhile enemies assurance against secret armour build-ups. Surprise by an adversary can be reduced by information acquired about his capabilities, his ambitions and the motivating forces pressing him to action. Self-surprise, or failure to anticipate, can be reduced by better analysis of the adversary's options and their comparative attractiveness from *his* viewpoint, not ours. And successful deception becomes less likely as the process of analysis extends beyond cloistered government corridors to include more participants, including even the mavericks whose doubts and concerns must be answered and not brushed aside as impertinent or unworthy.

As central intelligence thus grows to a democratic rather than merely a governmental responsibility, it will improve sufficiently to convince nations to resolve their issues by analysis and common effort, not by blood.

NOTES

1 Kent, Sherman, *Strategic Intelligence for American World Policy* (Princeton U.P., 1949)

8 United States and Soviet Strategic Technologies and Nuclear War Fighting: A Comparison

Patrick J. Friel

THE CONTRAST BETWEEN UNITED STATES AND SOVIET NUCLEAR DOCTRINES

The cornerstone of United States strategic policy with respect to the Soviet Union is deterrence through the possession of an 'assured destruction' capability; that is, the ability to inflict 'unacceptable' levels of damage on the Soviet Union even after absorbing an attack on United States strategic nuclear forces. This has included the capability to limit damage to the United States, using high accuracy missile systems to attack hardened Soviet military installations. Reportedly, the United States targeted some of its strategic forces against Soviet conventional forces in order to blunt a Warsaw Pact invasion of Western Europe. But the principal emphasis of United States policy remains assured destruction, and consequently most of the United States strategic nuclear missile warheads are small and inaccurate and can be targeted effectively only against soft urban areas. The inventory of United States warheads is large and they are deployed on a diverse number of strategic nuclear delivery systems (ICBMs, SLBMs, and long-range aircraft). There is little reliance on strategic defence, whether passive or active, since it is believed that in a nuclear war no one can win.

In contrast, the Soviet military literature provides evidence of a strategic doctrine that includes the ability to fight and win a nuclear war and survive as a national entity. Richard Pipes[1] and, earlier, Leon Gouré *et al.* suggest that the Soviets had articulated a nuclear warfighting and warwinning doctrine by the mid-1960s.[2] This does not necessarily mean that the Soviet Union is systematically planning an attack on the United States, but rather should general war break out,

98

their strategy would be to ensure survival and rapid recovery. The forces derived from a nuclear warfighting strategic doctrine would be quite different than those derived from the United States deterrence concept. A nuclear warfighting doctrine would emphasise capabilities which would be able to suppress United States strategic forces in order to minimise damage to the Soviet Union. There would also be a significant emphasis on strategic defence, particularly of those assets and personnel required for survival and rapid post-attack recovery.

This chapter attempts to show that the present and projected United States strategic nuclear forces are in fact accurate reflections of its strategic doctrine of deterrence. It also suggests that well-conceived nuclear warfighting doctrine involves the coordination of six diverse strategic capabilities. The development of this broad spectrum of strategic capabilities should be indicated by rather specific technical indicators. Soviet strategic technology programmes are examined to determine whether or not these technical indicators are present and support the view that the Soviet Union is systematically developing a nuclear warfighting capability. A comparative analysis of United States strategic programmes is made in order to show whether or not United States and Soviet strategic doctrine are in fact diametrically opposed. It is assumed that the strategic forces on both sides will be constrained by the numerical limits contained in the SALT II Treaty.

POTENTIAL UNITED STATES AND SOVIET STRATEGIC NUCLEAR FORCES UNDER THE SALT II TREATY

The SALT II Treaty will run to the end of 1985 and the Protocol to the end of 1981. SALT I produced a treaty that permanently limited strategic ballistic missile defences (ABM); the objective of SALT II is to limit strategic offensive arms. The terms of the Treaty are summarised in Table 8.1 and are taken from Burt.[3] The size and composition of the present United States and Soviet strategic forces are summarised in Tables 8.2 and 8.3.[4-6] At present, the United States has more than 2000 strategic nuclear delivery systems capable of delivering in excess of 9500 warheads while the Soviet Union has over 2500 delivery vehicles capable of delivering more than 7700 nuclear warheads.

The important difference between the United States and Soviet ballistic missiles is their throw-weights. The largest Soviet missiles have throw-weights of 3170 kg (7000 lb) and 6800 to 9000 kg (15,000 to 20,000 lb), respectively, three-and-a-half to ten times the size of Minuteman. The United States has agreed to define a 'light' missile as the Soviet 3170 kg (7000 lb) system and the 'heavy' missile as the 6800 to 9000 kg (15,000 to 20,000 lb) missile. This agreement, combined with

TABLE 8.1 SALT II limitations on strategic nuclear forces (Treaty expires
31 December 1985)

- 2250   Strategic nuclear launch vehicles
- 1320   ICBM/SLBM MIRVs[a] plus aircraft equipped with air-launched cruise missiles (ALCM) with range greater than 600 km
(370 miles)
- 1200   MIRV ICBMs plus SLBMs
- 820   ICBM MIRVs
- Number of warheads on deployed missiles cannot be greater than
tested configuration
- 326   'Modern' large ('heavy') ballistic missiles allowed for Soviet
Union–none for United States. No future deployment on
either side allowed
- 'Light' missile defined as SS-19/6 RVs,[b] 3170 kg (7000 lb)
- 'Heavy' missile defined as SS-18/10 RVs, 6800 to 9000 kg (15,000 to
20,000 lb)
- One 'new type' ICBM allowed for each side with 6, or 10 RVs
- No limit on 'new type' SLBMs
- 24–35 ALCMs with ranges over 6000 km (3700 miles) allowed on
'heavy' (B-52 class) bomber:
   Each 'heavy' bomber with cruise missiles counts against 1320 MIRV
   limit
- Significant transfer of weapons limited by treaty to third country
banned
- Protocol limitations (expires 31 December 1981):
   Ban on mobile ICBMs and air-to-surface ballistic missile testing and
   deployment
   Ban on deployment of cruise missiles with range greater than 600 km
   (370 miles)

---

[a] Multiple independently targeted re-entry vehicles
[b] Re-entry vehicles armed with thermonuclear warheads

the SALT II numerical limits, will clearly allow the Soviet Union to increase substantially the number of potentially accurate ICBM warheads (4566 at the time of writing (1979)). Using the characteristics of the present Soviet systems and the numerical limits of SALT II, the potential size of the Soviet strategic forces in 1985 can be predicted with considerable accuracy. This is shown in Table 8.4, using the data from notes.[4–6] It should be emphasised that this projection is not a speculation. It is based on high quality data from United States intelligence sensors on the size and number of warheads on each of the new Soviet ICBMs which have been extensively tested. As the table indicates, the total number of Soviet strategic missile warheads would be 9300 and the number of high yield, potentially accurate warheads would increase to over 6600, 70 per cent of the Soviet strategic missile warhead inventory. The yield and numbers of these weapons are high enough so that the Soviet ICBM force would have a significant capability to

TABLE 8.2 Present United States strategic nuclear forces (Total United States strategic nuclear delivery vehicles: 2057)

Ground-based ICBMs: 1054 (550 MIRVs, 504 single warheads):	
550 MMIII/3 MIRV 170 KT warheads/booster	1650 RVs
450 MMII/Single 1-MT warhead/booster	450
54 Titan II-9 MT	54
Total United States warheads in ICBM force:	2154
Sea-based forces: 41 SLBM subs, 656 launchers (496 MIRVs, 160 multiple warhead vehicles):	
28 Poseidons, 16 launchers per boat with 10 MIRV 50 KT warheads per launcher	4480
10 Polaris, 16 launchers with 3 MIRVs per launcher	480
3 Poseidons, Trident (4.8 MIRV 100 kt warheads per launcher)	384
Total United States warheads in SLBM force:	5344
Total United States strategic missile warheads:	7498
Total United States MIRVs:	1046
Strategic bombers:	
346 B-52s FB-111 each with six gravity bombs or SRAM missiles	2076
Total number of United States strategic warheads now deployed:	9574[a]

[a] The fourteen warhead option on Poseidon could increase the total to 11,366.

destroy ICBM silos with reasonable missile accuracies (0.2–0.15 nm CEP for 90 per cent kill probability with two warheads per silo). If the Soviets place the allowed number of cruise missiles on each of the bombers permitted, the total number of Soviet strategic warheads could be as high as 12,000. The SALT II Treaty legitimises the deployment of these forces. There is also a distinction between deployed warheads and a strategic reserve; the Treaty's numerical limits refer only to deployed forces. There is no prohibition on the number of missiles and warheads that could be produced and stored – a significant strategic reserve. There are many who believe that the Soviet Union has or will have a significant strategic reserve so that the useful strategic forces could be much larger than that prescribed by the SALT II limits. While it is true, as both President Carter and Senator Edward Kennedy have observed, that

TABLE 8.3   Present Soviet[4] strategic forces
(Total strategic nuclear delivery vehicles: 2509)

Ground-based ICBMs:	*Re-entry vehicles*	
MIRV ICBM launchers (758 MIRVs, 640 single warheads)		
150 SS-17/4 MIRV–0.5–1 MT warhead	600	
308 SS-18/10 MIRV–0.5–1 MT warhead[d]	3080	
300 SS-19/6 MIRV–0.5–1 MT warhead	1800	
	———	
Total ICBM MIRV warheads:	5480	
	═══	
Single warhead launchers		
All SS-9s retired – 7500 kg warhead 20 MT		
640 SS-11/13/1 MT warhead	640	
	———	
Total ICBM warhead inventory:	6120	
	═══	

Sea-based forces (63 SLBM submarines, 928 launchers)[b]	*Launch tubes*	*warheads*
19 Delta I submarines 12 SS-N-8 single warhead launchers	228	228
4 Delta II submarines 16 SS-N-8 single warhead launchers	64	64
10 Delta III 16 SS-N-18/3 MIRV[a]	160	480
29 Yankee submarines 16 SS-N-6 single warhead launchers	464	464
1 Yankee, 12 SS-N-17, 3–1 MT MIRV[a]	12	36
	———	———
Total SLBM launchers:	928	1272[b]
	═══	═══

Total Soviet strategic missile warheads		7392
		═══
Total Soviet MIRVs	930	
	═══	
Strategic bombers: 156[c]–2 gravity or ASMs per bomber	312	
Total number of USSR strategic warheads now deployed		7704
		═══

---

[a] This brings a total of 63, or one more SSBN that the Soviets are permitted under the SALT I Interim Agreement. Presumably the Soviets will retire one of their older SSBNs in order to keep within the SALT I guidelines.

[b] The Soviet SLBM inventory includes 75 additional SLBM launchers deployed on 24 golf and hotel-class submarines. While the hotel submarines are not counted under the SALT I ceilings, their launchers are giving the Soviet Union a total of 1003 sea-based launchers or 53 SLBM over the total agreed upon in SALT I. The official United States position on this issue is to assert that the launch tubes on the hotel-class are being dismantled and, therefore, are not to be counted in the SALT totals. The total of 87 SLBM submarines is also in excess of the 62 agreed in SALT I – See Ref. 4, 1980–81 edition.

[c] Not including Backfire.

[d] 18–25 MT, 7500 kg warhead version tested.

TABLE 8.4 Potential Soviet strategic offensive forces under SALT II Treaty. Total potential Soviet strategic nuclear launch vehicles: 2250

Ground-based strategic forces (820 MIRVs
plus 345 single RV launchers—Total: 1165)

326[a]	SS-18 boosters	10 RVs/booster	3260 RVs
494	SS-19 boosters	6 RVs/booster	2964 RVs
345	SS-11s[b]	1 RV/booster	345 RVs
Potential ICBM warheads			6569

Sea-based strategic forces (950 launchers/380 MIRVs)

34	Yankee/16 launchers SSN-6/17	
25–26	Delta/16 launchers SSN-8/18	
Potential SLBM RVs (three RVs/launcher—380 MIRVs allowed)		2750

Potential number of Soviet warheads (SLBM/MIRV/MRV and ICBM MIRVs)	9319

Strategic bombers: (120 TU-95 BEAR and MYA-4 BISON)

If each carries 25 cruise missiles	3000

Soviet RV yields

● Soviet MIRV ICBMs–RVs:	1–2 MT
● Soviet SLBM–RVs:	1–2 MT
● Large Soviet ICBM–RV:	15–20 MT
Total potential Soviet strategic warheads	12,319

[a] Including 18 SS-9/SS-18 launch sites used in R & D.

[b] (Possibly some or all high yield (15–20 MT) new RVs allowed under Treaty)

SALT II will require the Soviet Union to dismantle and destroy 300 strategic systems, the destructive power of these ten-year-old single warhead missiles would be more than replaced by missile systems carrying six or more high yield, accurate warheads.

The options available to the Soviet Union are straightforward since they have developed, tested and are deploying a spectrum of new missile systems which can maximise the number of their warheads within the launcher and high MIRV constraints of SALT II. The strategic weapon system options to implement the United States policy of assured destruction, however, have been in a state of flux for a number of years. The penetrating bomber option has been dropped, presumably because of the vulnerability of SAC bases to an attack by Soviet SLBMs and the enormous size of the Soviet air defences. A low vulnerability mobile ICBM would seriously compromise the verification issue and is banned by the Protocol until the end of 1981. Another minimum vulnerability system, called the multiple aimpoint (MAP) or the multiple protective shelter (MPS) system, involves a large number of silos and the missiles would be moved randomly from silo to silo; 200 new ICBMs would be deployed, each assigned to an MPS site of 24 to 30 silos. The number of hardened targets which the Soviets must attack would be increased to 4800 to 6000. The 'racetrack' mode proposed by the Carter administration is presumably still under consideration. While MPS would not deny verification, it would certainly make it more difficult and uncertain. In any event, a new generation United States ICBM such as the MX would not be operational within the life of the Treaty. Realistically, the only deployment options available to the United States before 1985 are weapons now under development, specifically the Trident I and Trident II missiles and the air-launched cruise missiles.[7]

In order to evaluate these two options, let us assume that the United States does not want to alter its plans to deploy what it considers to be an invulnerable sea-based ballistic missile system with an increase in the number of launchers and warheads in the Trident system. This would mean that the United States would have 736 MIRVs in the Trident/Poseidon systems during the life of the Treaty. The ICBM and cruise missile total, therefore, must stay within the MIRV constraints of SALT II with 736 MIRVs assigned to the sea-based forces. Consequently, there can be only 464 MIRV ICBMs. To deploy 200 new MIRV ICBMs, for example, the number of ICBM MIRVs would have to be reduced by 86 to stay within the 1200 MIRV ICBM plus SLBM sublimit. These silos would presumably be used to deploy 86 single warhead ICBMs. The United States can deploy 120 bombers equipped with cruise missiles (ALCM) within the 1320 total MIRV plus ALCM limit. The resultant United States strategic nuclear force using these options is summarised in Table 8.5. There would be an increase in the total number of United States strategic warheads to 14,000 with an increase in the ICBM MIRV warhead inventory to 2792 from 2154. The SLBM warhead inventory would increase 18 per cent (to 6560) and the force would include 3000 cruise missiles.

Of the potential SALT II United States missile warhead inventory, 70 per cent are SLBM warheads which would not present a threat to Soviet ICBMs. The number of accurate ICBM MIRV warheads would be 2000. The accuracy of these warheads would have to be extremely high to pose a threat to ICBM silos (0.08 nmi for a 95 per cent kill probability with two warheads). The remaining ICBM MIRVs (492 Minuteman III warheads) would presumably use the MK12A warhead, which is reported to have over twice the yield as the present Minuteman III warhead.[5] Even with the higher yield, the accuracy of the Minuteman III system would have to be half that reported (0.2 nmi)[6] for a high confidence kill of hardened ICBM silos. Thus, the potential United States ICBM MIRV force will not have and probably cannot have the correct combination of warhead numbers and a yield/accuracy combi-

TABLE 8.5 Potential United States strategic forces under SALT II

No change in planned United States SLBM forces
200 Trident I or II missiles replace 200 Minuteman IIIs (or a new
    MIRV missile–the MX)[a]
Minuteman III MIRVs reduced to 264 to stay within 1320 total
    MIRV limit and 1200 MIRV ICBM/SLBM sublimit
Bomber force retained at 346 and 25 cruise missiles added to 120
    bombers
Single warhead Minuteman IIs replace 86 Minuteman IIIs

Ground-based ICBMs: (464 MIRVs plus 590 single RV launchers):	*1054*
200 Trident II modified/10 MIRV 100–350 KT warheads/booster	2000
264 Minuteman III/3 MIRV 170 KT warheads/booster	792
536 Minuteman II/single 1 MT warhead	536
54 Titan II–single 9 MT warhead	54
Total potential United States ICBM warheads:	3382
Potential United States ICBM MIRV warheads:	2792
Sea-Based forces: (736 MIRVs):	
21 Poseidons, 16 launchers per boat with ten MIRV 50 KT warheads per launcher	3360
10 Poseidons, 16 launchers per boat with eight MIRV Trident I, 100 KT warheads per boat	1280
10 Tridents, 24 launchers per boat with Trident I missiles	1920
Total potential United States SLBM warheads:	9352
Total potential United States strategic missile warheads:	10,642
Strategic Bombers: (346):	
120 Bombers with 25 cruise missiles each	3000
226 Bombers with 7 gravity bombs or SRAM missiles.	1582
Total potential United States warheads in bombers	4582
Total potential United States strategic nuclear launch vehicles	2136
Total potential United States warheads	13,934

[a] In one version, the first two stages of Trident II would be the first and third stages of MX.
The number of warheads on the resultant MX would be ten and the yield more than
three times that of Trident I.

nation to present an impressive capability, from a military standpoint, to destroy the Soviet ICBM force (for a 2-on-1 attack on hardened ICBM silos). The United States cruise missile force allowed under SALT II would be very accurate, and could have a significant capability to destroy hardened missile silos. However, the total flight time of the aircraft and missile is about 10 hours and the missile could be susceptible to defence countermeasures. The hard target capability of cruise missiles as a reliable counterforce weapon, therefore, is clearly inferior to the ballistic missile.

The new United States ICBM would not even reach initial operational capability by the end of the Treaty period. The forces shown in Table 8.5 represent, therefore, only potential United States strategic capabilities. The proposed deceptive basing schemes cannot be implemented during the lifetime of the Treaty. Thus the United States ICBM force will remain vulnerable during the period of the Treaty; however, the new ICBM force would give the United States an important warfighting capability. While it would not have an impressive capability to destroy Soviet hardened missile silos, it would have a significant capability against targets hardened to several thousand kN/m^2(psi). Thus it would be possible to target Russian military installations and forces that would be used in an attack on western Europe. There would also be the capability to destroy some of the nuclear warfighting assets in the Soviet Union. However the potential United States forces would still mainly reflect the assured destruction doctrine.

THE WARHEAD REQUIREMENTS FOR UNITED STATES NUCLEAR POLICY: DETERRENCE THROUGH ASSURED DESTRUCTION

In order to determine the warhead requirements for the assured destruction policy, two questions must be answered: What constitutes deterrence and what constitutes assured destruction? The answer to both of these questions, from the United States viewpoint, was provided by Secretary of Defence McNamara in the early 1960s.[8–10] In this statement of United States policy, deterrence was defined as the ability to destroy at least 25 per cent of the Soviet population and over 50 per cent of their industrial capacity. He further estimated that this level of destruction could be realised by delivering 400 megaton-equivalent (MTE) nuclear warheads on the Soviet Union; these parameters can be placed in better perspective by considering an attack on the first 100 Soviet cities. An estimate of the total area contained within this target complex is shown in Table 8.6. The size of Soviet cities assumed is in reasonable agreement with the values given by Kemp.[10] Under these assumptions, the area contained within this 100-city target complex

TABLE 8.6 Assumed size of the first 100 Soviet cities

City rank	$R_{95}{}^a$ (Statute miles)	Unit area km² (miles²)	Total area km² (miles²)
1 (Moscow)	6.9	380 (150)	380 (150)
Next 35	5.8	270 (105)	10,030 (3675)
Next 35	4.6	170 (66)	5980 (2310)
Next 30	3.6	98 (38)	3880 (1140)
Total area in assumed target complex		18,830 (7275 miles²)	

[a] R_{95}: Radius of city containing 95 per cent of the population

would be about 7300 square miles. This target complex should contain about 25 per cent of the Soviet population[11] and 50 per cent of its industrial capacity, as indicated in Secretary of Defence Harold Brown's Annual Report for fiscal year 1979.[5] Using Glasstone's standard reference on the effects of nuclear weapons[12] the MTE required to place a 18,900 square kilometre (7300 square mile) area at risk for various overpressures from 40 to 80 kN/m² (6 to 12 psi) is shown in Table 8.7.

TABLE 8.7 Warhead requirement for United States nuclear policy: assured destruction. (100 cities with assumed total area of 7300 mi²)
[25 per cent population, 50 per cent of industrial capacity at risk[5]]

Overpressure		Megatonne equivalents (MTE) required[a]
41 kN/m² (6 psi)		161
68 kN/m² (10 psi)	McNamara's assured destruction	318
82 kN/m² (12 psi)	← ————————— →	400
50 KT warheads		170 KT
41 kN/m² (6 psi)	1186	524
82 kN/m² (12 psi)	2947	1303

United States warhead requirements to threaten next 200 Soviet urban areas (300 cities, 37 per cent of population, 67 per cent industrial capacity at risk[5]
City 100–200 R_{95} = 3.0 miles Additional area–12,400 km² (4800 miles²)
City 200–300 R_{95} = 2.5 miles
Poseidon warheads required for 300
  city attack   *1960* (or 13 Poseidon submarines)
Minuteman warheads required for
  300 city attack   875 (or 291 Minuteman III
                                                         missiles)

[a] $MTE = NY^{2/3}$
  N = Number of warheads
  Y = Yield-megatonnes

One can see that McNamara's criteria of 400 MTE corresponds to about 80 kN/m² (12 psi). As Glasstone indicates,[12] this would mean severe damage to even reinforced concrete buildings, indeed assured destruction. It can also be shown that above 400 MTE the marginal return for additional warheads in terms of destructive capability is small. Thus, as Kemp[10] has inferred, the 400 MTE definition of deterrence and assured destruction by Mr McNamara may have represented more a management tool than any particularly clear insight into what constitutes deterrence. As Table 8.7 indicates, if the more reasonable 40 kN/m² (6 psi) criteria were used (meaning severe damage to masonry buildings) the warhead requirements would be 165 MTE. In terms of 50 KT Poseidon class warheads, this would mean a requirement of about 1200 warheads delivered. For a 170 KT (Minuteman III class) yield, the requirements would be about 524 warheads. The bottom of Table 8.7 also shows the United States warhead requirements for a 300-city attack; an additional 775 Poseidon warheads (for a total of 1960) would be required. Thus, with 65 per cent of the 3200 Poseidon warheads on station, the United States could place at risk about 37 per cent of the Soviet population[13] and 67 per cent of its industrial capacity, again using the table of Soviet population/industrial capacity versus number of cities shown in the Annual Report of the Department of Defence for 1979.[5]

Thus, the assured destruction mission could be accomplished using 200 missiles of the Minuteman III class or about eight Poseidon submarines. Moreover, 300 Soviet cities would be placed at risk by about thirteen Poseidon submarines or 290 Minuteman III missiles. An on-station Poseidon force of 20 or 21 submarines would probably place at risk over 600 Soviet cities.

While it is clear that this may not be an exact target list, this analysis shows that the United States SLBM forces would place most of the urban areas in the Soviet Union at risk, excluding the threat of the tactical nuclear warheads in Europe and the not insignificant French and British ballistic missile submarine forces,[10] even after a successful Soviet attack on Minuteman and SAC bases.

AN ESTIMATE OF THE NUMBER OF STRATEGIC NUCLEAR WARHEADS REQUIRED FOR A SOVIET WARFIGHTING CAPABILITY

If the Soviet strategic doctrine is nuclear warfighting, one important capability would be the ability to destroy United States strategic offensive forces in the event of general war. The other important capability in nuclear warfighting would be strategic defence or the ability to mitigate retaliation, and this will be discussed below. Assuming that the United States SLBM force cannot be detected and is therefore invulnerable, then the primary United States strategic force which the Soviet Union must destroy would be Minuteman ICBM and the SAC bombers. After a long debate, it is now generally agreed that the quality and quantity of Soviet ICBM MIRV systems, the SS-18 and SS-19, will be adequate to threaten the Minuteman ICBM force in the 1980s. If the circular-error-probability (CEP) of these Soviet missile systems is 0.10 nmi or less, the number of warheads required to destroy Minuteman would be equivalent to the number of silos, almost independent of yield. On the other hand, it is difficult to conceive of a successful attack on Minuteman silos using a ballistic missile system in which the accuracy is not at least 0.2 nmi CEP. If one assumes that the Soviet Union can achieve a missile accuracy of 0.15 nmi CEP, the number of 1 megatonne warheads required for the destruction of Minuteman would be 2000, that is, two ICBM warheads per silo.

A Soviet counterforce attack would also include the approximately 100 airfields from which the bombers of the United States Strategic Air Command could be launched. The most effective Soviet attack capability would be SLBMs fired on depressed trajectories. The maximum flight time on these warheads would be 5 to 7 minutes from either coast. It is well known that most aircraft are relatively vulnerable to even a few kN/m^2 (psi) overpressure. Thus a single 1 megatonne burst could destroy all of the exposed bombers in an airfield which is several kilometres in diameter. Thus, about eight Delta or Yankee class Soviet submarines could place at risk SAC bombers located on 100 airfields. Only three of the Delta III class submarines with the SS-N-18 MIRV missiles would be required to execute the same mission. Even if it is assumed that the Soviet SLBM attack on SAC could be detected by infrared early warning satellites or the PAVE PAWS radar system located on either coast, the maximum time available to allow the SAC bombers to escape would be 5 to 7 minutes. The Soviet SLBM force would require only a few more warheads to destroy or disable the fraction of the United States Poseidon/Trident fleet in port at Charleston, South Carolina, and Puget Sound, Washington. Thus the warhead requirements for an attack on all of the strategic offensive forces located in the continental United States would be 2200 1 megatonne weapons, the majority of which would be accurate ICBMs.

If the Soviet strategic doctrine in fact emphasises nuclear warfighting, then the Soviet Union might not use warheads against the general population, although it may want to target industrial centres in order to destroy the United States war survival capability. Even in a warfighting strategic doctrine, therefore, the Soviets may target United States industrial centres and indirectly place at risk a substantial fraction of the

United States population. In any case, it would be instructive to consider the translation of an assured destruction policy on the part of the Soviet Union with respect to the United States urban/industrial complex. This analysis is not intended to infer that the strategic nuclear policy of the Soviet Union is a mirror-image of the United States deterrence doctrine. It was again assumed that the prime target complex would be the first 100 United States cities. The size of each of the targets and the total area within the target complex are summarised in Table 8.8 and again are in agreement with Kemp.[10] The total area within the target complex would be about 54,800 square kilometres (21,000 square miles). The population within this area is 126 million and would contain about 60 per cent of the United States industrial capacity. The addition of the next 100 cities to the target complex would increase the population at risk by only about 20 million. The warheads required to place this area at risk for overpressures of 40 and 70 kN/m² (6 and 10 psi) are shown in Table 8.9, which indicates that about 458 MTE would be needed to place this target complex at risk for a 40 kN/m² (6 psi) destruction criterion. The bottom of Table 8.9 shows the effect of large warheads; 40–5 megatonne weapons would place the 10 top top cities at risk. The population within this area would be 55 million and would contain about 30 per cent of the United States industrial capacity. The Soviets are reported to have a deployment option involving a very large warhead on the SS-18; the size of this warhead could be as high as 25 megatonnes. As Table 8.9 indicates, only fifteen of these massive weapons could pose a threat to the top ten United States cities. In addition, the detonation of such a large weapon at the optimum height of burst for maximum overpressure on the ground (about 8800 m or 29,000 ft) would result in a thermal flux directly under the detonation of 500 calories per square centimetre and at the edge of a 17 km (10 mile) radius city the flux would be 100 calories per square centimetre. At these thermal fluxes, almost all combustible

TABLE 8.8 Size of first 100 United States cities

	R_{95} radius	Area m²	(yds²)
1 New York	15	708	(846)
2 Los Angeles	18	1018	(1972)
3 Chicago	16	804	(960)
4 Philadelphia	14	616	(736)
5 Through 10	12	2262	(4215)
10 Through 25	9	3817	(6829)
25 Through 100	7	11,545	(22,111)
		20,769	(37,669)

● Population at risk–125 million
● 60–65 per cent of United States industrial floor space at risk
● Next 100 cities would add about 20 million population at risk

TABLE 8.9 Impact of Soviet nuclear attack on United States (100 cities–125 million population at risk)

41 kN/m² (6 psi)	458 (megatonne equivalents)
68 kN/m² (10 psi)	907

Effectiveness of high yield weapons on United States cities:

40–5 MT/41 kN/m² (6 psi), (13,720 km–5300 miles²), ten top cities, 55 million population, 30 per cent of United States industrial floor space at risk, or

15–25 MT at 41 kN/m² (6 psi) produces same damage

Conclusions:

United States extremely vulnerable to even a small attack
5 per cent of potential Soviet inventory adequate to deter United States (?)
– Even 1 per cent is staggering
Vast majority of potential Soviet inventory available for attack on United States forces

material will ignite to cause extensive fire damage in the target area.

These calculations show the incredible vulnerability of the United States urban-industrial complex to a nuclear attack. Thus, the ability to destroy the top United States urban centres with a few tens of megatonne class weapons should provide the Soviets with an adequate deterrent. From the United States viewpoint, the ability of the Soviet Union to destroy the top 100 cities with about 500 1 megatonne weapons constitutes a massive overkill. The Soviet Union would have a more than adequate deterrent with respect to the United States, with about 1 to 5 per cent of the total number of warheads that could be deployed in her long-range strategic forces.

To execute a counterforce mission against the Minuteman and SAC bomber bases as well as to destroy industrial targets in the United States, the Soviet Union would need no more than 2800 1 megatonne class warheads. Thus the residual number of warheads in the Soviet inventory allowed under SALT II would be substantially in excess of those required for both a warfighting and deterrence policy. It is the possible doctrinal asymmetry between the United States and the Soviet Union and the substantial residual Soviet forces that would be allowed under SALT II that has led many United States strategic analysts to the conclusion that the Soviet Union will achieve strategic superiority over the United States in the mid-1980s.

SOVIET UNCERTAINTIES IN A MINUTEMAN ATTACK

In planning such a drastic action as an attack on the United States Minuteman force, the Soviet planners are faced with three significant uncertainties. The first uncertainty would be the collateral damage to the civilian population that would result from such a large-scale attack on the Minuteman bases. If the collateral damage were high, then an attack on the Minuteman could, in fact, be considered an attack on the civilian population. The United States response could be an all-out attack on the Soviet Union. Department of Defence calculations of the collateral damage to civilian population from an attack on Minuteman involving two warheads per silo suggests that as many as 20 million Americans would die a dreadful death of radiation sickness. The calculations by Drell and Vol Heppel[14] indicate that an attack on Minuteman bases, as well as the four Titan II bases, could mean a lethal fallout of radiation on Chicago, Detroit, Cleveland, St Louis and as far east as Washington and Atlanta. In addition, there would be a significant amount of fallout in Canada, particularly along the border where most of the Canadian population is concentrated. Thus, the attack on the United States ICBM bases from the Soviet planners' viewpoint could easily be considered a population attack on the United States (and Canada?) and invite an immediate United States response.

A second Soviet uncertainty is re-entry vehicle fratricide. It is well known that the continuous impact of small particles at high velocities on re-entry system heat shields could cause significant surface erosion and eventual destruction of the vehicle. In addition, if the erosion process should be asymmetric, the vehicle could acquire some aerodynamic lift with a severe degradation in its accuracy. Thus, the timing and the geometry of the attack must be structured to avoid long-term flight of re-entry vehicles in the dust-cloud produced by previous detonations. The Soviets must plan the attack to destroy the southern part of each of the six bases first and work north; that is, the attack plan must include a 'south-to-north' walk. The geometry of a 'south-to-north' walk attack would be such, therefore, that a subsequent re-entry vehicle would not have to pass through the dust-cloud produced by a previous detonation. Such an attack, however, would mean that the northern part of each base would be attacked last and thus allow time for the launch of these missiles.

The RV fratricide uncertainty, therefore, leads to the third and perhaps most serious uncertainty; that is, the possibility that the United States will launch the Minuteman as a result of the detection of a large attack by the United States early warning systems. The first United States early warning system to be considered is the infrared satellites which continuously observe launches from the Soviet Union. These satellites are presently capable of detecting and tracking a launch with sufficient accuracy to determine the size of the attack and whether the azimuth of the attack is directed at the Minuteman bases. Consequently, these satellites will give 25 to 30 minutes warning of an attack directed at the Minuteman. Thus, the Soviet planner must consider the possibility that this 30 minute warning time would be adequate to launch the entire Minuteman force, with devastating effects on the Soviet Union. It seems reasonable, therefore, that a Soviet planner must consider deactivating the infrared satellites by a direct attack. These satellites are in synchronous orbit at an altitude of about 37,000 km (23,000 miles and consequently a missile flight time would be of the order of 5 hours. Thus, a direct attack on the satellite system would provide a more than adequate early warning of the possibility of large-scale Soviet hostile action. An alternative approach would be to place in orbit with the early warning infrared satellites an antisatellite system (for example, a high-power laser or a simple pellet-kill system) that would deactivate the satellite shortly before the initiation of an attack. However, a Soviet planner must then consider the United States early warning radar systems (the BMEWS at Flyingdales, England; Thule, Greenland; and Clear, Alaska); also the sophisticated phased array intelligence radar located in Shemya, Alaska. Even if the Soviet planner intends to attack these relatively vulnerable early warning sites, he must also consider the early warning system located at one of the principal targets, namely the Grand Forks Minuteman base. The long-range Perimeter Acquisition Radar (PAR) was installed at Grand Forks, North Dakota, as part of the Sentinel/Safeguard ABM system. This large, sophisticated phased array radar has been incorporated into the United States early warning system and could provide up to 20 minutes early warning of an attack. In addition, the United States has in place a large over-the-horizon radar early warning system. Thus, this multilayer United States early warning system ranging from space-based infrared satellites to a high-traffic, powerful phased array radar located at one of the key targets could easily provide an adequate amount of early warning to allow a launch of the Minuteman system. Thus, the possibility that the United States could obtain adequate early warning to allow a launch of Minuteman is the largest uncertainty in any Soviet plan to attack Minuteman. It is not obvious how one could reduce this uncertainty without an elaborate and sophisticated plan to neutralise all of the United States strategic early warning systems.

THE STRATEGIC CAPABILITIES REQUIRED FOR NUCLEAR WARFIGHTING AND A COMPARISON WITH STATED SOVIET STRATEGIC DOCTRINE

The substantial Soviet risk associated with an attack on Minuteman suggests that a nuclear warfighting capability involves more than just the possession of a sufficient number of accurate MIRV ICBMs to destroy Minuteman and SLBMs to destroy the SAC bases. A well-conceived nuclear warfighting capability should include the ability to prevent retaliation or mitigate its effect. In order to prevent the retaliation by United States SLBM forces or the launch of Minuteman while under attack, three strategic capabilities would be required: an antisatellite system to destroy the United States infrared early warning satellites in geosynchronous orbit, an antisubmarine system which would prevent the launch of the Poseidon/Trident system, in addition to the accurate ICBMs, MIRVs, and SLBMs required to destroy Minuteman and SAC bases. Mitigation of a retaliatory attack would be accomplished through a combination of active and passive defence; that is, civil defence, ballistic missile defence, and an air-defence system to counter the surviving United States manned bombers, some armed with cruise missiles. Thus, nuclear warfighting involves the coordination of six diverse strategic capabilities.

Many students of the Soviet military literature suggest that the Soviet strategic nuclear doctrine is, if necessary, to fight and win a nuclear war and survive as a national entity.[1,2] Pipes[1] indicates that stated Soviet strategic doctrine contains seven elements. It is interesting to compare the six technical capabilities required for nuclear warfighting

TABLE 8.10   Soviet   strategic   doctrine   and   required   technical/military
capabilities

Element of Soviet strategic doctrine	*Required technical/military capability*
Pre-emption	Real time coordination of SLBMs, ICBMs, antisatellite and ASW systems to destroy United States strategic missile and bomber forces
Quantitative superiority	Ability to execute counterforce strike with 75 per cent of the strategic force remaining (under SALT II limits)
Counterforce	Deployment of enough accurate warheads and ASW to destroy Minuteman, SAC and on-station SLBMs with minimum chance of United States launch-on-warning by destroying United States early warning satellites
Combined-arms operation	Integration of all six capabilities to destroy United States nuclear forces and annexe Europe
Defence	ABM, civil defence and air defence to minimise damage to Soviet Union, to political/military/industrial 'cadre' required for rapid recovery

and the elements of stated Soviet strategic doctrine, and this is shown in Table 8.10. Its first three elements – pre-emption, quantitative superiority, and counterforce – relate to those technical capabilities required to prevent retaliation. The key element in Soviet strategic doctrine is the emphasis on strategic defence which is reflected in their substantial programmes in civil defence, air defence, and ballistic missile defence. Pipes[1] suggests that the Soviet military doctrines of 'combined arms operations' would then include their armies and navies, a seventh capability in the present context. The large troop concentrations of Warsaw Pact forces in Eastern Europe are well in excess of reasonable defence requirements. They are there not only to launch a surprise land attack against NATO but to seize Western Europe with minimum damage to industry in the event of a strategic nuclear exchange with the United States. The task of the Soviet navy would be to clear all United States ships from the seas, to cut the sea lanes connecting the United States with its allies and sources of raw material.

There seems to be a close correlation between the six diverse technical capabilities required for nuclear warfighting and the key elements of Soviet strategic doctrine. If it could be shown that the Soviet Union is developing a significant capability in all of the required six areas, the Soviets may indeed be developing a nuclear warfighting capability with a strategic doctrine diametrically opposed to that of the United States.

TECHNICAL INDICATORS OF SOVIET NUCLEAR WARFIGHTING CAPABILITY

From the viewpoint of United States strategic technology, the six technical/military capabilities required for high confidence nuclear warfighting forces include a massive programme in research and development, field testing and deployment of complex and costly strategic systems. Fortunately (for world stability), modern intelligence sensors should be able to monitor the R & D and the field testing of strategic programmes of this size. Much information has been published in the United States press as well as in western Europe, on the status of the Soviet strategic system developments, presumably derived, at least in part, from data provided by these sensors. These published reports indicate that the Soviet Union has extensive R & D and field test programmes in five of the six technical areas required for a nuclear warfighting capability. The amount of published information on the sixth area, Soviet and United States ASW programmes, is not great. In any case, a nuclear warfighting strategy which relies on ASW would be very risky, in view of recent United States programmes to minimise the ASW threat to the United States SLBM force. It would be preferable for the Soviet Union to obtain a warfighting capability with respect to United States SLBMs by mitigating the effects of the attack through a combination of active and passive defence.

SOVIET PROGRAMMES TO PREVENT RETALIATION

THE ICBM MIRV PROGRAMME

The Soviet Union is developing four new ICBMs with a substantial MIRV capability.[4-6] United States industry and population are so concentrated that there is little justification for these new systems from an 'assured destruction' or 'mutual deterrence' viewpoint. One could readily conclude that these missiles have principally one mission, an attack on hardened United States military installations, particularly the Minuteman system. As shown previously, SALT II will legitimise the first capability required for nuclear warfighting, that is, accurate ICBM MIRVs, at a warhead inventory equal to three times that required to destroy the Minuteman force.

The importance that the Soviet Union places on its MIRV ICBM force can be seen in the reaction by Soviet Foreign Minister Andrei Gromyko to the Carter Administration's so-called comprehensive proposal in March 1977. The clear purpose of the proposal was to limit MIRV ICBMs (to 550) and thus mitigate the single issue which fuels the nuclear arms race now – at least from an American viewpoint – the vulnerability of Minuteman. In an extraordinary statement, Mr Gromyko criticised the proposal and accused the Carter Administration of trying to achieve 'unilateral advantages'. Thus, as Burt[3] has observed, 'What the Carter Administration viewed as a serious threat to strategic stability – accurate MIRV'd ICBMs – the Soviet leadership undoubtedly viewed as the cornerstone of its strategic power'.

THE ANTISATELLITE PROGRAMME

Since 1968, the Soviet Union has conducted at least seventeen antisatellite tests[15] with intercepts at altitudes around 500 km (290 miles). More tests have been reported recently. The capability of these interceptors is, therefore, restricted to low-altitude electronic and photographic reconnaissance satellites. However, these intercept systems are viewed in the United States as potentially destabilising and provocative. The flight time to the geosynchronous orbits of the United States early warning infrared and strategic communications satellites is 5 hours, so that the present Soviet antisatellite system is not a threat to these important United States space assets. However, it is not inconceivable that these intercept systems could be placed in orbit with United States early warning satellites and activated prior to the initiation of the Minuteman attack.[16] They might deny critical reconnaissance data to the United States during a crisis or prevent United States observation of the development of Soviet strategic systems and verification of an arms limitation agreement. By reference to United States deterrence concepts (but not to those of the Soviet Union), the development of these antisatellite systems seems to be unwarranted particularly since space-based nuclear weapons are banned by Treaty and it is well known that the United States has never considered space-based offensive nuclear weapon systems to be technically or strategically credible.

ANTISUBMARINE WARFARE

By the mid-1980s, the range of the United States sea-based ballistic missile forces will have been extended to as much as 8850 nautical km (5500 nautical miles). The current Polaris/Poseidon missiles have ranges of 3200 to 4000 km (2000 to 2500 nautical miles). The ballistic missile submarines on patrol operate, therefore, with an ocean area of 14 to 16 million square kilometres (9 to 10 million square miles). The deployment area for the present SSBN force is relatively close to the Soviet Union and subject to surveillance by air and naval forces operating out of home bases and susceptible to fixed acoustical systems comparable to the United States SOSUS (Sound Surveillance System). At a missile range of 8850 nautical km (5500 nautical miles), the submarines' operating area would increase to 296 million square km (95 million square miles). Many United States analysts have argued that such a vast deployment area would pose insuperable problems for any Soviet ASW programme. Both the enormous size of the area and its remoteness from Soviet bases would make the ASW task extremely difficult if not impossible. First, the Soviet ASW forces will have to increase by a factor of ten to cover the larger area and they must be capable of detecting the much quieter Trident submarine. The extended area would require much longer transit times, shorter on station cruises and would reduce the utilisation rate of the Soviet ASW forces. At-sea replenishment may even be required, implying a substantial increase in the logistical fleet train. Consequently, the total effort needed to cover the extended ocean area would be substantially greater than the simple factor of ten suggested by the additional area.

These long-range sea-based ballistic missile forces will also provide the United States with two new strategic capabilities. The first is the ability to launch from port. The extended range would allow missile launches from the Charleston (South Carolina), Bangor (Maine), and Puget Sound (Washington) bases to targets within the Soviet Union.

This capability, combined with shorter transit time required for these long-range systems to get on station, would mean that the warheads available to the United States at the initiation of a Soviet counterforce strike would be greatly increased, even if the attack warning time were only five minutes. The statement by Dr William J. Perry, Undersecretary of Defence for Research and Engineering, before the Senate Arms Services Committee on United States Strategic Nuclear Forces on 1 February 1979 (p. 11) indicates that the new submarine will spend more time at sea so that only one-third of the fleet could be attacked in port. The number of SLBM warheads on station, therefore, could be from 4600 to 5300, much larger than the present force of 3000 warheads.

The second capability provided by these long-range sea-based systems is even more significant. With the extended range, the submarines could operate relatively close to the east or west coasts of the United States, say within 800 to 1600 km (500 to 1000 miles). If United States naval forces could monitor the activity of any Soviet naval vessel capable of attacking the United States SSBNs in this area, then it may be possible to combine the low detectability of the long-range United States SSBNs with an active defence of the critical component of the United States strategic forces.

Thus, there are compelling technical reasons why many United States strategic analysts consider the long-range SLBM forces 'invulnerable'. It should be emphasised, however, that if the SSBNs on station would be the only surviving United States strategic forces, they could be regarded as simply 20 to 30 more relatively soft targets which, if detected and tracked, are easily destroyed. For example, is it possible to conceive of a 'technological breakthrough' in which the Soviet Union could locate each submarine with sufficient accuracy to launch 20 to 40 ICBMs equipped with warheads that penetrate the surface of the ocean and detonate near the submarine?

Thus, with the introduction of the long-range Trident I and II systems, the possibility that the Soviets could prevent a retaliatory launch of the United States SLBM force is not very great. Certainly, a Soviet warfighting plan which relied on the destruction of United States SLBMs on station would be very risky.

SOVIET PROGRAMMES TO MITIGATE THE EFFECT OF RETALIATION: PASSIVE AND ACTIVE DEFENCE

In order to develop a meaningful nuclear warfighting capability, therefore, the Soviet Union must be able to mitigate the effects of a United States SLBM attack through passive and active defence. It should be emphasised that, should the Minuteman/SAC attack be successful, the Soviets could tailor their passive and active defence systems specifically to accommodate a United States SLBM attack. They will also have a good knowledge of the technical details of the weapons in the SLBM force. The number of launch vehicles and many of the key technical characteristics of the warhead of the re-entry system in the deployed United States SLBM forces have been widely publicised and are available in a number of sources.[4-6, 10] The United States does not have penetration aids on many of the strategic missile systems but, rather, relies on local exhaustion of the interceptor stockpile with real warheads to suppress ballistic missile defences.

It has been suggested by Gouré[17] and others that the major objective of the large Soviet civil defence programme is, in fact, to mitigate the effect of a United States retaliatory strike, particularly by the SLBM forces. These analysts suggest that the Soviet Union would evacuate all the major urban-industrial areas in a crisis prior to the breakout of general war. Major industrial installations would be protected so that they could survive high overpressures, apparently up to 700 to 2000 kN/m^2 (100 to 300 psi). Prior to the attack on Minuteman, all major urban-industrial areas would be evacuated and the civilian population would be assigned to predetermined places, removed from the areas which could be threatened by the United States sea-based strategic forces. Thus, when the United States SLBM attack occurs, the major urban-industrial centres would be severely damaged, but the industrial capacity would only be marginally impaired. The civilian population, or at least a cadre of political and military leaders as well as industrial managers and skilled workers, would have been provided special protection. They would return to the cities immediately and the industrial capacity of the Soviet Union would be restored to pre-attack levels in 6 months. The surviving cadre of political, military and technical leaders would then re-establish the political and economic system after the war. This is the prime Soviet strategy to survive and recover after a nuclear war according to Gouré.[17]

However, to accept the argument that civil defence constitutes a principal feature of a Soviet warfighting capability, one must believe that the Soviet Union might not be deterred by the very real possibility of the substantial destruction of 300 to 600 Soviet cities in the first hour of conflict by attack from surviving United States SLBM forces, which could be modified to reduce the effectiveness of a Soviet civil defence programme; for example, all the warheads could be fused to detonate only on ground impact. The radioactive fallout from the groundburst of several thousand Poseidon class warheads would then be deposited over a substantial part of the Soviet Union. An additional source of stress to the Soviet civil defence would be the warheads of any surviving Minuteman missiles or SAC bombers. If only a few per cent of the

Minuteman silos survive, several hundred more warheads would be deposited on the Soviet Union. Any surviving SAC bombers would present an even greater problem. If only a few tens of these bombers survive, as many as 1000 cruise missiles could arrive over the Soviet Union ten hours after the United States SLBM attack. The destructive power of this force would be almost as large as the original SLBM attack. Thus, there are many United States analysts who believe that civil defence can be an effective nuclear warfighting instrument only if it is complemented with an active defence.

THE AMERICAN AND SOVIET PERSPECTIVE OF STRATEGIC MISSILE DEFENCE

The role of active defence in a strategic nuclear force structure derives directly from the strategic doctrine. In the United States strategic doctrine of deterrence, passive and active defence of the population is believed to be technically and economically infeasible. Defence is also perceived as strategically destabilising in the sense that any defence would be neutralised by a corresponding increase in the size of the Soviet offensive forces. From an American perspective, the defence components would be deployed in proportion to national value – that is, in proportion to population. This concept of urban defence would always fail if the number of offensive warheads targeted exceeded the number of interceptors in the defence inventory. Since the defence must protect the soft urban target, it must be extremely reliable; it must also be able to operate in the cluttered environment associated with a nuclear engagement. The defence must also be able to distinguish between the re-entry vehicles and any penetration aids in real time. Thus, a defence deployed from an American perspective to protect soft urban targets would probably collapse when faced with the large and sophisticated attack that could be mounted by the Soviet Union.

The conclusion that large-scale ABM using 'NIKE-X' technology and civil defence is impractical when applied to soft urban targets is based on an American analysis derived from the assumption that both the United States and the Soviet Union have the same strategic policy. However, let us assume that the defence objective is to protect areas that contain what the Soviet Union believes is 'national value', that is, a selected cadre with an industrial capability to ensure rapid recovery after a nuclear exchange. The ABM effectiveness analysis should be re-examined within the framework of a Soviet perspective of a warfighting strategy with passive and active defence: that is, the protection of a large number (500 to 1000) of small, hardened (350 to 2000 kN/m² – 50 to 300 psi) sites with a ballistic missile defence. The deployment of this ABM would not be proportional to the population, but would be distributed uniformly throughout all the sites. The Soviet Union could correctly assume that the only retaliatory strike by the United States will be a countervalue SLBM attack involving only low-yield warheads. The stockpile of interceptors required at each site would be reduced and the hardness of the sites will allow intercepts lower in the atmosphere. Thus, this ABM is less complicated and the operating environment is simpler. The technical credibility of the system would be higher since offensive penetration aids are more difficult to design for low altitudes. The shorter operating range of the terminal defence radars would also mean a substantial decrease in power and size so that the radar could be deployed rapidly.

The first consideration is the impact of small hardened sites on the strategic performance of Poseidon missiles. The impact of target hardness on the performance of Poseidon missiles is significant for a CEP of 0.3 nmi, the accuracy value reported by Collins.[6] The number of Poseidon warheads required for 350 and 700 kN/m^2 (50 and 100 psi) targets would vary from 5 to 80 for a high kill probability, so that the number of targets which the surviving Poseidon missiles could threaten would be drastically reduced. Above a target hardness of about 700 kN/m^2 (100 psi), the number of the small Poseidon warheads required for a high kill probability rapidly becomes prohibitive.[18] A ballistic missile defence at each site would increase the number of warheads required by the local defence missile inventory. Thus, if the number of these hardened sites were hundreds and each site were protected by only a few defensive missiles, the number of United States SLBM warheads required to exhaust the defence and destroy the site could exceed the on-station inventory by a factor of three or four.

This Soviet perspective of an ABM is in sharp contrast to the large-scale urban defence described previously to protect 'national value' – that is, the population and industry in the large urban areas. Such a defence would defend only the Soviet 'national value'; that is, warfighting and survival capabilities. The areas near these sites (and many must be near large cities) would be exposed to enormous damage. However, if the Soviet Union's nuclear doctrine is warfighting, involving a counter-force attack on the United States strategic forces followed by the absorption of United States SLBMs by a Soviet ABM/civil defence protecting select facilities and cadres, then a sound technical/strategic argument could be made that the defence would be feasible and would give the Soviet Union a decided strategic advantage, in striking contrast to the United States perception of ABM as applied to 'national value'.

The key technical capability required would be a rapidly deployable version of United States 'NIKE-X' technology which could be integrated with the Soviet civil defence programme. The Soviet Union has been reported to be testing a small sophisticated phased array radar and an interceptor of the United States Sprint class, the ABM-X-3 system.[4] There are also reports that the radar is transportable. This rapidly deployable ABM, combined with the Soviet civil defence, seems to many United States analysts to provide the key technical indicator of a high confidence, Soviet nuclear warfighting capability.

THE SOVIET AIR DEFENCE SYSTEM

The Soviet Union has had deployed for over a decade a truly massive air defence system involving 1000 sites and 10,000 supersonic surface-to-air missiles.[4] This massive deployment should have a significant capability against any manned penetrating bomber. The cruise missile, however, has greatly improved the penetration capability of these air-breathing strategic systems. If the surviving bombers carry ALCMs, the potential destructive power of each bomber would be enormous. For example, if 50 bombers each with 25 to 200 KT cruise missiles survive, they would have the same destructive power as the surviving Poseidon missiles, but without the ability to cover a large number of geographically dispersed targets. Thus, the surviving SAC bombers armed with ALCMs pose a much greater threat to the Soviet Union than the manned bomber alone. During the terminal phase the missile flies at altitudes of about 100 m (109 yards) and is guided to the target by a terrain-contour-matching radar (TERCOM). Accuracies on the order of 10 m (11 yards) are possible, as indicated by Tsipsis.[19] These missiles, therefore, when armed with 200 to 400 KT nuclear weapons could have a significant hard target capability. The radar cross-section of cruise missiles is low and, at these very low flight altitudes, will probably escape detection by the present Soviet radars until it is too late to launch the air defence missile. However, the technical problems associated with upgrading air defences to engage the cruise missiles are substantially less formidable than those associated with a ballistic missile engagement. In fact, there is only one technical issue, that is, the ability of Soviet ground-based or airborne radar to detect and track the cruise missile. Once the subsonic cruise missile is detected and tracked, it could easily be engaged by the supersonic surface-to-air or air-to-air defence missiles. There are two ways to improve the defence capability to detect cruise missiles. The first is simply to place a standard air defence radar on a tower. A second is to equip fighter aircraft with look-down radars. These improvements to the Soviet air defence system, while costly, are within the state-of-the-art and are permitted by SALT II (which limits cruise missile deployments but not countermeasures). In a well-conceived warfighting plan, therefore, the Soviet Union must not only execute an SLBM attack on SAC bases, but must also upgrade its air defence to absorb the cruise missiles launched by the surviving bombers. Recent reports suggest that the Soviet Union has already conducted some tests of these two techniques. In addition, the new SA-10 may have some cruise missile capability.

Of substantial concern to United States Strategic planners for over a decade is the possibility that the Soviet air defence system could have some ABM capability. United States studies in the early 1970s suggested that with some modest upgrading of the SA-5 radar, the Soviet air defence system could have a capability against the old Polaris re-entry system in which the re-entry vehicle slows down rapidly in the atmosphere. This modest 'upgrade' of the SA-5 would have no capability against the high performance re-entry systems on Minuteman III, Poseidon or Trident. However, the clandestine installation of the mobile ABM radar and the higher performance interceptor at these air defence sites would mean a major shift in the strategic balance of power to the Soviet Union. While there is no published evidence that the Soviet Union is engaged in such an improvement, there were Soviet tests using the SA-5 radar in 1973 and 1974 which involved tracking a ballistic missile during re-entry at the Soviet ABM test range.

The last of the six technical/military capabilities which could give the Soviet Union a strategic advantage is an ASW programme directed at the on-station United States SLBM systems. Congressional testimony suggests that the Soviet Union has a large ASW programme. However, in contrast to the other five capabilities required for nuclear warfighting, there are no published reports to indicate that the Soviet Union has conducted a test to track and destroy a long-range SSBN. The possibility that a Soviet ASW system could neutralise the United States SLBM force with the Trident system is small. Since there is hard, technical data in the public literature to suggest that the Soviet Union is developing five of the technical/military capabilities required (and has, in fact, deployed or is deploying strategic systems in four areas), the acquisition of similar data on the sixth area, ASW, would be strong evidence to support the thesis that the Soviet Union is systematically developing a nuclear warfighting capability. If Soviet strategy is nuclear warfighting, the Soviet Union is strongly motivated to complement the other five capabilities to neutralise the third leg of the United States triad.

COMPARISON OF UNITED STATES AND SOVIET STRATEGIC PROGRAMMES FOR A NUCLEAR WARFIGHTING CAPABILITY

A comparison of both United States and Soviet programmes in the six areas required for nuclear warfighting is shown in Table 8.11. The United States has not deployed a new missile system in over a decade

TABLE 8.11 Comparison of United States and Soviet strategic programmes for nuclear warfighting capability

Required nuclear warfighting technical/military capability	Present Soviet programmes	Present United States programmes

High accuracy MIRVs	• Four new ICBMs with MIRVs
	• SS-17, SS-18, SS-19 have payloads three to ten times larger than Minuteman III
	  – Warheads large enough to attack hardened silos with modest accuracy
	  – Mobile ICBM SS-X-16 under development
		• 75 per cent of United States MIRV warheads are inaccurate, low yield SLBMs – no counterforce capability
		• 550 MMIII MIRVs yield and accuracy are too low to attack hard targets (0.34 SSKP against 13,800 kN/m^2 (2000 psi) at 270 m (900 ft) CEP)
		• Some high accuracy programmes in development
		• No new missiles deployed in decade:
		  – Trident missiles and submarine in development to increase survivability
		  – Trident programme reflects deterrence policy not nuclear warfighting

Anti-satellite system	• Developing an extensive system
	• 30–40 field tests disclosed
	• Ground-based laser attempts to blind reconnaissance and early warning satellites(?) Very provocative
		• No programme in a decade
		• Modest non-nuclear R & D programme recently
		  – Response to Soviet programmes
		  – No tests until 1980s

ASW	• Large programme • Alarming if aimed at United States SLBMs • Very risky for nuclear war fighting since Trident programme • Very effective if directed at United States SLBM retaliation	• Extensive programme – Not oriented to destroy Soviet SLBMs (?)
Civil defence	• Large programme	• $100–$125 million – Negligible strategic value

ABM	• One operational site at Moscow— new radar 1980
	• Large programme on development of rapidly deployable ABM components
	• Extensive testing
	• Urban as well as hard site defence
	• Very effective if applied to hardened, dispersed sites and integrated with civil defence to US SLBMs
		• One site deactivated
		• $300 million R & D, only half for testing militarily useful equipment
		  – ICBM defence primary mission
		  – Some area defence technology
		  – No urban defence
		• Not more than ten tests planned for 1975–85
		  – No new ABM radars until 1984

Air defence	• 10,000 surface-to-air missiles at 1000 sites • Continuous R & D • Cruise Missile upgrade required – In progress (?)	• Air defence system abandoned for all practical purposes

and the introduction of MIRVs into Minuteman III and Poseidon was completed in the late 1960s. All the United States MIRVs have minimal hard-target capability and 80 per cent are SLBMs that could only be used for one mission, assured destruction. The long-range Trident I missile is nearing completion of its developmental phase and will soon replace about one-third of the shorter range Poseidon missiles. The new Trident submarine with the Trident II missile will have an initial operational capability in 1981. The Trident submarine and missile programmes are the major United States strategic nuclear initiatives over the past decade. They are also an unambiguous reflection of United States strategic doctrine—deterrence through the possession of a survivable assured destruction capability. The Trident programme does not provide the United States with a new capability which could improve the United States strategic posture with respect to the Soviet Union. The enormous investment in the Trident programme shows the extent to which the United States and the Western Alliance rely on a survivable SLBM deterrent force with no attempt to provide a significant nuclear warfighting capability.

The United States has had no antisatellite programme of any kind for over a decade and recently initiated a relatively modest effort (in response to the Soviet programme) which will not even be tested until the 1980s. The United States has no ABM sites and a $215 million R & D programme in ballistic missile defence, only half of which will produce equipment that could have any military capability. The United States air defence system involves 331 manned interceptors and almost all air defence sites with defensive missiles have been abandoned. The United States civil defence programme is small ($125 million) and has negligible strategic value. The United States ASW programme is large but is primarily oriented toward protection of the sea lanes and not toward the neutralisation of Soviet SLBM systems. The entire strategic forces budget in the United States is $9.8 billion[5] or 7.8 per cent of the United States defence budget.

It is fairly clear, therefore, that a detailed examination of United States strategic technology programmes shows that it would be impossible for the United States to develop a high confidence nuclear warfighting capability in the foreseeable future. Even though there has been a great deal of publicity about high accuracy United States programmes, none has been deployed. It is United States policy not to defend the country against a nuclear attack of any size using any delivery system, bombers, ICBMs, SLBMs, or cruise missiles and as Table 8.9 indicates, even ten nuclear warheads are devastating. Thus, the technical possibility of the United States developing a significant nuclear warfighting capability with respect to the Soviet Union is remote, even unthinkable from an American perspective.

The first part of this chapter attempts to show that a nuclear warfighting capability is extremely risky, even irrational, but through an 'American' analysis. However, an analysis of Soviet strategic technology programmes, particularly when compared to United States programmes leads one to the conclusion that the technical indicators suggest that the Soviet Union is systematically developing a significant nuclear warfighting capability. The harsh reality is that the Soviet Union has deployed or is deploying strategic systems in five of the six areas required. In addition, there is a significant R & D programme in the sixth (ABM), and even there the key technical characteristic (radar mobility) is that which would be required to contribute to nuclear warfighting. In sharp contrast, the key comparable United States programmes are essentially non-existent as deployed or deployable strategic systems and even the relevant R & D programmes are small. While it is impossible to ignore the very real risks of reciprocal mass destruction, the disturbing reality is that the Soviet Union is apparently willing to develop the option to fight and win a nuclear war and the published technical indicators seem to support that conclusion.

NOTES

1. Pipes, Richard, 'Why the Soviet Union Thinks It Could Fight and Win a Nuclear War', *Commentary*, Vol. 64, No.1 (July 1977).
2. Gouré, Leon, Kohler, Foy D., and Harvey, Mose L., *The Role of Nuclear Forces in Current Soviet Strategy* (Miami, Center for Advanced International Studies, 1974).
3. Burt, Richard, 'SALT II', *Foreign Affairs* (July 1978).
4. *The Military Balance—1978–79*, International Institute for Strategic Studies, pp. 4, 8 and 81 (London, 1978, and 1977 issue). Also (1980–1) pp. 88, 89, 90, 91.
5. *Department of Defence Annual Report – Fiscal Year 1979*, Washington, DC Department of Defence (2 February 1978), pp. 47 and 49.
6. Collins, J. M., 'American and Soviet Military Trends Since the Cuban Missile Crisis', Center for Strategic and International Studies, Georgetown University, (Washington, DC, (June 1978).
7. A 'partly common' United States SLBM/ICBM is apparently under consideration. The new missile would carry ten warheads and engineering development would be completed by 1985.
8. McNamara, R. S., *The Essence of Security* (New York, Harper & Row, 1968), p. 52.
9. Kaufman, W. W., *The McNamara Strategy* (New York, Harper & Row, 1964), pp. 138–47.
10. Kemp, Geoffrey, 'Nuclear Forces for Medium Powers', *Adelphi Papers Nos 106 and 107* International Institute for Strategic Studies (London, 1974).
11. About 70 million people based on a 1970 population of 241 million with a 1.2 per cent growth rate for a projected 1980 population of 275 million.
12. Glasstone, S. K., *The Effects of Nuclear Weapons* (with Nuclear Bomb Effects Computer Designed by the Lovelace Foundation), US Atomic Energy Commission (April 1962).

13. This would be 104 million, based on a 275 million total population estimate for 1980.
14. Drell, S. D. and Von Heppel, F., 'Limited Nuclear War', *Scientific American*, Vol. 235, No. 5 (November 1975), p. 27.
15. Freedman, L., 'The Soviet Union and Anti-Space Defense', *Survival*, Vol. XIX, No. 1 (January/February 1977), p. 16.
16. There have been recent reports of a substantial increase in Soviet antisatellite tests – fifteen launches in January and February of this year alone. The same source infers that the Soviet Union will conduct an antisatellite test at geosynchronous altitude (*Aviation Week and Space Technology*, 5 March 1979, p. 11).
17. Gouré, Leon, 'War Survival in Soviet Strategy, Soviet Civil Defense' (Miami, Center for Advanced International Studies; 1976).
18. However, if the Poseidon CEP were half that suggested by Collins[6] only 1.5–2 warheads would be required for a 90 to 95 per cent kill probability of a 700 kN/m^2 (100 psi) target.
19. Tsipsis, K., 'Cruise Missiles', *Scientific American*, Vol. 232 (February 1977), p. 20.

Part Four

Intelligence and Verification: The Case of Salt II

9 Verification

Jasper A. Welch

Verification, as an activity associated with international agreements, has a long history. It played a role in the first United States treaty dealing with arms control. That treaty, known as the Rush–Bagot Treaty, was negotiated with the United Kingdom over 160 years ago. Signed in 1817, it had both quantitative and qualitative provisions affecting naval forces on the 'American Lakes', and thus, compliance needed to be verified. As it turned out, the sides cooperated extensively, and since everything was out in the open in a relatively small area, verification with high confidence was easily achieved.

The growing number of treaties and agreements, particularly in recent years, attests to the importance of arms control as a factor in the foreign and national policy of the United States. The commensurate increase in the complexity and detail of these agreements makes verification a critical element of arms control and assures its continued place of importance in the future. Therefore, verification needs to be understood in the context of today's Strategic Arms Limitation Talks (SALT) environment.

As a technical term in the lexicon of arms control, verification refers to a process which assesses compliance with provisions of a treaty or agreement. Verification and national intelligence are very closely related. In fact, much of verification is the application of intelligence techniques to matters regulated by international agreements. The main difference is that intelligence attempts to determine weapon characteristics and military force activities, whereas verification assesses whether or not those characteristics and activities are in compliance with some specific treaty provision.

There are three basic purposes of verification. Clearly, it serves to detect violations of treaty provisions, thus giving timely warning of possible threats to national security. Verification also helps to deter violations by increasing the risk of detection and complicating possible evasion schemes. Finally, successful verification helps build domestic and international confidence in the viability of arms control agreements. A look at the elements of verification will shed light on the process itself.

The collection of intelligence data, or monitoring, is the first element in the verification process. If the capability to collect data by some means does not exist, then it is impossible to verify even the simplest of treaty provisions. This is why discussions which took place years before SALT I were so important in setting the stage for the SALT process.

The technical possibilities of reconnaissance by orbiting satellites were first explored in discussions subsequent to a late 1958 Geneva conference of western and Soviet *bloc* representatives concerning the reduction of forces in Europe.[1] Although that particular suggestion was not adopted, the way was paved by that, and other similar discussions, for managing the verification problem. By 1963, when the Limited Test Ban Treaty was signed, the phrase 'national technical means' (NTM) was adopted. The word 'technical', which can have very great or little significance, depending on one's perspective, was of Soviet origin and never precisely defined.

More recently, when President Carter spoke at the Kennedy Space Center, one element of NTM was referred to when he said, 'Photo reconnaissance satellites have become an important stabilizing factor in world affairs in the monitoring of arms control agreements. They make an immense contribution to the security of all nations. We shall continue to develop them.'[2]

The formal language of SALT I, both in the Anti-ballistic Missile (ABM) Treaty and the Interim Agreement, speaks of verification by NTM. These documents specify that assurance of compliance with treaty or agreement provisions will be provided through the party's use of NTM in a manner consistent with generally recognised principles of international law.[3]

A very natural question arises at this point. To what extent does NTM provide for credible verification of Soviet compliance? Three assumptions in a paper by Robert Perry of The Rand Corporation[4] provide a good framework for discussing this point:

(1) United States NTM can provide conclusive evidence of non-compliance with the terms of the agreements.
(2) No expansion of Soviet strategic capabilities could be concealed long enough, or well enough, to support the development of a serious Soviet threat to the established strategic balance.
(3) So long as the Soviet Union credits those assumptions, no serious effort to evade the terms of the arms limitation agreements will occur.

Whether or not NTM can provide the conclusive evidence of the first assumption depends on several factors. For instance, the provision itself is a factor. If it provides for an easily observable and distinguishable system by either banning deployment or permitting and counting all such systems, then non-compliance might be detected easily. If, however, the provision deals with something more complex like a qualitative constraint, detection of non-compliance might be extremely unlikely and evidence by NTM inconclusive at best. Of course, the capability of our NTM is also a factor.

A further factor, which applies to Perry's second assumption as well, is the timeframe during which conclusive evidence is expected or necessary to be collected. If the perception of stability is very sensitive to the least bit of non-compliance, then the time in which to collect conclusive evidence is much shorter than if stability is rather insensitive to small compliance deviations.

A way of looking at the third assumption is to picture a spread between what the Soviet leaders perceive as the risk of detection at some point in time and the delta in military capability achieved through non-compliance at that same point in time. If the perception of the first two assumptions is such that the delta in capability is still small when the probability of detection (risk) is high, then Perry's third assumption follows.

Implicit in Perry's assumptions is another element of the verification process: the analysis and evaluation of relevant data once it has been collected. This phase of the verification process is one of the real discriminators between national intelligence and verification, which I referred to earlier.

In verification, it is necessary to go beyond the logging and categorising of data. In many cases, unambiguous verification is not possible. A good treaty may have some provision for which compliance can be verified with less confidence than others. On the other hand, a wholly verifiable bad treaty would still be a bad treaty. The difficult task is to make a net assessment which takes into consideration factors such as the provision in question, the impact of non-compliance with that provision, monitorability, freedom to pursue United States options and United States hedges against non-compliance. The phrase 'adequately verifiable' is often used to connote this net assessment. I prefer to judge the provision as 'acceptable in terms of verification', but whichever phrase is used, it is instructive to examine further the contributing factors.

The formulation of a provision can go a long way towards enhancing verification. When formulating the treaty provisions, the negotiators attempt to make individual provisions convey precisely what is intended; no more and no less. You can imagine the difficulty of this task, particularly when two languages are involved. However, it is obvious that different interpretations of the same provision can cripple verification at its foundation.

When considering the impact of non-compliance, several aspects come to mind. First, there is the military aspect of what non-compliance can lead to in terms of capability, which can be translated into perceptions of power or actual 'breakout' potential. The military capability, in terms of various measures such as equivalent megatonnes (EMT) or numbers of strategic nuclear delivery vehicles (SNDVs), will be easier to quantify than the possible perceptions of this capability by third countries as well as the United States and the resultant political leverage.

The political aspect of 'blowing the whistle' is also important. The possible disadvantage of divulging the source of evidence must be weighed against the idea of permitting even a slight infraction to remain unchallenged.

This last aspect bridges over into the consideration of verification itself. We discussed earlier the problem of providing conclusive evidence of non-compliance using NTM. Verification, as it contributes to a net assessment of a provision, includes more than just our NTM capability. It is the capability to collect and evaluate all the available data in order to judge, with some level of confidence, whether or not the Soviets are in compliance with a treaty provision. The significance of this in understanding SALT verification is that with a given capability of NTM the contribution of verification to a net assessment of acceptability may vary from provision to provision. Acceptable confidence levels will vary directly with the strategic significance of the provisions. Finally, it is necessary to evaluate possible hedges to offset non-compliance should it occur. In the extreme, this hedge is treaty abrogation so as to permit unfettered programmatic response. However, there may be many alternatives between this and the other extreme of doing nothing. For example, a hedge may be a specific funded weapons programme, a research and development effort aimed at new technology, or a commitment to react in a specific way if a potential threat develops. Hedges, of course, if perceived as realistic possibilities and effective measures by the other side, can help to deter cheating.

After a provision has been examined in the light of these factors, a net assessment can be made as to whether or not the provision is acceptable in terms of verification. As an example of this assessment, let us look at a provision from the ABM Treaty. The provision states that no more than 100 ABM launchers and no more than 100 ABM interceptor missiles shall be deployed at launch sites.[5]

The provision is straight forward and appears to leave little room for misinterpretation. The impact of non-compliance could be significant if ABM launchers and missiles were to be covertly deployed in large numbers. Balancing this, however, are two things. First, this provision should be relatively easy to verify. Components of an ABM system are large, take considerable time to construct in place, and look different than other equipment that might be expected in the same area. Second, the United States has a hedge against non-compliance, should it occur. The Multiple Independently Targetable Re-entry Vehicle (MIRV), Penetration Aids, and the Triad force structure provide confidence against this type of breakpoint potential.

A net assessment of this provision indicates that since it is difficult to violate the provision without being detected, and since there is little probability of gaining any significant military advantage before being detected, the provision is acceptable from a verification point of view. A footnote to this assessment might be that introduction of a new technology ABM system could make verification much more difficult, and, in the extreme, could make the provision unacceptable. Such new technology systems are, however, constrained by another provision of the same treaty.

Some treaty provisions are not as straightforward as the example discussed; however, a forum does exist in which to address and resolve ambiguities. The Standing Consultative Commission (SCC) was chartered by the ABM Treaty, carried forward by the Interim Agreement, and reportedly provided for in SALT II. Its purpose is to 'consider questions concerning compliance . . . provide on a voluntary basis such information as either Party considers necessary to assure confidence in compliance . . . [and to] consider questions involving unintended interference with national technical means of verification . . .'.[6]

It is interesting to note that, in the verification process, issues have been placed before the SCC and have been satisfactorily resolved. For instance, an action initiated by the United States about a possible Soviet ABM radar on the Kamchatka Peninsula started discussions which eventually resulted in an identification by the Soviets of all their ABM test ranges. What had not been obtained during the SALT I negotiations was finally entered into the official negotiating record through the SCC forum.

As one looks to the likely conclusion of SALT II and beyond, there are some interesting questions to consider. One might ask how verification is to change to accommodate more sophisticated weapon systems and more complex treaty provisions. If verification is not to drive arms control, and there are good reasons why it should not, then verification must adjust to new schemes, to new and innovative ideas.

It is interesting to look, in this regard, at cooperation and regulated activities as a specific kind of cooperation. The simplest form of cooperation is one already provided for in the SALT I documents. In those documents, both sides agreed not to interfere with each other's NTM.

On the one hand, both sides were protected from having to make changes in current construction, assembly conversion, or overhaul practices. On the other hand, it was implicit that any such change which impeded verification would be challanged. The situation could be characterised as 'don't change your current practices and don't interfere with my NTM'. Verification is essentially a unilateral matter, whereas matters requiring active cooperation, such as regulated activities, have been addressed in the SCC. There are agreed procedures for such things as dismantling radars, ABM missile launchers, and submarines, and even exchanging one ABM site for another. The type of activity that has not been regulated yet is that which precedes the deployment of a weapon system. This area appears worthwhile to explore.

Cooperation can have benefits which go beyond the inherent increase in confidence engenders. For instance, there may be monetary benefits. If weapons tests were to be preannounced, expensive monitoring systems could be operated less frequently and for shorter periods. Other, less costly, equipment could be used to assure that testing activity was not taking place covertly.

It is important to catch the significance of this last point. Cooperation does not preclude the need for verification. Unilateral means of verifying the fact of cooperation must be provided. These means, however, may be less costly than those needed in the absence of cooperation. Categories where regulation could occur are:

Production: constraints on places where systems are produced or the way in which they are produced.

Testing: constraints on the times and places wherein systems can be tested.

Inventory/Deployment: constraints on the manner in which systems may be deployed.

Disposition: constraints on the manner in which the limited systems are removed from the inventory.

Certain aspects of some of these activities have been regulated in terms of frequency, location, time, and condition constraints. Often, more than one constraint applies to a particular activity.

The concept of regulated activity can be linked to real-world cases with which both sides are already familiar. In several cases, such as Intercontinental Ballistic Missile (ICBM) production, there are no restrictions. In other cases, such as the regulation of certain kinds of testing, considerable experience has already been gained – and precedents set. Although traditionally these activities have been monitored by NTM, cooperative measures would be developed to facilitate such monitoring. For example, the production count of heavy bombers would imply that they will be displayed after final assembly.

The basis for at least some types of cooperative measures is contained in the exisiting Strategic Arms Limitation (SAL) agreement with the Standing Consultive Commission mentioned earlier. During the SALT I period, both sides demonstrated acceptance of the requirement for cooperative measures and demonstrated adherence to agreed measures. The Soviets have agreed to cooperative measures, together with precisely regulated activities, when it served their purpose.

An example of this stood out in the Interim Agreement. In order to build and deploy new Nuclear-powered Ballistic Missile Submarines (SSBNs), the Soviets agreed to procedures for dismantling older ICBM launchers. They may well have dismantled them anyway, but a useful precedent was set for regulated activities which, through cooperative measures, facilitated United States verification of a specific provision. Opportunities to employ regulated activities become very apparent when one considers the life-cycle flow of a weapon system from R & D prototype through production and introduction into the inventory to disposition.

SALT has generally operated under the thesis that adequate verification can be maintained by monitoring the inventory and regulating certain parts of the disposition activities. The research, development and production phases should also be used.

R & D monitoring is useful in identifying potential new systems, and, thus, minimising surprises by orienting us toward future requirements. This stage can also be useful for identifying system characteristics, which, if measured, can aid verification. 'Agreed-to' design parameters would be even more helpful. But the prime concern on a day-to-day basis is always the Soviet current inventory and its capability.

Information on the Soviet inventory is potentially available by either direct count, or by subtracting disposition from production. Note the requirement that the information must be adequate to ensure compliance with any arms control provision to the extent necessary to bound satisfactorily the impact on our national security. As an example, a look at each of the three major strategic systems helps to illustrate how stocks and flows can aid in the verification and monitoring process. An examination of SSBN, aircraft, and ICBM life-cycles provides some useful observations.

SSBNs

A considerable experience base has evolved, especially during the production phase. There are only a few places where submarines are made; the facilities are unique; the process is slow; the pipeline is usually full; and the object is big.

The only condition required for effective monitoring is that production continue in the same fundamental way as in the past, and that there is no subsequent deliberate concealment measures or interference with NTM used to observe production.

By the time SSBNs became accountable within the strategic arms control framework, considerable intelligence-related experience with submarine development and operations already existed. Submarine production was known to take place in particular areas and under conditions which were known and understood in some detail. The time lines for such assembly extended over periods of many months. In the end, the SSBN appeared in its finished form, and was observed 'fitting out' in the open for an extended time prior to sea trials.

Monitoring the SSBN once it is in the operational inventory also can provide a reasonable estimate of the total number in inventory. There are relatively few SSBN ports; those facilities are unique in many respects; and SSBN port-calls tend to extend over many days or weeks. Thus, the opportunity for observation is typically both substantial and predictable.

Disposition of SSBNs involves a special class of industrial type activity that approximates the reverse of that required for production. The dismantling process usually takes place in particular, known locations. Considerable experience and precedent exist in negotiating the procedures for SSBN disposition. In fact, the Soviet Union has essentially appeared most cooperative in those measures involving the disposition of systems.

A separate but useful observation deals with the traditional view of the submarine acting as a 'first stage', transporting the subcontinental missile part-way to its target. Thus, there was no need to monitor the number of sublaunched missiles, *per se*. As SLBMs become truly intercontinental, that view needs to change. Since new generation SSBNs can reach targets from their home ports, they could also be launched effectively from landbased, perhaps covert, launchers.

STRATEGIC AIRCRAFT

As with with the SSBN, a substantial historical experience exists for strategic aircraft. There are only a few particular places where strategic bombers are made, and they are unique and well known. Once the airframe is produced, it is rolled out onto the flight line ramp where it is observable for an extended period of time prior to, and during, flight testing.

Deployed strategic aircraft are generally assigned to Long Range Aviation units. Which airfields are associated with these missions is open knowledge. A conceptual view of aircraft stocks and flows would take the system from production through primary and secondary (if any) operational uses, obsolete storage and, finally, disposition. In addition, some aircraft could go directly into some form of storage from production.

Monitoring is made easier by the fact that in contrast to fighters, which are routinely sheltered between flights (indeed, some fighter aircraft spend most of their operational life in shelters) strategic aircraft are typically parked in open ramp areas – observable to NTM on a day-to-day basis.

Once an aeroplane leaves the operational inventory, it is either placed in storage or destroyed. The United States obsolete aircraft storage area is at Davis-Monthan AFB in Arizona. Aircraft are stored in various 'mothball' conditions. In some cases, an attempt is made to keep certain aeroplanes in a condition which would allow them to return to operational status. In other cases aircraft are 'cannibalised' to provide spare parts. In still other cases, aircraft are destroyed in open, clearly observable salvage yards.

The historical monitoring of stocks and flows of SSBNs and aircraft is marked by familiar and observable practices which could provide procedural precedents. As we think about tomorrow's strategic systems, we should learn from those precedents and emulate them when appropriate.

ICBMs

At the time of the first SALT agreement, the characteristics that were dealt with in the provisions made the ICBM case similar to those for submarines and bombers. Monitoring ICBM launchers–rather than missiles themselves–apparently made verification manageable within the NTM state-of-the-art.

Technology was soon to complicate this situation, however. The advent of MIRV was a particularly complicating factor – to such an extent that a closely considered national decision was required before testing the first Minuteman III in 1968. The mobile ICBM adds another new dimension, complicating the situation even further.

Figure 9.1 on page 140 does not reflect the historical context, but it does bound the basic nature of the verification and monitoring problem – again in terms of stocks and flows. Note that in the production phase, *subsystems* are input to an assembly node from which an ICBM enters the national strategic weapons inventory.

While Figure 9.1 suggests many possible paths, we need to distinguish between two main-flow streams – overt (authorised) and covert (unauthorised). The overt flow represents data which typically contribute to formal estimates of the threat. As noted above, 'launcher counting' is currently the statistic used for inventory accountability and ICBM threat definition.

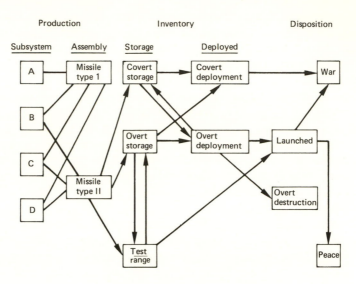

FIGURE 9.1   Strategic Missiles

But the potential for covert activity (including production, storage, and deployment) remains an issue which stimulates a continuous dialogue on the implications of Soviet cheating or 'breakout' activities. Cheating and breakout result when resources (including more than missiles) in either the covert storage or covert deployment modes enter the nuclear arsenal and alter the real threat (perceived threat as well, in the case of breakout).

The distinction between storage and deployment is an important one. As noted with aircraft, storage can involve partially assembled or fully assembled systems. In the case of stored ICBMs, the operational picture is not complete without the launcher and electronic support equipment needed for targeting and launching. For Minuteman-type systems, that support equipment is in the silo; for mobile systems, however, it accompanies the missile and is therefore integral to the accountability problem. The 'launcher' is not a hole in the ground, easily counted and monitored, but a largely self-contained mobile facility.

The time required to transition from storage to deployment is a function of the kind of storage. If 'full systems' are in storage, then the time to transition to deployment is small. It is short transition time possibilities that create an untidy environment for talking about absolute verification and monitoring. Bounding the production end of the process would be most helpful in reducing the possibility of greater-than-expected threats in any scenario.

As noted, current ICBM verification centres around the counting of 'launchers'. Neither the production nor disposition phases of the ICBM life cycle is accountable.

The potential impact of covert activities merit special – separate – attention. A total ban on covert storage and deployment could ease concerns by making systematic, large-scale covert activities more risky – even if production limits could not be obtained. In both the long-term and the short-term, such a ban would be useful.

A programme which relates verification and monitoring to a weapon system's life-cycle and could mitigate some of the concerns associated with covert activities could consist of the following five points:

(1) Control production of weapon systems
(2) Prohibit storage and deployment except as agreed in terms of location and numbers
(3) Introduce weapon systems into agreed deployment areas using agreed procedures
(4) Sample inventories using agreed procedures
(5) Dispose of deployed weapons and major system components in accordance with agreed procedures.

Acquisition of high confidence data in all areas would be ideal, but is hardly essential. Data from one life-cycle phase can compensate for data shortfalls in another. For instance, to the degree that production can be bounded, the need for precise verification of systems deployed is eased.

One of the keys to the process appears to be an intercommunity effort of those people involved in the various life-cycle phases of weapon systems. Such a group needs to react at the basic level when various designs are under consideration. Further, they need to devise 'peg-points' within, and between, the life-cycle phases which will enhance verification for the specific system and situation. This approach can lead to a valid net assessment of treaty provisions in terms of verification.

Verification is a complicated process with several elements, and it is sensitive to many factors. It is necessary in order to assure our national security, but verification is unattainable in the pure sense of 100 per cent confidence. However, through the careful formulation of treaty provisions and consideration of appropriate hedges, absolute verifiability of every provision may not be necessary to make a new treaty acceptable. There are still problems to solve, but our understanding of the process is increasing and verification appears to be workable.

NOTES

1. ACDA, Verification: *The Critical Element of Arms Control*, p. 18.
2. The White House, Remarks of The President at Congressional Space Medals Awards Ceremony, Kennedy Space Center (10 October 1978).
3. *Arms Control and Disarmament Agreements: Texts and Histories of Negotiations*, ACDA (Washington, DC 1975), pp. 134, 139.
4. Perry, Robert, *The Faces of Verification* (Santa Monica, CA, The Rand Corporation, 1977).
5. *The ABM Treaty and Interim Agreement and Associated Protocol*, US Government Printing Office (Washington, DC 1972).
6. *Ibid.*

10 Verification and Salt: A Different Line of Insight

Amrom Katz

My view about verification has developed over many years.[1] I hope that I have made progress along the route. I regard verification machinery, especially of the kind covered under the rubric of 'national technical means', as not being artifacts of nature. We are not operating the first four moons of Jupiter over the Soviet Union. Instead, we are operating man-made gadgets, and the other NTMs on the ground, as they were in Iran and Turkey, are also man-made gadgets. *The other side knows about them.* A bastardised Heisenberg's principle, which argues that there is interaction between the observer and the observed, is at work here. We are not picking up independent facts, just because we are exceptionally clever, have so much money, so much time, such good luck, and all that; there is interaction, there is feedback.

When I tell my friends in the intelligence community that they are profiting from a form of cooperation between the Soviet military leadership and the United States national intelligence system they say, 'What do you mean?' or words to that effect. What I mean is simple. To the extent that deterrence has been the name of the game, it has been a factor. But what makes a deterrent? Let us try a simple example. Suppose someone nearby has a gun of which I know nothing. He cannot deter me with that weapon. He can ambush me, astonish me, surprise me, assassinate me, cause me acute discomfort and pain, and aggravated assault (not in that order), but he cannot deter me. To deter me, *I have to know the weapon.* Therefore, the fundamental requirement for a deterrence system to function effectively is that each side has to have a disclosure apparatus. Now it would be a complete waste of time for me to detail to a well-informed readership the enormously elaborate, interconnected, well-wired United States disclosure apparatus. It would take twenty minutes just to sketch the bare outline of this wiring diagram on a blackboard. But it exists, and it is our way of doing things.

The Soviet disclosure system – that interests me more at the moment – is easier to talk about because there is not much to it. It has two components, one qualitative, the other quantitative. The qualitative component is the Moscow dragstrip, where they drag things through once or twice a year. Now, no matter how impressed we are and how useful this is, they are giving us excellent opportunities to photograph this, which we do, and to be impressed by it. But nobody is deterred by one each or five each missiles. One is deterred by order of battle, by force disposition, by information on the Soviet R & D activities (community derived), by vigour and success of space shots – things like that. To impress not only the United States, but to impress China, the Soviet satellites, our allies, the third world, the Soviet leaders depend exclusively on the free services (free to them, that is) of an otherwise extremely well-funded internationally certified, honest broker, CPA. Who is it? *Believe it or not, it is the United States national intelligence system, which is doing their work for the Soviets.* It is clear that we have been benefiting from a form of cooperation by the Soviet Union.

Now, again, my friends in the intelligence business say, 'If you say they are cooperating with us, why do we have to work nights and weekends?' Well, by 'cooperating' I do not mean that Dobrynin goes in every Monday morning to the DCI's office and delivers him a list of events and channel numbers to tune in on for the next week. It is not that kind of cooperation. For lack of a better term, it is a form of non-non-cooperating. They have not made impossible things which they could have made impossible; they were willing to leave them difficult. And all sorts of things follow from that. One, if they had an incentive to cooperate, what would change that incentive to cooperate to an incentive to hide? Lo and behold, I find the signature of a SALT treaty does exactly that; it furnishes them an incentive.

General Welch has stated that: 'There are three basic purposes of verification. Clearly, it serves to detect violations of treaty provisions, thus giving timely warning of possible threats to national security.' Agreed. But, I would add an additional clause: ' . . . but by remaining mute, you give silent assent to what is going on, not deliberately, but by failing to speak out'. He continues, 'Finally, successful verification helps build domestic and international confidence in the viability of arms control agreements. A look at the elements of verification will shed light on the process itself.' But then *I* would add to that: ' . . . but certification done in error may coat a bitter pill with euphoria'. So, there is always the other half of the statement, the unvoiced part – that has to be weighed as if built in automatically.

We have heard discussion of what is in and what is out of the Treaty. Here we have a very fundamental and logical dilemma, because we do not want to put anything in the Treaty that is not verifiable; everybody has agreed to that. Also, we do not want to leave anything out that is significant. Now the only solution of these two inequalities is that only things that are verifiable are significant, and only things that are insignificant are unverifiable. Unfortunately that is not so.

Apart from that, we have the enormous debate between the two factions of SALT. Both of them are American. I will call them the white hats and the black hats. And since I am an erstwhile physicist, I will have the physicists wear the white hats and the lawyers wear the black hats. The physicists want, and argue the case in favour of, precise statements. They argue with SALT I: we allowed sloppy statements, elastic statements; the Soviets pushed to the limits and beyond, and they got away with it. The lawyers can respond – and they have a good point too – that ambiguity and elasticity protect against future unimagined situations; that if we are very precise about what we say, we may define out of the Treaty something which we would like to have covered. So they argue the case of ambiguity. The Russians do not argue this much at all. They just witness our argument and participate in it from time to time.

General Welch writes:

> It is interesting to note that, as a result of the verification process . . . issues have been placed before the SCC (Standing Consultative Commission) and have been satisfactorily resolved. For instance, an action initiated by the United States about a possible Soviet ABM radar on the Kamchatka Peninsula started discussions which eventually resulted in an identification by the Soviets of all their ABM test ranges.

That is one way of saying it. Another way of saying this, which, I argue, has equal validity, is that we found an ABM radar on the Kamchatka Peninsula and we said: 'Hey, what about that?' They said: 'If it pleases you to regard that as an ABM range, so be it'. We wrote to them and said, in effect (I am paraphrasing this, obviously; the language is much longer and more convoluted):'If you will only say that that's an ABM test range, we'll go away happy'. So they answered: 'If you're willing to believe that, go ahead and believe it. It is up to you.' This is not quite a verbatim account but that, to my reading, essentially and fairly discusses what happened.

The problem with the antisatellite activity in the Soviet Union is that it has gone on unchallenged for quite a long time. It always struck me as exceptionally odd that we never once said to them: 'Hey, look, we want to talk about this. What are you guys doing? What is it all about?' This never did. Now, the subject is up for negotiation, and we still do not have a sensible theory as to how they would use this, what they would do it for, what the penalties would be, and so forth. But that is under negotiation so we will not talk about it, except to note that, to my taste, the Outer Space Treaty of 1967 seems to be both broad and specific enough to cover the case of antisatellite activities. Specifically, I recall that Article IX of that treaty should be consulted on this.

What are 'national technical means?' Everybody has a sneaking suspicion that they know that what was discussed was not exactly meant by this. I suspect that nobody really has a coherent, limiting, unique, precise definition. I suspect that we could be very embarrassed if one day the Soviet leaders say: 'Your reference to "national technical means" and the discussion of the history of the word "technical" [which General Welch has discussed briefly] usually ignores the clause that always accompanies it. "Each party shall use national technical means of verification at its disposal in a manner consistent with generally recognised principles of international law." ' So what are we going to do if they say: 'Which are your "national technical means", and what are your espionage satellites?' That opens up a new can of worms, and I will leave it open for anyone who wants to go fishing.

Another spherical fiasco, and this is about the only word that I can think of to describe it, is the continuing interchangeability of 'launchers' and 'missiles'. The most conspicuous use of these two words interchangeably is in Lodal's long piece[2] in which he supplies us a footnote that where he uses the term missiles he means launchers: 'the term "missiles" is shorthand in this connection. Technically the number of missiles is not limited by the treaty. Rather, the treaty's limits apply to missile launchers.' Why he had to use that kind of shorthand in a paper that is some 40 or 50 pages long is not obvious.[3] We got ourselves into a lot of trouble because of that. We were quite surprised by the Soviet Union going to cold-launch techniques after we signed the interim agreement of 1972. There are several explanations why they did this, one of which is that they could put a bigger missile in a smaller hole, because the diameter of the hole includes room for the flame to come out for hot-launch missiles. That is one explanation. Another is that after a cold launch, the silo can be reused quickly. The best explanation, to my taste, is that this would enable them to super-harden the missile silo by constructing a necking down at the top of the missile silo, and, thus needing a smaller door to seal the silo which is the most vulnerable part of the silo to an air blast directly overhead. This considerably increases the hardness of that particular feature. We were quite astonished by this. There was and is all this nonsense (left over from SALT I) about the silo diameters, silo sizes (10 per cent to 15 per cent was the phrase used, I think). And there was no agreement of whether it was volume, length, or length plus radius, or diameter, and so a lot of ambiguity resulted.

General Welch's life-cycle arguments are well worth reading. I find that we usually observe these developments during a life-cycle of a weapons system when the weapon is in the adolescent stage. We are usually some years behind. What we give our intelligence analyst to work with is not what he would really like. What he would really like is the name of the designer, and a long distance and lengthy phone call to him twice a week at an early stage of the design; our analyst would like copies of the laboratory tests on materials, the inside tests on components and all that. All we have to offer him is a picture taken from a great distance on a clear day after the gadget has been completed and they (the Soviet leaders) take it outside and unwrap it. That always happens late in the game. Under the circumstances, it is quite remarkable what our analysts are able to accomplish.

I am not as much concerned as others have been with brand new weapons and our ability to keep up with new weapons, because I am deathly afraid of being killed by an old weapon. For the victim there is no consolation whatsoever were he to be killed by an obsolete weapon of clumsy design, delivered by an 'inaccurate' missile, launched by an unsophisticated leader who has heard a poor analysis by a primitive strategist. One is just as dead. Those neutrons are just as fresh and speedy as those in a new weapon. While we guard against failure of our 'C³' system (Command, Control, and Communication), we need to ensure that we do not inadvertently install an 'O³' system: Overhead, Overheard, and Overlooked.

NOTES

1. See Amrom Katz, 'Verification of SALT: The State of the Art and the Art of the State', The Heritage Foundation, Washington (April 1979) for a detailed discussion of these matters.
2. In *Foreign Affairs* (Winter 1978–79), p. 246.
3. The Salt II Treaty, with its Agreed Statements, Common Understandings, and exegesis by Secretary Vance, is full of examples of the equation and interchangeable usage of ICBM launchers, strategic nuclear delivery vehicles, strategic arms, and ICBMs.

    Perhaps the most compact official collection of examples of this fuzziness is found in 'SALT II Basic Guide', US Department of State, Bureau of Public Affairs (May 1979) (Department of State Publication 8974). On page 3 this pamphlet states: 'The treaty restricts the US and the Soviet Union to an equal, overall total of *strategic nuclear delivery vehicles*. . . . Units to be included under this ceiling are *land-based ICBM launchers*. . . . Under these limits, the Soviet Union . . . will have to remove about 270 *strategic nuclear delivery vehicles* from its weapons inventory.' (my emphasis)

    The fact is that there is *no limit* on ICBM missiles. We do not know what they do with their old missiles, we do not know how many missiles have been produced, and we tend to dismiss the possibility of overt deployment.

11 SALT II: Who Is Deceiving Whom?

Richard Perle

The title of these remarks – 'SALT Verification: Who is Deceiving Whom?' – seems to pose the question of whether we are deceiving the Soviets or the Soviets are deceiving us. In fact, we have been deceiving ourselves; and the Soviets, for their part, have been only too pleased to help us do so.

That, surely, is the lesson of SALT I, an agreement that we hoped and believed would seriously constrain the growth of Soviet strategic offensive forces. It was an agreement that would 'halt the momentum of the Soviet strategic build-up', that would make the future course of Soviet strategic weapons development more predictable, that would reduce the risks of a nuclear confrontation between the superpowers. We now know that the SALT I interim agreement was none of those things. It did not halt the momentum of the Soviet strategic build up or enable us better to predict future Soviet developments or prevent the sort of strategic crisis that erupted in October 1973 when the United States went on a strategic nuclear alert following the mobilisation of seven Soviet airborne divisions. The build-up continued and even intensified. Soviet spending on strategic weapons actually increased following the 1972 agreement. Neither the momentum of the Soviet program nor American faith in the effacy of arms control slowed, much less halted.

One of the principal reasons that SALT I failed to meet the expectations of its makers is that the Soviets shrewdly negotiated an agreement whose constraints proved quite irrelevant to their planned increases in strategic forces. The proposed limits that they knew would not impede their momentum, constraints that left them free to continue their build-up. American efforts to build into the agreement limitations on the Soviet drive to acquire a capacity to destroy at least the land-based component of our strategic deterrent were either rejected by the Soviets or rendered ineffective through beguiling definitions and well-crafted loopholes. In achieving this result the Soviets had a distinct advantage: they knew as much about our future plans and a great deal more about their future plans than we did. They were thus in a position, as we were not, to design treaty limitations whose effects were predictable and whose loopholes were exploitable by them alone. The Soviets had, moreover, the inestimable advantage of catering to American willingness to believe, despite the absence of convincing evidence, that they, like we, wished to limit the competition in strategic arms in a manner that would affect both sides equally. In short they facilitated our natural tendency toward self deception.

It is not that we did not try to bring about constraints in SALT I to inhibit the growth of Soviet strategic forces. We proposed, for example, that launchers for light missiles should not be convertible into launchers for heavy missiles, a provision designed to reinforce the agreement's ceiling on strategic launchers. Faced with analyses that showed that the conversion of light into heavy missiles would enable the Soviets to acquire a force large enough to threaten our Minuteman missiles in a preemptive strike we insisted on limiting the light into heavy conversion of missile silos. The Soviets readily agreed – and the interim agreement contains just such a provision than even spells out the percentage increase by which missile silos can be enlarged. However, when the United States sought to obtain Soviet agreement on the maximum size of a missile that could be based in an enlarged missile launcher the Soviets were not so accommodating. They refused to agree to a common definition of the terms 'light' and 'heavy' as those terms applied to ICBMs.

During the course of the negotiations the United States side had come to believe that for ideosyncratic reasons, often having to do with a Russian historical tendency to extreme secretiveness, it was not possible to obtain Soviet agreement to precise definitions. It was a belief encouraged by the Soviet negotiators. Indeed, it has become a persistent theme in American thinking about arms control and the Soviets. So when we encountered the Soviet refusal to agree to a precise quantitative definition of the terms 'light' and 'heavy' we resorted to stating a definition of our own. This 'unilateral' definition distinguished between light and heavy missiles in terms of the Soviet SS-11: any missile having a volume greater than the SS-11 was, according to our definition, deemed to be a 'heavy' missile; and no conversion of light missile launchers to house a missile larger than the SS-11 was to be permitted. The willingness to regard the Soviet refusal to agree to our definition as a mere quirk of Soviet negotiating style rather than a deliberate device for eventual circumvention of the purpose of the agreement was greatly facilitated by the ease with which we indulged in unfounded optimism and self-deception.

The rest is history. Shortly after the treaty was signed and approved by the Congress, the Soviets flight tested, for the first time, the SS-19 – a missile that greatly exceeded the size of the SS-11 and was therefore, according to our definition, clearly a 'heavy' missile. Subsequent analyses proved that the SS-19 had been in development while the negotiations were taking place and that the Soviets had made a specific effort to assure that nothing in the agreement would interfere with its eventual deployment. A Soviet program of converting their 'light' missile silos to accommodate the 'heavy' SS-19 quickly followed.

The American SALT bureaucracy then went through a two-year struggle to decide how to deal with the SS-19. If we were to stand by our unilateral definition it would constitute a violation of the agreement – and if there is anything the Administration wished to avoid it was reaching the conclusion that the Soviets were violating SALT II even as SALT II was under negotiation.

In the end we applied what might be termed the 'buttered matzo rule'. Let me explain. It seems that around the Jewish holiday of Passover there was, in a certain place, a traditional ceremony in which a group of rabbis would carry a giant buttered matzo to the top of a mountain. On one occasion as the rabbis were struggling to get the giant matzo up the mountainside, a great gust of wind flung the matzo into the air and blew it to the ground – buttered side down. In haste and dismay a Talmudic court was convened to define the meaning of this ominous event. After three days of prayer, study and discussion, the court reached the conclusion that the rabbis had buttered the wrong side.

And thus the government of the United States concluded that the SS-19 was not a heavy missile and instructed its SALT II negotiators to propose to the Soviets that any missile larger than the SS-19 would be regarded a heavy missile. The Soviets, in SALT II, agreed.

How easy it is to extenuate when one wishes to. For that is what we did with the SS-19; and no one should be surprised if we find ourselves invoking the 'buttered matzo rule' with respect to some of the provisions of the SALT II treaty.

I have written at some length about the SS-19 because it is a good example not only of our tendency to self-deception but of the Soviet strategy of nurturing that tendency. Nowhere in the record of the SALT I negotiation did the Soviets indicate that they would not agree to our definition of a heavy missile because they had under development a missile that would qualify as heavy if the definition were agreed. If anything they encouraged us to believe that the failure to reach agreement on a definition was a minor technical matter because agreement had been reached on the definition of a launcher for heavy missiles. They pressed for a loophole; we permitted it to become a noose.

During the SALT I negotiations we insisted that each side limit the construction of certain ABM radars to agreed operational sites and to existing test ranges. The Soviets agreed; but they would not specify what their existing test ranges were. When we inquired they said that each side knew the location of the other's test ranges. As we believed we did in fact know the location of the Soviet ABM test range we resorted, again, to a unilateral statement, declaring the location of our ranges and stating that the Soviet ABM test range was at Sary Shagan. The Soviets said nothing to contradict our statement. Some time later we discovered a new ABM radar at a Soviet site on the Kamchatka Peninsula. Somehow we managed to conclude, not that Soviet silence in the face of our unilateral statement had been deceptive, but that we had failed to count the Kamchatka facility among Soviet test sites at which it was permissible to erect new radars.

The claims that eight years ago were made for SALT I are now being made for SALT II; the disappointed expectations of the first agreement are rapidly becoming the self-deceptions of the second. Thus the Administration argues that under the SALT II treaty the Soviets will actually have to reduce their strategic forces by 10 per cent. Now it is true that the treaty will require the Soviets to dismantle some 250 obsolete launchers that they otherwise might keep in the inventory. But this fact taken alone obscures the more important fact that between now and 1985, when the treaty is supposed to expire, we expect the Soviets to add several thousand new strategic warheads to their inventory. For each launcher retired from the force some twenty warheads will be added. Yet one again hears claims about inhibiting the growth of Soviet forces, halting the momentum of their build up, 'capping' the arms race. This treaty, like its predecessor, is constructed so as to allow the Soviets to continue augmenting their strategic forces as they see fit. The Soviets have instructed their negotiators to agree only to constraints that leave their programs unaffected; and we have embraced the result. Thus through a combination of loosely drawn limitations, concessions to Soviet demands and loopholes and ambiguities we have once again negotiated the illusion, but not the reality, of limitations on Soviet strategic forces.

We have, for example, persuaded ourselves that the SALT II treaty will prevent the Soviets from deploying new types of ICBMs. Over and over Administration spokesmen have pointed to the limitation on new types of ICBM as a central achievement of SALT II. The fact is, however, that the Soviets have succeeded – with cooperation from our negotiators – in getting a definition of the term 'new type' that will permit them to complete the development of all the ICBMs we believe they intend to complete during the period of the treaty – the so-called 'fifth generation'. It is interesting to note that the term 'new', as used in the treaty, has nothing to do with the concept to temporal sequence. An ICBM is 'new' or 'old' depending on some (but by no means all) of its quantitative and qualitative characteristics, not on the date of its development or the advancement of its technology. In the strange world of SALT treaties we may well see 'old' ICBMs developed years after 'new' ones.

The simple truth is that we were out-negotiated by the Soviets on this issue. They succeeded in protecting their fifth generation of missiles under development by refusing to agree to constraints that would have caused them to scrap or significantly modify them. We tried – and failed to halt the fifth generation and we ought not to deceive ourselves into believing otherwise.

There is yet another sort of self-deception in the SALT II treaty that is rather more serious – not from a strategic point of view, but from the more important perspective of maintaining some standards of integrity in the way we conduct negotiations with adversaries; it has to do with the Backfire bomber.

We have made many estimates over the years of the Soviet Backfire bomber and all of these estimates, including those that ascribe to it the most modest capability, conclude that the Backfire has the capacity to attack targets in the United States on plausible third country recovery missions. The intelligence community has therefore concluded that the Backfire has intercontinental capability, but the Soviets have told us otherwise.

As the treaty is shaping up the Soviets will make a statement, outside the treaty itself, to the effect that the Backfire is not capable of operating at intercontinental ranges; and we will accept the statement.[1]

I believe that we would be better off if we acknowledged that we have agreed to permit the Soviets to go on building the Backfire at their current rate of 30 per year outside the aggregate ceiling established in the treaty because we wanted an agreement and the Soviets insisted upon it. We should not legitimise a Soviet statement that we believe to be false. We should not fool ourselves into believing that we are justified in accepting Soviet assurances when we have intelligence that falsifies those assurances. When the Secretary of Defense says, as Harold Brown did in April 1977, that ' . . . these (Backfire) bombers . . . have a combat radius sufficient for some strategic uses . . .', the President ought not to accept a statement by Mr Brezhnev to the contrary. Even more than the resolution of the Backfire issue, the integrity of our position is at stake. By the way Backfire was handled, it has been diminished.

Unhappily, the verification standard that we now apply to international arms control treaties is rapidly declining. Until recently the view was widely accepted within the government that we ought not to enter into treaties unless compliance with them could be verified. We felt it unwise to enter into treaty limitations unless we were reasonably confident that the other party could not cheat without our knowing it.

That does, after all, seem a reasonable standard for verification: that cheating be detectable.

The current Administration is about to sign a SALT II treaty that contains major provisions that we cannot verify – that is, there are a number of provisions that the Soviets could violate with a high degree of confidence that we would not be able to detect their violations. Quite apart from the consequences for our security, if they should in fact choose to exploit our inability to detect violations, the decline in the old standard of insisting on verifiable agreements is troubling. Furthermore, the decline is a general one. We have been negotiating toward the conclusion of a comprehensive ban on nuclear testing, despite a consensus among experts that it is not verifiable. We have put forward a number of proposals for arms controls in the Indian Ocean, many of them unverifiable. We have discussed with the Soviets limitations on the development of anti-satellite systems; limitations that are, in large measure, unverifiable. The Department of State continues to urge that we negotiate limits on the transfer of conventional weapons to the countries of the Third World – with little apparent regard for the fact that these limits would be largely unverifiable.

When the American people hear their senior officials pronounce the SALT II treaty 'verifiable', they surely think that we have sources and methods of intelligence gathering that are able to detect violations of the treaty provisions should violations occur. They will be astonished to discover, as the debate over SALT II unfolds, that administration spokesmen mean something quite different. When they say that the treaty is 'verifiable', they mean that such cheating as could take place without our knowledge will not shift the strategic balance against us. Of course they do not specify what sort of change in the strategic balance would constitute a shift, and from everything one can gather about their conception of the United States Soviet strategic relationship, any alteration in the strategic balance is, by definition, ruled out.

I think it is clear that the Administration has resorted to a novel definition of the word 'verify' in order to justify their claim that they will be able to verify Soviet compliance with the SALT II treaty. So long as they remain the arbiters of the strategic balance they can lay claim to an ability to verify the treaty whether we can detect violations or not. In short, Soviet violations may be undetectable but compliance will be verifiable!

Recently President Carter made a speech on the SALT II treaty. He said, 'The bottom line is that if there is an effort to cheat on the SALT agreement, including the limit on modernizing ICBMs, we will detect it.' Later in the same speech, he said: 'The treaty must and will be verifiable from the day it is signed'. Both of these statements are false, and a little detail about them would perhaps be valuable.

The limits on the deployment of new types of ICBMs, to which I referred earlier, cannot be verified. That is, the Soviets could violate those limits and we would not be able to detect it. The limits with respect to the testing and deployment of new types of ICBMs provide that an ICBM is 'new' if it differs in certain parameters from ICBMs already tested or deployed. The parameters include such measures as launch weight, throw-weight, length, diameter and so forth, and the maximum permitted departure from existing missiles, for several of the critical parameters, is 5 per cent. We cannot verify within 5 per cent, however, and this was the case even before we lost critical intelligence facilities in Iran; since the loss of those facilities our verification capability has been significantly weakened. Moreover, we are unlikely, in the near term, to restore even our earlier ability to measure Soviet compliance, despite some ill-founded assurances from the Secretary of Defense that we will recover the SALT relevant collection assets within a year. Of course, there is a mad scramble on to compensate for the loss of Iranian bases – not so much because the intelligence gap is a serious one for our security, but because it affects the treaty – and therefore the debate on its ratification.

In addition to the limits on the testing and deployment of new types of ICBMs, there are a number of other provisions in the treaty that cannot be verified. We do not know how to verify Soviet compliance with the range limit on ground and sea-launched cruise missiles, for example. If the Soviets were to violate the 600 kilometre (370 mile) limit on, say, sea-launched cruise missiles, there is a significant chance that we would not discover they had done so until a United States Navy ship was hit from 700 or 1000 kilometres (430 or 620 miles) away by a Soviet cruise missile with a nominal range of 600 kilometres (370 miles). That, surely, is not the verification technique the Administration has in mind when it claims that if there is an effort to cheat, we will detect it.

We cannot verify the clandestine production of mobile ICBMs. Indeed, we cannot even account for ICBMs that we know were produced and previously deployed but are not now in evidence. Therefore we cannot verify whether they are or could be made readily operable. We cannot verify the treaty provision banning the conversion of SS-20 missiles into SS-16 missiles. We cannot verify improvements to the Backfire bomber, even though the Soviets have pledged not to increase the capabilities of the aircraft. So in a number of important respects the Treaty simply is not verifiable, and the Administration would do far better to own up to that fact and go to the American people with the argument that they are prepared to take the risks inherent in a treaty that has unverifiable provisions, rather than continuing to insist, by resort to a private definition, that the Treaty is verifiable. I believe that in the end, after extensive hearings and Senate debate, the

Administration will be forced to concede that there are unverifiable provisions in the treaty.

Now the argument is sometimes put forward that, even if we could not detect Soviet cheating, the Soviets would not cheat, because the costs to them would be so high. One thing I am sure about, following the approval of the SALT II Treaty, is that there will be no desire, on the part of the Administration that negotiated it, to catch the Soviets cheating. There clearly was no such desire on the part of the previous Administration; every time it had a close call to make on whether the Soviets were complying with SALT I, they decided either that the Soviets were in compliance (and we had been careless in drafting the treaty) or that their willingness to stop violating the treaty was sufficiently responsive to our concerns.

I do not think that the costs to the Soviets of cheating on the SALT II treaty are likely to be very high – at least to the Soviets. They would be high to any United States administration, which would then be faced with the necessity to do something about it. Even if we could be confident of detecting Soviet cheating – and, as I have indicated, we cannot – the last thing we will want to do is precipitate an international crisis over Soviet compliance with the agreement that is the centerpiece of an admittedly ragged detente. The Soviets know that; but for self-deception, so would we.

There is another reason why our ability to verify Soviet compliance with the SALT II treaty is in doubt: the treaty is too vague in too many places to establish a clear dividing line between compliance and non-compliance. In order for any treaty to be verifiable certain conditions must be met. First, the treaty must be drafted with sufficient precision for a definitive judgments about compliance to be made, if all the necessary information about Soviet performance were available. Second, there must be a reasonable expectation that the necessary information, much of it technical in nature, will be available. Third, the treaty itself and the information necessary to measure performance must be sufficiently intelligible, in the real world of politics, for a convincing case to be made in the event that there is evidence of non-compliance. The SALT II treaty fails on all three counts. Because there is so much that is imprecise in the treaty (despite the self-serving claim by its chief negotiator that it is a masterpiece of legal draftsmanship) it is almost certain that the information necessary to establish compliance will prove to be unobtainable; and it will prove impossible to make a convincing case that a violation has taken place.

To take one example, the treaty provides that the throw-weight of only one missile may differ by more than 5 per cent from some other, existing missile. But there is no agreement on the throw-weight of the existing missiles. Thus any American assertion that this particular provision has been violated would require us first to establish the throw-weight of an existing missile and then the throw-weight of some 'new' missile from which it differed by more than 5 per cent. Even if the data were available – and it is not – try, in the real world, to assert that a treaty has been violated on the strength of mathematical formulas that impute numerical values to reference data indicated by squiggles on an oscilloscope or data bits intercepted in transmission from a test launch and processed by a computer. President Kennedy realised the importance of *intelligible* evidence when he dispatched photographs of Soviet missiles in Cuba – missiles that Mr Gromyko sore did not exist. How willing would he have been to challenge the Kremlin's claims if, instead of photographs, he had only an arguable interpretation of a vague phrase evidenced by a series of computer generated digits!

One final point, and this on the subject of deception. I was enormously interested in what Professor Jones had to say, but as I listened to him I kept thinking that, if there is a Professor Jones on the Soviet side, we are in deep trouble. We are terribly vulnerable to Soviet deception because we do not take deception seriously. We assume that the Soviets are essentially straightforward in the way they organise and manage their military programmes. We assume that they will do things in the future the way they have done in the past and that we will have the benefit of their cooperation as we seek to monitor their compliance with the treaty.

We depend to a disconcerning degree on the unwarranted assumption that the Soviets will not alter their standard practices so as to diminish our ability to monitor their strategic military programmes. From the Soviet point of view, a little deception would go a long way. We will be fortunate beyond any reasonable expectation, if they do not exploit our vulnerability in this regard.

NOTES

1. At the Vienna summit, the Soviet Union, made the following statement: ' . . . the Soviet side states that will not increase the radius of action of this (Backfire) airplane in such a way as to enable it to strike targets on the territory of the USA. Nor does it intend to give it such a capability in any other manner, including by in-flight refuelling'.

12 The Adequacy of SALT Verification

Albert Carnesale

Let me start with some lessons from SALT I that have been important in framing SALT II and will be important in the ratification debate. One such lesson is that unilateral statements may be worth the paper they are written on, but no more. A unilateral statement by the United States that clarifies something they intend to do may be helpful, but we cannot expect our unilateral statements to impose constraints on the Soviet Union. If the Soviet leaders refuse to agree to accept a particular constraint, they probably have some reason for doing so. Our making a statement that says, in effect, 'We wish you would have agreed to such and such a provision', cannot substitute for Soviet acceptance of the provision.

We also learned from SALT I that silence on the part of the Soviet leaders does not indicate consent or agreement. I will return to this point later.

Another lesson from SALT I is that, if there is a fuzzy area between prohibited and permitted activities, Americans tend to view actions in the fuzzy area as prohibited, while the Russians tend to view them as permitted. The Soviet Union is very legalistic in this sense: what is prohibited is prohibited; what is not prohibited is permitted. We must avoid the establishment of fuzzy areas in SALT II.

Let us look at some of the issues raised by Richard Perle (Chapter 11 of this volume), particularly those which illustrate mistakes made in SALT I which are unlikely to be made again. Consider first the replacement of the SS-11 by the SS-19. In the SALT I negotiations, we tried hard to get the Soviet Union to agree that anything larger than the SS-11 was a heavy missile. They refused to accept this definition. Later, they tested and deployed a new missile, the SS-19, which was heavier than the SS-11. Did this action constitute a violation of the 'freeze' on heavy missiles? No. We might not have liked what the Soviet leaders did, but it certainly could not be characterised as cheating. What they did was not in accordance with our unilateral statement, but it was not in violation of the SALT I agreements.

The ABM radar at Kamchatka is another example. You will recall that SALT I permits ABM testing only 'within current or additionally agreed test ranges'. We tried to get the Soviet leaders to specify the locations of their test ranges, but they would not. We said we were aware of the current ABM test range near Sary Shagan, and they said nothing. Did their silence indicate their acknowledgement that the Sary Shagan facility existed, that it was the only Soviet test range and, therefore, that there was no test range at Kamchatka? Evidently not. Soviet silence is not to be interpreted as a clear statement of anything.

Let me turn now to some general questions about verifiability. As I understand him, Mr Perle defines a verifiable agreement as one which precludes cheating in ways which could escape detection. That means that if a provision is to be verifiable, the adversary must not be able to cheat at all. Moreover, if any level of cheating were possible, Mr Perle would find the proposed agreement unacceptable. I disagree with him. In my view, it would not be in our interest to accept such a rule. I believe, for example, that if we could constrain the Soviet Union to 103 heavy missiles, such a constraint would be in our interest even if the Soviet Union could by cheating secretly achieve a level of 104. The Soviet leaders now have 308 heavy missiles; I would prefer to see them with 104.

A reasonable guideline for 'adequacy' of verification is far more in our interest than any clearly unattainable theoretical standard. I am not going to try here to define what constitutes adequate verification, but I will pose some questions which should be addressed in determining whether verification is adequate. These are: What are the ways in which the Soviet Union might cheat? What would be the likelihood of successful cheating at various levels? What would be the costs and benefits – economic, military, and political – to the Soviet leaders of such cheating? What would be the risks to United States security of successful Soviet cheating? What would be the risks and benefits to United States security of not having the proposed constraint on either Soviet or American forces? Finally, would the net benefit of having the constraint exceed the net benefit of *not* having it?

One of the considerations in developing answers to these questions is verifiability – but it is only one among several. Any constraint which is clearly in the United States interest, even if not verifiable to the level of Mr Perle's perfection standard, should be acceptable to us. Actually, this is an oversimplification, for it can be misleading to look at a single constraint in isolation. One must examine the entire agreement as a package. An acceptable package may contain some provisions which, by themselves, do not appear to be in our interest, provided that the benefits of other provisions outweigh all of the disadvantages.

If there has been any consistent 'gap' in the Soviet–American competition, it is an information gap, and it has been (and remains) in the Soviets' favour. They have easy access to detailed information about our strategic forces and programmes, but we must work hard to find out about theirs. SALT agreements and the verification provisions they include, as imperfect as they may be, help to reduce the effects of this asymmetry. The information gap remains, SALT or no SALT, but it is mitigated in our favour by SALT.

It is important to keep in mind that verification and intelligence are not identical. Consider the continuing debate over our ability to determine the characteristics of Soviet missiles undergoing flight tests. For obvious reasons, we want to learn as much as we can about the missiles and their performance during the tests. This would be true with or without SALT. Intelligence relevant to any Soviet military matter is of value to us. Verification of whether the Soviets are in strict compliance with a particular provision of an arms control agreement may be of greater or lesser value. If, under SALT II, the Soviet leaders were to test (as their one new type of ICBM) a new, solid-fuelled, small, highly accurate ICBM, we would want to learn as much as possible about it, including some characteristics unconstrained by SALT (such as accuracy and reliability). Such intelligence information would be of far greater importance to us than would be the answer to the verification question of whether a new version of the SS-11 was more than 5 per cent heavier than the older model. In some cases, our intelligence requirements exceed our verification requirements.

On the matter of new types of ICBMs, Mr Perle found it odd that the definition of a new type does not include the concept of time. That observation is an interesting one, especially coming from him. Suppose age were the parameter which determined whether a missile was of a new type. How would Mr Perle determine whether the tested Soviet missile were seven years old, four years old, a week-and-a-half old, or just born? An age criterion clearly would be unverifiable. If age had been the criterion employed in the agreement, Mr Perle would have been first to protest its unverifiability. He cannot have it both ways. As an aside, I point out that there is an easy way to solve the problem of our inability to verify as well as we would like the constraints on testing new types of missiles; namely, delete the provision. Would Senator Glenn or Mr Perle be happier then? I doubt it, even though the verification problem would no longer exist. But this particular constraint is one that the United States wants to see imposed; it was not a Soviet proposal. This constraint, even though not perfectly verifiable, is clearly in our interest, and we should not be forced by faulty reasoning to abandon it.

A similar point can be made about the production of mobile ICBMs. Nobody can claim that the Soviet Union could not produce and store some mobile ICBMs clandestinely. Indeed, it is possible (though hardly plausible) that there are thousands of mobile ICBMs stored covertly in the Soviet Union today. I doubt it, but it is not impossible. If Mr Perle lacks faith in our ability to detect and count mobile ICBMs in the Soviet Union, he has a problem whether or not these systems are constrained by SALT. How would his problem be made worse if there were a ceiling on the allowed number of mobile ICBMs? On the contrary, he should be somewhat relieved, because the SALT agreements contain corollary constraints which bolster our intelligence collection capabilities.

Mr Perle also expresses concern about the verifiability of constraints on upgrading the Backfire bomber. This problem too would disappear if no such constraints were imposed, but it would be replaced by a far more difficult problem – an unconstrained Backfire force. He also deals with the Backfire as a strategic weapon. He might have mentioned that, according to Soviet strategic concepts, our forward-based systems (in other words, our aircraft in Europe and on carriers within range of the Soviet Union) are strategic weapons. The United States does not accept this categorisation. We maintain that these weapons systems are not strategic because they are not intended for use in a strategic role. We have not claimed that they were not capable of attacking targets in the Soviet Union. To some extent, the forward-based systems issue is analogous to the Backfire issue.

A meaningful analysis of SALT II must include an examination of the whole SALT II package. Mr Perle, quite appropriately, has selected for discussion those provisions which raise the toughest verification problems. But a complete analysis must also consider all of the other provisions, such as those which constrain the number of heavy missiles and the number of warheads per missile.

Suppose verifiability were the only test of whether a provision were acceptable to the United States; then, in light of the asymmetry between the American and Soviet societies, we would limit only American weapons. Such an agreement would be verifiable, but clearly unacceptable. This absurd example serves to demonstrate that perfect verifiability must not be employed as a criterion for acceptability.

A SALT II agreement, even though imperfectly verifiable, can make important contributions to our national security. We must not sacrifice such an agreement on the domestic political altar of absolute verifiability.

Part Five

Surprise: The Technological Factors

13 Technology and Lead Time: Soviet Experimental Technology

Clarence A. Robinson Jr

Massive Soviet research and development strategy over the past ten years is now paying off for the Soviet Union in the capability of both strategic and tactical weapons systems. The Central Intelligence Agency (CIA) estimates that the Soviet Union is outspending the United States in the defence area by 25 per cent to 45 per cent, and that portion of the USSR's defence budget dedicated to research, development and acquisition is about 75 per cent greater, according to Dr William Perry, Under-Secretary of Defence for Research and Engineering.[1] The actual military hardware being built in Russia and deployed over the past five years supports these estimates: 50 submarines to twelve for the United States; over 1000 new, modern intercontinental ballistic missiles to 280 for the United States; and over 10,000 tanks to 3600 for the United States.[2]

Since 1977, for example, the Soviet Union has surprised the United States by demonstrating significant new capabilities in areas where the United States has been clearly superior, including a look-down, shoot-down radar capability in an interceptor aircraft; improved ICBM accuracy; and high-speed computers. The Soviet Union has acquired strong capabilities against aircraft carriers operating within striking range of its territory and diversified its inventory of antiship missiles on nuclear-powered submarines and surface vessels. Soviet helicopter and vertical/short takeoff and landing carriers have entered the inventory. These are principally armed for antisubmarine and antiship missions. The massive Soviet effort in military technology is producing such advanced weapons as an improved antisatellite system, an advanced submarine, and unconventional technologies such as high energy laser weapons and charged particle beam weapons. According to Dr Perry: '. . . in particular, in the high energy laser field, they [USSR] may be beginning the development of specific weapons systems'.[3] But spending

163

alone is not the total problem. The Soviet Union is producing graduates of technology institutes and universities at four to five times the United States rate. There has been a 30 per cent growth rate in research institutes since 1960, with aerospace, missile and propulsion leading the way. The Soviet Union has a clear lead over the United States in areas of high pressure physics, welding, magnetohydrodynamic power generation, antiship missile technology and chemical warfare. Other Soviet strengths are in titanium fabrication, high frequency radio propagation and explosive power generation.

The total national commitment to the development of fusion energy in the Soviet Union, together with technology leads in these other areas, has provided the basis for an intense particle beam and high energy laser weapons programme.

Early in 1979, a group of 53 United States physicists and engineers completed and presented a plan to Dr Perry to develop technology for a particle beam weapons programme in the United States. In assessing Soviet technology in the particle beam weapons area, the group concluded that the Soviet Union is five to seven years ahead of the United States.[4]

To counter the Soviet momentum, the group, headed by scientists from the Los Alamos Scientific Laboratory, recommended a $315 million particle beam technology effort in the United States based on four generic types of beam weapons leading toward proof-of-principle experiments. To reach beam weapons deployment from the initial five-year programme will require another five or six years and another $800 million. Some $40 million will be earmarked for the development of the technology for a space-based neutral beam system based on the Army's Sipapu development at Los Alamos. That basing mode seems to offer great promise in solving some of the technology problems involved.

Much has been said by those on both sides of the issue of whether or not charged particle beams can be developed for weapons application, and just how clear the evidence of Soviet beam weapons development really is. The dichotomy appears to centre around what the Russians are doing at Semipalatinsk, a facility in Soviet Central Asia. The facility is often referred to under the acronym PNUTS (possible nuclear underground test site). In 1978 the Air Force's block 647 early warning satellite positioned in geostationary orbit over the Indian Ocean detected high levels of thermal radiation in the atmosphere in the general vicinity of Semipalatinsk. That information was relayed to the ground monitoring station at Buckley Field, Denver, Colorado. That was the seventh time in recent years when the venting of radiation and nuclear debris has been detected in the area of Semipalantinsk. In this instance, a United States weather reconnaissance aircraft over the Aleutian Islands a few days after satellite detection was also able to detect debris in the atmosphere normally associated with the detonation of nuclear weapons. From the location of the debris and the winds aloft, it was determined that the material came from Soviet Central Asia. United States intelligence experts concluded that there appeared to be no known sizeable nuclear detonations at the time the debris was discovered. These same experts believe that the Soviets are experimenting with miniaturised explosive generators for pulsed power formation directly applicable to beam weapons use.

Most of the controversy over particle beam weapons development stems from a number of public statements made by Major-General George Keegan after his retirement as chief of intelligence for the Air Force, and most are related to his information on the Semipalatinsk facility. There is little doubt that much of the information made public about the installation at Semipalatinsk is accurate. Photographic reconnaissance satellites produced evidence of the assembly above ground of gores of thick steel for a large sphere which was moved underground in caverns blasted from rock. The spacecraft cameras also recorded thick-walled building construction and what appear to be transformers and huge capacitor banks.

There are a number of physicists and engineers in the United States who are convinced that explosive generators to power beam weapons are being developed and tested at Semipalatinsk, but there are others who, while not outright sceptical, counter that there is no hard evidence that beams are being propagated at the facility. But even discounting the work at Semipalatinsk, there is no doubt that there is a widespread effort in the Soviet Union to produce directed energy weapons – particle beams and high energy lasers. That effort is coordinated and controlled by Y. P. Velikhov at the Kurchatov Institute of Atomic Energy in Moscow.

There has been an interchange between American and Soviet nuclear physicists and engineers working in the fusion energy and related fields for a number of years. When these scientists exchange visits and discuss pure physics there is a language and knowledge of physics that transcends national politics. Moreover, Soviet academician Askarian provided one of the keys to the kind of technology the Soviet Union is pursuing for fusion energy programmes which have a direct application to particle beam physics.[5] In his paper on micro-explosions to magnify magnetic fields to accelerate particles, Askarian explained that a hollow deuterium–tritium shell containing a metal case is used in an experiment in which the centre of the pellet is subjected to a megagauss magnetic field penetrating the deuterium–tritium shell which is imploded with a laser. The field is amplified through the procedure to 10^8 gauss. The deuterium–tritium is compressed 10^4 fold and undergoes the thermonuclear process of fusion, which in turn implodes the magnetic field in such a fraction of time that the field travels with the metal at 10^{11} gauss. The particles tend to follow the field lines and this amplifies the energy of the particles (protons in this case) to the field lines to 100 MeV. As the particles receive the energy, collisions tend to produce 10^{18} pi-mesons which decay releasing 10^{18} high energy neutrinos. This is said to produce an unprecedented acceleration of particles in a contained volume to achieve more directed energy.[6]

In a similar exchange of information, Soviet physicist Leonid I. Rudakov of the Kurchatov Institute caused a sensation when he provided information to the United States physics community.[7] The basic message from Rudakov's paper was that the Soviet Union had achieved a breakthrough which could enable production of a thermo-nuclear weapon yield capability within the same weight constraints by a factor of 10 to 100. Rudakov described electron beam experiments with yields of 3×10^6 neutrons. His advances in electron beam pellet fusion are based on the concept of transforming laser and electron beams into soft X-rays to compress fusion fuel. The release of the large amounts of energy in this process could provide power for beam weapons application, according to United States experts involved in beam weapons technology development.

Rudakov's experimental parameters were 1000 joules deposited on a deuterium–deuterium pellet target for 30 nanosec. The cone of the solid deuterium target is covered by a spherical cap of gold and embedded in a sphere of lead. The electron beam is focused on the gold cap, not over the bulk of the spherical pellet with the resultant neutron yield. Rudakov has demonstrated that an electron beam directed against the metal foil which shields the deuterium–deuterium pellet of fusionable material produces a highly non-linear plasma. Hard X-rays are converted to soft X-rays which in turn produce isentropic compression of the pellet. Rudakov claims to have produced high density electron beams of 10 million amperes per square centimetre at over 1 MeV particle energies with his prototype Angara 1 reactor. The second generation device, Angara 5, is being built at Efremov Institute in Leningrad and is slated to be operational in 1980. The physicist believes he has demonstrated breakeven fusion, albeit over a relatively small area. With Angara 5's 48 beam modules to heat the pellet from all sides simultaneously, the electron beam is guided along the pellet chamber containing a molten lithium blanket for heat exchange and tritium breeding, and a uranium blanket for plutonium breeding. Pellet fusion is considered by many United States physicists to be important to Soviet high energy weapons power sources.

The beam weapons work in the USSR is not structured as a beam weapons programme *per se*, even though the development effort has been placed under the PVO Strany air defence forces, according to

United States intelligence officials. Instead, it is a programme that cuts across a broad spectrum of Soviet science and industry. It is dependent on technology advances from several areas that feed into directed energy weapons development.

During his United States visit and in published papers, Rudakov said that the ignition of thermonuclear pellets with relativistic electron beams by the Soviet Union 'is oriented about well known technology of relativistic beam generation—pulses of 40–60 nanosec with energy up to 100 kilojoules (kj) per device'.[8] According to Rudakov, accelerator technology efforts in the Soviet Union are being concentrated in three areas which include inductive storage devices with transfer times in the range of 10–100 microsec, the LN-20 machine using collapsing aluminum liners, and deuterium—tritium ignition with net energy through compression of the mixture by the collapsing liner alone. With the inductive storage devices, massive liners can be accelerated to speeds of 10^5 cm/sec. It is possible to compress and adiabatically heat magnetised plasmas and provide thermal isolation for particle densities up to 10^{19} and temperature equivalent to 10^4 MeV. The LN-20 machine is used to reach a hundred-fold compression of the preplasma in the liner. The device is fed energy from a 2 megajoule (mj) fast-capacitor bank, and the metal liners are accelerated to speeds of greater than 10^6 cm/sec. Liners driven to such speeds can compress plasma to a particle density of greater than 10^{22} cm^3, and can heat it to thermonuclear temperatures. Achievement of deuterium—tritium ignition and net thermonuclear energy through the compression of the mixture by the collapsing liner is based on speeds greater than $1.5–2 \times 10^7$ cm/sec. This means it is no longer necessary to use a magnetic field to isolate plasma.

During the past year the attitude toward beam weapons development by the United States has shifted from one of scepticism to one of caution and prudence for the country to continue technological development to avoid Soviet surprise. The general attitude in the United States physics/engineering community is that such weapons may be possible within a reasonable time. In a Los Alamos Scientific Laboratory study on particle beam technology an assessment of the capability by the United States *vis-à-vis* the Soviet Union revealed:

(1) The Soviet Union could field a proton-charged particle beam weapon between 1980–83. It appears to lack only an efficient accelerator technique and started work on an autoresonant accelerator prototype in 1974. The United States could not produce such a weapon before 1986, and lacks everything except steering magnets developed for the Navy's electron beam Chair Heritage programme designed to destroy cruise missiles for shipboard point defence.

(2) Aircraft-based proton-charged particle beam weapons could be

deployed by the Soviet Union between 1983–86 after pulse power technology is perfected. The earliest date for a similar United States system is estimated to be 1990.

(3) Space-based neutral beam weapon could be fielded by the USSR between 1986–89. Previous Soviet experience in putting an electron beam in space provides a definite advantage. The Soviet deployment could be sooner if pulse power technology evolves more rapidly. The United States is in the infancy stage on technology except for power generation and could produce a space-based particle beam by 1990 at the earliest.

From frequent contacts with Soviet physicists, United States physicists believe that rapid Soviet progress toward achieving a beam weapons application is possible. Soviet developments in directed energy weapons related areas include:

(1) Location of the particle beam weapons development headquarters at Sarova near Gorki, and the testing of a ground-based advanced electron accelerator there under the direction of M. S. Rabinovich, a physicist from the Lebedev Institute in Moscow, who is believed to be running the particle beam technology effort for Velikhov. Experiments are said to have been conducted at Sarova to determine beam effects against targets. Such tests in the United States are not slated until late 1982 in the Chair Heritage programme.

(2) Use of manned Soyuz spacecraft, unmanned Cosmos spacecraft and Salyut space stations to conduct eight electron beam propagation experiments.

(3) Construction of a new powerful accelerator at Sarova (dubbed the four sevens machine for the superscript used in four of its parameters). It is expected to be a proton beam device and the development is under the direction of A. I. Pavlovskiy.

(4) Joint Soviet–French Araks experiments using a Soviet electron beam accelerator to propagate a beam from French Eridan sounding rockets. A series of tests goes back to 1975, and they will continue through 1982. Rocket launches have taken place from the Kerguelen Islands in the Indian Ocean to study the injection of energised electrons in the ionosphere and the magnetosphere.

(5) Testing of a compact hydrogen fluoride high energy laser weapon for use on a spacecraft at Krasnaya Pahkra, a large underground installation some 48 km (30 miles) south of Moscow, and at Sary Shagan near the Chinese border. The system may soon be tested on a dedicated Cosmos spacecraft, and there is evidence that laser experiments may have been carried out on the manned Salyut space station.

It is believed that the Soviet Union is developing the hydrogen fluoride laser as an antisatellite mechanism to replace the present system of exploding a spacecraft to destroy another satellite, a system that has been tested seventeen times over the past few years with flybys of Soviet antisatellite systems at a 447 m/s (1000 mph) within a kilometre of a Soviet spacecraft target to be an estimated success.

Both the Army and the Air Force are developing technology for placing high energy lasers on United States spacecraft: the Army for ballistic missile defence and the Air Force for space defence. The vacuum of space is ideal for propagation of laser beams which, unfettered by the atmosphere, can destroy targets thousands of kilometres away.

Laser power units have been developed in the United States which can provide sufficient energy for space-based weapons. And with the advent of the space transportation system – the shuttle – lasers will be carried into orbit in shuttle loads and placed on large spacecraft assembled on orbit. The United States now plans to flight-test its own miniature intercept technology antisatellite vehicle in 1981 in response to the Soviet system. The use of both space-based and ground-based laser systems by the Air Force for the antisatellite role is also a distinct possibility unless there is an agreement between the United States and the Soviet Union for a moratorium on antisatellite tests. Army/Los Alamos officials also are convinced that within three years from approval a variant of the antiballistic missile defence Sipapu space-based neutral beam weapon for space basing could be used for antisatellite missions. Pointing and tracking technology would not be nearly as critical for that mission and the system could provide useful data for continued United States beam weapons development.

Meanwhile, the Air Force is continuing development of its miniature vehicle for either ground or aircraft launch. The device will operate with an infrared homing seeker and destroy targets by placing a pattern of penetrator rods in the path of a hostile spacecraft. Vought Corporation is doing the development work for the Air Force based on technology earlier developed for a non-nuclear warhead for use on antiballistic missile defence interceptor missiles.

The principal use of the Soviet charged particle beam weapons is for antiballistic missile defence. Whichever side first perfects the use of a particle beam weapon with efficiency in destroying the other side's ICBMs will have the potential for nuclear blackmail in world power politics, and could force the other side to back down by threatening to neutralise the ICBM and submarine-launched ballistic missile forces.

Apollo X astronaut Tom Stafford, now a Lieutenant General who heads Air Force research and development, recently told the Congress that, if directed, space testing of the miniature vehicle for antisatellite missions could be carried out to validate weapons performance.[9] It would be tested against a cooperative target instrumented to determine performance.

In the present fiscal year the $73 million allocated for the antisatellite programme used for the fabrication of the developmental hardware and 25 flights will be simulated using drop tests.

In the coming fiscal year the Air Force plans to spend $85 million on anti-satellite technology. In addition to accelerating development of the miniature vehicle, it will be used to complete high energy laser advanced weapons system efforts with concentration on kill verification, pointing and tracking.

The United States position in context of the Outer Space Treaty is that 'peaceful' does not mean non-military, but, rather, non-aggressive. The treaty provides that the use of military personnel for scientific research or for any other peaceful purpose shall not be banned. Under current law there are activities that are not prohibited in space. Among them are the testing and placement in space of the necessary methods and means to preserve law and order and security, hardening of satellites to protect them from interference or attack, and the testing, development and placement of antisatellite systems in space is permitted according to Major-General Walter D. Reed, Air Force Judge Advocate General.[10]

Another area of technology in which the Soviet Union has made progress in recent years is antisubmarine warfare. The Soviet Union has developed a more powerful, narrow beam radar for use on a spacecraft to detect changes in sea life caused by nuclear-powered submarines passing through a given stretch of the ocean. The Soviet radar satellite for ocean surveillance came to public attention in 1978 when Cosmos 954 re-entered the atmosphere and spread its radioactive material used to power the radar over areas of northern Canada. The spacecraft is the type the Soviet Union has used for years to keep track of United States vessels in adverse weather or at night. It weighs about 2700 kg (6000 lb) with 450 kg (1000 lb) dedicated to the nuclear reactor used to power the radar. The high-frequency transmitter onboard is powered by about 45 kg (100 lb) of enriched uranium U-235 used for reactor fission.[11]

The Soviet Union also demonstrated new ASW technology during Okean 75 in the Pacific Ocean's Mariana Trench. During that exercise the Soviets used six Russian ballistic missile submarines to test the new equipment, giving the names of United States fleet ballistic missile boats to their submarines for the test. The Soviets have developed a device to detect the radioactive nuclides deposited in the ocean by the heat exchange from the reactor in nuclear-powered boats. The device was successful in locating Soviet vessels at ranges of over 160 nautical km (100 nautical miles) at substantial depths, but the submarines of the Soviet Union are not considered as efficient as the United States—

designed reactors which place less material in the water during the heat transfer. Still, continued perfection of the device could imperil United States submarines. Other Soviet technology for ASW is evolving such as variable depth-towed array listening devices. These already are deployed on the Kiev-type VTOL carriers used primarily for anti-submarine operations.

With the deployment of the fourth generation of ICBMs continuing with its great advantage in throw-weight, the Soviet Union will soon have more than 6000 re-entry vehicles on the missiles. These can be used to pattern-bomb some 30 or more areas of the ocean with a 80 nautical km (50 nautical mile) radius each and have a high confidence that any United States submarine in the area would be destroyed. Such an attack would mean that through various means United States submarines with ballistic missiles have been localised to an area of uncertainty corresponding to the 80 nautical km (50 nautical mile) radius. Satellite-borne sensors represent one capability in this purpose and the Soviets have undertaken considerable activity in this area.

The Soviet military effort continues to increase steadily and to pay off in terms of both improved research and development capabilities and in the deployment of new weapons systems. The Soviet Union has repeatedly surprised the United States since the SALT I Interim Agreement was signed in 1972 with the pace of its technology and the improved quality in weapons systems. Some of those surprises include:

(1) Deployment of four new ICBMs with modern improvements such as a cold launch pop-up technique permitting the removal of silo shielding to allow the increase of the missile's size in the silo. It also provides for a reload capability of the silo.

(2) Accuracy demonstrated with ICBMs, particularly the SS-18 with its one-tenth nautical mile circular error probable, and with SLBMs such as the SS-NX-18. Stellar inertial guidance systems are also being tested on Soviet ballistic missiles.

(3) Development and testing of a phased array radar system for antiballistic missile defence. Produced by the design team for the SA-5 air defence radar, the new ABM system is not only accurate in filtering out decoys, but it is also transportable.

(4) Prototype testing of a new high-velocity antiballistic missile interceptor missile which operates within the atomsphere at hypersonic velocities guided by the phased array ABM radar system.

(5) Deployment of the Delta 2 class submarine, a lengthened version of the Delta 1. The nuclear powered vessel has 16 SS-N-8 SLBMs with a range of 6430 nautical km (4000 nautical miles) and torpedo tubes.

(6) Construction of the Typhoon boat, a follow-on to the Delta 2 with all-titanium hull, the largest titanium structure ever built. The new

submarine is designed to operate with the SS-NX-18 SLBM which will have multiple independently-targetable re-entry vehicles with a 6430 nautical km (4000 nautical mile) range capability.

(7) Development of three new Soviet bombers. One of these aircraft is the variable geometry wing aircraft Defence Secretary Harold Brown mentioned in testimony to the Congress early in 1979. [12, 13] It has the performance characteristics of the United States-cancelled Rockwell International B-1 bomber. The Soviet bomber will have a 11,750 nautical km (7300 nautical mile) unrefuelled range and operate at Mach 2.3 dash speeds.

(8) Testing of a 1200 kilometre (646 nautical mile) cruise missile from the Tupolev Tu-26 Backfire bomber, and improved inlets on the Backfire to extend its range.

(9) Three new Soviet aircraft – two fighters and a ground attack aircraft with designs that show that the Soviet Union has made a conscious decision to concentrate on sophisticated technology for adverse weather/night operations at standoff ranges. The fighters, the Ram K and L, are close approximations of the United States Grumman F-14 and Northrop/McDonnell Douglas F-18, respectively.

The Soviet Union has made impressive progress over the past fifteen years in developing and fielding military forces. The technological quality of their systems has moved dramatically closer to that of the United States. This qualitative advance, when coupled with their overwhelming numerical superiority, underscores the need for United States technology as a counterpoint.

CONCLUSION

The Carter Administration plans to spend between $400 and $500 million in an intensive multi-year technology programme to overcome the ten-year lead by the Soviet Union in antisatellite weapons development and testing. A contract has already been awarded to the Avco Corporation for ten spacecraft targets to be tested against the Vought Corporation's miniature intercept technology vehicle. Space tests are planned for the early 1980s. [13]

The primary counter to the Soviet killer satellite programme is the Vought design, but the USAF has at least two backup systems: one is an antisatellite device designed to go into orbit, fly an orbital rendezvous with the Soviet spacecraft, and then to detonate, sending hot metal at the target; the other is an antisatellite ground-based laser weapon. [14]

The Vought antisatellite weapon will be carried aloft under the McDonnell Douglas F-15 fighter aircraft. The warhead is a cluster of small rocket tubes surrounding a terminal homing sensor package. An onboard computer manoeuvres the warhead by firing the rocket tubes based on sensor inputs. Once in position, the rocket tubes become projectiles fired at the enemy spacecraft.

The miniature intercept vehicle would be launched using a combination of solid rocket motor from the short-range attack missile (SRAM) and the Thiokol Atlair 3 solid rocket motor for the Scout launch vehicle. Once fired from the F-15, it flies directly to the orbital altitude of the target and manoeuvres for intercept, making it an air-to-space missile.

The Defence Department is also concentrating on force multipliers, applications of technology which allow significant increases in military effectiveness or significant decreases in equipment costs, in order to maintain United States technology against the momentum of Soviet research and development.

In one area, the Pentagon will concentrate with increased emphasis on technology demonstration programmes where promising technology is selected and demonstration hardware is built and field-tested to determine capabilities and weaknesses. The demonstrations can be accomplished quickly and relatively cheaply because the equipment does not have to meet military specification. The budget is being increased by 17 per cent in the coming fiscal year for technology demonstration programmes.

The Defence Department science and technology programme for fiscal year 1980 will emphasise high-leverage technologies, as stated by Dr William J. Perry, Under-Secretary of Defence.[15] They are:

(1) Precision-guided munitions technology to capitalise on advances made in microelectronics and signal processing. Payoffs are in areas of adverse weather and long-range uses as well as short-range improvements.

(2) Directed energy technology where efforts will be concentrated on identifying scientific and engineering uncertainties associated with laser and particle beam technology, and on determining the feasibility of directed energy weapons for the 1980–90 environment.

(3) Very high-speed integrated circuits to achieve major advances in an order of magnitude reduction in size, weight, power consumption and failure rates and a hundred-fold increase in processing capacity. Integrated circuits with these capabilities will allow important advances in cruise missiles, satellites, avionics, radar, undersea surveillance, electronic warfare, communications and intelligence systems.

(4) Advanced composite material where efforts are directed at improving survivability and accuracy of advanced re-entry vehicles and to improve the structural performance of a wide variety of military systems.

(5) Manufacturing technology to develop techniques to reduce costs across the wide spectrum of defence production. Examples include the areas of composite materials fabrication, advanced inspection methods, and improved ammunition production.

NOTES

1. The Fiscal 1980 Department of Defence Programme for Research, Development and Acquisition, P 1–1.
2. CIA Document SR 79-10004, *Dollar Cost Comparison of Soviet and United States Defence Activities*, 1968–78, p. 4.
3. Fiscal year 1980 Posture Statement by the Honorable William J. Perry to the 96th Congress, pp. 1–6.
4. *Aviation Week and Space Technology* (2 April 1979), p. 12.
5. In Askarian the *Journal of Experimental and Theoretical Physics* (January 1979).
6. This technique provides the means to use energy to accelerate particles. In an earlier paper in 1978, co-authored with his immediate superior, physicist M. S. Rabinovich, Askarian explained the use of asymmetric amplification of the magnetic field to achieve acceleration of particles to multi GeV energies.
7. During the Gordon Conference on Plasma Heating in Mirimar, California (30 June 1976). Rudakov presented the same material at the Lawrence Livermore Laboratory (2 July 1976), at the Sandia Laboratory, New Mexico, on 3 July 1976 and at the Naval Research Laboratory in Washington (6 July 1976).
8. *Aviation Week and Space Technology* (16 November 1978), p. 16.
9. United States Air Force Fiscal Year 1980 Budget Estimates; Statement of Lt.-General Tom Stafford, pp. 2–39 (12 March 1979).
10. Remarks by Major General Walter D. Reed, JAG, to the American Astronautical Society, Houston, Texas (31 October 1978).
11. *Aviation Week and Space Technology* (6 February 1978), p. 22.
12. *Aviation Week and Space Technology* (26 March 1979), p. 15.
13. Secretary of Defence, Fiscal Year 1980 Posture Statement to the 96th Congress, p. 73.
14. Sahlin, Harry L. (trans.), 'A Soviet Paper on Laser Target Heating, Symmetry of Irradiation and Two-Dimensional Effects on Compression', Lawrence Livermore Laboratory (13 December 1977).
15. In his Fiscal Year 1980 Posture Statement, pp. 1–44.

14 ASAT: At Home and Abroad

Edgar Ulsamer

On 11 May 1978, President Carter committed the nation to a new space policy by signing Presidential Decision Memorandum 37. (PDM 37), a policy statement that breaks new ground by projecting the principle of a nation's sovereign rights in space and the right to defend them. This policy also asserted that any nation's space systems are national property and are entitled to free passage and unhampered operation. PDM 37 commits the nation to activities in space in support of its right of self-defence and thereby strengthens national security, deterrence, and arms control agreements. In the absence of an agreement to comprehensively limit antisatellite capabilities and their use, the United States will vigorously pursue development of its own capabilities. The United States space defence programme will include an integrated attack warning, notification, verification, and contingency reaction capability which can effectively detect and react to threats to United States space systems.

At this time, the Administration is solidifying its negotiating position on a two-phased accord with the Soviet Union to limit or bar the use of satellite interceptors. The initial accord, meant to be of unlimited duration, but providing for a one-year cessation of ASAT testing, is to be of limited scope. The principal objective is to prohibit both sides from permanently damaging, destroying, or displacing–and by the latter is probably meant kidnapping–of satellites through the use of a space shuttle or by taking over each other's satellite or satellites such as NATO's or Warsaw Pact's in which either side has an interest by electronic means.

An antisatellite (ASAT) testing moratorium, in effect for one year only, can be viewed as not impeding this nation's ASAT programme, which is not ready for space demonstration as yet. Conversely, however, it would seem preordained that the United States arms control enthusiasts will crusade mightily to extend such a cessation of weapons tests once it is on the book. Such an agreement would merely extend the provisions of SALT II concerning the inviolability of our national technical means of verification to military satellites in general. At some future date, perhaps after the United States has demonstrated its own ASAT in space, the two superpowers, according to present White House plans, are going to negotiate a comprehensive treaty that would seek to do away with both sides' arsenals of weapons and capabilities that can permanently damage, destroy or displace the other side's satellites. Issues such as the development of electronic space warfare capabilities, ground-based lasers that irradiate spacecraft with sufficient thermal energy to cause them to overheat, and space-based beam weapons are not covered by the initial agreement, other than by the basic prohibition against waging war against the other side's spacecraft.

The Administration's willingness to proceed with an ASAT treaty seems to be at odds with the generally accepted findings that Soviet dismantling of its existing ASAT capabilities and facilities cannot be verified without cooperative measures, including on-site inspection. This is so for two reasons. The Soviet Union uses a booster for an ASAT that also serves as the launch vehicle of several other unrelated space and missile systems. Further, the Soviet Union could launch an ASAT from boosters not now used for this purpose. It would be quite easy to launch an ASAT riding atop an alternate booster vehicle from a Soviet site, not associated by United States intelligence with this type of mission. Verification, therefore, seems to be almost impossible. But several other considerations weigh in on the other side of the argument. The Soviet ASAT system, even though under test since the early 1970s, is still of limited scope and has encountered several failures. The supporters of a limited ASAT accord argue, also, that while the Soviet ASAT system has been improved, the advances appear to be minimal. There is no evidence that the Soviet Union is about to flight test a direct-ascent interceptor, a weapon needed to reach geostationary orbits. With Soviet ASAT tests to date confined to about 600 kilometres (370 miles), some of this country's most crucial satellites seem to remain well beyond the reach of the existing Soviet space weapon. If this is so, then it will be in the United States interest to persuade the Soviet Union to freeze their ASAT development and test programme before it can take a major technological step forward. Buttressing this line of reasoning is the further contention, possibly founded more on optimism than certainty, that the United States has at its disposal the technologies that will outdistance the Soviet ASAT capabilities, once the White House authorises programme go-ahead. Further, since the homing and interceptor requirements of conventionally armed exoatmospheric ballistic missile defence interceptors far exceed the skill levels needed to kill a satellite on a fixed orbit, some experts contend that the United States ASAT programme gets a free ride from ballistic missile defense

(BMD) research. Thus, they claim, an ASAT treaty is not tantamount to technological stagnation so far as space weapons are concerned. Conclusion of some form of ASAT accord appears to be a high-priority concern of the Carter Administration and is said to be part of a 'peace package' that is to be launched as an extension of SALT II.

The initial ASAT weapon under development is a miniature vehicle capable of being launched either by ground-based missiles or aircraft. An offshoot of a homing interceptor developed by the United States Army as part of its ballistic missile defence programme, the miniature interceptor weighs about 15 kg (35 lb) and kills hostile satellites by impact, but without explosion. Impact speeds range from 10,970 to 43,800 km/h (10,000 to 40,000 ft/sec) depending on altitude and location. For ballistic and lower orbital altitudes, such as, presumably, photo-reconnaissance spacecraft, the miniature interceptor would be carried by heavily modified variants of such missiles as AGM-45 Shrike or AGM-69 SRAM; the latter would be launched from F-15 aircraft. The United States, therefore, could have an ASAT capability wherever F-15s are deployed. The homing interceptor uses rocket motors that, on command from the weapons seeker, bring it on a collision course with the target. For intercepts at high orbital altitudes, the miniature ASAT would be launched by a space booster from either Cape Kennedy or Vandenberg Air Force Base. But this phase of the ASAT programme is dormant at present. The Air Force, if so directed, will conduct operational space tests, and this weapon against the cooperating target satellite carrying the special instrumentation to evaluate ASAT performance is scheduled for 1982.

The Air Force also is pursuing advanced ASAT systems. These alternate approaches could provide a mixed force which would complicate Soviet defence. Countermeasures to the Soviet ASAT include a range of techniques and devices that can boost survivability of United States military satellite systems. These include proliferation of the number of satellites that perform a given mission; designing satellites so that they are not easily observed and placing them in orbits beyond sensor surveillance range; hardening satellites against laser radiation; and employing decoys to deceive and manoeuvre capability to evade an attacking interceptor.

By way of conclusion, attention should be focused on one aspect of the Soviet military space programme of grave concern. It is a fact that the Russians seem to be well on their way toward a manned command-and-control spacecraft that can perform along the lines of the United States E4B national emergency airborne post. Such a capability, coupled with a clearcut Soviet effort to capitalise on this country's lopsided dependence on sophisticated command, control, communications and intelligence C^3I systems with relatively vulnerable nodes in both space as well as on the ground, could decisively handicap the United States in the opening phase of a strategic nuclear war. This development is doubly portentous because of doctrinal and force structure-related advantages that accrue to the Soviets. This asymmetry stems mainly from the Soviet Union's commitment to a pre-emptive strategic posture, as well as her reliance on ICBMs which can be controlled and executed more easily through a far more survivable C-cubed system. It follows then that the United States ASAT capability of threatening manned Soviet and other vital spacecraft is indeed needed to deter Russian attacks on this country's command and control systems either in space or on the ground.

15 Technical Feasibility of Directed Energy Weapons in Strategic Defence

Patrick J. Friel

In view of the heavy emphasis laid by some upon directed energy weapons in evaluating problems of strategic surprise, an analysis is in order here of the technical feasibility of the development and deployment of such weapons.

PARTICLE BEAM WEAPONS

Since the early 1960s, the United States has maintained a programme designed to study the application of directed energy weapons to ballistic missile defence. These directed energy sources include charged particle beams (protons and electrons, primarily the latter), neutral particle beams (hydrogen atoms) and high power lasers. Charged particle beams cannot be used in the exosphere since the beam would be deflected by the earth's magnetic field. The possibility of using electron beams in endoatmospheric terminal defence was examined extensively by the United States in the 1960s. Those studies indicated that while it may be possible to propagate a lethal beam in the atmosphere, the beam was not very stable. In addition, the applications studies showed that the power required is enormous, the pointing and tracking requirements were severe and the system would be easily saturated in a large attack. The auxiliary sensors required to operate a ground-based electron beam weapon were also vulnerable to a variety of penetration aids. Therefore, it appears that the application of electron beam weapons to endoatmospheric defence is impractical.

In recent years, the United States has also evaluated the use of neutral particle beams of hydrogen atoms[1] in a space-based ballistic missile defence. Charged particle beam research in the United States and the Soviet Union has shown that it is feasible to produce an intense collimnated beam of H⁻ particles using available particle accelerator systems. Techniques have been developed to remove the electron without causing the beam to diverge, so that it may be possible to propagate a narrow, intense beam of hydrogen to long distances. The interaction of a high energy H^0 beam with a re-entry vehicle could cause the formation of a lethal dose of protons in a weapon. However, the application of this neutral beam technology to exospheric ballistic missile defence presents some formidable technological and engineering problems. If it is assumed that there is a practical range at which a narrow beam could be maintained at about 1000 km (620 miles), the number of satellites required to ensure coverage of a given missile silo field would be twenty (the great circle length divided by 1000 km–620 miles). Complete coverage of the United States would require a large number of orbits filled with satellites. Also, if it is assumed that the irradiation times required to produce a lethal dose of protons in the RV is significant, for example, of the order of ten or more, then the beam would have to be retargeted to each of the enormous number of aimpoints associated with a large scale Soviet attack on Minuteman. In addition, the beam would have to be precisely pointed (0.05 micro-radians or less) during the illumination period. Therefore, the satellite beam weapon system would easily be saturated in a large Soviet attack. The accelerator associated with a space-based neutral beam system could be quite large . . . many tens of metres. Research programmes in progress in the United States suggest that the technology required to develop a smaller acceleration system may be available in the future.

However, it is not impossible to imagine 100,000 kg (220,400 lb) launch weight payloads for a single beam weapon satellite. Assuming a 20,000 kg (44,000 lb) launch capability for the shuttle for a 1000 km (620 mile) orbit, over five shuttle loads would be required for each station. Then too, the beam must not look too close to the earth or the atmosphere will strip away an electron and the beam will be deflected in the earth's magnetic field. A reasonable minimum altitude would be about 200–300 km (120–180 miles) so that Soviet ICBMs or SLBMs on depressed trajectories simply could not be engaged. The beam weapon satellite will also require an auxilliary sensor to locate the RVs. If low orbit satellites equipped with long wavelength infrared sensors are used, they are vulnerable to direct attack and could be susceptible to relatively simple midcourse penetration aids. A space-based radar would also be susceptible to the same threats, particularly electronic countermeasures. Thus, even if the very difficult scientific problems are solved, the technological and engineering problems associated with a space-based neutral beam weapon are formidable – to say nothing of the costs which would be staggering. In addition, the total weapons system could be easily saturated and would be vulnerable to penetration aids and tactics. Thus, it can be predicted with reasonable confidence that the neutral particle beam research in progress will not lead to a space-based weapon system in the foreseeable future.

However, the United States should continue research on the possible use of neutral hydrogen beams as weapons with emphasis on the production of intense, sharply collimnated hydrogen atom beams and the design of smaller accelerators. The latter would include the collective accelerator in which an H^- would be accelerated along with a 'bunch' of electrons. The collective accelerator design should be much shorter than conventional designs.

The objective of this research would not specifically be oriented toward weapon systems development, but rather to prevent 'technological surprise' particularly since the Soviet Union is reported to have an active programme in this field.

LASERS IN BALLISTIC MISSILE DEFENCE

In its R & D programme in ballistic missile defence, the United States is also evaluating the potential of high energy lasers both as sensors and weapons. One application that has been given considerable attention is space-based laser weapons. ICBMs are most vulnerable during the boost phase of their trajectories. If a high power laser system could illuminate the upper stage of the booster during launch with enough energy to melt the skin (aluminum is a typical booster material), prior to RV deployment, the booster would probably be destroyed. In order to characterise the technical credibility of space-based laser weapons in ballistic missile defence, it is necessary to consider some of the key technical parameters. It can be shown that a reasonable thickness of aluminum will melt when $200-500$ joules/cm^2 of energy are absorbed. Since aluminum reflects 95 per cent or more of the incident energy in the infrared region, the amount of infrared energy which the space-based laser would have to deposit on the booster at launch would be $40000-10,000$ joules/cm^2. A reasonable projection of the power of infrared chemical lasers and the size of the optics that could be available and placed in orbit by the space shuttle is a $10-20$ megawatt (mW) laser using 15m reflecting optics. Using these parameters and kill criteria the laser weapon would be placed in a circular polar orbit at 3000 km (1860 miles). A space-based laser of this size does not appear to be beyond the projected state-of-the-art over the next 25 years and probably could be placed in space with a one or two space shuttle load (space-based optics of this size – about fifteen times anything deployed thus far – and the space deployment of a laser with this power would indeed be a remarkable technological feat in itself). However, while the size of the space-based laser system may not be beyond the projected state-of-the-art, several other factors must be considered if this technology is to be applied to ballistic missile defence. Two important factors are the time available to the space-based laser to illuminate the boosters and the size of the attack. The maximum time available for the space-based laser to illuminate a given booster during its launch phase is about 200 sec. Thus, it can be shown that for a 1000 booster Soviet attack over 150 of these space-based weapon systems would be required to insure that no RVs would reach targets in the United States. Assuming an illuminated spot size of 0.5 m, the 'jitter' of the optical system must be 0.05 microradians or less. The laser system must also act cooperatively with another passive optical sensor system which initially acquires and tracks the booster. The passive sensor hands the booster location over to the laser system which must accurately illuminate the target for as much as 10 sec and rapidly switch to another target. Thus, the system would be rate-saturated in a large Soviet attack, as in the neutral beam weapon. The auxiliary passive sensor would again be vulnerable to penetration aids. It should also be emphasised that, if the requirement that no Soviet MIRV payload impact on all of North America (that is, the United States and Canada) were placed on the space-based laser, the access time for the laser beam to illuminate the booster would be substantially less than 200 sec.

These various technical uncertainties are compounded by the largest technical uncertainty of all, the possibility of effective offensive countermeasures. The most effective countermeasures would simply be to place a highly reflective coating on the upper stages of each booster. For example, NASA has developed surface coatings for planetary entry vehicles (such as, Saturn atmospheric entries in which the radiant heat transfer rate is as high or higher than that of laser weapons) which will reflect 99.9 per cent or greater of the incident radiation. These coatings, together with insulation, could be very effective laser weapons counter-measures and they have not been comprehensively evaluated.

Thus, space-based laser weapons represent a formidable application of laser optics and space technology to ballistic missile defence. While the technical parameters associated with such a system are not outlandish, it is difficult to believe that this technology could have a strategically significant impact over the next 25 years. The United States R & D programme in ballistic missile defence will continue to investigate the technical feasibility of all directed energy weapons, primarily from the viewpoint of avoiding 'technological' surprise by the Soviet Union.

In recent years there has also been an attempt to integrate lasers with

LWIR sensors which would provide the search/acquisition function for the laser. The primary application of lasers in this context would be as tracking/discrimination and homing/fuzing sensors (a laser for these applications, of course, is a very different device from one intended to be a booster kill system). The annual expenditure for these applications of lasers has been as high as 10 per cent of the advanced development budget in ballistic missile defence. However, a meaningful, large scale laser field experiment comparable to those in progress with LWIR sensors has not been identified as yet. The reason for this is that the ranges associated with midcourse defence are large and the laser power/aperture and waveforms required for most of these space-based applications (except short range fuzing) are beyond the projected state-of-the-art.

It has been reported that a budget of $300 million over the next five years for directed energy weapons is being considered.[2] To put this figure in the proper perspective, the same publication also reported that the budget for the total Air Force programme in missile and space surveillance is about $115–$120 million per year. Thus, if the $300 million directed energy weapon technology programme were approved, the annual budget would be about half of the Air Force's missile and space surveillance budget – a substantial distortion in the United States military space programme. There is little chance that the research in space-based neutral particle beams or lasers will lead to viable weapon systems in the next ten or possibly twenty years. On the other hand, we may have to rely on a variety of space-based sensors for our very survival during the same time period. From this perspective, a directed energy weapon technology programme equal to 50 per cent of the Air Force's missile and space surveillance technology programme seems incredible.

In addition, if those responsible for the United States strategic technology programmes were really concerned about the possibility of any beam weapon compromising the United States strategic deterrent forces, a massive countermeasures programme would be initiated immediately. Two examples of such a reaction are the United States MIRV programmes to ensure the suppression of any Soviet ballistic missile defence and more recently, the Trident submarine programme to minimise the effectiveness of Soviet ASW. The total United States investment in these two programmes has been $40–50 billion. The countermeasures programme for directed energy weapons in the United States strategic technology programme is zero or miniscule (a small programme to counter high energy lassers). The absence of a United States countermeasures programme is a strong indication that the United States strategic technology community does not take the possibility of a viable space-based directed energy weapon seriously, at least for the foreseeable future.

NOTES

1. A substantial part of the neutral beam research in the United States and the Soviet Union is in direct support of the controlled thermonuclear reactor program. The neutral beam would be the 'fuel' for a system which would contain the plasma with a magnetic field.
2. Robinson, Clarence A., *Aviation Week* (2 April 1979), p. 12.

Part Six

Surprise: Political and Psychological Factors

16 Surprise in Diplomacy

Michael I. Handel

Research on the subject of surprise has thus far been limited to its use in war. Current literature on military surprise thoroughly explores topics such as the optimal use of surprise in tactical and strategic planning; methods of anticipating surprise; and the frequent occurrence of intelligence failures despite strong evidence of an imminent attack. The development of the theory of military surprise has, however, reached the point of diminishing returns.[1] At this stage, the study of surprise should expand in new directions.

Surprise is an inherent part of human affairs; it can be found in domestic politics, foreign policy, economics, and technology, as well as in military affairs.[2] Wherever it occurs the act of surprise includes certain common elements. The initiating side always makes an un-expected move in order to improve its position – the surprise is calculated to throw the adversary off balance and put him on the defensive. If successful, the surprise enables the initiating side to pursue more freely a new course of action in the face of weakened resistance. In addition, the side that wants to avoid *being* surprised collects and analyses all available information in order to minimise the impact of such an event. By applying present theories of military surprise to other areas of study, it will be possible to refine existing concepts, and gain new insights into the general process of surprise.

The development of a general theory of surprise must be preceded by the development of specific theories and case studies on the non-military manifestations of surprise. This article explores the role of surprise in one non-military area – that of foreign policy.

In the political process, surprise occurs on two basic levels: the internal and the external. On the internal (domestic) level, political surprise involves an unexpected change of government through a *coup d'état*, a revolution, or an election; and it can also result from the formation of a new political coalition or the nomination of an individual to an important governmental position. A political surprise on the domestic scene of one country can have important, unforeseen repercussions on the international system.[3]

On the external political level, a surprise is any unexpected international move that has a direct impact on one or more states. Such a manoeuvre might be the outcome of collaboration between two or more states (for example the Rapallo agreement between Germany and the Soviet Union in 1922, the Ribbentrop–Molotov Non-Aggression Pact of August 1939, Nixon's China diplomacy 1969–71, and the so-called 'Sadat peace initiative' of November 1977). An external surprise can also result from a unilateral move (such as the Soviet Union's recognition of Israel in 1948, the construction of the Berlin Wall in August 1961, and Sadat's expulsion of Soviet military advisers from Egypt in 1972).

This chapter discusses political surprise as a tool of foreign policy, and is concerned particularly with cases of diplomatic surprise involving collaboration between two or more states.

DIPLOMATIC SURPRISE: DEFINITION AND IMPACT

In diplomacy, surprise facilitates the reorientation of foreign policy. It creates a new situation through which the side initiating the surprise can avoid stalemates and secure important advantages.

A major diplomatic surprise does not occur frequently; diplomats usually practise what George Liska, in *Beyond Kissinger*, calls 'routine diplomacy': 'Routine diplomacy smooths and implements established relations with the aid of only marginal adjustments (i.e. it is the opposite of surprise). Its most constructive performance is in evolving formulas of mutually acceptable compromise which permit the existing configuration to endure and avoid thus the risks of convulsions of radical change'.[4]

The means to facilitate radical change are found in a major diplomatic surprise – the tool of what Liska calls 'creative diplomacy'.

Creative diplomacy rearranges the setting within which negotiations for compromise occur . . . the supreme expression of creative diplomacy is the 'diplomatic revolution' (i.e. a major diplomatic surprise): a fundamental recasting or reversal of existing alignments which automatically marks a major stage (and a rare turning point) in the evolution of an international system. Revolutionizing diplomacy is not, therefore, to be confused with revolutionary diplomacy . . . Creative diplomacy can be either offensive or defensive in strategic purpose; and the transformation sought may be for repose as well as for major or continuing change.[5]

A major diplomatic surprise is best defined as follows: 'A situation in which at least two states make an unexpected change in allegiance that has an important impact on the real or expected division of power in the global system'.

A major diplomatic surprise is global in impact and either directly involves the great powers or has implications that transcend the regional level.[6] An unexpected agreement between Chile and Argentina, Peru and Chile, or Uganda and Tanzania, does not seriously affect global stability or the global balance of power. The agreement between Germany and the Soviet Union in 1939 not only affected the European balance of power, but also influenced Japanese–Russian relations:

That the impending conclusion of the German–Soviet non-aggression pact has caught all the other Powers entirely unawares, and has decisively altered the balance of power, not only in Europe but throughout the world, in favour of the Axis Powers with all that that implies, is the first reaction of the American press, which was itself completely taken by surprise.[7]

A United States–Chinese agreement could also have a major impact on the international division of power by eventually changing the global order from a loose bipolar to a multipolar system. It could affect Europe and NATO by encouraging the Soviet Union to concentrate power on the Chinese border and to develop better relations with the European states. This might influence the Soviet Union to adopt a more conciliatory stance in the SALT talks or, alternatively, push them into greater efforts to attain strategic superiority. An understanding between Israel and Egypt is regional in the sense that it could transform the balance of power in the Middle East and lead to a succession of new treaties and alliances in the region. But this type of situation also has global implications since it could lead to a new level of involvement for the superpowers.

A diplomatic surprise can arise within any type of international system. The difference in various types of systems, as far as diplomatic surprise is concerned, is to be found in the frequency with which surprises occur. In the classical balance of power system, diplomatic surprise can be expected to occur more frequently than in a tight bipolar system; more in a multipolar system than in a bipolar system; and more in a loose bipolar than in a tight bipolar system. The impact of a diplomatic surprise, as will be shown below, stands in inverse relation to its probability.

The definition of the classical balance of power system, according to Morton Kaplan in *System and Process in International Politics*, demonstrates this relationship. Actors in a balance of power system are loyal to their own interests and to the maintenance of equilibrium in the system in general, but not to specific states or ideologies. One of the principal rules of the balance of power system allows and requires states to make rapid and unexpected shifts in alliances in order to enhance their own power and maintain systematic equilibrium. The continuous shifting of alliances is a trait of the system, and despite the higher frequency of manoeuvres, they are still surprising.[8] As a matter of fact, it is one of the best means for maintaining the system because it facilitates the smooth and rapid transition from one alliance to another. In this system, the larger the number of major actors, or centres of power, the higher the probability of surprise.

The theory of international systems distinguishes between homogeneous and heterogeneous (or revolutionary) systems.[9] In a homogeneous system, such as the classical balance-of-power system, all actors share a common ideology, so that ideological conflicts do not impede shifts in alliances. One potential ally is not highly preferable over another, and alliances can be rapidly made and broken. These diplomatic surprises are, therefore, of lower intensity than those in heterogeneous, revolutionary, bipolar, or multipolar systems.

In a heterogeneous or revolutionary type of international system, the actors adhere to different, competing ideologies. Obviously, their opposing ideologies hinder communication or the formation of new alliances. Diplomatic surprise is less likely to take place in this environment – but once it happens, it has a radical impact upon the distribution of power in the system, and is thus more surprising. The ideological differences in a multipolar heterogeneous European system, which is divided among democratic, fascist, and communist states, are barriers to the formation of alliances. Given the intense ideological conflict between Nazi Germany and Communist Russia in 1939, a treaty uniting them behind a common cause seemed to be an extremely unlikely event. Once such a treaty was actually signed, it had a powerful impact on the European division of power. Prior to the completion of the treaty, the British had been repeatedly warned that Soviet Russia and Nazi Germany might reach some agreement, but they ignored and misinterpreted the contradictory signals. The warnings were dismissed with the attitude that the treaty was 'inherently impossible'. . . . 'The British counted confidently on ideological estrangement between Fascism and Communism. . . .'[10]

During the height of the Cold War, ideological competition was intense. The great powers made extensive efforts to prevent the defection of small allies, and were ready to punish them if they did. In this hierarchical bipolar world, the defection of even a relatively weak and unimportant state could have global repercussions: the Russian–

Egyptian arms deal of 1955, or the 'defection' of Cuba to the Eastern *bloc*, are good examples of this situation.

A more recent example of surprise agreements between the adherents of competing ideologies is the United States – China *rapprochement* of 1970–71. Experienced observers of the more than twenty-year-long propaganda war between the capitalist and communist systems assumed that the two states would be unable to negotiate effectively with each other, let alone reach an agreement to establish diplomatic relations and collaborate in the international system. Analysts of Middle Eastern politics felt that, after five wars and 30 years of intense propaganda warfare, it was unlikely that Israel and Egypt would enter into direct and productive negotiations. In the above cases of heterogeneous systems, longstanding ideological rivalries and preconceptions made it difficult for observers to anticipate changes in political orientation.

All of these unexpected moves across ideological barriers have one clear common denominator: *the states involved preferred their national interests to their ideological commitments.* The political intelligence analyst can derive an important lesson from these cases; that is, he should concentrate on power calculations and national interests rather than on ideological commitment and rhetoric, because power politics will prevail in the long run.

The problem of anticipating a major surprise in international politics is directly related to the more familiar problem of forecasting and prediction. This problem has received much attention, either directly or implicitly, in the classical theories of *realpolitik* and 'interests' as developed by Thucydides (common interests are the best agreement between states); Machiavelli (the ideas of *necessitas* and *raison d'état*); and finally Hans Morgenthau (the concept of interest defined in terms of power). According to these theories the most important foreign policies of states can be predicted and identified because they operate on a logic of their own, and do not depend on a particular leader. Therefore, an external observer will be aided in his prediction of the actions a state will take once he perceives the state's *basic* interests. Thus, if China feels directly threatened by the Soviet Union and is not strong enough to defend itself against the threat, it must seek help from another country. The only country with strength sufficient to counter the Soviet threat is the United States, so China has no choice but to turn to the United States. Similarly, if any German government (regardless of the form of government) between the two World Wars had wanted to occupy Poland (it was the goal of many German politicians during the Weimar Republic when Germany was too weak to act), then sooner or later Germany would have had to seek an agreement, albeit a temporary one, with the Soviet Union.

When a certain trend in the foreign policy of a state contradicts its own basic interests, then the state will eventually change this trend. It was against the interests of the United States and China to ignore each other when their common enemy, the Soviet Union, was becoming increasingly powerful. Collaboration would enable them to maximise their power; and even if the process of *rapprochement* was protracted and hidden from public view, in theory, it should not have surprised any political analyst familiar with the principles of *realpolitik*.

Such theories are useful for predicting major long-range trends but not short-range events ('tactical level') or minor surprises. The literature of forecasting in international politics is of greatest relevance to the political intelligence analyst.[11] Human misperceptions act as a powerful filter between the theoretical world of *realpolitik* and the realities of action, and they weaken the strength of the theory. This is not the context in which to develop an elaborate critique of the theory of *realpolitik*–but it is important to note that the theory is still of use as discussed above. Perhaps in each important political intelligence analysis in international diplomacy, a procedure could be developed in which one analyst prepares a strictly theoretical assessment according to the theory of *realpolitik* and power politics, while another analyst independently compiles a prediction based on available data. Corroboration of the two types of analysis might reveal interesting discrepancies and contradictions, and thus help to amplify signals that had been weakened through the screening process of perception.

DIFFERENCES BETWEEN MILITARY AND DIPLOMATIC SURPRISE

Unlike its military counterpart, diplomatic surprise can be positive in nature and it often has long-range effects. Therefore, the military intelligence analyst and the political analyst must approach the study of surprise with different goals in mind. The military analyst seeks to develop theories and techniques that will help him to avoid the critical and costly moment of surprise. His analysis attempts to answer a practical question concerned with *immediate decision*, and it is also the basis for momentous decisions. The political analyst is not just interested in averting an unexpected diplomatic manoeuvre. Instead of focusing on the moment of surprise alone, he is also concerned with the historical process that continues after the surprise has taken place. His analysis must attempt to foretell the surprise *and* it must also examine the long-range effects that the new situation might have on the international system.

The intention of the side that initiates the military surprise is to attain immediate short-range military objectives: to throw the adversary off balance; to dictate the direction and pace of developments; to maintain the ability to dictate the direction and pace of developments; and to win a decisive military victory. Diplomatic surprise also has an immediate dramatic impact, but its most important effects do not usually take place immediately after the moment of surprise. For example, the Rapallo agreement led to the long-range economic and military cooperation between Germany and the Soviet Union. In the long run, it helped to legitimise their acceptance and presence in world affairs. The United States–China diplomacy and Sadat's surprise visit to Jerusalem represented only the *begining of a process* which led to agreements in 1979, and they will continue to have an effect in the future. The Ribbentrop–Molotov agreement of 23 August 1939 somewhat differs from the cases mentioned above. Germany's desire to form a non-aggression pact stemmed from its intention to acquire immediate benefits – that is, to clear the way for an attack on Poland. Comparatively speaking, this treaty had swift results and was terminated in June 1941.

DIFFERENCES IN THE PREDICTION OF MILITARY AND DIPLOMATIC SURPRISE

Another way in which military surprise differs from diplomatic surprise is in its greater complexity. A military surprise can occur on a large number of levels and involves any combination of the following elements: surprise in terms of timing, area or areas chosen for the attack; strategy and tactics employed; use of new military doctrines; technological surprise in the employment of new weapons systems; unexpected goals, and so on. The complex interaction between the possible modes of surprise makes it much more difficult to hedge against a military surprise attack in all but one respect (which will be discussed below). In theory, the task of predicting a diplomatic surprise is simpler. But in practice, political intelligence analysts commit the same perceptual errors as their military colleagues and thus render their task more difficult. The number of possible major shifts in the foreign policy of any given state is limited; hence, they should be easier to predict. A few examples will clarify this point.

Early in 1921, both Germany and the Soviet Union were faced with only two viable major foreign policy choices. They could (1) improve their diplomatic relations with the Western democracies or, (2) turn to each other. If they chose the latter option, they would have to improve bilateral relations despite all earlier animosities and conflicting interests, and break the isolation imposed on them by the Western democracies. Initially, both the Soviet Union and Germany preferred the first option, although they never wholly relinquished the second; therefore, in order to keep both options open, they negotiated simultaneously with the Western democracies and with each other. Having met with the obstinate, uncompromising, and shortsighted attitudes of England and France, they had no choice but to turn to each other. For this reason alone, the Western powers should not have been so surprised by the ensuing German–Soviet agreement.

In 1939, history repeated itself again. Once Hitler decided to dismember Poland, he faced two major choices in order to accomplish his goal. Given his earlier moves in Austria and Czechoslovakia, he could be expected to first make an attempt to obtain either British and French consent, or Russian consent. When he failed to receive the open or tacit agreement of the West for such a move, he could *only* turn to the Soviet Union. The Russians desired security through a reliable defence agreement with Great Britain and France – or through an understanding with Germany itself. Again, both sides initially attempted to research an angreement with the reluctant French and British governments, and then paralleled discussions in the West with direct negotiations with each other. Moreover, the Soviet Union and Germany gradually developed a common interest in preventing the other from reaching a separate agreement with Britain and France. The Western democracies should have anticipated the Ribbentrop–Molotov agreement, which was as much the outcome of their own policies as it was the result of German and Soviet policies; yet the agreement came as a 'bombshell' and the two Western powers were, in fact, surprised. The British subsequently tried to counter the Russian–German surprise with a bombshell of their own. The ratification of the Anglo-Polish Treaty on 25 August 1939, did succeed in surprising Hitler, but it came too late to alter the course of events.

In the case of the United States–China relationship, surprise could only come from one direction. After the Chinese Communists gained power in 1949, the United States–Chinese relationship steadily deteriorated into the direct military conflict of the Korean War, and remained hostile until the late 1960s. Therefore, the only direction which a major diplomatic surprise could take would be the radical improvement of diplomatic relations.

Sadat's surprise visit to Israel is analogous to the United States–Chinese *rapprochement*. In this case all sides, including the Israelis, were caught unaware. For the second time, Sadat wrecked the conceptions of Israeli policymakers and the intelligence community. This time, however, he disproved not a military, but a political, conception. This was a political 'Ramadhan'. Nevertheless, in light of the limited number of new diplomatic options, and Israel's own contribution to Sadat's move, the Israelis should not have been so surprised. They were not so much surprised by Sadat's initiative itself as much as they were by the speed of his decision and his offer to come to Jerusalem. The Israelis, after all, had made the first contacts with Sadat; had initially offered to meet with him on neutral ground such as Geneva or Rumania; offered the return of the Sinai for a peace agreement; and warned him against a Libyan assassination plot.[12] The range of possibilities for diplomatic surprise could be further narrowed because any move by Sadat in a negative direction would not have surprised anyone given the history of Arab–Israeli relations. The only real diplomatic surprise initiated by an Arab state would have to be a positive one.

In principle, diplomatic surprise should be easier to predict than military surprise because, in the long run, the logic of foreign policy or *raison de'état* makes certain choices appear inevitable. Under both internal and external pressures, a process that appears likely to occur in the distant future becomes feasible much sooner. For example, it is reasonable to assume that the United States and China would not have remained in their estranged state forever. In principle, the United States–China *rapprochement* should not have surprised anyone, for after two decades of conflict, the only new direction could be one of *rapprochement* and collaboration. Political circumstances such as the American desire to get out of Indochina, the desire to counter the power of the Soviet Union, and President Nixon's need to score points in public opinion polls for the coming election, created a favourable environment for *rapprochement* and brought the two states together much earlier than was expected. For their part, the Chinese needed the United States in order to strengthen their position *vis-à-vis* the Soviet Union, to get a seat in the United Nations, and to guarantee future economic and technological aid. In spite of all the available signals preceding the actual move, observers in the United States, the Soviet Union, and other interested parties (Taiwan and Japan, for instance), were taken by surprise.

The limited range of options for a major diplomatic surprise is narrowed by the particular political circumstances at any given point. During the summer and autumn of 1977, Sadat may have been considering three basic courses of action. His first choice was to go to war. Sadat had already chosen this option in the autumn of 1973 with a limited measure of success. Egypt did gain some political points from the war, but it did not win, nor did it succeed in liberating much of the Sinai. With Egypt's relative military weakness and Israel's substantial growth in military strength, another war did not appear to be a viable alternative. In war Egypt would pay a high military and economic price, and Sadat would risk paying the ultimate political price of being ousted from office. His second option was to preserve the *status quo* and pursue earlier policies of prolonged and frustrating negotiations with Israel through a third party. At best, these negotiations would lead to yet another separation agreement without the return of the whole Sinai Peninsula. Sadat did not want Soviet participation in the bargaining process, but he realised, on the other hand, that there was a clear limit to the pressures the United States would bring to bear on Israel. This option was not promising either. Thus, he was left with a third, untried, option – a comprehensive settlement. He could try to gain United States support, thereby inserting a wedge between the United States and Israel. Then he could accelerate the political process with a direct dramatic move.[13] Choosing the third option did not preclude a later return to the second or the first options. The long years of inertia and minimal success made the choice of a fresh alternative almost inevitable. The course of action that cannot be avoided is dictated by *raison d'état* or what Machiavelli called *necessitas*.

There is only one factor which makes a diplomatic surprise more difficult to detect than a military one. In diplomacy, secrecy can be more easily maintained in the preparatory stages. A military surprise attack must include a large number of participants, the movement of troops and supplies, a period of intensified communication, and the concentration of the formations necessary for the attack. Major diplomatic moves such as the German–Russian negotiations in 1939, the United States–Chinese exchange of signals in 1971–72, or the Egyptian–Israel contacts in the autumn of 1977 could be made by a very limited number of top diplomats and their close aides. They could also be directly negotiated in face-to-face meetings between top leaders (such as King Hussein's secret negotiations with Israeli leaders in Israel). Military intentions can often be corroborated by examination of material evidence and capabilities. The intelligence analyst can compare declared intentions of peaceful coexistence and *détente* with the development of military hardware. If he observes that a state is building a substantial offensive military capability, he will doubt its intentions and therefore continuously re-evaluate them in the light of these developments; the political intelligence analyst cannot re-evaluate his conclusions in light of any 'objective' material evidence.

It must nevertheless be emphasised that complete secrecy is impossible even in diplomacy. Important signals indicating a possible dramatic diplomatic move are rarely absent. For example, Hitler and Stalin exchanged many public signals prior to commencing negotiations. In his anniversary speech to the Reichstag on 30 January 1939, Hitler omitted his customary diatribe against communism and the Soviet Union. On 10 March 1939, Stalin signalled back by declaring that the Soviet Union would not let itself be drawn into a senseless conflict with Germany on behalf of the weak Western democracies. This signal was not lost on the Germans. An additional public signal occurred on 5 May 1939, when the Russians announced that Commissar for Foreign Affairs

Litvinov 'had resigned'. Litvinov has been a well-known advocate of closer collaboration with the Western democracies. Then, beginning in May 1939, the German newspapers restrained their attacks on the Soviet Union.

In the case of the United States—China accord, public signals took the form of positive moves toward China by President Nixon and National Security Adviser Kissinger in 1969. The United States allowed the automatic validation of passports for scholars, journalists, and Congressmen who wished to visit China and gave permission for American tourists to purchase Chinese goods up to a maximum of $100 (July 1969). The $100 limit was lifted in December 1969. In 1970, Nixon's special report to Congress on United States foreign policy included many positive references to the Chinese. On 1 October 1970, China's National Day, an American visitor, Edgar Snow, was shown standing near Chairman Mao. On the same occasion, Mao expressed his dissatisfaction with the Soviet Union and made sympathetic remarks directed at the United States. On 26 October 1970, Nixon became the first American president to refer to mainland China as the 'People's Republic of China'. On 6 April 1971, the American pingpong team was invited to visit China, and eight days later, they met with Chou En-lai in Peking. When Nixon announced on 15 July 1971, that he planned to visit China, the surprise was complete because these signals had not been perceived as leading to a change in policy. Nixon described the surprise in the following words.

> At 7:30 on the evening of July 15, 1971, I spoke to the nation from a television studio in Burbank, California. I talked for only three and a half minutes, but my words produced one of the greatest diplomatic surprises of the century. . . .
>
> Despite the almost miraculous secrecy we had been able to maintain, the China initiative was actually one of the most publicly prepared surprises in history.[14]

There is greater ease in maintaining secrecy in diplomatic conduct, but the emission of signals is still an integral part of the process. These signals, like the signals preceding a military attack, are usually ignored and do not contribute to the prevention of an impending surprise.

These two types of surprise also differ in the order of complexity involved in assessing the *intentions* and *capabilities* of the participants. In the study of military surprise, analysts must give equal attention to these two factors and their intricate interaction. In the study of diplomatic surprise, attention must be skewed in favour of intentions. In this respect, the difference between military and diplomatic surprise is one of emphasis. In both cases, surprise is used to amplify force and compensate for weakness – but that is where the similarity ends. Obviously, the launching of a military surprise requires a certain minimum level of capabilities. The greater the capabilities, the more attention the intelligence analyst should devote to how capabilities would influence intentions.

This is not a major consideration for the political analyst who does not deal with actions that require the *immediate* use of capabilities. A political move does not necessarily need a minimum level of military or other capabilities to back it up. In fact, the opposite is true. The political analyst should become *more* alert when a state's power is weak relative to its most important goals, because diplomatic activity is often intended to compensate for the lack of capabilities. For example, the Rapallo agreement allied two exhausted states whose capabilities had been seriously damaged during the First World War. In the case of the Ribbentrop–Molotov Treaty in 1939, the Soviet Union entered into a non-aggression pact with Germany because it realised that war with Germany would be disastrous as long as the Western democracies remained remote and impotent. Even if Stalin realised that the Soviet Union would eventually have to fight Germany, the non-aggression pact was still advantageous because it gave the Soviet Union time to prepare for war. Hitler wanted a treaty with the Soviet Union because Germany was not strong enough to fight a war on two fronts.

The People's Republic of China drew closer to the United States because it did not want to face the powerful Soviet threat alone. To a lesser extent, the same was true for the United States. Sadat did not come to Jerusalem because of a longstanding ideological devotion to peace. He came because Egypt had not been able to accomplish its goals (for example regaining the Sinai) through the use of military capabilities. For its part, Israel realised that its military capabilities would not hold out indefinitely in a protracted war against all Arab states.

THE ADVANTAGES AND DISADVANTAGES OF MILITARY AND DIPLOMATIC SURPRISE

Another important difference between the two types of surprise is that military surprise offers only advantages to the attacker while diplomatic surprise involves a tradeoff. Surprise is the multiplier of any military force and is a fundamental characteristic of military planning because it throws the enemy off balance, dictates the course of war on the attacker's terms, reduces his casualties, and makes victory easier to achieve.[15] However, diplomatic surprise is always a compromise – it is a political decision that entails both benefits and costs.

When Rathenau decided to sign the treaty with Russia at Rapallo, he knew it would undermine Germany's relations with the Western democracies. Similarly, Hitler's decision to sign a treaty with the Soviet Union without consulting his allies, Italy and Japan, may have cost him dearly in the later stages of the war. When Mussolini took his 'revenge' and attacked Albania without consulting the Germans, he embroiled Germany in a Balkan war at a strategically difficult time. As for the Russians, the signing of an agreement with fascist Nazi Germany damaged their political standing with the communist parties of Europe, and convinced the Europeans that Russian interests took precedence over communist ideology. From a historical perspective, this was one incentive for the development of Euro-communism and diverse communist ideologies.

In his visit to Jerusalem, Sadat also had to pay a substantial price. He alienated almost all of the Arab states, thus losing much of his prestige in the Arab world. Sadat obtained the Sinai Peninsula and American economic and military support for Egypt, but he sacrificed the bid for Arab hegemony. It was a clear choice of Egypt first, which was contrary to the spirit of Pan-Arabism.

In addition to the price that must be paid in the external sphere, there is always a price to be paid on the domestic scene. The reversal of a policy to which the state, and many interest groups within the state, have long been committed engenders sharp criticism. The leaders responsible for the change in policy must therefore be sure that they have adequate domestic political support with which to implement the desired new policy.[16]

It is easier to undertake a major diplomatic revolution in an authoritarian state than in a democratic one: government-controlled mass media sells the new direction in foreign policy to the people and overcomes political objections. This does not mean that internal opposition to such moves is non-existent. Of course, when Stalin and Hitler were at the peak of their power and in full control of their parties and political systems, they faced no real opposition. But in Egypt, Sadat is in a more difficult position. He has had to contend with opposition from the army, religious groups, and political parties from both the left (those who follow the Soviet line) and the right (the nationalistic and Pan-Arab groups), and he had to fire two foreign ministers during the peacemaking process.

The leader of a democratic country, however, faces stiffer opposition. President Carter's decision to establish full diplomatic relations with the People's Republic of China and unilaterally sever relations and treaty obligations with Taiwan brought him under attack in Congress. He paid the price for bringing President Nixon's China policy to its logical conclusion. In Israel, Prime Minister Begin encountered strong criticism of the negotiations with Egypt from both his own party and the opposition. Since he could secure the delivery of certain goods by himself, Sadat found it difficult to understand why Begin had to undergo the lengthier process of obtaining government and Knesset approval. Soon, Sadat realised the advantages this system held for him, and he learned to manipulate the Israeli opposition forces in his favour. The difficulties involved in calculating the costs and benefits of a decision to implement a controversial new policy can offer some explanation for the infrequent occurrence of major diplomatic surprises.

The major differences in military and diplomatic surprise are summarised in Table 16.1.

TABLE 16.1 Differences in military and diplomatic surprise

Military surprise	*Diplomatic surprise*
1. The potential source of a threat can be known, but the large variety of possibilities for surprise in terms of time, place, method and weapons make effective forecasting difficult.	1. The possibility of a major diplomatic surprise can, in principle, be more easily anticipated because of the relatively limited variety of forms it can assume.
2. Immediate impact – the price paid by the surprised side is heavy and immediate, if the surprise succeeds.	2. Impact is short and/or long range. Surprised parties are not usually subject to immediate danger. The costs involved may not be immediate or high.
3. Offers *only* advantages to the attacking side.	3. Always involves a tradeoff between goals, interests, or political allies.
4. Equal importance must be attached to the enemy's *intentions* and *capabilities* and the complex interaction between the two factors.	4. Attention must mainly, though not exclusively, be paid to intentions. Capabilities are not a limiting factor in non-coercive diplomacy.
5. The emission of signals prior to a large-scale military operation is impossible to avoid. Troops and *matériel* have to be concentrated for the attack.	5. Easier to control the emission of signals prior to a major surprise since decisions are made by a very small number of top officials.

As far as the failure to be able to predict a surprise is concerned, the differences between the two types of surprise are minimal. Theories developed in the study of military surprise serve as valid explanations for the inability to avoid a diplomatic surprise. These theories are concerned with the following subjects: signal-to-noise ratio; deception (the ambiguities of evidence); rigid concepts and fixed perceptions projected on the enemy; pathologies in communication and organisation; uncertainties and inherent contradictions in intelligence work (paradoxes in perception); and repeated unsuccessful warnings and alert fatigue (the so-called 'cry wolf' syndrome). In this context, it is not necessary to repeat these theories since they would add nothing new to our understanding of surprise.[17]

THE PATTERN OF DIPLOMATIC SURPRISE

The most interesting cases of major diplomatic surprise fit a common pattern which can be divided into three basic stages (Table 16.2). During the first stage, one or both of the sides re-evaluate their basic interests and conclude that a reorientation in their related foreign policies is necessary. During the second stage, they establish a dialogue to determine whether or not an agreement can be reached. The third stage follows once an agreement is reached and made public.

STAGE I

Both sides begin to realise, at first independently of each other, that their earlier policies must be revised. Often these policies have gradually become obsolete, as a look at familiar examples will demonstrate. The United States embargo on China, as well as the ban on American visits, had lost much of their original purpose by the 1970s. President Sadat may have realised that peaceful bargaining was a more efficient way to regain the Sinai. Changing circumstances and goals are important in this process. Hitler's decision to occupy Poland took precedence over his reluctance to collaborate with communist Russia. Likewise, Chinese anti-American policy gradually weakened when faced with the mounting Soviet threat in the 1960s.

A reorientation of basic policy is facilitated by a change in leadership. A new leader or government may initially appear to support older policies until he/it is better established because it is dangerous to provoke opposition during the period of political transition. Nevertheless, the new and uncommitted leader will often find it easier to change the order of national priorities at a later stage. General de Gaulle, for example, found it easier to reverse France's policy toward Algeria after his return to power in 1958. In Israel, Begin was not committed to the same goals as the Labour Party which had been in power from 1940–77. Sadat did not have Nasser's commitment to war

TABLE 16.2 Patterns of Diplomatic Surprise

Case study	Type of system	Stage I	Stage II	Stage III	Were warning signals available?
The Ribbentrop–Molotov agreement	(1) Multipolar (2) Heterogeneous (3) Revolutionary (4) Conflicting ideologies	Stage I begins with Hitler's decision to attack Poland in October/November 1938. For the Soviet Union, perhaps after the Western Powers' demonstration of weakness during the Munich Crisis and Russia's isolation.	Early signalling by leaders begins around January–March 1939. Lower level contacts intensify from May 1939 onward.	On 21 August 1939 German radio announces the German–Soviet intention to sign a non-aggression pact. Agreement signed on 23 August 1939. War on Poland 1 September 1939.	Yes, a large number of signals both covert and overt.
Nixon's China diplomacy	(1) Loose bipolar (2) Heterogeneous (3) Ideological competition	(1) Nixon considers a new approach towards China since 1967. (2) The Chinese since the deterioration of relations with the Soviet Union.	Signalling by the United States starts in 1969. Exchange of messages. Negotiations start in 1970. Kissinger's secret visit to China 9–11 July 1971.	On 15 July 1971 President Nixon announces his intention to visit China–relations finally established in January 1979.	Yes, a fair amount of open signals.
Sadat's peace initiative	(1) Regional system in terms of the Arab–Israeli conflict is tight bipolar (otherwise multipolar) (2) Heterogeneous (3) Extreme ideological conflict	(1) Sadat offer. (2) Begin's election, perhaps before. (3) In Israel after Begin's election summer and autumn 1977.	Israel signals by warning Sadat of a Libyan assassination plot (July 1977). Promises Sinai back for peace. Direct secret negotiations between ministers in Morocco mid-September 1977.	On 9 November 1977 Sadat declares he is ready to address the Israeli parliament. On 19 November 1977 Sadat arrives in Israel.	No public signals.

Table 16.2 (*cont.*)

Was the use of deception important?	Major third parties surprised	Mediator states	Type of leaders and domestic system	Short and long-range results
Secrecy was more important than deception. Some deception to cover up the conversations was used by both sides.	*Opponents* (1) Western Allies (2) Poland *Allies* (1) Italy and Japan (2) Communist parties of Europe	Italy for Germany, and Bulgaria for the Soviet Union, played a minor mediating role.	Both authoritarian leaders and authoritarian systems.	(1) Partition and occupation of Poland. (2) Economic agreements (3) Weaken anti-German front.
No deliberate deception but some 'tactical deception' to maintain secrecy.	*Opponents* (1) Soviet Union *Allies* (1) Japan (2) Taiwan (3) North Vietnam (4) South Vietnam	Use was made of good offices of Romania, Pakistan, France.	Chinese authoritarian. United States leadership in foreign policy is strong (otherwise democratic).	Ease way out of Vietnam: United States–Chinese diplomatic relations; counterbalance Soviet power; for Nixon domestic popularity before election year.
Secrecy was perfect—no deception.	*Opponents and allies* (1) United States (2) Soviet Union (3) Arab States	Moderate role played by Romania and Morocco.	(1) The system and leadership of Egypt are authoritarian. (2) The Israeli leadership is strong and the system is democratic.	Egyptian–Israeli Peace Treaty: Sinai back to Egypt; Reduce Soviet role in the Middle East; economic development in Egypt increases United States influence.

against Israel or collaboration with the Soviet Union. After a token victory in 1973, he could afford to change the policy of confrontation with Israel, and change the order of priorities to an 'Egypt first' policy. The first stage involves a prolonged gestation period and the search for new alternatives.

Secrecy can be maintained during the first stage, since the number of decisionmakers participating in the formation of high-level foreign policy is small. Hitler, Stalin, de Gaulle, Sadat, or Begin are leaders who did not consult a large number of other politicians before making major decisions. It is, of course, important that a similar revision of national interests occur on both sides, but each step in the re-evaluation process need not be synchronised – one side may be further ahead or in a greater hurry. In the Ribbentrop–Molotov case, Germany and the Soviet Union began to recognise the need for a policy change at about the same time; however, Hitler was under pressure to reach an agreement by 1 September 1939, which was the latest date he had set for his attack on Poland. The severe time-limit forced him to make many concessions to the Russians. The latter were not in a hurry, but they could ill-afford to refuse Hitler's offers and the corresponding pressures for speed. In the negotiations between Egypt and Israel, both sides were interested in reaching a settlement, but Sadat was ahead of Begin in his decision and insisted on a faster pace.

During the first stage, both sides frequently use foreign mediators who are not necessarily told the exact meaning of the messages they convey. The Israelis and Egyptians used the good offices of Romania and Morocco. The United States employed the good offices of the French, Romanians, and Pakistanis in order to signal their change in policy to the Chinese. When the preliminary feelers have proven successful, the parties establish direct contact. Symmetrical interests are not necessary, but the existence of a common, viable interest is, of course, essential.

STAGE II

At this juncture, each party must determine to its own satisfaction that the other party is serious in its intentions. Secrecy is crucial, for each side must be able, if necessary, to withdraw without losing face or undermining existing relationships with his other allies should the move fail. During the negotiations between Nazi Germany and the Soviet Union in 1939, most exchanges were oral, and the few documents which did exist were not written on official paper. Care is taken to keep direct contacts behind a veil of secrecy. Kissinger's trip to China through Pakistan was covered by an elaborate deception plan, as was the meeting between Israeli Foreign Minister Dayan and Egyptian Deputy Prime Minister Hassan el Tohamy in Morocco in 1977. Successful preservation of secrecy allows the two sides to build confidence in each other. Should a leak occur, both sides would be quick to deny any contacts, and subsequent renewal of these contacts would be more difficult. In the first and second stages, *some* signals are transmitted publicly.

In addition to the open exchange and emission of signals, secret information may be passed to other states. As more and more people participate in the preparations for discussions and cover-up plans, the chance of a breach of secrecy increases. Participants who object to the new policies may try to inform third parties. Prior to the Ribbentrop–Molotov agreement, Germans who opposed Hitler warned the British intelligence and foreign offices several times that Hitler was making overtures to the Soviet Union. Although preconceptions, excessive noise, and deliberate deception make a clear analysis difficult, alert observers may detect significant changes at this stage.

The intricate process of action and reaction continues until the intentions of each side are clear. At this point, the negotiations are usually accelerated and culminate in the surprise agreement. Nazi Germany and the Soviet Union exchanged signals (stages 1 and 2) for at least half a year before concluding the non-aggression pact. According to some analysts, President Nixon sent signals to the People's Republic of China in his Foreign Affairs article of October 1967, spreading the United States–China exchange of feelers over a period of approximately three years.

After basic decisions have been made at the highest level during the first stage, lower level officials can continue the talks. The negotiations do not always directly concern political issues; sometimes, the two sides begin with the less binding subject of economic and cultural relations. Early German–Soviet contacts were made by low level economic representatives. The preliminary United States– Chinese exchange of signals also concerned economic or cultural matters (such as the pingpong team invitation). Finally, the parties progress to a discussion of the political issues that were only mentioned indirectly in previous talks.

The re-evaluation of earlier fundamental policies continues throughout the first and second stages. These two stages are overlapping phases in which the evaluation of basic interests and policies occurs first, but does not come to an abrupt end as the second stage begins. No one is certain of the final course of action until the last moment, so both sides keep their options open. The continuation of earlier policies while negotiations are in progress, and conflicting trends within the political élite of each state substantially increase the signal-to-noise ratio. The predicament of the political intelligence analyst was summarised by a bewildered British intelligence officer after the failure to anticipate the Ribbentrop–Molotov agreement:

In general, we feel ourselves, when attempting to assess the value of these secret reports, somewhat in the position of the captain of the Forty Thieves when, having put a chalk mark on Ali Baba's door, he found that Morgiana had put similar marks on all other doors in the street and had no indication to show which mark was the true one. In this there were passages in many of our reports which told against the probability of a German–Soviet *rapprochement*. We had no indications that these statements were in general any less reliable than those in a contrary sense.[18]

STAGE III

The new course of action is made public as soon as an understanding is reached. All that remains is to establish the final details of the agreement and to devise strategies and tactics to counter the objections of third parties. Diplomatic surprise is theoretically simpler to forecast, but in practice the record of timely warnings is no better than that of military surprise. Most often, third parties are totally surprised despite the available indicators. It can strike observers 'like a bombshell' (as Churchill described the Ribbentrop – Molotov non-aggression pact). President Nixon's engendered the following reaction from some observers: 'The moment the president completed his surprise announcement, the cameras switched to the studio commentators for a reaction. They were all flabbergasted, and one anchorman was literally speechless as he looked out into the living rooms of America. The country was stunned and so was the world.'[19]

There is still much to learn about the use of surprise in diplomacy. The failure to warn against surprise and prepare countermoves can have serious implications, as historical examples clearly demonstrate. Had the British and French been more alert to the signals indicating a possible Soviet – German agreement in 1939, they could have taken diplomatic or military steps to block or hinder the conclusion of such an agreement. They could have tried to disrupt the conversations between Germany and the Soviet Union by convincing or pressuring the Polish government to consent to the presence of Soviet troops on their soil in the event of a German attack. In addition, they could have outbid the Germans by recognising the Soviet Union's right to an extended sphere of influence along the Baltic, and they might have shown that they were seriously negotiating by sending higher ranking officials to participate in the talks. Strong statements concerning the British and French readiness to come to the aid of the Poles might have been served as a deterrent to the Germans. The Western democracies *did* make such a statement, but only *after* the signing of the Ribbentrop – Molotov agreement.

If fully aware of the contacts between the United States and the

People's Republic of China in 1970–71, the Soviet Union may have tried to 'blow up' a successful *rapprochement* by disclosing the contacts, conducting an intense propanda campaign, or obstructing the contacts by other means.

The Arab oil embargo that was imposed in the wake of the Yom Kippur War in 1973 caught Western Europe and the United States by surprise although, between 1967 and 1973, there were enough signals available to indicate the Arab intention to use the oil weapon as part of their war against Israel. A thoughtful evaluation of these signals might have stimulated the planning of countermeasures (for example, a new policy for storing oil, the earlier development of alternative sources of energy and better political coordination between Western countries), and eased the psychological pressure – that is, the sense of helplessness and frustration.

The United States might not have been so anxious to invite the Soviet Union to the Geneva conference if it had been aware of the Egyptian – Israeli contacts during the autumn of 1977. It might *at least* have prepared contingency plans and avoided being completely surprised by Sadat's trip to Jerusalem.

The revolution in Iran was anticipated by Israeli intelligence. Israel had a greater incentive than the United States to know what was happening in Iran because it was highly dependent on oil from that country; as a result, Israel arranged for alternative oil supplies in time to avert a crisis.

Avoidance of a diplomatic surprise requires not only good intelligence, but also the detailed preparation of contingency plans. There is an urgent need to prepare a set of major case studies on non-military surprise, (cases comparable to Pearl Harbour, Barbarossa, and the Cuban Missile Crisis). In the age of nuclear deterrence, in which the likelihood of a direct military confrontation between the two superpowers has declined, more and more competition and energy will be diverted to political and economic manoeuvring. As recent events have demonstrated, surprises confined to the political level can be very unpleasant, but can also present new opportunities.

NOTES

1. Handel, Michael I., *Perception, Deception and Surprise: The Case of the Yom Kippur War*, Jerusalem; The Leonard Davis Institute at the Hebrew University; Jerusalem Papers on Peace Problems (1976); or an abbreviated version in 'The Yom Kippur War and the Inevitability of Surprise', *International Studies Quarterly*, Vol. 21, No. 3 (September 1977), pp. 461–503; or Betts, Richard K., 'Analysis, War and Decision; Why Intelligence Failures are Inevitable', *World Politics*, Vol. 31, No. 1 (October 1978), pp. 61–89.

2. Technological surprise, especially as it occurs in war, is an area of great potential interest. At present, no theoretical study on technological surprise is published. However, Dr Zeev Bonen, the former head of the Israeli Armament and Development Authority, has made some interesting observations on this subject (*Technological Surprise* mimeo). He suggests that a technological surprise 'out of the blue' is rare if not impossible. 'If the equipment is produced in small quantities, as, for example, in the U-2 case or the A bomb (or Enigma) in World War II, it may be kept secret for a long time' (p. 5). Even in the cases he cites, technological surprise was avoidable. His research points to a dynamic of failure similar to that in military and diplomatic surprise. The weakest link, according to Bonen, is not in the intelligence acquisition or analysis process as much as in the lack of acceptance of intelligence reports by decisionmakers. For example, he examines one of the classical case studies of technological surprise – that of the launching of the first Russian Sputnik – and draws the following conclusions.

> The launching of the Sputnik came as a major surprise and shock to the American public abruptly challenging American supremacy. Was the Sputnik a technological intelligence surprise? Definitely not. The information was given directly and clearly by the Russians themselves on various occasions before the actual launching (October 4, 1957). . . . Obviously there was no intelligence surprise. The information was freely available. It was a problem of acceptance. The Americans did not take the Russian challenge seriously. Their strong belief in American technological supremacy was a very effective filter that discounted and rejected the possibility of being overtaken by the Russians in the satellite race (pp. 8–9).

See also, Krieger, F. J., *Behind the Sputniks* (Washington, DC. Public Affairs Press, 1958); and York, Herbert F., *Race to Oblivion*, (New York, Simon and Schuster 1971), pp. 106–125. Another area of interest in the general study of surprise is that of disasters as surprise. See Turner, Barry A., 'The Organizational and Interorganizational Development of Disasters', *Administrative Science Quarterly* (September 1976), Vol 21, pp. 378–397. See also, Turner, Barry A., 'Research Note: A Comment on the Nature of Information in Channels of Observation', *Cybernetica*, Vol. 20, No. 1 (1977), pp. 39–42.

3.   . . . The CIA was dumbfounded [by Begin's election]. The agency was so sure that the leader of the Likud opposition had no chance of unseating the Labor party, that it hadn't bothered to work out an analysis of the situation which the United States would face if Begin won. Director of the CIA, Stansfield Turner, had to try to explain the omissions to the President. The problem (a commonly recurring one) was that American officials in Israel spoke mainly with the 'ins', who assured one another that what they didn't want to happen could not possibly take place. (Zion, Sidney and Dan, Uri, 'Untold Story of the Mideast Talks', *New York Times Magazine* (January 1979), p. 22; see also *Time Magazine* (15 June 1977).

For Iran see Mansur, Abul Kassim (*nom de plume* of a former State Department official with intimate experience in Iranian affairs), 'The Crisis in Iran: Why the U.S. Ignored a Quarter of a Century of Warning', *Armed Forces Journal* (January 1979), pp. 26–33; and Mansur, Abul Kassim, 'U.S. Must Heed Honest Reporting on Special Allies', *Washington Star* (4 March 1979), p. D1. See also United States Congress Permanent Select Committee on Intelligence, Staff Report, *Iran: Evaluation of U.S. Intelligence Perform-ance Prior to November 1978*, Committee Print (January 1979); also Leaf, Jesse James, 'Iran: A Blind Spot in U.S. Intelligence', *Washington Post* (8 January 1979); and McArthur, George, 'Iran Intelligence Gap Not Unique: Restraints Hamper U.S. Agents Abroad', *Los Angeles Times* (11 March 1979); Morgenthau, Hans J., 'The Limits of Intelligence', *New Leader* (15 January 1979), p. 4.

4. Liska, George, *Beyond Kissinger: Ways of Conservative Statecraft* (Baltimore, The Johns Hopkins University Press, 1975), p. 25.

5. Ibid, pp.25–26.

6. A distinction should be made between diplomatic surprise and a *new diplomatic initiative*. A new diplomatic initiative is a *new* but expected move in a state's foreign policy. It *does not break* with earlier policies – whereas, a diplomatic surprise is not only unexpected but also breaks away from earlier policies. Thus, a new Soviet or American initiative in the SALT talks, or a new United States effort to 'mediate' between Israel and the Arab states is *not* a diplomatic surprise.

7. Quoted from a report to Berlin by the German *chargé d'affaires* in Washington, DC, in which he discusses the impact that Ribbentrop's impending trip to Moscow to sign a non-aggression with Soviet Union would have on the international system. Documents on German Foreign Policy, Series D, Vol. VII (1939), p. 180.

8. For the characteristics of the balance of power system see Gulick, Edward Vose, *Europe's Classical Balance of Power*, (New York. W.W. Norton 1967); Kaplan, Morton A., *System and Process in International Politics* (New York, Wiley and Sons, 1967), part 1; Butterfield, 'The Balance of Power' in Butterfield, Herbert and Wight, Martin (eds.), *Diplomatic Investigations* (Cambridge, Mass.; Harvard University Press, 1968), pp. 132–148, 149–175; Morgenthau, Hans J., *Politics Among Nations*, 5th ed. (New York, Alfred A. Knopf, 1973), pp. 167–224; Haas, Ernst B., 'The Balance of Power – Prescription, Concept, or Propaganda', *World Politics* Vol. 5 (July 1953), pp. 442–477; Hoffman, Stanley, 'Balance of Power', *The Encyclopedia of the Social Sciences* (old) Vol. II, pp. 395–399; Kim, Kyung-Won, *Revolution and International System* (New York, New York University Press, 1970).

9. For the multipolar system, see Aron, Raymond, *Peace and War*, Garden City, NY, Doubleday, 1966), pp. 94–149; and Hoffman, Stanley, *Gulliver's Troubles* (New York, McGraw Hill, 1968), pp. 3–52. (The term multipolar is actually inexact since by definition there can be only two poles.)

10. Taylor, A.J.P., *The Origins of the Second World War* (New York, Atheneum 1968), p. 229.

11. The fact that major diplomatic surprises do occur is, of course, an excellent critique of the theories of *realpolitik* from a psychological point of view. Despite the logic of *realpolitik*, perceptions of decision makers and intelligence analysts continue to interfere with what logic ought to tell them. See, for example, Friedländer, 'Forecasting in International Relations', *Futuribiles* (Geneva, Librarie Droz, 1965); Knorr, Klaus and Morgenstern, Oskar, *Political Conjecture in Military* (Princeton, NJ, Princeton Center of International Studies (November 1968), Policy Memorandum No. 35.

12. For the story of the Israeli – Egyptian early contacts, see Zion, Sidney and Dan, Uri, 'Untold Story of the Mideast Talks', pp. 20–22, 46–53; and *New York Times Magazine* (28 January 1979), pp. 32–38, 42–43; and *Time* (14 August 1978), pp. 17–18. See also, el Sadat, Anwar, *In Search of Identity*

(New York, Harper and Row, 1978), p. 306; Golan, Tamar, 'Meetings in Morocco', *Maariv Weekend Magazine*, pp. 7–9; Porat, Y., 'Dayan's Fingerprints', *Yediot Aharnot* (5 May 1978), p. 3.
13. This analysis is based on a lecture given by the former Israeli Chief of Intelligence, Major-General Shlomo Gazit, 'The Israeli – Arab Conflict After Camp David', mimeo (no date), p. 5. See also Sadat, *In Search of Identity*, pp. 271–313.
14. Nixon, Richard M., *The Memoirs of Richard Nixon* (New York, Crosset and Dunlap, 1978).
15. A common misunderstanding concerning military surprise attacks is that a true surprise has taken place only if the war, or the offensive it has begun, ends in victory. This is a logical fallacy, since there is no connection between the two. The side that initiates a very successful surprise attack may ultimately lose the war (for example the Nazi attack on Russia in 1941, the German offensive in the Ardennes in 1945, the Japanese attack on Pearl Harbour in 1941, and the Arab attack on Israel in 1973). The major decision is whether or not to go to war. Once one side decides to go to war, it is naturally interested in maximising its gains in the opening move and destroying the highest possible portion of the enemy's forces. Whether that side wins or loses in the end does not matter. A surprise attack always strengthens the surprising side and weakens the surprised side. Every side wants to avoid being surprised, for even if it has the strength to recuperate from the initial shock, the price it pays will be higher (in other words had the Japanese attack on Pearl Harbour or the Arab attack on Israel failed, they would have lost the war much sooner). In most (though not all) cases, the attacking side expects to emerge victorious. If the two sides have roughly comparable capabilities, then, when one side launches a surprise attack, it substantially increases the chances of winning. (The Japanese and Arab attacks are unusual in the sense that the attacking sides did not plan on winning – but rather planned on making temporary gains that would improve their political bargaining positions.)
     The same holds true for diplomatic surprise. Sadat may, in the long run, lose his gamble for peace or even his control over Egypt – but that does not mean that his surprise diplomacy failed to *initially* bring Egypt some benefits.
16. It is interesting to speculate whether there is a certain personality type of political leader who is more inclined to use surprise as a political tool against friends and enemies alike, in domestic as well as in foreign policy. Do Stalin, Hitler, Khruschev, de Gaulle, or Sadat have any personality traits in common, or did they operate in a similar political environment or political system? Hitler and Sadat used surprise tactics frequently in both domestic and foreign politics. A highly authoritarian type of leader, who is the only *major* decisionmaker in his country, can more easily resort to the use of surprise. He does not have to consult others, so it is not difficult to maintain secrecy. A democratic type of leader who functions in a democratic political environment will find it more difficult to maintain secrecy and resort to abrupt policy changes. Authoritarian leaders do not necessarily act creatively or on intuition only when they decide to change the course of their policy. They try, however, to reach such decisions without consultation or teamwork. They make swift decisions against little or no opposition, and do not hesitate to get rid of those who may object to their new policies (Stalin's dismissal of Litvinov, or Sadat's firing of two foreign ministers, for instance). The leader in a democratic system usually has to consider public

opinion, interest groups, political allies and opponents, etc. It is not only an authoritarian leader, but also a non-democratic or closed political system that is more conducive to political surprise. It is, as a matter of fact, difficult to separate the two. But authoritarian leaders can rise to power in democratic systems. President de Gaulle was a leader with little tolerance of opposition. He ruled in a non-democratic fashion and imposed his opinion and discipline on his cabinet. He certainly chose the astonishing and unexpected, and did not hesitate to break away from longstanding policies. Surprise can thus be seen as a characteristic of a certain *political style*; hence, it is typical of Hitler and Sadat who have raised it to the level of an intuitive political act.

> Sadat made his decision to come to Jerusalem on his peace initiative as best as is known, completely on his own, a personal decision not based on advisors, aids, or any staff work. No wonder he has also surprised in his decision even those who are the closest to him . . . and so, in a dramatic move, in a 'typical Sadat surprise', he chose the course of making peace (Major-General Gazit, 'The Israeli – Arab Conflict After the Camp David Agreements', mimeo (no date), p. 5.
> See also Heikal's testimony on Sadat's surprise decision to expel the Soviet experts from Egypt in July 1972: Heikal, Mohamed, *The Sphinx and the Commissar* (New York, Harper and Row, 1978), pp. 242–244.

17. Allison, Graham, *Essence of Decision: Explaining the Cuban Missile Crisis* (Boston, Little Brown, 1971).
18. Aster, Sidney, *1939: The Making of the Second World War* (New York, Simon and Schuster 1973), p. 318.
19. Kalb, Marvin and Kalb, Bernard, *Kissinger* (Boston, Little, Brown, 1974), p. 298.

17 Soviet *Bloc* 'Disinformation' and other 'Active Measures'

Ladislav Bittman

THE PASSIVE AND ACTIVE ROLES OF INTELLIGENCE SERVICES

'Disinformation', 'Provocation', and 'Black Propaganda'[1] operations – in journalistic jargon usually called 'dirty tricks' – historically are not new phenomena. The Roman emperors used the weapon of political and/or strategic deception against their adversaries, just as did British or German commanders in the First World War or the Second World War. It was the 'Cold War' which started a new period in the history of disinformation, when the Soviet *bloc*, and also Western countries, established professional institutions for *mass production* of deception ploys against each other.

Mammoth intelligence services are the inevitable byproduct of the division of the world along political, military, economic, and ideological lines. They exert influence on the decision-making processes of government agencies and officials at the highest level. To an increasing extent, intelligence services also are emerging as active co-authors and executors of foreign policy.

Two basic thrusts characterise the activities of intelligence services. The first, categorised as the 'passive' or information-gathering role, has to do efforts aimed at the collection of a wide range of (usually classified) information on an adversary – his strengths, weaknesses, plans, and intentions. The second thrust comprises the 'active' role played by intelligence services. These include special covert operations, called 'active measures' in communist countries; they differ substantially from overt policy or official propaganda.

Even the passive or information-gathering function of an intelligence service includes, of course, an active element – namely the manner in which information is selected and evaluated. Every intelligence service, and a communist intelligence service in particular, is influenced by the political system of the state concerned. In communist countries, the intelligence apparatus is allied ideologically with the most regressive elements of the party and government. The harsh acts of day-to-day repression perpetrated against 'class enemies' at home and abroad, exceed even the limits of the law as defined by the legislative codes of the communist states themselves. This exposes communist intelligence services to the constant risk that the more moderate leaders of their respective countries, for various reasons – sincere or tactical – might take action against the security apparatus, in the form of purges, the criminal prosecution of individuals, or temporary curtailment of their activities. For this reason, that apparatus identifies itself politically with the most regressive and most dogmatic elements in the Party and government, since they appear to offer the best protective umbrella. The politically reactionary atmosphere of the communist security apparatus substantially limits the objectivity of the information it generates. The information passed on to the highest ranking representatives of the party and government is not an objective picture of reality, but an excerpt, concealing a number of distorting elements.

The second major thrust of the work of the intelligence community consists of special operations. Today, these an integral part of the overall foreign-policy effort of the Soviet *bloc*. Until the late 1950s, Soviet *bloc* special operations were designed and conducted by individual territorial, operational departments without a well-orchestrated, long-term strategy. The situation changed in 1959, when the KGB established the so-called 'Department for Active Measures'. In subsequent years, all intelligence services of the client states of the Soviet Union followed the Soviet example. (The Czechoslovak Department for Active Measures was created in February 1964, and for two years the author of this study served as its Deputy Commander.)

OBJECTIVE AND SUBJECTIVE CONDITIONS FOR SPECIAL OPERATIONS

One of the most important *objective* conditions affecting the conduct of special operations is the political situation in the country targeted, namely its weaknesses, mistakes, problems and the shortcomings of its domestic and foreign policies. The vast majority of special operations are parasites that feed upon an adversary's vulnerabilities and seek to inflame any festering malaise that may plague his politics. The successes of anti-American special operations conducted particularly in the developing countries (sometimes even through very primitive means), are related directly to such problems of American foreign policy as failure to understand the internal problems of some of these states, insensitivity to the national pride of foreign partners, and frequent alliances with régimes easily labelled as right-wing because of their demonstratively anti-communist attitudes.

The failure or success of Soviet *bloc* special operations depends also on: The level of sophistication of the target country; the quality of its government bureaucracy, including the counterintelligence and intelligence components; quality of the mass media, and the general level of its population's political and cultural sophistication. While in the 1960s, for example, it was very difficult to lend credibility to a forged document in the United States, this was readily feasible in Africa, Asia, or Latin America. The editors of Western European or American newspapers were suspicious of anonymous letters with enclosed documents, whereas the press of the developing countries was quite willing to use them – if the documents were in tune with their xenophobic views.

The most important *subjective* factor affecting the conduct of special operations is the size and skill of the intelligence services in the Warsaw Pact countries: The quality of the networks of agents; the ability to analyse situations properly; the choice of the most effective scenario or methods and channels of communication; the quality of technical and organisational execution of projects; and the degree of rigidity in the internal bureaucratic structure of the apparatus. The scope and quality of special operations, of course, is affected also by the natural urge for quick and easy success. Consequently, they often become stereotyped, which constitutes the first step toward their exposure.

Do ethical norms and principles influence the conduct of special operations? This question, of course, forms part of the ethical dilemma of all intelligence services. Their activities are amoral in terms of the daily habitual violation of the legal norms of foreign countries, and sometimes even of their own state, not to speak of universally recognised ethical principles.

In this ethical conflict, the pragmatic interests of the operator will always triumph in the end. All intelligence services, if they are to be effective, stage foreign operations which grossly violate the laws of their adversaries. For that matter, the effectiveness of any intelligence service is directly proportional to the degree to which it is prepared to break the laws of its adversary. The complexity and top secret nature of intelligence operations may sometimes cause an intelligence service to violate the laws of its own country. In the case of the communist services, operations have been carried out which even were in direct conflict with the basic tenets of Marxism–Leninism. Thus, eithical problems appear to do nothing to pose an obstacle to mounting special operations.

THEORY AND PRACTICE OF SPECIAL OPERATIONS

The manner in which special operations are developed is reminiscent of the work of a physician who examines his patient carefully, and proceeds then to not cure him but to prolong his illness and hasten his demise.

Special operations are a kind of a game where the players belong to one of the three basic categories: (a) The Operator—author and conductor of an operation; (b) The Adversary—this can be a foreign state as a whole, its ruling authorities, or even individual citizens. From the standpoint of communist intelligence, the United States and the Federal Republic of Germany are most often cast in the adversary role; (c) The Unwitting Agent—a game player who without being aware of his true role, is exploited by the Operator as a means of attacking the Adversary. An Unwitting Agent also can wind up being the target of countermeasures taken by an Adversary, who mistakes him for the real Operator. The role of Unwitting Agent is most often assigned to personalities and agencies in developing countries. The roles of Adversary and Unwitting Agent are not circumscribed necessarily by national frontiers, even though this is most often the case. The role of Adversary and Unwitting Agent can be played also by governmental agencies, institutions, or even individual persons within a given country.

BASIC GAME-PLAN VERSIONS

(1) The Operator strikes at an Adversary indirectly, through an Unwitting Agent. The Operator gears his efforts toward influencing the actions of the Unwitting Agent who voluntarily, though unaware, takes on the role of (indirect) Operator and strikes at the Adversary on his own initiative, even at the risk of becoming the target of countermeasures by the Adversary.

(2) The Operator strikes at the Adversary, who defends himself, but, in view of the lack of clear and concrete evidence to the contrary, mistakes the Unwitting Agent for the real Operator. The Unwitting Agent thus becomes the target of countermeasures taken by the Adversary, takes action to defend himself, and this, in turn, gives rise to the trading of charges and accusations between the Adversary and the Unwitting Agent, rebounding to the advantage of the Operator. The latter can include this eventuality in his basic operational plan, but he can also resort to this tactic on a continguency basis.

(3) The Operator strikes directly at the Adversary, who is unable or unwilling to interpret such an attack as a hostile act; rather, he perceives it as being essentially a consequence of his own shortcomings or regards it as an element of the natural course of events and does not categorise it as an attack *per se*.

(4) The Operator strikes simultaneously both directly at the Adversary and through the Unwitting Agent, assuming that his thrust will trigger another exchange of hostile moves between the Adversary and the Unwitting Agent. In order to use this version of the game-plan, the Operator has to be able to convince both the Adversary and the Unwitting Agent, or at least one of them, that the Unwitting Agent is the (real) Operator *vis-à-vis* the Adversary, and that the Adversary is the (real) Operator *vis-à-vis* the Unwitting Agent.

All these intertwined relationships between the Operator, Adversary, and Unwitting Agent share one common characteristic: The initiative, impetus, or triggering of an attack emanate always from the Operator, who conceals his identity, either by hiding under a cloak of anonymity or by launching his moves indirectly, via the Unwitting Agent or even the Adversary himself.

However, these variations constitute merely ideal situations, in which the real Operator is able to keep his role in the game secret. There are, of course, instances in which the Operator is partially or completely exposed and subjected to countermeasures taken by the government of the target country. This, however, happens rather rarely. Even though an Adversary occasionally may 'break the code' of some operation, usually he does not have enough evidence to identify the Operator or to prove his guilt beyond a shadow of a doubt.

Special operations include the risk that the Operator's own mass media and governmental agencies also may be taken in by disinformation campaigns. This problem is totally disregarded by communist intelligence services (since negative byproducts are more easily subject to control in their case). They pay attention mainly to operational risks posed by the possibility that the identity of an agent and his case officer may be exposed. The rule of 'minimal risks', which is supposed to be observed, has an adverse impact on the quality of special operations. Instead of using 'human' disinformation channels, (in other words, agents) communist intelligence gives priority to 'paper operations', consisting of forged documents sent through the mails which, of course, become stereotyped and, consequently, less effective.

If we take into account the number of intelligence services conducting special operations around the world today, the total sum would form a barely comprehensible hodgepodge of operators, adversaries, and unwitting agents, a kaleidoscope of a game in which these roles are traded back and forth and attacks and counterattacks are intertwined. Consequently, there is the risk that the Operator may fall victim to his own intrigues and attacks. During my fourteen-year intelligence service experience, this happened many times. Today, intelligence services acting as instigators of international games constitute an important factor which not only distrupts the natural flow of information, but also exerts direct influence on political, diplomatic, military, and economic relations between countries.

THE CHARACTER AND QUALITY OF ANTI-AMERICAN OPERATIONS

On 6 February 1978, *Time* magazine published an analytical story comparing the strength and weaknesses of the KGB and the CIA, and evaluating the qualities of the major intelligence services around the world. The ten best included also the Czechoslovak and the Polish services.[2] I agree. But the authors totally underestimated the East German service, which was not mentioned at all, although it is very effective in Western Europe, Latin America, Africa, and in the Arab world.

For some years, the German Democratic Republic has played a role following closely behind the Soviet Union and Cuba in providing not only technical, military and political aid to some African countries, but also 'internal security' assistance and support to black 'liberation movements'. East Germany's broad involvement in Africa apparently began in the early 1970s, at the urging of the Soviet Union. The full extent of the East German commitment has not been disclosed publicly, evidently because the East German leaders have been successful in concealing their paramilitary and intelligence involvement.

In 1978, General Hoffman, Defence Minister of the German Democratic Republic, visited military installations in several African countries and admitted that during his trip he discussed 'further military cooperation' in Tunisia, Algeria, Angola, Guinea, and the Congo. Apart from these countries, East German military and security experts operate also in Ethiopia, Libya, and South Yemen. In 1978, East Germany signed a ten-year cooperation pact with Libya, according to which 450 East German advisors are to be stationed there.[3]

The East German, Czechoslovak, Polish, Hungarian, and Bulgarian services are subordinated formally to their governments, but they are directed mainly by the KGB. Moscow is informed about every operational detail of their activities, including the identities of recruited agents. Russian advisers influence the planning of each operation and assess the results. No important decision is made without them.

Western experts believe that the KGB has five times as many operatives involved in foreign intelligence, as the CIA and the Western European intelligence agencies combined. I believe that this is a realistic assessment. With reference to a 'major European intelligence service' as a source, the abovementioned article in *Time* magazine claims that 24 per cent of the Soviet diplomats accredited to embassies in Western Europe are KGB agents, and about 35 per cent of the 136 diplomats accredited to the Soviet embassy in Washington are believed to be members of the KGB, while others serve as TASS correspondents, trade representatives and Aeroflot employees. The authors of the article do not take into consideration the fact that, in addition to KGB staff members, Soviet intelligence and security services, a network exists of the so-called ideological collaborators among Soviet diplomats and Soviet foreign trade and media employees, bringing the proportion of individuals involved in espionage on United States territory close to the 80 per cent mark.

According to the long-term action plan formulated in Prague, 1964–65, under the guidance of Soviet advisers, the United States is the 'Principal Antagonist', followed by other NATO countries, with the Federal Republic of Germany as another primary target.

In 1965, Czechoslovak intelligence conducted about 115 'active measures' abroad. Considering the fourteen years that have elapsed and the tendency of the Soviet *bloc* apparatus to grow and expand, I assume that the 'annual production' has at least doubled. The range of deception games or 'active measures' is quite broad but, considered individually, their impact is usually not global. The typical disinformation campaign normally has limited impact. Their main value, from the point of view of the perpetrators, lies in their cumulative effect.

The Soviet *bloc* intelligence services distinguish three basic types of 'active measures':

(1) Black Propaganda,
(2) Disinformation, and
(3) Influence Operations.

Black propaganda – actually disinformation designed to deceive the public at large – is the weapon most often used against opponents of the Soviet Union. It takes many forms: rumours, leaked documents (either forged or genuine), campaigns organised in the world press with the help of journalists acting as agents (wittingly or not), books, radio and television programmes; actually, any communication channel can be used to disseminate anti-American messages. A substantial part of 'black propaganda' campaigns are based on forgeries.

Some readers may recall the United States 'Operation Camelot' – a public opinion research project financed by the Pentagon and conducted, during the early 1960s, in Latin America. When the information about this politically sensitive project reached the Latin American press, President Johnson cancelled it. However, it gave Czech disinformation experts an idea how to hurt America's image. Prague manufactured an American questionnaire asking a series of very personal and politically sensitive questions, including the names and political sympathies of intimate friends of the recipient. The pseudo-survey was constructed as part of a campaign to disseminate an image of continuing brutal United States interference in the internal affairs of several Latin American countries. The completed questionnaires were to be sent to American embassies. Recipients were carefully selected for their well-known anti-American bias; of course they were outraged. For several months, the press in Latin American countries (and, subsequently, in the United States itself) lambasted Washington for this alleged survey, completely ignoring the possibility that it could be a Soviet *bloc* provocation.

Anti-American forgeries, a typical product of Soviet *bloc* intelligence, reappear again and again, particularly in developing countries. The House Intelligence Committee, in a 96-page report published in September 1978, revealed that 'forgeries of apparent Soviet origin have been appearing with increasing frequency in 1977'. The report cited as an example a bogus letter purportedly written by Herman Eilts, the United States Ambassador in Cairo, to the American Ambassador in Saudi Arabia. The phony letter had Eilts calling for the overthrow of the Sudanese government. It turned up at the Sudanese Embassy in Beirut.[4] Undoubtedly, it originated in Prague's or Moscow's forgery kitchen.

Disinformation is a well-designed message containing both true and false information, leaked to an opponent to deceive him. Disinformation is intended to dupe the decisionmakers: politicians, intelligence and foreign policy experts, military strategists, or scientists, rather than the public at large.

Egypt's President Nasser, for example, for a long time was a victim of a long-range disinformation game, which significantly affected his foreign policy. Soviet, Czechoslovak and East German intelligence deeply penetrated the Egyptian intelligence service in Cairo, as well as outside Egypt. Many items reaching Nasser actually were pseudofacts, manufactured by disinformation in Moscow or Prague and leaked to the Egyptians: fabrications about American policy toward Egypt, devious American plans to overthrow Nasser's régime—anything that would hurt the American position in Egypt. It was a far-reaching and successful operation, that ended only when Sadat made the decision to break with the Soviet Union and to purge drastically his security agencies. Immediately after Egypt's rift with Moscow, Sadat—himself a German agent during the Second World War against the British—ordered mass arrests of Moscow's followers and sympathisers in the intelligence service. Egypt's secret service has still not recovered completely.

In the spring of 1979, *Time Books*, a subsidiary of the *New York*

Times, published a book, *The Coming Decline of the Chinese Empire*, by Victor Louis, a controversial Soviet journalist known for his association with KGB. It forecast an uprising by China's ethnic minorities against Peking, eventual Soviet military intervention, and subsequent disintegration of the People's Republic of China.

According to Victor Louis, growing nationalism in China would explode in a series of ethnic revolts which 'may start at any moment'. The Turkic peoples of Sinkiang would express their desire to unite with their brothers living in Soviet Central Asia, the inhabitants of Inner Mongolia would look for unification with the Mongolian People's Republic. Hundreds of thousands of Soviet volunteers would 'come to the aid of their brothers in blood and faith', and, while the Soviet government would have to tolerate this outburst of ethnic, proletarian solidarity, the Chinese would retaliate and attack the Soviet Union. The military conflict would end in the collapse of what Louis calls the Chinese Empire.

The Soviet press as a communication channel between the Soviet élite and domestic and foreign audiences is highly centralised, a well-orchestrated machine which does not allow explosive ideas, like the eventuality of a Soviet–Chinese military conflict, to be published without careful evaluation by the security agencies. The book was undoubtedly written by Victor Louis–it shows his typical style and argumentation appealing to Western readers–but there is also no doubt that the topic was designed, and the unorthodox, politically sensitive content was shaped by Soviet disinformation strategists. Harrison Salisbury, who was asked by the American publisher to write an introduction, calls the book a 'political perversity seldom seen . . .', material of 'spurious content, dubious logic, and flagrant untruth'.

Officially a Soviet journalist and a Moscow correspondent for the London *Evening News*, with the lifestyle of a successful American businessman, Victor Louis has been described by Western journalists as 'controversial' so often, that it has become a fixed appendage to his name. Son of a Russian Jew of French origin, he served after The Second World War as a messenger for the New Zealand and Brazilian embassies in Moscow, was accused of spying, arrested, and spent almost a decade in Stalin's concentration camps. He reappeared in Moscow in the late 1950s, offering *avant-garde* paintings and ikons to foreigners. Later he became known as an 'independent' journalist and middleman, trying to sell to Western publishers unauthorised versions of controversial political manuscripts, like the memoirs of Stalin's daughter, Svetlana Alliluyeva, and Khrushchev's memoirs, versions in both cases substantially changed from the original.

Although Victor Louis denies any KGB connection, his frequent trips abroad, luxurious lifestyle, and, above all, the character of his articles published in the Western press, leave little doubt that every step he makes and everything he writes is directed and controlled by Soviet intelligence. To lend more credibility to his message for Western consumption, he avoids the openly propagandistic, doctrinaire tone typical of most Soviet journalism.

Following a trip to Taiwan in 1968, as the first Soviet journalist who had been allowed to visit the island after The Second World War, Louis wrote an article for the London *Evening News,* speaking about growing underground opposition to Peking's authority, with dissident Chinese leaders pleading allegedly for Soviet military intervention and pointing to the eventuality of a military conflict between the Soviet Union and the People's Republic of China. Peking reacted angrily and accused the Russians of 'despicable provocation against the Chinese people', but shortly afterwards agreed to resume negotiations with the Soviet Union. The warning contained in Louis' article was, it appears taken seriously by Peking.

What is the meaning of Louis' latest message? American lay readers of *The Coming Decline of the Chinese Empire* may find his observations and predictions unorthodox and amusing, but the book is not primarily addressed to them. It is designed for Chinese, as well as American decision-makers. For the Chinese, it is intended to be another serious warning that their anti-Sovietism has crossed the limits Moscow is willing to tolerate. It states, to all intents and purposes, that the Soviet leaders are ready to use every available tool and channel to disturb the internal balance and security of China and to provide support to local revolts and to dissent, including the religious separatism of Tibet, if Peking does not change its policy. The message for Washington is not stated in the same manner, but it is clear: do not concern yourselves about growing Soviet military strength, it is not intended to affect your wellbeing–the primary adversary is not America, but communist China.

The third category of communist 'active measures' consists of so-called *Influence operations*–behind the scene manoeuvres, subsuming disinformation and black propaganda as well, with the objective of disrupting the political, military and/or economic system in the target country. This type of operations sometimes involves the use of 'influence agents', individuals occupying important positions in an adversary government. Rather than merely supplying secret information, they are to act, to make far-reaching decisions, in accordance with Soviet instructions.

In March 1975, the Mexican government accused the CIA of instigating the stoning of President Luis Echeverria-Alvarez by a gang of youths at Mexico National University. The Mexican President, who suffered a slight head wound, said, 'Fascist youths manipulated by the CIA' were to blame.[6] Neither the United States nor the Mexican press mentioned the possibility that the incident might have been a Soviet *bloc* provocation intended to widen the gap between Mexico and the United States. In the mid-1960s, for example, Czechoslovak intelligence had close contact with several radical groups in Mexico and orchestrated a series of similar provocations against the United States. The charge that it was a right-wing group sponsored by the CIA, trying to sabotage the reformist efforts of President Echeverria, is clearly in tune with Soviet interests: To create rifts and prevent closer cooperation between Mexico and its northern neighbour. The March 1975 timing, when the CIA was under investigation and thus less likely to be able to convince the media that it had not been involved, is another indication of Soviet *bloc* involvement.

One of the major targets for influence operations is the American army in the German Federal Republic. Soviet *bloc* intelligence uses a variety of techniques to paralyse the readiness and alertness of the American units stationed there. One of the means employed is hard drugs. Representative Glenn English, Chairman of the Congressional Task Force on Drug Abuse, revealed in June 1978, that virtually all of the heroin being used by American military personnel in West Berlin, and more than 65 per cent of the heroin used by American servicemen in West Berlin, and more than 65 per cent of the heroin used by American servicemen in West Germany, came from East Germany.[7] The data were furnished to the Congressional Task Force on Drug Abuse not by the CIA, but by the Drug Enforcement Administration. The fact that the use of hard drugs among American servicemen is increasing represents a serious threat to NATO's defence capability. The East German and Soviet intelligence agencies will undoubtedly continue irritating this unhealed wound as long as possible.

For a long time, neither the Italian nor the American press suspected any link between the Soviet *bloc* and the Red Brigades. After all, the Italian Red Brigades are known not only as opponents of the Italian government, but also of the Italian communist party. It was only in April 1978, after the kidnapping of the former Italian Prime Minister, Aldo Moro, that this hypothesis was discussed publicly. Both the Italian and United States governments opened an investigation into whether a link exists between Italian terrorists and Eastern Europe.

Czechoslovakia became the major suspect. Giangiacomo Feltrinelli, the Italian publisher who founded the Red Brigades, was found dead in 1972 with a false passport bearing 22 Czechoslovak-stamped entries. Several sources indicated that Czechoslovakia had provided assistance to the Red Brigades, including weapons, money, false documents and help in traveling in and out of Western Europe, as well as assistance to other West European terrorist groups, including the Red Army Faction in West Germany (known to the public as the Baader – Meinhof gang).[8]

Although journalists in communist countries are not informed about the real nature of these well-orchestrated 'Black Propaganda' operations, reports about them can also be found from time to time in the Soviet *bloc* press. The problem of the Red Brigades or other West European leftist terrorists, however, is a very sensitive subject, and not only because communist intelligence services are involved. The published reports are sketchy and highly selective, avoiding mention of the techniques and brutality of the methods of the Red Brigades, because Moscow is afraid that in-depth, comprehensive reporting could stimulate individuals in Soviet *bloc* countries to employ the same means against the communist establishment.

Several recent incidents indicate that Soviet *bloc* intelligence is reinstituting its most drastic methods, namely, assassination. In the 1960s, to my knowledge, the Czechoslovak intelligence did not carry out any operation of this kind and I assume that the same can be said about other Soviet *bloc* services. In October 1978 a Bulgarian defector, Georgi Markov, became the victim of an 'umbrella attack', near Waterloo Bridge in London, and died four days later in London hospital. The British authorities at first did not believe the victim's claim shortly before his death that he had been stabbed with a poisoned umbrella. When surgeons in the hospital were asked to investigate the victim's body thoroughly, they found, under his skin, a poison pellet one-fifteenth of an inch in diameter. An identical pellet was discovered in the back of another Bulgarian defector, stabbed with an umbrella when he was entering an escalator in the Paris Metro.[9] He survived for reasons not yet clear.

THE FIRST AMENDMENT ISSUE AND SOVIET *BLOC* DISINFORMATION IN THE UNITED STATES

The current situation in the United States offers many opportunities for Soviet disinformation specialists to become involved and exploit unresolved problems, particularly the dispute between the Executive and the press over First Amendment issues, and the leaking of confidential information and documents to the press.

American democracy is rooted in the constitutionally guaranteed concept of a free press. A reporter has the *right*, even the *obligation*, to seek information from any official of any rank, in order to present the public with an accurate picture. Many journalists stress that, without this guarantee, the press would become no more than the official spokesman of Government. Terence Smith says with good reason that 'When this relationship is perverted by Government officials who suborn newsmen or newsmen who lend themselves to subordination, that system goes awry'.[10] He is also right when he says that 'the tradition of government openness to reporters, even in the intelligence field, is found only in the United States. Even in Britain the contacts between a correspondent and intelligence officials are likely to be much more narrow and constrained than those of their American counterparts.' American journalists are on alert whenever the government takes measures they consider dangerous to the concept of freedom of the press. However, they do not take into consideration the possibility that the American mass media may be penetrated or exploited by *foreign* governments, and Soviet *bloc* intelligence, in particular.

During my assignment as a disinformation expert, the Czechoslovak Department for Active Measures operated on American territory. However, at the time it was rather difficult to orchestrate long-term 'Black Propaganda' operations systematically by misusing American mass media as a communications channel. In the mid-1960s, American newspapers were very cautious when handling controversial information leaked from anonymous sources, particularly documents dealing with sensitive, national security issues.

The implications of the 'Pentagon Papers', leaked to the newspapers, and the growing gap between the Executive and the press that followed, visibly changed the situation. In July 1971, the cover of William F. Buckley's conservative *National Review* surprised readers with a bold headline: 'The Secret Papers They Didn't Publish'. The fourteen-page article quoted memoranda not published in the *New York Times* and the *Washington Post*, but supposedly leaked to *National Review*. The alleged documents, appearing over the signatures of former Secretary of State, Dean Rusk, and Admiral Arthur Radford, one-time Chairman of the Joint Chiefs of Staff, recommended draconian measures against North Vietnam, including a 'demonstration drop of a nuclear device' and 'the use of nuclear bombs where militarily suitable', if Hanoi did not respond to American peace proposals. Newspapers, networks, and wire services gave the supposed documents wide publicity. The *Washington Post* printed the story on the front page, and the Voice of America broadcast it around the world. William Buckley, bombarded by telephone calls, disappeared. When he returned to New York City, he made a surprising statement: the *National Review*'s papers had been 'composed *ex nihilo*' – out of nothing. It was a hoax Buckley used to demonstrate that 'forged documents would be widely accepted as genuine, provided their content was inherently plausible'. He said also that he had acted to demonstrate the ethical vacuum in which 'the *New York Times* has instructed us that it is permissible to traffic in stolen documents', but 'they have not yet instructed us on whether it is permissible to traffic in forged documents'.[11]

Mr Buckley proved his point, but the gap between the executive and the press widened, particularly after the Watergate affair. An increasing number of politically sensitive and even secret foreign policy documents was leaked to the press.

Who leaked them? – apparently, some Senators, Congressmen, their staff members, lawyers, government bureaucrats, army officers, even CIA staff members. Although the government officially condemns leaks, unofficially it uses the technique for its own purposes to promote certain policies, or to damage the reputation of vocal critics. It is hard to blame newsmen for this widespread practice. Many journalists, including those with a distinctively conservative philosophy, consider 'leaking' a positive phenomenon. They call leaks 'the safety valve of democracy', and seem to think that, without them, the country would obtain only official controlled news. In many cases, they may be right. In others, the journalistic scoop seems to be more important than the 'safety valve of democracy'.

In September 1975, a picture of Henry Kissinger reading a document labeled 'TOP SECRET SENSITIVE EXCLUSIVELY EYES ONLY CONTAINS CODEWORD' was published not only in the United States, but also in Italy and the Netherlands. The Italian photographer, Franco Rossi, who covered the European Security Conference in Helsinki for an Italian weekly, took several pictures of Gerald Ford and Henry Kissinger from a balcony. When he developed the film and made the prints, he was surprised. One picture showed Ford passing a note to Kissinger and it was perfectly legible. Twenty minutes later, when Kissinger opened his briefcase and started reading a document, Rossi took another picture. His camera recorded a report on diplomatic relations between Paris and Hanoi, based on information from 'a CIA source with excellent access' in the French Foreign Ministry.[12] The publication of this picture did not exactly help to improve strained French–American relations.

Soviet *bloc* intelligence officers sent to the United States are generally surprised by what they call the political naïveté and credulity of many Americans. From the press or chance contacts, they are able to obtain information for which they would have to pay a high price in a West European country. In Europe, both East and West, the tradition of state secrets is deeply rooted. In America, it means very little. With relatively few exceptions, journals are willing to publish politically sensitive, including secret, documents, regardless, in many instances, of possible negative consequences for the United States *vis-à-vis* the Soviet Union or even *vis-à-vis* our allies. In many instances, the KGB learns more about the 'principal adversary', the United States, from American publications, than from reports of secret agents.

An anecdote circulating among the Soviet *bloc* espionage community illustrates this particular advantage enjoyed by Soviet intelligence: A

Russian officer, stationed in the United States, finishes writing a cable, based on secret information for which he had to pay a few thousand dollars. He is ready to hand the cable to a radio communications operator, when he returns to the desk to add one more sentence, 'For a more comprehensive and reliable report, read today's *New York Times*'. (Of course, depending on the city, one may substitute the name of the appropriate newspaper.)

A series of 1974 and 1976 amendments to the Freedom of Information Act, encouraging maximum disclosure of data dealing with national defence, foreign policy and law-enforcement investigations, opened widely the archives and safes of government agencies, including the Pentagon, the FBI and the CIA. The new anti-secrecy policy of the Freedom of Information Act created new problems, however, reflecting the traditional conflict between the pragmatic realities of running a government and the democratic ideal of free flow of information. Allen Weinstein says that 'today, more than three out of every five FOIA requests are filed not by scholars, crusading congressmen, public interest advocates and enterprising journalists for whom the act was intended', but rather by the business community, imprisoned felons, people under criminal investigation, and – what is even more interesting – by foreign governments. 'Since the FOIA allows anyone in the world to request and possibly receive government files,' Allen Weinstein says, 'the FBI and the CIA regularly process and occasionally ship documents to requests from Communist and third world countries.'[13]

The FOIA offers the communist countries not only the opportunity to receive important information about their major adversary without any operational risk, but also new territory for international games, including disinformation, black propaganda, and influence operations. The fact that anybody – even foreign agents – can request and receive politically sensitive material from government files, for little more than the price of a postage stamp, has made America's allies particularly cautious and hesitant when dealing with United States agencies, including the State Department or the CIA. They are afraid that classified information shared with the United States could be obtained easily by hostile governments or published in the American press. For Soviet deception specialists, it opens the door to another area of international games playing upon this fear, trying to widen the gap between the United States and its allies, and to paralyse American foreign policy efforts and measures.

If someone at this moment had the magic key that would open Soviet *bloc* intelligence safes, and looked into the files of secret agents operating in Western countries, I am sure he would be surprised. A relatively high percentage of agents is to be found in the journalistic profession. A journalist in a libertarian country may constitute a significant asset to an intelligence service. He can be investigative, professionally curious, without raising suspicion. After all, it is his vocation to obtain important, even highly sensitive information. This is true particularly of the United States, with its tradition of an aggressive press, in an adversary posture. A major newspaper, in fact, is a highly effective intelligence-gathering system. Considering the volume and quality of domestic and foreign news collected, evaluated and published every day in a major paper with, perhaps, some 700 staff members, it constitutes a much more efficient and productive service than the KGB or the CIA.

It is impossible to make a realistic assessment of how many and what kind of documents have been leaked to the American press by Soviet *bloc* services in recent years. Mass media would probably object to this kind of research, suspecting either FBI or CIA involvement. I assume that many American secret documents that Soviet *bloc* intelligence has been able to obtain, after a while are 'recycled' back to the United States. The value of any document is limited in time, and when it loses its informational value for Soviet decision-makers, it can be used for black propaganda purposes. The document may be leaked to the American press on the assumption that its publication either would hurt the Administration's public image, widen the gap between the United States and its allies, or damage American interests in some other way.

Is there a solution to this complex and sensitive problem of 'leaking'? It would be a grave mistake to blame only the press for the situation described. The First Amendment guarantee of freedom of the press assigns to the mass media the role of a watchdog. American journalists, of course, are on guard whenever press freedom is threatened or an official attacks the press. In this country, the press plays a more important role than in any other libertarian country. In a system of two major political parties without substantial philosophical differences, only the press constitutes real opposition. To deprive the press of its rights would deprive American democracy of one of its main pillars. What bothers me, however, is the fact that relatively few American journalists are aware of the significant potential for abuse current interpretations of freedom of the press offer to Soviet *bloc* intelligence. These so-called disinformation and black propaganda operations not only injure the United States, they constitute violations of First Amendment rights, they place American journalists in the invidious position of unwitting victims and messengers of the 'Big Lie'. The press should be more cautious when receiving anonymous leaks. Anonymity is a signal indicating that Soviet *bloc* agencies might be involved. Soviet or Czech intelligence would rarely endanger an important agent by instructing him to leak a document and to reveal his identity as a source. Despite the fact that leaking is a common practice here, in one way or another revealing himself as a source could threaten the agent's security.

That is precisely why, in most cases, disinformation documents (whether forgeries or genuine), are leaked to the press by intelligence services through anonymous channels.

NOTES

1. These are the terms employed in the professional jargon of Soviet *bloc* intelligence services.
2. 'KGB: Russia's Old Boychiks', *Time* (6 February 1978), p. 25.
3. Lentz, Ellen, 'East Germany's Role in Africa Debated', *The New York Times* (2 August 1978), p. A7.
4. *The Boston Globe* (18 September 1978).
5. *Time*, (28 May 1979), p. 17.
6. See report, 'Mexico Blames CIA for Stoning', *The New York Times* (18 March 1975).
7. Weinraub, Bernard, 'East Germany Linked to Increase in Use of Heroin by US Troops', *The New York Times* (2 June 1978).
8. Burt, Richard, 'US Studying Possible Connection of the Italian Terrorists to Prague', *The New York Times* (28 April 1978), p. A3.
9. See 'The Spy with the Furled Umbrella', in *The Boston Globe* (8 October 1978).
10. In his article on 'CIA Contacts with Reporters', *New York Times* (25 December 1977).
11. See 'Buckley's Prank', in *Time* (2 August 1971), p. 43.
12. *Time* (8 September 1975).
13. Weinstein, Allen, 'Open Season on Open Government', *The New York Times Magazine* (10 June 1979), p. 74.

Part Seven

Intelligence:
The Economic Factor

18 Intelligence
The Economic Factor

Richard Mancke

The rise of the United States to global pre-eminence, during and immediately following The Second World War, derived less from military or diplomatic genius than from the enormous size, diversity, flexibility, and technical sophistication of the American economy and the ability of the nation to mobilise and project economic power during international crises in order to advance its political and strategic interests. Beginning on a modest scale in the late 1950s and early 1960s, three developments—Japanese and West German basic and mass-consumer goods industries out-competing many of their United States counterparts; growing official and popular scepticism about the doctrine that what was good for the United States business was good for the United States; and the success of the Organisation of Petroleum Exporting Countries (OPEC) in cornering control over the world's crude oil trade—eroded the United States dominant international economic position. In 1979, the United States was no longer dominating the industrialised non-communist countries that belong to the Organisation for Economic Cooperation and Development (OECD) and economic power was shifting steadily and rapidly from the OECD to OPEC.

In view of the causal linkage between America's economic power and its global political–strategic status, three categories of economic intelligence are vital for assessing the ongoing changes in the international power balance: First, acquisition of a factual database about domestic economic conditions and policies in other countries. Second, construction of a database of sufficient quality to support plausible projections of future international economic events and trends. (In the 1970s, the two international economic events having the most deleterious political–strategic consequences for the United States were the need to abandon fixed exchange rates, with the resultant sharp decline of the American dollar, and the rise of OPEC. Neither was anticipated by the United States government's top political–economic strategists.)

Third, the development and utilisation of an analytical framework suitable for evaluating the economic significance of the two types of data.

Events in the 1970s confirm, it is suggested here, that American efforts to acquire and analyse economic information have suffered from two principal shortcomings:

(1) The principal architects of the overall strategy of the United States (for example, the President's National Security Adviser(s), the Director(s) of the CIA, and the Secretaries of Defence and State) have been both poorly versed in economics and preoccupied with the direct threat posed by the Soviet Union, including Nikita Khruschev's fatuous boast that the Soviet economy quickly would overtake and overwhelm that of the United States. Hence, their factual knowledge about (and interest in) economic conditions, policies, and trends, both within and between important non-communist countries, has been sparse. However, with the exception of the Soviet 'great grain robbery', the economic events that have resulted in the diminution of the United States international economic power during the 1970s did not emanate from the communist states, but rather from America's non-communist trading partners.[1] This suggests the importance of broadening the scope of the intelligence community's assignment to include more extensive collection and assessment of economic information from the non-communist countries and to incorporate the results of such analysis in the policymaking process.

(2) United States political–security strategists have demonstrated almost no awareness of the fact that American domestic economic policies have frequently had deleterious international ramifications. In short, there has been an artificial separation of domestic and international problems in the economic sphere. Both shortcomings are illustrated graphically by Washington's misassessments of the problems and opportunities arising from changes in domestic and international markets for petroleum products.

PROHIBITING EXPORTS OF ALASKAN OIL

The peak sustainable output of Alaska's Prudhoe Bay oil field is about 1.6 million barrels per day; known adjacent fields probably could produce an additional 200 to 400 thousand barrels per day. However, even though world oil prices have exploded upward since 1972 and worldwide recession is threatened because of the oil shortages caused by the sharp and sudden cutbacks in Iranian production during 1978–79, Prudhoe Bay was producing only about 1.1 million barrels per day during the spring of 1979. The cause of this anomalous behaviour stems from current legislation requiring that all oil traversing the 2 million barrel per day capacity trans-Alaskan pipeline – connecting Prudhoe Bay to the port of Valdez – must be sold in the United States. However, because of transportation and refinery bottlenecks, in 1979 United States markets could only consume about 1.1 million barrels per day of Alaskan oil, and daily consumption will grow only by about 100 to 200 thousand barrels each subsequent year.[2] The cheapest and quickest way (by several years and hundreds of millions of dollars) to circumvent these bottlenecks so that Prudhoe Bay and environs could begin producing at peak capacity would be by allowing the export of any increase in the output of Alaskan oil above 1979 levels.[3]

Since the early 1970s the principal argument against exporting Alaskan oil has been that such exports would be offset by a corresponding rise in United States oil imports thereby strengthening OPEC and increasing United States vulnerability to, and therefore the likelihood of, future oil embargoes. Shortly before being elected Vice President, Walter Mondale argued this point dramatically in United States Senate debates:

> It seems very strange to me that as we try to do everything we can to deal with the energy problems we have in America that the first significant thing we would do would be approve a pipeline, the purpose of which is to export massive quantities of US oil outside our borders. That is what has been admitted here. The answer is that we will swap US oil for something else. What is that something else? That something else is the very Middle East oil we have trouble getting today. In other words we would be back in the frying pan. It seems to me this is utterly suicidal for this country.[4]

In the context of the 1978–79 worldwide oil shortages, the weakness of the above argument is obvious: if production of Alaskan oil in excess of 1.1 million barrels per day cannot be exported, it will not be produced. Thus, the decision to disallow exports of Alaskan oil simply implies that during 1978–79 world output was at least one-half million barrels per day lower than it otherwise would have been. This is not an inconsequential volume – being roughly 25 per cent of the net reduction in worldwide crude oil output that has occurred since political turmoil began in Iran. A firm commitment that an additional, hitherto unexpected, one-half million barrels per day of crude oil would begin to be sold as soon as practicable (probably by mid-1980 if the decision were made in mid-1979), would help to assuage the panic that was gripping world oil markets in spring/summer 1979. However, as of mid-1979, there was no prospect that such a decision would be made.

MEXICAN OIL: OPPORTUNITIES SQUANDERED[5]

Since the OAPEC oil embargo in 1973–74 there has been one highly favourable event on the international oil scene: the discovery of enormous quantities of crude oil and natural gas – almost certainly at least 100 billion barrels of (relatively easy to produce) recoverable reserves of crude oil and natural gas equivalents – in the south-eastern Mexican states of Chiapas and Tabasco and the adjacent offshore waters of the Gulf of Campeche. Mexico's strategic location, coupled with the very real domestic as well as bilateral political–economic problems raised by the large and growing influx of illegal Mexican aliens, has caused the United States to develop a legitimate self-interest in promoting the political stability of the Mexican government, more amicable bilateral relations, and rapidly rising living standards, especially for poorer Mexicans.

Any improvement in Mexico's economic and political prospects, in all probability, will rebound to the benefit of the United States. The fact that Mexico has petroleum reserves sufficient to allow a large, steady, year-to-year expansion in the production and export of crude oil and natural gas, creates an economic climate conducive to rapidly rising Mexican living standards. These considerations provide sufficient justification for the United States to make a commitment encouraging Mexico to expand its petroleum production. However, from the United States perspective, there are even better (and more selfish) reasons: expanded production of Mexican oil and natural gas would help to reduce United States vulnerability to sudden interruptions in oil supplies and would help the United States to satisfy its basic energy needs more efficiently. After evaluating these benefits and concluding that they are substantial, it becomes all the more puzzling to review the paradoxical way in which United States policies have actually discouraged the expansion of Mexico's petroleum industry.

REDUCING VULNERABILITY TO SUPPLY INTERRUPTIONS

In the years following the OAPEC embargo, the security of United States oil supplies has continued to deteriorate. With the exception of a temporary reversal in 1977–78, attributable to completion of the trans-Alaskan pipeline, United States production of crude oil has continued to fall. Moreover, imports from the relatively secure sources of supply in nearby Canada and Venezuela also have fallen substantially. As a result, the United States depends increasingly on more distant sources of oil, such as Iran, Nigeria, and the Arab states; moreover, sea transport lines have become more vulnerable. The basis for the present oil insecurity of the United States is twofold: First, the interests of the small group of countries in control of the bulk of the world's exportable oil production differ from the interests of the United States on a variety of political and economic issues; second, the United States is becoming more dependent on distant sources of oil at a time when its principal rival, the Soviet Union, is growing in naval strength. Increased imports of Mexican crude oil and natural gas offer a partial remedy to these threats.

The development and sale of Mexico's petroleum will help to reduce Western dependency on Arab oil. While sharing a common interest with other oil exporters in wanting to maintain or raise per barrel oil revenues, Mexico is not an OPEC member and would be unlikely to join any embargo or production cutback that is motivated by Middle Eastern politics. In particular, the Mexicans have no nationalistic, cultural, political, or religious reasons for supporting an Arab campaign against Israel. Moreover, to do so would be unprofitable, since Mexico is currently selling oil to Israel. While Mexico, at some point, may refuse to sell oil to the United States or other countries for political reasons, the motivation for such a refusal is likely to be different from that of OPEC.

Technical characteristics of the new Mexican oilfields require that large quantities of natural gas be produced in association with (that is, as a byproduct of) crude oil. However, the Mexican economy's ability to consume natural gas is limited. Hence, if Mexico's crude oil production is to continue expanding at recent rates, large quantities of essentially costless (in the economic sense of near zero opportunity costs) natural gas will be available for export. Because of the high cost of gas liquefaction, the United States offers Mexico its only commercially feasible natural gas export market, at least throughout the mid-1980s. Any surplus natural gas that cannot be exported must be flared. Therefore, if political complications can be resolved, Mexico has strong financial incentives not only to export natural gas to the United States but to avoid the gas-wasting consequences of an embargo. In sum, the United States should regard the political security of imports of Mexican natural gas as being substantially greater than that associated with imports of OPEC oil.

Another important reason why expanded exports of Mexican petroleum would enhance the energy security of all importers lies in its psychological value. The OPEC countries are well aware that Mexico has huge petroleum reserves, the estimates of which are increasing rapidly as exploration continues. The mere knowledge that what is a growing new petroleum source seems likely to reduce the power of other oil exporters to influence the West with implicit threats of an oil embargo.

Finally, Mexico's geographical location enhances the oil security of the United States in two ways. First, Mexico is distant from the numerous sources of conflict that could disrupt the critical flow of oil from the Middle East and Africa. Second, being adjacent to the United States, the vital sea lanes are short and, in the event of conflict, would be relatively easy to defend.

ECONOMIC BENEFITS

World oil prices will be based on Persian Gulf plus freight pricing as long as the Persian Gulf producers continue in their present role as the residual suppliers for all the major oil-importing nations. Therefore, the United States cannot expect to reduce the prices it pays for imported fuels merely because it substitutes Mexican oil and gas for OPEC oil. Nevertheless, rising imports of Mexican petroleum promise two potentially significant benefits for the United States: (1) A sizeable reduction in total spending for energy, because increased imports of relatively more secure Mexican oil should reduce the need to commence large-scale commercial production of higher cost domestic alternatives, such as synthetic oil or gas made from coal, oil shale, nuclear power, and solar energy, and (2) a sharp reduction in capital demands and, as a corollary, less rigid capital stock requirements.

POLICIES OF THE UNITED STATES

Policies to promote expanded imports of Mexico's crude oil and natural gas would yield substantial benefits to the United States by encouraging Mexico to expand its petroleum production and by reducing United States reliance on oil imports from eastern hemispheric OPEC sources. The fact that the United States offers the only potential large market for Mexico's natural gas exports suggests two reasons why expanded imports of this product would be especially desirable. First, since Mexico would be unable to divert natural gas shipments to other foreign markets, it would be very costly for it to halt sales to the United States. Therefore, politically inspired interruptions in United States supplies of natural gas are especially unlikely. Second, since Mexico's natural gas is produced in association with crude oil, and since Mexico is reluctant to raise its crude oil production as long as the associated natural gas must be flared, one of the most efficacious ways for the United States to encourage Mexico to expand its crude oil production would be to allow the otherwise worthless natural gas to be sold in the United States market. Unfortunately (and paradoxically), as of mid-1979 the United States government had done nothing to promote the rapid expansion of Mexico's petroleum industry. Even worse, the United States was pursuing energy policies that actively discouraged large imports of Mexican natural gas.

In 1977, in order to prevent wasteful flaring of associated natural gas,

Mexico's national oil company, Pemex, prnposed building a giant 840-mile pipeline or *gasoducto* that would link the oil-fields of Chiapa–Tabasco with the northern industrial centre of Monterrey and, by early 1980, would connect with the United States natural gas grid at the Texas border near Reynosa. The 1.2m (4 ft) diameter *gasoducto* would be the largest natural gas pipeline ever laid in the western hemisphere – its designed capacity was 2.7 billion cubic feet per day, equivalent to nearly 400 thousand barrels per day of crude oil, and the estimated cost of delivering gas to the Texas border was only $0.40 per thousand cubic feet. Mexican industries were expected to be able to consume only about one-quarter of this gas. However, Pemex anticipated that any surplus – estimated to be 2 billion cubic feet per day (or about 300 thousand barrels per day of crude oil equivalents)–would be readily marketable within the gas-hungry United States. Assuming daily exports of 2 billion cubic feet at the $2.60 per thousand cubic feet price sought by Pemex, the *gasoducto* would have been paid fully after just one year's operation. Even at the $1.75 per thousand cubic feet proposed for new domestic natural gas in President Carter's 1977 energy plan, the payback period would have been less 20 months.

In August 1977, Pemex signed letters of intent to sell natural gas to six United States interstate pipelines. Under the terms of the letters of intent, Pemex would begin immediately to deliver 50 million cubic feet per day of natural gas from fields located directly across the Texas border. However, upon the *gasoducto's* 1980 completion, Mexico's daily natural gas exports would rise to 2 billion cubic feet. The United States companies agreed to pay $2.60 per thousand cubic feet and there would be further price hikes if heating oil prices were to rise.

The proposed natural gas deal was unacceptable to President Carter. His National Energy Plan called for fixing the price of new domestic natural gas at $1.75 per thousand cubic feet and United States gas transmission companies were paying only $2.16 for natural gas imported from Canada. In addition to an unacceptably high price, the Mexican gas deal had a second major defect. Because the pricing formula linked future prices for Mexican gas to the price of imported fuel oil, the effect of the agreement was indirectly to peg prices for Mexican gas to the price of imported crude oil. Acceptance of this principle would have undercut the Administration's rationale for maintaining price controls of domestic crude oil and natural gas. Faced with these problems, the Carter Administration believed its only recourse was to kill the proposed Mexican gas deal.

Mexico has had a long history of stormy relations with the United States over energy matters. Thus, Mexico's President Portillo had been criticised severely for supporting the *gasoducto*, a scheme the political opposition compared unfavourably to the Panama Canal. Portillo had defended his position by pledging that Mexico would receive a 'fair' price for whatever gas it would be unable to store or consume domestically. Mexico could earn profits if it was to export its natural gas to the United States at any price greater than $0.40 per thousand cubic feet. Nevertheless, in view of President Portillo's public commitments and the two facts that (1) six United States companies had voluntarily agreed to pay at least $2.60 per thousand cubic feet, and (2) late in 1978, the United States appeared to have approved a deal to pay $3.42 per thousand cubic feet for liquefied natural gas from Indonesia, it was politically untenable for Mexico to accept less than $2.60 on its United States sales. In short, the United States decision not to allow imports of Mexican natural gas to the $2.60 price led to a sharp deterioration in United States–Mexican relations. These relations are likely to worsen as long as Mexico is forced to flare ever larger amounts of natural gas because the United States has closed its borders to Mexican imports.

There are no villains in the *gasoducto* story; domestic constraints forced both countries' presidents to adopt positions from which compromise will prove difficult. (In light of the sharp rise in world oil prices since 1978, this statement may be too strong. In mid-1979, natural gas at a price of $2.60 per thousand cubic feet would be a bargain compared to imported crude oil.) However, the issue certainly illustrates one of the flaws in the continued commitment of the United States to natural gas price controls. Crude oil and natural gas are close substitutes, but, because it is much cheaper to transport, crude oil is the more valuable product. Early in 1978, imported crude oil cost about $14 per barrel delivered to Texas refineries. Since 200 m³ (7000 cubic feet) of natural gas has an energy content equivalent to about one barrel of crude oil, Mexico would have been unable to sell its natural gas for more than $2.00 per thousand cubic feet if the United States had not been enforcing domestic price controls. More precisely, the United States gas transmission companies were willing to pay $2.60 for Mexico's natural gas only because of the conjunction of two United States policies: First, price controls on interstate natural gas were holding the average price to less than $1; low interstate prices caused shortages of natural gas. Second, other regulations required gas companies to practice 'rolling-in', that is, higher cost imported natural gas is combined with lower-cost domestic gas; the customer's price is based on the combined product's average costs. As long as the rolled-in price is less than the price for an equivalent ꟾuantity of crude oil, the gas transmission companies find it profitable to import natural gas, even if the price is higher than the price of an equivalent quantity of more valuable crude oil.

If the United States had not been enforcing natural gas price controls during 1977, no gas transmission company would have been willing to pay more for Mexican natural gas than the price for an equivalent amount of imported crude oil delivered to the Texas market. Thus, regardless of the assessment by the two presidents (or anyone else) as to what was the 'fair' price, the maximum price for Mexican natural gas sold in the United States would have been somewhat less than $2 late in 1977. If market forces rather than government policies had been allowed to determine this price, it seems likely that a natural gas deal beneficial to both countries would have been consummated late in 1977, and that presidential disagreements over what constitutes a 'fair' price would not have led to deteriorating bilateral energy relations.

Because of its enormous petroleum potential, Mexico's role on the world oil scene will grow steadily in importance. Rapid development of Mexico's petroleum will decrease the energy vulnerability of the United States. Yet, to date, the United States has done nothing to encourage Mexico's oil industry. Even worse, during 1977–78, high State Department and Department of Energy officials adopted a rather bullying approach towards Mexico. In October 1978 the *Wall Street Journal* provided a lucid criticism of the United States position towards Mexico in an editorial:

> The second huge cost has been the utter derangement of our relationship with Mexico. Because it embarrassed the lobbying effort [for the President's Energy Plan] with $2.60 price, a deal to import huge quantities of Mexican gas was busted by the administration. The Mexicans, understandably resent this, as they must resent the current claims that, oh well, they'll come back and sell it to us anyway . . . . Beyond that, the resentment adds to a growing foreign-relations problem with Mexico. Here we have a nation of 65 million, growing rapidly. It has justifiable grievances against the US on subjects like tomato tariffs and Colorado River water. Illegal immigration is an irritant, building up a huge Mexican minority in the US, much of it in areas where Mexico has irredentist interests. With the wrong change of government, this mixture could evolve into a pressing problem of national security.
>
> The Carter energy proposals were intended to solve the problem of energy supplies, and to protect the national security. It will be ironic, though it seems entirely likely, if their most lasting consequence turns out to have been missing the key chance to cement relations with Mexico, head off a potential security problem and insure easy access to our most readily available supplies of energy.[6]

SHORTAGES OF IRANIAN OIL

Between the summers of 1978 and 1979, Iran's exports of crude oil fell by about 2 million barrels per day. Because of the knife-edge nature of the worldwide oil supply–demand balance, a sustained cutback of this magnitude precipitated huge oil price hikes and, primarily in the United States, physical shortages. However, when the Iranian turmoil was just beginning, United States policymakers had reasoned that, since imports of Iranian oil constituted a far smaller fraction of total United States oil imports than of the total imports of most other major industrial countries (especially Japan), the United States therefore would be relatively unaffected by the Iranian shortfall. Why was this analysis so mistaken? The answer appears to be an inability to apply elementary economic reasoning and the adoption of a misguided policy.

Suppose that, at the time of the Iranian cutbacks, all of the oil traded internationally was purchased under long-term contracts and none of the oil imported into the United States came from Iran. Nevertheless, in the absence of any countervailing policies, the United States would still experience a reduction in oil imports roughly proportionate to that suffered by all other substantial oil importers. This paradoxical outcome (not to economists but to United States policymakers in the fall of 1978) has a simple explanation. Specifically, as soon as any large buyers of Iranian oil had suspicions of a production cutback, they would call oil brokers and attempt to buy some of the oil being sold in other markets, including the United States. Even though this oil was all under long term contract, the higher the price premium offered by Iran's crude-short customers, the more oil would be sold to them either by oil companies who could choose to rely on *force majeur* clauses to abrogate existing contracts or by customers who would choose to reap the profits available to all who resold some of the oil delivered to them under their long-term contracts. The just described process would continue until the net reduction in the total amount of oil traded internationally was shared by each major oil importing country roughly in the same proportion as that country's share of the total world oil trade. The only difference between this example, and the more realistic case where a substantial fraction of the oil traded internationally is not under long-term contract, would be that the equilibrating process may work slightly more rapidly and the price premiums offered by Iran's customers may not need to be quite as high.

Variants of the above explanation have been offered repeatedly by economists in an attempt to explain why United States policymakers were being foolhardy when they asserted repeatedly that, as long as the United States did not consume oil from those regions from which supply interruptions were likely, the United States economy would be insulated from the ill effects of a sudden oil supply interruption. However, in the fall of 1978, even economists would not have predicted that the United States would actually bear a disproportionate share of the cutback in Iran's oil exports. Though unanticipated, this unfortunate outcome has a simple explanation: when world oil prices began rising in the aftermath of the Iranian cutbacks, the Department of Energy warned the oil companies that they might not be allowed to pass through to consumers any higher costs because they paid a premium to acquire imported oil. As a result, the companies cut back their imports into the United States and some of the oil that otherwise would have been burned in United States cars and trucks went, instead, to other countries. The upshot of this misguided policy directive (only reversed late in May, after fuel shortages had paralysed much of California) was that the United States suffered more severe oil shortages than any other major oil-importing country.

CONCLUSION

ECONOMIC DATA AND ANALYSIS

Only elementary economic analysis and a modest knowledge of the relevant economic data were necessary in order to evaluate the three policy failures discussed in this paper. Specifically, most strategists aware of the two facts that in 1978–79 Prudhoe Bay could (and would) have been producing an additional one-half million barrels of oil per day, if this oil were allowed to be exported, and that a 2 million barrel per day cutback in world oil supplies had caused oil's world price to rise roughly $10 per barrel, would conclude that the United States ought to allow this oil to be exported. Similarly, I suspect that the United States might have responded very differently to Mexico, during 1978–79, if policymakers had appreciated the huge size of Mexico's petroleum reserves and the fundamental economic and political problems Mexico's President Portillo faces. Finally, the Iranian example illustrates faulty economic analysis.

NEW APPROACHES TO ECONOMIC INTELLIGENCE

These examples also illustrate a more general point: until senior United States political–strategic policymakers stop deceiving themselves about the nature of the international economic problems and opportunities facing the United States, we will continue to be surprised by a plethora of disasters and squandered opportunities. In short, it is absolutely essential that the scope of the intelligence community's economic assignment be broadened and that there be an end to the artifical separation of domestic and international problems in the economic sphere.

NOTES

1. On 8 July 1972, President Richard Nixon announced the conclusion of a three-year agreement between the United States and the Soviet Union involving the largest grain deal in history between the two countries. The transaction, which ultimately totalled more than $1.1 billion, was fraught with scandal and mismanagement on the part of the United States Department of Agriculture and the major United States grain dealers. The agreement provided for long-term credits to the USSR through the Commodity Credit Corporation to purchase grain from private United States concerns. Subsequent investigations indicated that the six principal grain companies selling wheat to the Soviet Union benefited from advance notice of the deal through individuals within the Agriculture Department, and were able to reap windfall profits, at the expense of farmers and consumers, by purchasing wheat early and placing future orders at significantly lower prices. Moreover, the Soviet Union was able to purchase this grain at bargain prices by taking advantage of: (1) the Agriculture Department's failure to keep abreast of current market conditions, and (2) the payment of unnecessary subsidies to United States exporters. The ultimate insult to United States economic intelligence came in the autumn of 1973 when it was revealed that the Soviet Union in fact was reselling this grain at far higher prices to third party countries such as Italy.
2. Both Prudhoe Bay crude oil and indigenous California crude oil are relatively heavy; that is, they have a high specific gravity. Heavy crudes are not a good feedstock for making gasoline – the petroleum product most in demand on the West Coast. Thus, West Coast refineries find it necessary to mix domestic heavy crudes with imported lighter crudes. For this reason, the West Coast can only consume about 900 thousand barrels per day of Alaskan oil.
   There are no pipelines connecting the West Coast with states east of the Rockies. Thus, the only way to ship Alaskan oil to the rest of the country is on tankers, either through the Panama Canal or around the tip of South America. In addition to high costs, there is a shortage of United States flag tankers which are the only type that can legally deliver oil between two United States ports. Thus, only 300 to 400 thousand barrels per day of Alaskan oil can be transported to the rest of the United States.
3. Additional pumping capacity must be installed before the trans-Alaskan pipeline can begin delivering 1.6 to 2.0 million barrels per day; installation of this capacity would take about one year.
4. United States Senate, Joint Hearings Before the Committees on Interior and Commerce, *Problems in Transporting Alaskan North Slope Oil to Domestic Markets*, 94th Cong., 2nd Sess., Washington, US Government Printing Office (1976), p. 273.
5. For support of the assessments of Mexico's oil potential see Richard Mancke, *Mexican Oil and Natural Gas: Political, Strategic, and Economic Implications* (New York, Praeger, 1979). Much of the discussion in this section is based on material in Chapter 7 of that book.
6. 'Reviewing the Energy Debacle', *Wall Street Journal*, (19 October 1978), p. 22.

Part Eight

Intelligence Management

19 American Strategic Intelligence: Politics, Priorities, and Direction

Richard K. Betts

The American intelligence community has been a political football in recent years. It has been buffeted ideologically: from the left for abuses in covert political action and domestic surveillance, from the right for analytical failures to appreciate the Soviet threat. The community has been guilty on both counts, but not as guilty as many of the critics contend. Intelligence has also been buffeted institutionally, caught between conflicting demands of a Republican Executive and a Democratic Congress in the mid-1970s and shaken by a rapid and confusing sequence of reorganisations and jurisdictional turf fights which are not yet fully resolved. Little wonder, then, that our professional intelligence apparatus is suffering from a profound malaise.

The turmoil of recent years has exposed a number of problems that must be obvious to anyone who reads a newspaper, but the most publicised of these problems are not the most crucial. The spotlight has focused on constitutional issues of secrecy and civil liberties, and personality issues of incompetence or malevolence in top-level leadership. The role of Congress has been most visible in dealing with these controversies, especially the former. The role of the executive branch has been less apparent to interested laymen, in part because the executive has been caught up in dealing with – curing or exacerbating, depending on one's perspective – some of the less prominent but more essential problems in intelligence acquisition and production. The public focus on lurid details of subversion abroad and legal arguments about withholding of information at home has obscured the substantive problems of adapting the Byzantine complexity of the United States intelligence establishment to better ways of functioning in a world of changing challenges. These issues make bad copy for journalists.

Congress today plays a much more active role and has a bigger mandate. But it cannot address all of these problems definitively. It can challenge the administration's priorities, change the direction of certain institutional developments, and constrain emphasis in intelligence programmes through its appropriations power. A broad organisational strategy and detailed plans for improving the collection and evaluation of intelligence, however, can only come from the executive. By the same token, an essay as brief as this cannot discuss these problems comprehensively or even treat selected ones in depth sufficient for thorough understanding. I will survey some of the most salient and enduring issues, many of which boil down to two general problems: priorities and politicisation.

CONTINUING PROBLEMS AND CHANGING ADMINISTRATION

United States intelligence has to do more these days. Changes in the international monetary system and the decline of American economic hegemony, for instance, place a higher premium on information and analysis about the global economy. Emergence of non-military challenges as major issues, however, is an additive problem for intelligence; it does not make the traditional needs of strategic intelligence any less imperative. President Carter spent no less time thinking about the strategic balance than did Eisenhower. But the profusion of issues does complicate the administration of the intelligence community. Organisational units grow, proliferate, widen the span of control for leaders of the bureaucracy, diffuse their attention, and thus increase the policy and control problems that flow from creeping bureaucratisation. This is inevitable. Even *within* the area of military intelligence the substantive burden has grown as new weapons, nuclear and conventional, evolve, and force structures grow in complexity.

As the intelligence bureaucracy has grown, it has prompted several managerial responses. Among these is a cyclical emphasis on centralisation in order to improve coherence, control, and efficiency. This is inhibited both by the norm of maintaining competition between intelligence agencies (to minimise surprise by maximising the range of views presented) and the conflicting interests of national authorities and separate departments. The tension between these goals, in combination with other pressures, pushes each administration into a round of reorganisational tinkering. From the mid-1960s to the mid-1970s, for example, the executive branch commissioned a half-dozen major studies on how to reduce 'unnecessary' duplication of expenditure and activity.[1] President Nixon reorganised the intelligence apparatus after the 1971 Schlesinger Report; Ford reorganised again in 1976,[2] coincident with the Congressional investigations; less than two years later Carter reorganised,[3] after a bruising intrabureaucratic battle over a Presidential Review Memorandum study on intelligence functions and jurisdictions.

Each time offices and titles were renamed, abolished, or created, and coordination procedures were amended. Structure was altered, process was decreed, but it was often difficult to trace – other than from a worm's eye view – the specific changes these moves wrought on functional output: the volume, character, and accuracy of data collected and analyses produced. Nixon's replacement of the Office of National Estimates (ONE) with the group of National Intelligence Officers (NIOs) was a major change, the effects of which left few professionals indifferent. But while all held opinions on whether this made National Intelligence Estimates (NIEs) better or worse, it is difficult for an external observer to discern from conversations or gossip any consensus on how the change made estimates consistently or predictably different in accuracy from what they would have been otherwise. (This is, of course, difficult to measure other than subjectively, and it is even questionable that accuracy is a valid criterion).[4] The Team B critics, for instance, did not argue that estimates on Soviet capabilities and objectives were any more or less *erroneous* under ONE than under the NIOs.

There may also be less to recent reorganisations than meets the eye.[5] For example, Ford and Carter both upgraded the membership of the group charged with making recommendations on covert action and collection, vesting responsibility in units with cabinet-level members (the Operations Advisory Group for Ford, the National Security Council's Special Coordination Committee [SCC] for Carter). Previous units responsible (at various times the 10/2 Panel, Operations Coordination Board, 5412 Committee, Special Group, 303 Committee, and 40 Committee)[6] had often been at the Under-Secretary level. But Ford's and Carter's executive orders continued to recognise the time constraints of top leaders by providing that the cabinet members could send designees to meetings in 'unusual circumstances'. Cabinet-level scrutiny of covert activities is probably higher now less because of this organisational change than because of the bigger substantive change; there are simply far fewer covert activities to scrutinise than in past decades.

Carter also created a consumers' committee in the Policy Review Committee of the NSC. It is structually similar to Kissinger's old NSC Intelligence Committee which was eventually abolished because over-burdened members lacked the time or interest to vitalise it.[7] Carter abolished the President's Foreign Intelligence Advisory Board, but created a functionally similar Intelligence Oversight Board. The most confusing of the latest changes – but potentially the most significant –

were the reorganisation of the CIA's Directorate of Intelligence (DDI) and the Intelligence Community Staff. The new National Foreign Assessment Centre appears to be little more than the old DDI with the NIOs folded in. The principal result of these latter two moves so far has been to obfuscate the traditional distinction between CIA as one agency among several and the collective coordinating function of intelligence community organs – a blurring that was apparently intended.[8] (One friend still working on the NSC staff confessed to being as confused as I am about the new lines dividing CIA and community units.)

So what? The point is that there is a strong inference of '*plus ça change, plus c'est la même chose*'. Administrations are always dissatisfied with how the intelligence community does its job, (never recognising the policymakers' tendency to expect too much from intelligence and to blame intelligence failures for their own mistakes), and always try to find a structural fix. But structural adjustments do not always produce meaningful changes in process. The structural fixes – with some exceptions, especially the original formation of CIA in the late 1940s – rarely do more than shift emphases at the margin. Much more significant are subjective differences in the attitudes and operating styles of successive DCIs. This does not mean that organisational shuffling never matters. Indeed, while it occasionally creates new problems it sometimes yields improvements. Current centralisation measures such as establishment of the Resource Management Staff under a Deputy to the DCI will probably constitute a major change in comparison to previous attempts. Most fundamental problems are never solved, though, because they are inherent in the nature of the intelligence function.[9] And while the intelligence community is afflicted by increasing demands imposed by growing complexity in the range of foreign political and economic problems it must interpret for policymakers, it also faces the same increase in challenges, as well as the traditional problems, in strategic military intelligence.

Two examples reflect the latter point. One is the traditional highest priority of defence intelligence: strategic warning. The trauma of our greatest historic failure in this area – Pearl Harbour – is what determined the formation in 1946–48 of the modern intelligence community as we know it. The failure of this fundamental reform to prevent later surprises, such as in the Korean War, prompted subsequent revisions in executive organisation for the warning function. The latest were the establishment of a Strategic Warning Staff for the Director of Central Intelligence (DCI) several years ago and, even more recently, an NIO for Warning. Rapidly improving modern technology also provides greater support for the most critical aspect of warning: speed in the consultation of warning officers and communication of alert messages up the chain of command. For example, several novel conferencing systems have been instituted: a National Operations and Intelligence Watch Officers Net to facilitate secure voice contacts between operations centres of the CIA, Defence Intelligence Agency (DIA), National Security Agency (NSA), State Department and its Bureau of Intelligence and Research (INR), the Joint Chiefs of Staff's J-3, and White House Situation Room (whereby any two watch officers can issue an 'advisory' on their own authority which is channelled laterally and vertically through executive departments); a National Operations and Intelligence Analysts Net for parallel consultation by analysts in these organisations; and a Conference Text editing system to help analysts prepare alerting memoranda without leaving their own headquarters.[10] The intelligence community did perform well in predicting China's 1979 invasion of Vietnam.[11] But, given China's peculiarly symbolic political goals in the invasion, it is far from certain that they wanted to conceal their intentions before the invasion. In any case, it is also far from certain that communications crucial to warning have been perfected. Periodically in the past crises exposed deficiencies in worldwide communications – in the 1964 Tonkin Gulf crisis, the 1967 Israeli attack on the *Liberty*, the 1968 *Pueblo* seizure – and periodically reviews of the system were undertaken to fix it. But as recently as the *Mayaguez* crisis of 1975 inadequacies still existed, prompting yet another set of recommendations for rectification.[12] The track record does not inspire confidence in any final solution. Moreover, in the worst sort of crisis whatever passive deficiencies there are could be compounded by active enemy interruptions.

The second example is the most recent of high-priority strategic intelligence responsibilities: verification of arms control agreements. When SALT first became a prospect the DCI was very wary of committing the community to fulfil the verification mission by guaranteeing detection of Soviet cheating:

> The problems this posed for the CIA's virginity in policy matters became apparent when the first discussions took place on the proper approach to the impending SALT negotiations. Richard Helms initially refused to have anything to do with verification and was not prepared to sign any document promising an ability to verify an arms control agreement. After being told the President did not want negotiations held up over this, Helms entered into a compromise. This involved a recognition . . . that there could never be 100 per cent certainty in verification. The formula accepted was to make a judgement on the number (n) of a given missile (a) that would have to be involved in a violation . . . before it would be strategically significant. Then a calculation was to be made of the probability that the Russians would deploy (n) $\times$ (a) without being detected. For an

agreement there would have to be a 90 per cent probability of detection . . . . It was also agreed that the CIA should not have to make the final judgement on compliance. It was accepted that this was a policy decision, not merely a 'technical' finding.[13]

SALT verification is a special challenge because the intelligence problem is inseparable from political problems that exist in several dimensions. First, the *degree* of confidence in detection of Soviet compliance that is satisfactory is a domestic political issue that leads the administration to prod the intelligence professionals to promise as much as they can. Second, the degree of verifiability is contingent on policy decisions about what provisions to accept in an agreement – for instance, whether or not missile telemetry encryption should be allowed under SALT II. Third, what is allowed under an agreement may leave enough ambiguity to make it susceptible to different interpretation by both sides, leading to a change in the intelligence rules-of-the-game *after* ratification. For example, 'a unilateral Soviet redefinition of what is a "permissible" type of NTN [National Technical Means of Verification – viz., surveillance and communications monitoring mechanisms], passive and legalistic in nature. could exclude some "means" from whatever nominal protection is afforded by the curiously worded non-interference clauses of SALT'.[14] Fourth, physical capabilities for verification are wrapped up in international political controversies. When the United States arms embargo led Turkey to shut down intelligence bases monitoring Soviet territory, more important bases in Iran took up some of the slack. Now the United States facilities in Iran are lost, and the most geographically appropriate substitutes are politically denied (in Afghanistan by a Soviet client government, in Pakistan by a government whose United States foreign aid has been cut off because of transgressions against American nuclear non proliferation policy). Turkey reopened the bases there in 1978 for one year, but at the time of writing is driving a hard bargain for foreign aid in exchange for extension of the agreement.[15] The Turkish bases cannot compensate for the losses in Iran anyway. It appears that the United States will have to rely on a combination of stopgap measures (such as use of U-2s) for a while until technical development can produce a surveillance mechanism that compensates satisfactorily for the lost bases.[16]

These political problems only compound the actual difficulties of intelligence *per se*. The old imperative that bedevilled the national security bureaucracy in the 1950s – determination of what numbers and which kinds of strategic forces the Soviet Union had – is no longer a problem (though it could become one again if mobile systems are allowed and deployed). The pressing problems in evaluating Soviet strategic forces today and thus the arena of most dispute depend more on qualitative, managerial, subjective, and philosophical issues: missile accuracy and reliability, command and control procedures and options, perceptions or beliefs of Soviet leaders about what options their forces can give them, and operational doctrine and force employment plans. Wide uncertainties about these factors make analysis inseparable from political debate between hawks and doves. This also makes the position of the DCI more delicate by making him more susceptible to charges of bias – no matter what answers the NIEs provide.

Even if collectors and analysts could produce unambiguous proof of unequivocal conclusions, such as detection of a Soviet SALT violation, decisionmakers would still face problems in the entanglement of intelligence and policy. For example, they might be constrained from even *revealing* knowledge of the violation for fear of endangering the security of intelligence assets and techniques. Which need should take priority?[17] Convoluted linkages between intelligence and policy infect most important issues and complicate the basic problem of establishing requirements for collection of information and evaluation and use of that information.

REQUIREMENTS, ASSETS, AND MISSIONS

A recurring complaint among both policymakers and intelligence professionals has been the inadequacy of mechanisms for translating consumers' needs into collection guidance and establishing coherent topical priorities for acquisition and analysis of data. There has been no lack of effort to address the problem. A succession of overlapping committees and planning documents have tried to rationalise the process. In the Ford administration, for instance, the DCI alone had a 'Directive' (a matrix of 120 countries against 83 intelligence topics, with numerical priorities assigned from one to seven for each country), 'Perspectives' (defining 'the major intelligence problems policymakers will face over the next five years'), 'Objectives' (detailing resource management), and 'Key Intelligence Questions' (KIQs, identifying 'topics of particular interest to national policymakers').[18] The departments had their own comparable documents, such as the Pentagon's 'Defence Intelligence Objectives and Priorities'.

The fate of the KIQs illustrates the frustration that seems to accompany many attempts at innovation in setting requirements. They were designed to get all of the intelligence agencies to respond to policymakers' needs rather than just to more parochial operational requirements of the separate departments. DCI William Colby says he intended a KIQ to do what the acronym (pronounced 'kick') sounded like it would do: jolt collectors into responsiveness.[19] But Colby faced the problem of all DCIs since the office was created – insufficient authority to implement his central community-coordinating responsibility. He could not force genuine response from the State and Defence Department agencies. Although NSA made some good efforts, the Church Committee concluded, 'Defense-controlled agencies do not give priority to non-military questions even though such questions are established as priorities in the DCI's guidance'. Colby even had trouble enforcing the guidance on CIA, the agency answerable directly to him.[20]

Even without the barrier of departmental independence, the KIQs were problematic. Almost every topic was embodied in them in some form, and they introduced an additional layer in the apparatus. James Schlesinger called the formalised requirements 'aggregated wish lists'.[21] Moreover, the policymakers who consume intelligence seldom *tried* seriously to define what they need; indeed many had no idea. 'Therefore, intelligence requirements reflect what intelligence managers think the consumers need, and equally important, what they think their organisations can produce.'[22] Some professionals, it should be noted, are not worried by this. John Huizenga, Director of ONE before it was abolished, argued that the requirements process was 'the most over-bureaucratized aspect of intelligence management. . . . The larger the requirements apparatus, the less meaningful collection guidance will be; well-trained collectors mostly know what to collect.'[23] Henry Kissinger also apparently lost no sleep over consumer responsibility. 'I don't know what kind of intelligence I need,' he is reported to have said, 'but I know it when I get it.'

In the past, given the limits to the DCI's authority, intelligence community priorities were the net sum of different agencies' priorities rather than the deductive result of an informational grand strategy. This certainly did not shortchange traditional strategic intelligence. In FY 1975 over half the community's effort in expenditure terms was devoted to military subjects; only 6 per cent was focused on political and economic concerns. Two-thirds of resources were directed toward the Warsaw Pact and NATO. One-fourth was allocated to Asia (mostly to China); 7 per cent to the Arab–Israeli conflict; less than 2 per cent to Latin America; and less than 1 per cent to the entire rest of the world.[24]

Since the congressional investigations the executive branch has made significant efforts to impose real control on priorities. Ford's 1976 executive order extended the DCI's authority over resource allocation and Carter extended it further. The key to implementing such broad authority is in building bureaucratic strength in the community staffs designed to aid the DCI in directing the collection and analysis activities of the various intelligence agencies. The Ford administration did this with large increases in the size of the Intelligence Community Staff under

George Bush. The Carter–Turner régime accelerated this trend, also creating additional deputies to the DCI. The most obvious innovation designed to rationalise requirements was the establishment of a National Intelligence Tasking Centre under one of those deputies. The internal gossip that filters out to external observers, however, suggests that as of this writing the Tasking Centre (or Office, or Staff, as it has been variously billed in public) is still a rather amorphous entity yet to become organised.

Even if the latest ambitious efforts at structural fixes succeed in rationalising the requirements process better than previous attempts, big problems are left unresolved. An old one is that collection outpaces analysis, and critics have accused Turner of aggravating the situation by skimping on the hiring of analysts and spending lavishly on procurement of technical collection assets.[25] For years the volume and quality of raw intelligence grew exponentially, while analytical capabilities grew modestly.[26] Data gluts accumulated and remained unprocessed for long periods of time, and backlogs cause other inefficiences beyond wasted collection.[27]

Related to this phenomenon are the continuing disagreements over the proper relative emphasis on technical collection from sophisticated sensors and reconnaissance capabilities, on one hand, and human intelligence (HUMINT, in professional jargon) or classical espionage, on the other. The former offers the allure of precision, and reliability, the absence of political controversy about employment, and high quality data on strategic military capabilities; the liabilities of technical collection are that it is extremely expensive, not versatile, and cannot yield information on enemy intentions. HUMINT is less expensive (though not cheap), offers the potential for discovering *something* about intentions, but suffers from the facts that it is ideologically controversial and there are often major uncertainties about the reliability of information it provides. As one insider put it, 'Nobody has ever believed a piece of HUMINT, no matter its pedigree, unless he found it compatible with his personal predisposition.' Another major problem is the long time it takes to develop a human network and the short time horizons of leaders. Political authorities often lose interest in HUMINT investments whey they discover that they may not get much from them until ten or twenty years down the road.

The tension between technical collection and HUMINT comes out in other ways, too. One of the reasons behind the intelligence failure to predict the Iranian revolution was that political guidance inhibited human intelligence operations that could have made contact with the opposition movements. The discouragement of such contacts was due to the Shah's suspicions and demands. Keeping the Shah happy, however, was not just a foreign policy interest but an intelligence interest as well. It seemed necessary in order to secure the technical collection bases in Iran, which some worried he would shut down if he suspected American collusion with his domestic enemies.[28] Monitoring of Soviet missile tests appeared clearly at that time to be more important than finding out what 'weak' opposition movements in Iran were doing. In the end, of course, we lost both—the Shah *and* the bases. But before the revolution, both policy and intelligence needs appeared to justify foregoing HUMINT that hindsight shows would have been invaluable.

HUMINT has also been constrained in recent years by the collapse of intelligence security. Since the invention of xeroxing, the Ellsberg case, the Anderson Papers, Philip Agee's publication of names of case officers and agents, the sensational deluge of memoirs by covert operations veterans, and day-to-day revelations of investigative reporting, it has become nearly axiomatic that any information is vulnerable to leakage. This introduces domestic political constraints, with liberals opposing many traditional clandestine operations on principle, promotes responses of greater security that interferes with distribution of intelligence products, and aggravates constraints on collection opportunities. Deputy DCI Frank Carlucci claims publicity has led foreign sources in numerous instances to hold back for fear of exposure, citing even the Freedom of Information Act with its generous exemptions as a threat to the security of their identities and roles.[29]

Of course, information security has always been a problem, which led to the elaborate system of 'compartmentation' that restricted dissemination of highly classified data to those with 'need to know'. While enhancing secrecy, however, compartmentation ramifies harmfully in the analytical functions of the intelligence community. The Cunningham Report of 1966 noted the adverse effects on 'cross-discipline cooperation';[30] the Church Committee discovered that CIA analysts were kept ignorant of certain American strategic R & D programmes, which detracted from their ability 'to assess completely the reasons for countermeasures that were being taken in the development of Soviet strategic forces';[31] the permanent Senate intelligence committee's staff blamed compartmentation indirectly in the community's failure to predict the 1973–74 oil embargo and price rise, because analysts were unable to verify the credibility of clandestine sources for information from CIA's Directorate of Operations (DDO) and relied instead on embassy reporting.[32] Finally, compartmentation hinders high level rationalisation of requirements. DDO resisted formation of a Human Resources Committee on the old United States Intelligence Board, for fear that secrecy of sensitive operations would be compromised.[33]

William Colby tried to reduce the insularity of the clandestine service and encourage more interaction with other parts of CIA,[34] but it is uncertain how far such cross-fertilisation can go. Colby was fired by

Ford and reviled by some intelligence professionals in part for encouraging too much openness. Public pressure for reduction of secrecy has abated, indeed the drift is back toward more effective restraints on information and the executive branch is searching harder for ways to guarantee information security than ways to loosen the lid.[35] The internal tension between security that protects collection sources and dissemination that improves finished analyses will probably continue.

However many technical collection mechanisms there are producing more data than can be digested, there is still some competition for control of large shares of assets, particularly satellites. The most enduring competition is the 'national' versus 'tactical' split. (This is no titanic struggle, but budgetary considerations do promote sharing of assets and hence some uneasiness over control authority.) National intelligence refers to information needed by high authorities (such as the DCI and Secretaries of State and Defence) to help them make policy decisions; tactical intelligence is data required by commanders for planning and execution of operational missions. Some technical collection systems are applicable to either purpose. The Strategic Air Command, for instance, can justify a wide range of demands for control over certain systems by claiming they are necessary for implementation of limited nuclear options, which require high levels of capability for damage assessment and survivable command communications. National needs are generally associated with peacetime, and tactical ones with wartime. But this distinction is not easy to operationalise. The Secretary of Defence theoretically is supposed to take authority over technical collection systems from the DCI in wartime, but how would the transition be accomplished rapidly and efficiently in the confusion that would attend the outbreak of conflict?

This brings us to another grey area between operations and intelligence, and one that has become a central defence programme issue in this administration:'C^3/I', or Command, Control, Communications, and Intelligence. The growing recognition of the linkage of these functions in defence strategy has been forced by recognition of Soviet capacity to attack United States and NATO communication systems as well as by the American shift away from the nuclear retaliatory targeting concept of mutual assured destruction. A conventional conflict in Europe, where electronic warfare would be a major impediment to coordination of large forces, or unspasmodic nuclear combat that unfolds over a period of days rather than hours, would place a premium on preservation of working systems for quick information gathering, processing, and transmission. For a limited nuclear war, intelligence becomes integral to command rather than just a primarily prewar function.

Wartime survivability of information systems and command channels has long been a weak spot in American strategic posture, and the Carter Administration has made improvements a top defence priority. In 1977 the offices of Intelligence and C^3 and Telecommunications were merged and other related elements were reorganised in the Office of the Secretary of Defence (OSD).[36] In development of actual system capabilities much remains to be done. Halfway through the Carter adminstration Secretary of Defence Harold Brown reported that 'current systems which support rapid situation assessment and control in crisis are deficient'.[37] A large number of programmes are in progress to expand and upgrade system capabilities and management. In fact, the FY 1980 defence budget allocates over \$9 billion for C^3/I (which compares with less than \$11 billion for strategic forces) out of a total Budget Authority of \$135 billion.[38]

Consolidation of C^3 and intelligence functions does not obviate the national/tactical tension. Some of the professional military worry that the centralising reorganisations may turn commanders into 'figure-heads, unable to make decisions and left with little or no real-time information with which to make those decisions even if allowed to'.[39] Plans were reportedly afoot to have all intelligence funnelled directly to headquarters where it would then be analysed and transmitted to commanders as headquarters saw fit. Reductions in funding for Navy over-the-horizon targeting programmes were criticised on the grounds that 'the fleet commander is now faced with possessing an over-the-horizon arsenal of weapons and no logical way of using it'.[40] Timely alert of national authorities and coordination of data for policy decisions, however, is also critical, so the national/tactical competition (though much milder than this discussion suggests) is likely to continue. Another example of the entanglement and tradeoffs between intelligence capabilities and operational requirements – and arms control nego-tiations as well – is the area of antisatellite warfare innovations. Tacti-cal warning and attack assessment depend on the invulnerability of surveillance systems. Controversial aspects of strategic weapons com-petition and SALT are, thus, like verification, tied closely to intelligence-gathering innovations.

POLITICISATION OF ESTIMATES: SUBTLE, INNOCENT, AND UNAVOIDABLE

One of the longest-standing articles of faith among many theorists of intelligence is that analysis must be segregated from policymaking. Otherwise, analysts' independence will be compromised and their conclusions will begin to pander to what leaders want to hear. Others have argued against these principles because they are an unrealistic application of 'pure science' norms to areas where fact and value are inseparable and judgment must preside, and they risk encouraging misdirected production priorities, not providing the topical *kinds* of analyses that consumers need, offering good but irrelevant estimates. Whatever the merits of the ideal of separation between intelligence and policy perspectives, it is very difficult to institutionalise thoroughly. Policy can be prevented from corrupting analysis directly, but indirect and even unrecognised impacts are unavoidable – and some are necessary. When unfortunate influences of policy preferences on collection or evaluation are prevented in intelligence production they may still come to the fore in consumption.

Iran is the most obvious recent case in point, in terms of both information gathering and interpretation. Largely because of the political inhibitions mentioned before, CIA issued *no* reports based on sources in the religious opposition in the two years before November 1977.[41] Even if this gap had been plugged, however, consumers might not have been receptive. One analyst complained, 'until recently you couldn't *give* away intelligence on Iran'. As the House Intelligence Committee staff concluded, 'Policymakers were not asking *whether* the Shah's autocracy would survive indefinitely; policy was premised on that assumption'. Interest focused more on intelligence about the Shah's government itself.[42] The principal CIA analyst on Iran before 1973 claims that he wrote reports predicting the dissidence the Shah's policies were producing, but the reports were suppressed because they contradicted policy.[43] And despite the shock of Iran, it is possible that political imperatives could produce similar fiascos elsewhere.[44]

Politicisation of analysis is usually thought of as crude corruption, officials consciously bending conclusions to suit policy. This rarely occurs. Less obvious, but quite important for understanding the role of intelligence, are the ways in which policy and estimates are *intrinsically* linked. It is well recognised that policy draws on estimates (after all, that is what intelligence is for), but less appreciated are the ways in which accurate estimates must draw on policy. Projections of foreign military capabilities years into the future cannot be independent of American strategic initiatives. Simple action–reaction models of the arms race have been persuasively debunked, but there *is some* interdependence of policy adaptations between adversaries.[45] To the extent that leaders alter defence posture in response to estimates of future Soviet programmes, procurements, or deployments, the American changes will have some effect – not necessarily a mechanistic matching of weapon-for-weapon or countermeasure-for-measure – on Soviet strategy. Similarly, good estimates of a future Soviet energy crisis cannot be based simply on a straightline projection from current trends in oil production and consumption, but must take account of what Soviet policy might do to address the implications of such a projection.[46] The latter example is an awesomely difficult challenge, but at least it is one that astute intelligence professionals can address within the current bureaucratic rules-of-the-game, by spinning out alternative 'if . . . then' propositions. The former example, however, presents more difficulties, because intelligence agencies have usually been directed *not* to assess American policies or capabilities. This prohibition was designed to minimise the politicisation of estimates, keeping them from embroilment in the controversy of policy debates.[47] In this case, the norm of protecting the political purity of analysis constrains either the accuracy or salience of the analysis.

All is not lost, of course, because other agencies of the government, outside the intelligence community, can make these judgements. That is the purpose of 'net assessment' exercises – comparing and evaluating the capabilities and policies of the United States *vis-à-vis* the Soviet Union – and interagency studies combining intelligence and policy contributions. The latter have been known recently as PRMs (Presidential Review Memoranda), and before that as NSSMs (National Security Study Memoranda). The former function has been performed in various ways and places over time. Under Eisenhower net assessments were done by a Pentagon group reporting to a secret NSC subcommittee; for Kennedy and Johnson they were done primarily in the Systems Analysis Office of OSD; in the Nixon Administration there was a net assessment unit on the NSC staff under Andrew Marshall, who moved to OSD James Schlesinger and remains in the same position under Harold Brown. During 1971 Nixon, Kissinger, and Melvin Laird encouraged the proliferation of net assessment staffs in different agencies or offices (such as the Defence Directorate of Research and Engineering.)[48]

Net assessment remained nearly taboo for professional intelligence estimators. When questioned by the Senate Intelligence Committee at his confirmation hearings DCI Stansfield Turner affirmed his opposition, in the interest of avoiding 'an intrusion into the defence planning process'.[49] This division of labour may be quite proper. Indeed, CIA has been berated for underestimating simple and static numbers of Soviet missile deployments. In the current climate of statistical warfare in the SALT II debate, with partisans on both sides brandishing charts and graphs and using complex dynamic analyses of United States–Soviet strategic force interactions as empirical 'proof' for preferred strategies, an intelligence agency would not escape outraged attack if it tried to present a comprehensive net estimate in this area. But to the extent that 'intelligence' means the data and analysis required to alert and inform policymakers, it is important to realise that important forms of this intelligence are self-generated, and cannot be expected from intelligence professionals.[50]

Crude politicisation of estimating is certainly undesirable. It can only discredit the estimators. Although it may get them more attention – something they need and policymakers would do well to give them more often – it would come to identify them with factions, and their evaluations of data would command no more respect than the views of any combatant in the policy arena.[51] This can happen involuntarily, when decisionmakers parade intelligence analyses to buttress policy as occurred to some extent in 1978 when the Carter administration defended its allegations of Cuban involvement in the second Shaba – Zaire crisis. The evidence turned out to be circumstantial – satisfactory for supporters, who did not need convincing, and insufficient for sceptics.[52] *Most* intelligence is circumstantial, but ambiguity does not play as well before TV cameras as within the analytical world. Unfortunately, this sort of politicisation seemed to occur on the issue of SALT verification. Being honest in saying verification capabilities were less than perfect, DCI Turner got himself into hot water with some policymakers.[53]

A complete quarantine of intelligence from contamination by policy, on the other hand, is impractical; if accomplised, its effects could also be undesirable. To begin with, government decisionmaking is never perfectly coherent, deliberative, rational, and free from subjective or illogical inclinations. And the safest way to ensure that no one criticises estimates for being politicised is to make them so cautious, so sterile, and so thoroughly hedged – a grey-coloured mush – that they are un-informative. In being politically neutral in this extreme sense they become politically permissive, giving policymakers an excuse for whatever they want to do for normative reasons because they are not constrained by empirical disconfirmation of their premises. At the beginning of the Carter administration Harold Brown found it easy to justify a $2.8 billion reduction in the FY 1978 defence budget by citing his own 'judgement' of Soviet capabilities, which he justified in turn by the 'substantial spread' in intelligence estimates.[54]

One way to avoid mush is to encourage numerous and contrasting sharp, argumentative estimates, and let the most persuasive one prove itself in the market of ideas and advice. This is the norm of 'fostering competition', which everyone in recent years seems to approve. A perfect intellectual market within the government, however, depends on the time consumers can spend on scrutiny, comparison, and reflection (not to mention which side in the debate has lined up the best lawyer). This time varies inversely with the level of authority and responsibility.[55]

The coordination and clearance process – whereby each department ensures that an NIE reflects its view – should therefore encourage the explicit incorporation of dissents (this used to be done in footnotes, but is now in italics within the text) more than other usual means of accommodating divergent views: negotiation of controversial statements down to an unobjectionable and mushy lowest common denominator. All these considerations highlight another tension and tradeoff in intelligence evaluation. Intelligence analyses that have the most impact on decisionmakers must take risks with their own credibility. Impact comes from jolting originality, willingness to go out on a limb and not rub the sharp edges off an appraisal, but such tendentiousness necessarily short-changes other possible explanations and increases the danger of being demonstrably wrong and thus failing in the most obvious imaginable way to inform policy. Intelligence analyses that run the fewest risks of being wrong, on the other hand, are those that may turn out to be least useful to high officials. Multiple clearance and consensual softening tends to make analysis bloodless, failing to inform policy with creative insight. Both risks and payoffs are high in the former approach and low in the latter. An example of the negative aspect of the logic of the latter was one analyst's complaint that CIA is 'a typical bureaucracy, and the interest is in not being wrong more than in being right'.[56]

IMPROVING INTELLIGENCE: WHAT CAN BE DONE?

Most of the dilemmas of executive strategy for organising and utilising strategic data and analysis are only malleable, not soluble. The traditional highest priority need – assets for strategic and tactical military warning – is probably being fulfilled about as well as it can be. Strategic surprise can still happen, but it is less likely to happen for lack of early warning than for lack of proper appreciation of such warning or response to it. Intelligence capabilities for wartime, *beyond* warning – and thus intelligence capabilities relevant to enhancing deterrence as well – are more problematic, as the Carter–Brown–Turner régime's C^3/I programme emphasis suggests. The solution here is to follow through with innovations already planned, but the solution is only partial since the national/tactical competition affects the issue. Warning and wartime C^3/I may be the highest priorities but they are not the only priorities and the probability is that the threat requiring their implementation is so remote in comparison with needs for national intelligence that the answer for the warning mission cannot be simply to focus all effort on tactical requirements.

SALT verification may the most pressing substantive challenge for the community, but in terms of process the biggest current need for clarification of intelligence policy is to strike a better balance between emphasis on collection and on analysis, and to enhance analytical capabilities by rebuilding morale and stabilising organisation. Given the miniscule proportion of the intelligence budget that was being spent on analysis in the 1970s, a shift in expenditures of even a fraction of 1 per cent would expand the resources of evaluative units substantially while degrading collection capabilities infinitesimally. A marginal realignment of priorities of this sort would require Congressional cooperation, through authorisations and appropriations, but this presents no likely barrier. The House Intelligence Committee's 1978 annual report remarked: 'The attention of the intelligence community appears to be directed primarily to increasing collection, while other fundamental problems go relatively unattended. These include analytical problems which cannot be attributed to lack of data'.[57] It is the executive branch that has to decide how much collection compared to analysis it wants. (Given the constitutional competition between the two branches, Congress may be reluctant to fully endorse organisational centralising initiatives by the executive. In the authorisations for FY 1979 the Senate Intelligence Committee cut the executive's budget request for the Intelligence Community Staff by well over 10 per cent.)[58]

More money for analysis, however, is not the essence of the current problem. Much of the intelligence community, especially CIA, is in modest disarray due to organisational and personnel turbulence and weak morale. Outsiders are most aware of this problem in the clandestine service because of publicity about Turner's mass firings in DDO. This process began much earlier. Few realise that James Schlesinger fired more people than Turner. The clandestine service, judging from press reports, is now about half the size of what it was – 8500 – at the peak of operations in South-east Asia in 1969 (when there were almost 1900 covert operations personnel in Vietnam and Laos alone).[59] Turner, nevertheless, precipitated the most internal resentment, due to his administrative abrasions and problems beyond DDO. There is less *élan* in the CIA, to say the least, than there used to be.

Reasons for this are numerous, complex, hard for an outsider to trace thoroughly, and some may be normal disappointments that loom larger as other compensating advantages recede. One minor example that could probably be fixed without awesome difficulty is the dampener government publication norms put on analysts' incentives. Analytical papers are often published without the author's name on them. Any academic knows how his incentives to produce high quality work would be affected over time if most of his articles were published anonymously. (The obverse problem is one that flows from the ponderous coordination and clearance process. Often an anlyst will find the final paper so altered from his original intent that he will not *want* his name on it.) The CIA analyst's superiors know what he has done, and quality may be reflected in salary raises, but he must still forego much of the professional recognition that academics value. This is compounded by classification, although public dissemination of certain analyses has been encouraged in recent years. The latter trend should also be continued if the DCI wants estimates to be influential. The best way to guarantee that a policymaker will take a report seriously is to have a story about it published in the *New York Times*.

It is difficult to perfect specific incentives for collectors or evaluators while at the same time establishing broad administrative norms to control a vast bureaucracy. For the latter, general standards and rules-of-thumb have to be devised which can prove to be counterproductive in some of their particular ramifications. One officer caught in Turner's reduction in force complained, 'the problem with the system . . . is that we have a quantitative approach to collection. Rather than rate people on the value of the product they provide or the information they collect it's . . . how many intelligence reports a guy can write.' He claimed this created incentives to waste time interviewing people who have no real useful information, just to be able to file a report, and that incentives to meet a quota even prompted case officers to dress up an unproductive interview to the point of near fabrication.[60] Development of non-quantitative norms that can be used as practical management evaluation tools, though, is difficult.

The most sensational aspect of recent controversy about intelligence management has been the focus of criticism – from outside as well as within the community – on Admiral Turner. It is hard for an observer to be sure how much of the criticism was genuinely directed at Turner's individual faults and how much was resentment that would be directed at *any* DCI who came to office at the time he did. Moreover, although Turner has been criticised for excessive 'interference', 'politicisation', and other sins of activism, the intelligence community needs an aggressive DCI if it is to grapple with the raft of problems it faces. And while replacing Turner might strike some critics as an improvement, it would aggravate the chronic instability of top leadership that has plauged the community. There have been five different Directors in the past six years, a turnover rate that would disrupt even a small organisation.

Buffeted as the institutional framework for intelligence collection and evaluation has been, the community has still continued to perform reasonably well on many issues. Even if it limps through the current malaise and confusions and disputes sort themselves out gradually rather than rapidly and decisively, it may do its job adequately. The strategic intelligence challenges we face, however, demand high quality rather than just satisfactory results. The need to assess Soviet beliefs, perceptions, and doctrines concerning nuclear war is an example of one of the most critical of those challenges, since those issues are becoming the crux of the United States strategic debate. They may have been less important earlier in a world of decisive American strategic superiority – intelligence 'mistakes' that complicated a crisis might have been compensated for by the United States capability to intimidate Soviet leaders when the chips were down. Now, in an era of parity or, as some believe, emerging Soviet superiority, there is less margin for error. This area of intelligence needs as much dispassionate and disinterested analysis as possible because of the gravity of the problem, but the gravity of the problem makes it nearly impossible to prevent the entanglement of policy and estimates – the politicisation bogey. It is nearly impossible to write any analysis (that is sharper and more useful than grey mush) on a controversial subject without appearing partial. There again is the nagging dilemma underlying so much of any executive strategy for improving intelligence.

NOTES

1. US Congress, Senate, Select Committee to Study Governmental Operations With Respect to Intelligence Activities, *Final Report, Foreign and Military Intelligence* (hereafter cited as Church Committee Report), Book I, 94th Cong., 2nd Sess. (1976), p. 341.
2. Executive Order, 'United States Foreign Intelligence Activities' (18 February 1976).
3. Executive Order, 'United States Intelligence Activities' (24 January 1978).
4. See Chan, Steve, 'The Intelligence of Stupidity: Understanding Failures in Strategic Warning', *American Political Science Review* LXXIII, no. 1 (March 1979), p. 173.
5. For a general survey of administration intelligence initiatives in Carter's first year see Bonafede, Dom, 'The CIA Under Turner–The Pleasure of His Company', *National Journal*, XI, no. 51 (17 December 1977).
6. See Church Committee Report, Book I, pp. 48–53, and Book IV, pp. 51, 70–71.
7. 'The NSIC was established in late 1971, and had one 30 minute meeting a month later. Over two and a half years elapsed before the next meeting, which lasted for a little over an hour.' Macy, Robert M., 'Issues on Intelligence Resource Management', in United States Commission on the Organization of the Government for the Conduct of Foreign Policy (cited hereafter as Murphy Commission), *Appendices* (Washington, DC; Government Printing Office, June 1975), vol. 7, p. 53.
8. See 'National Foreign Assessment Center', Attachment to Memorandum for All NFAC Employees from Director Robert Bowie and Deputy Director Sayre Stevens (11 October 1977) (unclassified), pp. 1–2. In a way, this is a return to the original rationale of the 1940s that CIA *would* be a genuinely *central* agency for national intelligence, a concept that quickly

eroded as departmental intelligence units reasserted their autonomy.

9. See Betts, Richard K., 'Analysis, War, and Decision: Why Intelligence Failures are Inevitable', *World Politics* XXXI, no. 1 (October 1978), pp. 67–73, 85–87.

10. Belden, Thomas G., 'Indications, Warning, and Crisis Operations', *International Studies Quarterly* XXI, no. 1 (March 1977), pp. 192–193.

11. Aspin, Les, 'Intelligence Performance on the China–Vietnam Border', press release (26 March 1979).

12. See Report of the Comptroller General, 'System to Warn US Mariners of Potential Political/Military Hazards: SS *Mayaguez*, A Case Study', in US Congress, House, Committee on International Relations, Reports, Seizure of the *Mayaguez* Part IV, 94th Cong., 2nd Sess. (1976), pp. 1–57.

13. Freedman, Lawrence, *US Intelligence and the Soviet Strategic Threat* (Boulder, Westview Press 1977), p. 46.

14. Perry, Robert, 'Verifying SALT in the 1980s', in Christoph, Bertram (ed.), *The Future of Arms Control: Part I: Beyond SALT II*, Adelphi Paper No. 141 (London, international Institute of Strategic Studies, Spring 1978), p. 18. There is precedent for differences in Soviet intepretation of SALT I treaty constraints in the dispute over definition of 'new' heavy missiles. For an optimistic view of prospects see Aspin, Les 'The Verification of the SALT II Agreement', *Scientific American* (February 1979).

15. Meyer, Cord, 'The U.S. Stake in Turkish Bases', *Washington Star* (31 March 1979), p. 11; Bradsher, Henry, 'Monitoring Sites in Turkey Feared Run Down', *Washington Star* (7 April 1979), p. 5; Lawton, John, 'Turkey Demands More US Aid for Use of Bases', *Washington Post* (9 May 1979), p. Al.

16. Burt, Richard, 'U.S. Plans New Arms Monitoring', *New York Times* (31 March 1979), p. 5; Burt, 'U.S. May Use Modified U-2 Plane to Monitor Soviet Missile Testing', *New York Times* (4 April 1979), pp. Al, A13.

17. See Perry, Robert, 'Verifying SALT in the 1980s', p. 17n. Similarly agonising tradeoffs are suggested in reports about Winston Churchill's decisions in the Second World War. One observer claims Churchill allowed Conventry to be bombed in order to avoid revealing the British 'Ultra' secret, the ability to decode German communications; others deny this. In another instance, Churchill agonised but decided to risk 'Ultra' and authorised attack on an Axis convoy during the North African campaign. See Axelrod, Robert, 'The Rational Timing of Surprise', *World Politics* XXXI, no. 2 (January 1979), pp. 230–1.

18. Church Committee Report, I, pp. 83–4.

19. Colby, William and Forbath, Peter, *Honorable Men: My Life in the CIA* (New York, Simon and Schuster 1978), p. 361.

20. Church Committee Report, I, pp. 83–4, and IV, p. 87: 'DIA and DDO have responded to the KIQs only insofar as they were consistent with their respective internal collection objectives'. In FY 1975 'only 7 per cent of DIA's attache reports responded to KIQs', ibid., I, p. 91.

21. Ibid., I, pp. 90–347.

22. Ibid., I, p. 18. This, in turn, often comes out to producing the same things they have produced in the past. Most resources are not very flexible in the short run.

23. Huizenga, John W., 'Comments on Intelligence and Policymaking in an Institutional Context (Barnds)', in Murphy Commission. *Appendices*, vol. 7, p. 43.

24. Church Committee Report, I, pp. 347–8. These figures are only suggestive, and do not prove that outputs are proportional to inputs.

25. Schemmer, Benjamin F. (*et al.*), 'The Slow Murder of the American Intelligence Community', *Armed Forces Journal International CXVI*, No. 7 (March 1979), p. 52.

26. Church Committee Report, I, p. 18. A vexing problem is uncertainty over whether *more* analysis is needed, whether analytical assets are stretched too thin, or whether the problem is quality rather than quantity of coverage. And how many analysts of obscure areas that pose only *potential* problems should be kept on the shelf–'just in case'–if they have nothing to do but twiddle their thumbs most of the time.

27. 'Backlogs in processing and analysis lead to duplicative efforts across the board, since the results of preceding collection missions are not always available to plan and manage current missions. Moreover, the rush to keep pace with data disgorged by the technical collection systems encourages superficial scanning, increasing the probability that potentially important pieces of information will be overlooked.' Ibid., I, p. 344.

28. Hoagland, J., 'CIA–Shah Ties Cloud Iran Data', *Washington Post* (17 December 1978), p. A21.

29. Carlucci, Frank, on-the-record remarks at meeting of the Council on Foreign Relations (New York, 21 March 1979).

30. 'Foreign Intelligence Collection Requirements: The Inspector General's Survey', (December 1966), quoted in Church Committee Report, I, p. 348.

31. Church Committee Report, I, p. 268.

32. US Congress, Senate, Select Committee on Intelligence, *Staff Report, US Intelligence and the Oil Issue, 1973–1974*, 95th Cong., 1st Sess. (1977), pp. 3–4.

33. Church Committee Report, I, p. 86.

34. Ibid., p. 86.

35. Changes in political climate and legal norms are often unsynchronised. In the early 1970s dissatisfaction with executive secrecy and discretion bubbled up in Congress, but it took several years before this opposition was translated into effective restraints on Presidential power through legislation on war powers, freedom of information, and the Hughes–Ryan Amendment of 1974. The latter, in combination with establishment of permanent intelligence oversight committees in both houses requires the executive to report all covert operations to seven committees of Congress. Now sentiment has drifted back in the other direction, toward reinforcement of secrecy, but the government is stuck with revelatory norms of the mid-1970s. Intelligence charters were conceived a few years ago as means for the control of covert activities, including surveillance and communications intercepts. The period in which they have developed in drafting, however, was that in which the climate changed, and the charters have reportedly evolved into more permissive writs for the intelligence agencies than were earlier anticipated. See Lardner, George, 'Changing Climate May Stymie Intelligence Agency Bill', *Washington Post* (10 July 1978), p. A2; Nossiter, Bernard, 'Effort to Curb Spy Agencies Turns Into a Permission List', *Washington Post* (31 March 1979), p. A2; Nossiter, 'US, Hill Differ on Intelligence Charter', *Washington Post* (16 March 1979), p. A4.

36. See Dineen, Gerald P., 'C³ I An Overview', *Signal: Journal of the Armed Forces Communications and Electronics Association* (November/December 1978).

37. Department of Defence, *Department of Defence Annual Report Fiscal Year 1980* (Washington, DC, Government Printing Office (January 1979), p. 238. Chairman of the Joint Chiefs of Staff David Jones reports that 'the Post-Attack Command and Control System (PACCS) . . . will remain timely and sufficient for MINUTEMAN force execution plans', and shortcomings in NATO C^3 will require more integration of reconnaissance and target acquisition and better signal collection coordination. Organisation of the Joint Chiefs of Staff, *United States Military Posture* (Washington, DC), Department of Defence, January 1979), p. 43.
38. DOD, *Annual Report*, Appendix A.
39. Hartman, Richard, 'The New Game Plan', *Electronic Warfare/Defence Electronics* (November 1978). An insider with no patience for this complaint maintains cynically, though not unbelievably, that 'if the communications somehow survive and work, the field commanders will just pull the plugs'.
40. Ibid
41. US Congress, House, Permanent Select Committee on Intelligence, *Staff Report, Iran: Evaluation of US Intelligence Performance Prior to November 1978*, Committee Print (January 1979), p. 2.
42. Ibid., p. 6. State's INR did not even have a full-time analyst on Iran, and produced no reports on the country in 1978.
43. Leaf, Jesse James, 'Iran: A Blind Spot in US Intelligence', *Washington Post* (18 January 1979).
44. Collection of political intelligence concerning opponents of a regime is likely to be most inhibited in nations where it might someday be needed most, strategically important states with autocratic, potentially unstable regimes. . . . 'A foreign nation may permit the CIA to operate . . . against the Soviet Union but not against its own local officials' . . . going against the wishes of the local government may risk the loss of important opportunities for gathering information on the Russians. . . . Intelligence sources say in CIA's situation in Saudi Arabia parallels . . . Iran. . . . 'Nobody, but nobody, is going to do anything to upset the royal family.'
McArthur, George, 'Iran Intelligence Gap Not Unique: Restraints Hamper US Agents Abroad', *Los Angeles Times* (11 March 1979). For exculpatory views of intelligence failures such as Iran see Morgenthau, Hans J., 'The Limits of Intelligence', *New Leader* (15 January 1979), p. 4, and Betts, 'Analysis, War, and Decision', pp. 62, 69–71, 88–89.
45. See Betts, Richard, K., 'Nuclear Peace: Mythology and Futurology', *Journal of Strategic Studies* II, No. 1 (May 1979), p. 90.
46. See Thomas Blau's manuscript, 'Energy, Intelligence, and Security'.
47. This norm was established early. In strategic NIEs there was supposed to be a 'strict absence of reference to US policy and forces . . . at the insistence of Sherman Kent who did not wish to get drawn into debates on US military programmes'. Freedman, *US Intelligence and the Soviet Strategic Threat*, p. 41.
48. Ibid., p. 51, and Kraft, Joseph, 'CIA Reshuffling – Potentially Good, Possibly Just Political', *Boston Globe* (11 November 1971), p. 23.
49. US Congress, Senate, Select Committee on Intelligence, *Hearings, Nomination of Admiral Stansfield Turner*, 95th Cong., 1st Sess. (1977), pp. 76–7. Representatives of intelligence agencies do *participate* in interagency studies.
50. There have been rumours on the 'outside' that there is a new mandate to

include 'Red–Blue' (Soviet versus United States) comparisons in future NIEs.

51. See Freedman, *U.S. Intelligence and the Soviet Strategic Threat*, pp. 192–3.
52. See Goshko, John, and Russell, Mary, 'Turner Gives Hill Evidence of Cuba Role', *Washington Post* (6 June 1978), pp. A1, A16; Goshko and Russell, 'US Releases Summary of Its Evidence', *Washington Post* (15 June 1978), pp. A1, A17; Lowenthal, Abraham, 'Carter Should Be Skeptical About His Own Intelligence', *Los Angeles Times*, July 16, 1978, p. 2E; Gwertzman, Bernard, 'Carter's Case on Cuba Not Proved, Foreign Relations Chairman Says', *New York Times* (19 June 1978), pp. 1, 3; Burt, Richard, 'Lesson of Shaba: Carter Risked Serious "Credibility Gap"', *New York Times* (11 July 1978), p. A2.
53. Burt, Richard, 'US Says Arms Talks Have Now Resolved Virtually All Issues', *New York Times* (19 April 1979), pp. A1, A13.
54. Binder, David, 'Brown Sees Chance of Strategic Accord With Soviet in 1977', *New York Times* (27 January 1977), p. 6.
55. Betts, 'Analysis, War, and Decision', pp. 78, 88.
56. Leaf, Jesse, quoted in Seymour Hersh, 'Ex-Analyst Says CIA Rejected Warning on Shah', *New York Times* (7 January 1979), p. 3.
57. US Congress, House, Permanent Select Committee on Intelligence, *Annual Report Pursuant to Section 3 of House Resolution 656, 95th Congress, 1st session*, 95th Cong., 2nd Sess. (1978), p. 6.
58. US Congress, Senate, Select Committee on Intelligence, *Report to Accompany S. 2939 (Calendar No. 679)*, 95th Cong., 2nd Sess., pp. 4–5.
59. Binder, David, 'Cutbacks by CIA's New Director Creating Turmoil Within Agency', *New York Times* (10 December 1977), pp. 1, 13. The firings were due to overstaffing and a bunching of clandestine service officers in the top grades. Turner wanted to increase mobility opportunities for younger officers.
60. Jordan, Donald S., quoted in Kendall, John, 'Ousted CIA Official Continues Criticism', *Washington Post* (2 January 1978), p. A3. A quantitative standard for analytical production was also criticised in the Senate Select Committee *Staff Report, US Intelligence Analysis and the Oil Issue, 1973–1974*, p. 5.

20 Intelligence Problems as Viewed from The White House

John P. Roche

This chapter reflects a different perspective. Unlike most of the contributors, my major contact with intelligence was as a wholesale consumer. One of my major tasks in the White House was to try to protect President Johnson from surprise and deception. I suppose on an average day I would consume maybe 100 pages of raw intelligence material plus summaries.

From that viewpoint the contrasting perspectives represented here strike me as comparable to a debate on reorganising a museum. Let us move the surrealists from one corner to another and put the French moderns in that room instead of this room, and so on. I suppose my feeling about this is based on the appalling existential experience that I have had, where you are sitting suddenly at 3.00 in the morning in the Situation Room and the President of the United States, despite his naval background, is saying, 'What happened to that boat?' (the *Pueblo*) and nobody can tell him what happened to that boat.

Unfortunately, I have been in that position. The thing that used to worry me a great deal (and I say this not in great pride, but rather with a certain amount of terror) was that maybe the President might take my advice.

In this context, during the last week of May 1967 I will never forget the night LBJ gathered us and put the following question: An attack carrier, the *Intrepid*, is en route from Norfolk to the Seventh Fleet. It is west of Malta heading for Suez. Once it is in the Canal, Nasser can sink some barges fore and aft and it will remain there as the Suez Hilton. Should we turn it and its destroyers around to take the Cape route?

Meditate on the options and their potential signals. If we turned the carrier around, Nasser might construe it as a sign of our welshing on Israel in the tense period before the war began. On the other hand, if the carrier was 'accidentally' disabled in the Canal (which it almost filled in width), what would we do?

Having laid out the options, the President asked each of the six or seven of us what we thought he should do. He listened, thanked us, went off to decide. I spent a couple of sleepless nights after he decided to push the carrier through, but the ship made it. It is all very well to have the courage of your convictions, but a recognition of their possible consequences is also essential.

Now, if you are in search of decisions rather than conclusions – this is to say, if you have to get an answer rather than a term paper or a dissertation, and there is a clock going – you find yourself trying to get essential information fast. I trust that perhaps the reorganisations that are discussed in this volume may have made it possible for the President of the United States today to have assets at his disposal faster, but I rather doubt it.

Let me now just run through a few of the kinds of situations that I was involved in, in either a direct or indirect sense.

There has been a great hue and cry, for example, about the second Tonkin Gulf episode. I have done some intensive research on this in documents which, if the Senate Foreign Relations Committee ever gets around to, will be declassified – executive hearings and so on. I am convinced that there was no second Tonkin Gulf episode, but the people making a decision to react had every reason to believe that there was. The reason for this, of course, was that the *Turner* and the *Maddox* were out there, and they had a 'black box.' Suddenly out of the 'black box' came instructions to the North Vietnamese PT boats – 'Go get those ships!' They were in 'clear' (not encrypted, but simply in Vietnamese). The Vietnamese translator with the 'black box' went running to the Commodore and said that the North Vietnamese are coming after him. At that point the Commodore said, 'Shouldn't we pull further out to sea? They got us confused with that Alpha 33 operation' – a covert radar busting operation on some islands. It was the middle of the night, total confusion, and as Johnson later said, 'Probably they were shooting whales'.

But in terms of the evidence, you had these North Vietnamese messages that said, 'Go sink those ships'. Those, when they were presented to the Joint Senate Foreign Relations and Senate Armed Service Committees, were very persuasive. That is to say, 'Here are their messages; here's what they told them to do'. Here you had a situation where the COMINT evidence was too good, and the HUMINT was bypassed. [Ronald Lewin tells a similar story with regard to the bombing of Coventry in his splendid *Ultra Goes to War*. The key piece of information was HUMINT: a German pilot boasting of the *Luftwaffe's* plans in a bugged POW cage. But all hands were concentrating on the mysteries of Ultra and the pilot's remarks came to light after Coventry had been levelled. I will return to this point later.]

Let us move on, in terms of my own pessimistic point of view, to the problem when you suddenly have something utterly unpredictable happen. For instance, you are in the 'greatest airborne communication centre in the world' – Air Force I – returning from Adenauer's funeral. There is a coup in Greece. All the secure communication systems are out dead. Walt Rostow is hiding under a bench listening to the BBC; the President is roaming up and down yelling, 'Who couped who? What's going on in Greece?' We did not find out exactly what happened until we got to Andrews and got a land line. This was rather unnerving, to say the least.

To get back to the case that was most difficult, the *Pueblo*. Here we had everything wrapped up in one package. You get the 'Mayday' from the *Pueblo*. At roughly the same time, you had a raid on 'the Bluehouse' (the President's palace in Seoul) by communist commandos. The question was, 'Are they opening up a second front in Korea? Will the South Koreans want to pull back the two ROK divisions in Vietnam?' All these things were packed in one box. The President has Rostow call CINCPAC. The duty officer at Ft Smith says sadly: 'Mr Rostow, it's an awful long way out there'. Mr Rostow thanked him. We got the CINCUNK in Korea. Rostow says: 'Is the recce going up?' And they said, 'Well you know it's pretty bad, unfortunately, our SR-71 is down'. 'Got anything else up?' 'Well, everything else has nuclear arms. We're unlocking stuff; we're going to try to get a plane up there' [an F106, I think]. Meanwhile, in the White House we are trying to figure out whether this is a Soviet or North Korean action, or some cowboy who wants to get himself the Navy Cross, North Korean Branch.

In the middle of it a Russian Admiral gets on from Wonsan (a Soviet warm-water port which, by the way, has one of the tightest air defence systems in Asia, so you could not send even a Piper Cub in to find out what was happening). The Russian Admiral is in 'clear' that is, in Russian, to the Admiralty and says, 'Good God, those crazy [expletive deleted] Koreans went and grabbed an American ship on the high seas, a spook ship!' So you throw that one into the computation. Is it disinformation? All this is happening when you're sitting around a table trying to figure out what you are going to do.'

Finally Czechoslovakia – and I have some scars on this. In about late June and July 1968, I was convinced, on the basis of unclassified evidence, FBIS, that the Soviets would sock the Czechs. I used to read all the communist broadcasts, starting in Pyongyang and running right around, every morning. Out of Bratislava messages in German and Ukrainian were coming about communism with a human face. The Soviets are very sensitive about this because they have not quite achieved the new Socialist Ukrainian man. So I went down to the basement, to Rostow's place, and I said, 'These people are nuts! Are they going to try to turn on the Ukraine?'

So, in the course of things, we sent a plain brown envelope over some Czech transom, suggesting that maybe they might take it a little easy. But they kept on going, at which point I started trying to find out what Soviet military movements were. They did a beautiful job with this one, they had Warsaw Pact manoeuvres. Every tank had a radio. They were jabbering away, you just could not sort anything out. I had a rather interesting experience at this point with Zbig Brzezinski, who was convinced that the Soviets would not move on Czechoslovakia because world opinion would not permit it. He was 'bridge building' at the time. The day after they went in, I sent him a cable in Munich. I said, 'Like I told you, Zbig, bridges are for walking on'. He did not reply.

The fundamental problem here is how do you get the information you have? Not the information that they are in force and have the capability to go into Czechoslovakia, but what they are going to *do*. I recall so vividly from Roberta Wohlstetter's book[1], that the key action cable in determining the attack on Pearl Harbour was in a consular code. It was sent from the Japanese Consul General in Honolulu on December 6 1941 and said in part 'There is considerable opportunity for surprise attack. . . . The battleships do not have torpedo nets.' This was not decoded because it was a simple code (PA-K2), anybody could do it. They were doing the big ones, *Magic*. It was not transcribed until the 27 December, at which point somebody said, 'Oh, my gosh, there it was all the time'. Well, it was.

Now, how do you put these things into the decisionmaking process? One of the reasons I am somewhat terrified is that I have seen the President of the United States, in critical situations, naked. I suspect the same thing has happened to Presidents since. How do you decide, for example, the question, 'What are they planning?' Well, that is an interesting question; maybe they are not planning anything. Maybe sometimes they are just as confused as we are. Maybe they are playing by ear. You have to be leery of the notion that there is *a* plan, what I call the reification of uncertainty. It is easy, too easy, to discern a massive master plan when, in fact, they may have a general purpose, but they have not yet figured out the fine print.

To conclude, I really cannot deal with this kind of issue in an academic context, because I spent so much of my time just dealing with disinformation with the great North Vietnamese 'peace offensive'. I was in charge of damage limitation on the North Vietnamese peace offensive. They had this marvellous setup. A Vietnamese circus performer in Fort Lamy would tell somebody at a cocktail party, 'All they have to do is stop the bombing, and we'll stop the infiltration'. Back comes a 'critic' top secret cable from Fort Lamy, saying 'North Viets are willing to move. We have evidence of this.' (There was actually a 'top secret' cable once from the Consul General in Nassau about what an East German told him at a reception – probably the only cable in history from the Bahamas with that classification.) Harriman would get himself roused in his little office over there with Chet Cooper and they would go whooping around. Of course, there was no water in the well. Then the press would say, 'The President rejected another negotiation'. Oh, was that a beautiful job they did on us! Spectacular! You could plot the calibrations on a graph. (As I say, my scars ache.)

The problem seems to me to be one of how to bring all this information that has been collected, analysed and so on, to a head in time for it to be useful to the President of the United States.

I frankly think the President needs a personal intelligence staff. That is, not people attached to the intelligence community – one of our curses in the Vietnam war was the way George Carver and his crew at CIA fed the President and Walt[2] the kind of analyses the latter wanted to hear – not people attached to the NSC, but people whose job it is to just sit around and read all this stuff. Read it, and read it, and try to make some sense out of it, try to find patterns. Because if you wait for the stuff to come in from across the river, usually, in my experience at least, it comes along too late.

NOTES

1. Roberta Wohlstetter, *Pearl Harbour* (Stanford University Press, 1962)
2. Walter Roston

21 United States Intelligence Activities: The Role of Congress

Thomas K. Latimer

The question of what role Congress should play in the intelligence and counterintelligence activities of the Government is relatively new. Of course, Congress has always had some impact on intelligence activities beginning with the creation of the Central Intelligence Agency by the National Security Act of 1947. Both the Senate and House Armed Services Committees, as well as the Appropriations Committee of both Houses, were briefed to some extent on the CIA's operations and on its budget for each fiscal year.

However, in 1974 public allegations of massive misdeeds by the Central Intelligence Agency, the FBI and other intelligence agencies caused the Senate and House to re-examine the role of Congress in overseeing the activities of the nation's intelligence services. In the process which has unfolded over the past five years, Congress has exercised increased control over the intelligence services primarily in five separate but associated areas: Investigative, Oversight; Budget authorisation and appropriation; Legislation; and Substantive.

The sudden reality of determined congressional investigation created a cultural shock wave throughout the intelligence community which had been accustomed to dealing with only a few, very senior members of Congress and revealing very little about their operations. Moreover, the managers of the intelligence services had taken for granted the general acceptance of Congress and the public that their work was necessary and that they were performing well. The glare of publicity on the previously clandestine world plus the hard probing of the Senate and House Select Committees on Intelligence forced a dramatic change in the relationship between the intelligence agencies and the Congress.

That new relationship now has been worked out for the most part and the result has been a constructive one for the services, for Congress and for the public.

INVESTIGATIVE

In the first phase of developing this new relationship the primary emphasis was on the investigative role of Congress. Following upon allegations in the press of massive illegal activities by intelligence services, the Senate created a Select Committee to Study Governmental Operations with respect to Intelligence Activities.[1] That committee–known as the Church Committee from its Chairman, Senator Frank Church of Idaho–spent fifteen months thoroughly investigating and studying the intelligence activities of the United States. In July 1975, the House followed suit and established its own Select Committee on Intelligence,[2] known as the Pike Committee from its chairman, Republican Otis Pike of New York. The Pike Committee finished its work in February 1976. Both Committees recommended that permanent, follow-on committees be established to monitor systematically the activities of the intelligence services.[3]

In the case of both the Church and Pike Committees, allegations of misdeeds by the intelligence services were investigated thoroughly. But both Committees, in keeping with their charters, went beyond the questions of abuses and into issues related to the very structure and quality of the intelligence process.

Those investigations initially met with considerable resistance on the part of those being investigated. Out of the prolonged and agonising struggle between the Committee that wanted information and the intelligence services that were reluctant to provide certain information and adamant against providing other information came several import-ant lessons for Congress and the Executive Branch.

From the viewpoint of Congressional Committees, it became very important to be able to ask precisely the right question of the right official in order to get needed information. Persistence was also discovered to be a necessity. Within each element of the intelligence services there are officials who believe that cooperation with Con-gressional oversight committees is not only necessary and inevitable, but that it can be a constructive factor in the operations of those intelligence services. Persistence on the part of the oversight committees tends to encourage and to reinforce the efforts of such officials in their internal bureaucratic struggles.

The Executive Branch also learned that Congress was serious about exercising its oversight responsibilities toward the intelligence activities of the government. One result of that realisation was a responsible effort on the part of senior Administration officials outside the intelligence community, beginning in President Ford's Administration and continu-ing to the present, to work out procedures whereby the oversight committees can gain access to the information they seek while assuring the protection of intelligence sources from unauthorised disclosure.

Not all of those procedures have been finally worked out to everyone's satisfaction but both the oversight committees and the Executive Branch are approaching the problem in a spirit of comity which must exist for the Legislative and Executive Branches of our government to work together in this difficult area.

Congressional insistence on exercising its constitutional role of investigating and overseeing the executive branch in operating the clandestine intelligence activities of our government is in keeping with the wisdom of the Founding Fathers who built into our Constitution mechanisms to check the concentration of too much power in either branch. In the area of intelligence operations, which must be secret to remain effective, the checking and balancing role of Congress is especially important because the usual role played by an informed public is greatly diminished by the very fact that our nation's intelligence activities operate best when little information about those activities is made public.

To quote *The Federalist Papers* on the necessity of each branch of our government checking and balancing the other:

To what expedient, then, shall we finally resort for maintaining in practice the necessary partition of power among the several departments as laid down in the Constitution? The only answer that can be given is, that as all these exterior provisions are found to be inadequate, the defect must be supplied by so contriving the interior structure of the government as that its several constituent parts may, by their mutual relations, be the means of keeping each other in their proper places.[4]

But the great security against a gradual concentration of the several powers in the same department, consists in giving to those who administer each department the necessary constitutional means and personal motives to resist encroachment of the others. The provision of defence must in this, as in all other cases, be made commensurate to the danger of attack. Ambition must be made to counteract ambition. The interest of the man must be connected with the constitutional rights of the place. It may be a reflection on human nature, that such devices should be necessary to control the abuses of government. But what is government itself, but the greatest of all reflections on human nature? If men were angels, no government would be necessary. If angels were to govern men, neither external nor internal controls on government would be necessary. In framing a government which is to be administered by men over men, the great difficulty lies in this: you must first enable the government to control the governed; and in the next place oblige it to control itself. A dependence on the people is no doubt the primary control on the government, but experience has taught mankind the necessity of auxiliary precautions.[5]

Despite the difficulty the American people have in knowing whether or not the intelligence activities of their government are proper and effective, the public attitude toward intelligence is an important factor in the way Congress approaches its oversight role. The Congress, in turn, helps shape the image the public has of the intelligence services. Over the past five years that interactive process seems to have shaken out several concerns which Congress and the public share.

OVERSIGHT

One is a concern that the intelligence services be used against foreign activities hostile to our nation's security and that they not be used to violate the constitutional rights of American citizens. This concern resulted in the establishment of restrictions on the activities of intelligence services by the last two Presidents; first by President Ford[6] and then by President Carter.[7] In addition, the Attorney General in each of those Administrations issued voluminous guidelines for the conduct of intelligence activities to limit the danger that they would infringe on the rights of American citizens. That concern has also led to the enactment of one piece of legislation, 'The Foreign Electronic Surveillance Act of 1978'[8] which, for the first time requires the Executive Branch to obtain a warrant in order to engage electronic surveillance of an American citizen or permanent resident alien for national security purposes. Prior to the enactment of that legislation Presidents had relied on the inherent power of their office to approve such surveillance without a warrant. This concern has also led to proposals for the enactment of an omnibus bill which would provide legislative charters for the major intelligence services (CIA, the National Security Agency and the counterintelligence arm of the FBI). It would also provide a list of particular activities which would be proscribed for those services.

Finally, concern over the need to guard against any future violations of the rights of Americans was a primary factor in the creation of the Senate Select Committee on Intelligence in 1976[9] as a permanent follow-on to the Church committee and the establishment of the House Permanent Select Committee on Intelligence in 1977.[10]

Both the resolutions stated that their purpose was 'to provide vigilant legislative oversight over the intelligence and (and intelligence-related)[11] activities of the United States to assure that such activities are in conformity with the Constitution and laws of the United States'.

There can be little doubt about the chilling effect Congressional scrutiny can have on the clandestine activities of our intelligence services. Proponents of more vigorous efforts in the area of so-called 'covert actions' of the CIA[12] assert that enactment of the Hughes–Ryan Amendment to the foreign Assistance Act of 1974[13] which requires the appropriate committees of Congress be informed whenever the President makes a determination that such a covert action is necessary has been followed by a dramatic decrease in the use of such activities.

BUDGET REVIEW

Another concern which has developed out of the examination of intelligence over the past five years is that of the amount of money which is being spent on intelligence. Public concern over this issue is muted because for security reasons the debate is conducted in secret sessions between the oversight committees and the Executive Branch and in executive sessions among the Committees themselves.

Nonetheless, one of the major areas of Congressional impact upon the intelligence activities of the government is via the budgetary process. Both Houses of Congress recognised the importance of providing their intelligence oversight committees leverage over the intelligence services by giving them control over the budgets of the services. The resolutions establishing both select committees provided that no funds could be appropriated to carry out intelligence activities 'unless such funds shall have been previously authorised . . .', and in each House the select committees present the authorisations bill annually to their respective Houses for approval.

It is through the annual budget review process that the oversight committees can develop an in-depth understanding of exactly for what purposes the taxpayers' money is spent on intelligence. The Committees look at the budget not only agency-by-agency but functionally as well; that is, how much is being spent on collection, processing and productions. The committees also scrutinise the budgets from an appropriations viewpoint; that is, how much is spent for purposes such as research and development, procurement, operations and maintenance, personnel, and retirement.

In short, the Director of Central Intelligence and the heads of each agency in the intelligence community appear before the oversight committees and the Appropriations Committees of both Houses each year to justify in detail the amount of money being requested to operate his agency for the coming fiscal year.

Both the Senate and House Select Committees examine the budget request for the National Foreign Intelligence Programme which is developed by the Director of Central Intelligence. According to Executive Order 12036, it includes the budgets for:

(A) The programs of the Central Intelligence Agency;

(B) The Consolidated Cryptologic Program, the General Defense Intelligence Program, and the programs of the offices within the Department of Defense for the collection of specialized national foreign intelligence through reconnaissance except such elements as the Director of Central Intelligence and the Secretary of Defense agree should be excluded;

(C) Other programs of agencies within the intelligence community designated jointly by the Director of Central Intelligence and the head of the department or by the President as national foreign intelligence or counterintelligence activities;

(D) Activities of the staff elements of the Office of the Director of Central Intelligence.

In addition, the House Permanent Select Committee on Intelligence is also responsible—a responsibility shared with the Armed Services Committee—for reviewing that part of the Department of Defence budget which goes to those activities defined by the Secretary of Defence and the Joint Chiefs of Staff as 'Intelligence-related Activities'.[14]

In sum, intelligence-related activities are those activities within the Department of Defence but outside the National Intelligence Programme which: Respond primarily to operational military commanders' tasking for time-sensitive information on foreign entities; respond to national level intelligence tasking of systems, the primary mission of which is support of operating forces; train personnel for intelligence duties (funds for training Defence Department personnel are all contained in one programme in the overall Defence budget); provide an intelligence reserve; or are devoted to research and development of intelligence or related capabilities.

The intense scrutiny the oversight committees give the intelligence budget requests enables them to achieve several of their key responsibilities. For one thing, it would be extremely difficult if not impossible for the intelligence agencies to undertake any significant action in violation of the law without spending considerable money for that action. The thorough budget review, which includes visits to field operations, rules out any such possibility. Secondly, it is through the budget review process that the committees are able to determine whether or not there is any unnecessary duplication of collection, processing and production of intelligence.

The House, which tends to go into greater detail than does the Senate in examing Administration budget requests, includes the intelligence-related activities of the Department of Defence in the responsibilities of its Select Committee on Intelligence both to ensure that no unnecessary duplication of capabilities occurs between the operations of the 'national' programme and those of the Defence Department and to serve as a double check to make certain that needed capabilities do not slip between the cracks with neither the national intelligence nor the Defence budgets providing such capabilities.

SUBSTANTIVE QUALITY OF INTELLIGENCE

A third major concern which has engaged the attention of the Congress over the past half decade is that of how well our intelligence services support our policymakers and Congress. That concern was reflected in the language of both Senate Resolution 400 and House Resolution 658 which created the Senate and House Select Committees on Intelligence. Both committees were charged with the responsibility to 'make every effort to assure that the appropriate departments and agencies of the United States provide informed and timely intelligence necessary for the executive and legislative branches to make sound decisions affecting the security and vital interests of the Nation'.

Both resolutions also charged their respective select committee to make a study and report back to each House of Congress on 'the quality of the analytic capabilities of United States intelligence (and intelligence-related activities)[15] and means for integrating more closely analytic intelligence and policy formulation'.

Both select committees have taken their responsibility in this area very seriously. Each has conducted its own independent series of studies on the quality of intelligence. Mention of a few of those studies will provide an indication of the scope and depth of those studies and a measure of the concern of the committees over this issue.

One such study was conducted by the Senate Select Committee on Intelligence Subcommittee on Collection, Production and Quality. It addressed the question of how well the United States intelligence community had analysed the 1973 Arab oil embargo.[16] One of the key findings of that study was that certain public sources had done as good or a better job of analysing major issues involved in the oil crisis than had the intelligence community. The study also concluded that there had been ample data available to intelligence analysts. They simply failed to analyse adequately that data. The Central Intelligence Agency countered with its own classified assessment of how well it had done on the oil problem.

In the process, issues were illuminated which the management of the Central Intelligence Agency might not have noticed without such an outside study.

On the House side, one of the first studies the Permanent Select Committee on Intelligence undertook was to examine the interaction between the policymakers and their intelligence support services to determine how well that interaction is occurring, particularly in the vital area of 'warning intelligence'. As defined by the Select Committee's Subcommittee on evaluation, warning intelligence encompasses 'the range of intelligence collection, processing, analysis and reporting of data which is intended to provide our policymakers sufficient lead time before an event occurs to develop our own course of action to either deter, alter or respond to the impending development'.[17]

Quality analysis in the warning intelligence area certainly has to be considered one of the primary functions of the intelligence community. A major reason for the establishment of the Central Intelligence Agency in 1947 was the perception that the surprise attack on Pearl Harbour could have been avoided if the United States in 1941 had had a focal point for the correlation and distribution of all the then available intelligence.[18]

The Subcommittee on Evaluation study on warning intelligence discovered, however, that in 1978, some 31 years after the Central Intelligence Agency was created, no focal point existed within the United States Government for warning intelligence. Simply by opening up this subject for study, the Subcommittee found itself as a gathering point for the many separate views on warning intelligence that existed throughout the intelligence and defence communities.

That study examined the warning process in detail, focusing on lessons learned – and not learned – from past crises such as Pearl Harbour, the Korean War, the Cuba Missile Crisis, the Soviet invasion of Czechoslovakia and the Yom Kippur War of 1973. The study found that after each 'intelligence failure' to provide timely warning, a major effort was begun to improve the collection of more data and yet in virtually no case had lack of data been a major factor in the failure to adequately anticipate the crisis. Improvements in analysis and in the integration of analysis with policy formulation have lagged far behind improvements in the collection, processing and dissemination of data.

As a direct result of that Subcommittee's study of indications and warning and its spotlighting of the absence of a focal point for warning leadership in the intelligence community, the Director of Central Intelligence assigned a senior intelligence officer to provide such a focus. That was a major first step in improving our nation's warning intelligence but the Subcommittee study pointed out that much remains to be done. One such area where improvement is needed is in crisis management. That entails better management of the flow of information which, during crises, threatens to overload the system. The study also concluded that an important improvement in warning intelligence would be for the analysts to ask the necessary questions relating to the crisis. Richard K. Betts takes this idea a step further in his examination of intelligence failures, and suggests the intelligence analysts might perform a useful function by offering the policymaker difficult questions, thus serving as a 'Socratic agnostic'.[19]

The thrust of the Subcommittee study was that improvements can be made in the analysis of warning intelligence, despite the fact that difficulties will always persist. Betts has observed that it is illusory to believe that intelligence analysis can be improved substantially by altering the analytical system. Both the Evaluation Subcommittee's study on warning intelligence and Betts' analysis stress the importance of policy level interaction with the intelligence analysts in the warning process, although he places the heavier blame for failures on the policymakers.

> By the narrower definition of intelligence, there have been few major failures. In most cases of mistakes in predicting attacks or in assessing operations, the inadequacy of critical data or their submergence in a viscous bureaucracy were at best the proximate causes of failure. The ultimate causes of error in most cases have been wishful thinking, cavalier disregard of professional analysts and, above all, the premises and preconceptions of policymakers.[20]

Without wishing to denigrate the role of receptivity by the policy levels of warning intelligence, it is nonetheless difficult to support that sweeping a judgement. In the case of the 1973 Arab attack on Israel, not only was there no intelligence warning, the very morning of the attack the CIA disseminated an assessment that there would be no attack, an assessment agreed to by the rest of the intelligence community. Policy levels were not alerted in 1968 to the impending Soviet invasion of Czechoslovakia.

To be sure, Betts broke down the problem of what he calls 'strategic intelligence failures' into three categories: (1) attack warning; (2) operational evaluation; and (3) defence planning. Here we are primarily discussing his first category. He notes, however, that some problems cut across all three categories and it is in that context that he attributes the ultimate causes of error to policymakers.

Discussion on this point sometimes suffers from a difference in perspective over precisely what it is that a policymaker expects in the way of support from the intelligence community. In the area of warning intelligence, the policy levels (we are talking primarily about staff officers who brief, talk to and prepare issue and decision papers for the President, Cabinet and Subcabinet officers) are usually satisfied with a fairly general type of warning such as: 'the odds that country X will invade country Y within the next month have risen from 1 in 10 to 50–50 in the last two weeks because of the following factors'. Too often outside observers and even intelligence analysts themselves think that warning analysts have failed in their mission if they are unable to pinpoint the precise day, time and place of an attack weeks in advance.

Two recent examples show on the one hand how poorly the intelligence community can do in providing warning, and conversely how well they can do.

There is not much question that the intelligence analysts failed to provide the policy levels adequate warning of the Iranian revolution. A thorough study of the performance of the intelligence community on Iran was conducted by the House Permanent Select Committee on Intelligence Subcommittee on Evaluation.[21] It concluded that:

> Clearly, policymakers were not served as well as they needed to be. Weaknesses in the intelligence community's performance in this case are serious. . . . [The Staff Report went on to note, however, that] simplistic charges of 'intelligence failure' do not accurately describe the situation. Such charges blind us to the importance of user attitudes in any warning process. In the case of Iran, long-standing US attitudes toward the Shah inhibited intelligence collection, dampened policymakers' appetite for analysis of the Shah's position, and deafened policymakers to the warning implicit in available current intelligence.

In short, the Study concluded that in the case of Iran, there was a failure 'to which *both the intelligence community and the users of intelligence contributed*' (emphasis in the original).

In the second case, that of China's invasion of Vietnam in February 1979, the policy levels by their own testimony before the Oversight Subcommittee of the House Permanent Select Committee on Intelligence were provided adequate warning. The Chairman of the Oversight Subcommittees, Les Aspin (Democrat, Wisconsin), noted in a study following hearings on this subject that 'the intelligence community provided sufficiently accurate, timely notice of impending Vietnamese and Chinese actions that policy makers could prepare options and take certain actions in anticipation of hostilities'.[22] Representative Aspin went on to note that 'the policymakers' active efforts to find out what the intelligence community knew kept channels of communication open'. Aspin further suggested that steps already taken by the Director of Central Intelligence to make differences of opinion inside the intelligence community known to policymakers should be 'continued and strengthened'.

This last comment by Aspin deserves a closer look because it points to the fact that the quality of warning intelligence can be improved. In his study on the performance of the intelligence community on the China–

Vietnam clash, Aspin points out that the Strategic Warning Staff, a small CIA-chaired interagency group of analysts housed in the Pentagon, had been well out in front of the regular intelligence analytical groups at the CIA, the Defence Intelligence Agency and the State Department's Bureau of Intelligence and Research in issuing warnings that China would invade Vietnam.

In recent years, Directors of Central Intelligence have made an effort to incorporate differing analytical views into the text of National Intelligence Estimates which are the major analytical products of the intelligence community. Aspin's comment was directed at the desirability of expanding that practice even further to allow the views on warning of the Strategic Warning Staff or other analytical groups to surface to the policy level.

One impression left by the studies on Iran and China–Vietnam is that the performance of the intelligence community in the warning area is spotty. Of course, one does not wish to push too far the contrast between the performance of the intelligence analysts on Iran and on China–Vietnam because analytically they presented quite different problems for the analysts and vastly different problems for the policymakers.

At first blush, the two case studies might seem to confirm the thesis that the success or failure of the warning process depends directly upon the degree of willingness of the policy levels to interact with the intelligence analysts. Certainly, that is an important factor, at least when the warning process works.

There is no way to force policymakers to interact with the intelligence analysts. However, it is a relatively rare occurrence when policy levels deliberately refuse to listen to good, sound warning intelligence. In the case of China and Vietnam, the policy levels at State, Defence and the National Security Council staff knew they were getting good warning and were looking for it. In the case of Iran, the few warning signals that were sounded by intelligence analysts, primarily at the State Department, did not impinge on policy level ears, perhaps because they were deafened by the longstanding United States attitudes toward the Shah.

Ultimately, much depends upon the senior levels of the intelligence community having informed convictions and the courage of those convictions. Weakly sounded alarms, negative consensus and carefully hedged warnings are unlikely to get a reception at the policy levels. Granted that warning intelligence is almost always freighted with doubt; by its very nature, warning intelligence requires a degree of prescience beyond the ken of normal intellectual attainment.

But it can be done better. In evaluating current and past efforts at warning analysis by the intelligence community, it is necessary to keep in mind the relative lack of attention to analysis on the part of the managers of intelligence ever since 1947. The Directors of Central Intelligence have traditionally thought of themselves as chief clandestine operatives of the United States Government rather than as the premier analysts. In so far as any DCI has considered that he has a job more important than running the CIA's clandestine operations, he has tended to concentrate on his role as controller of the intelligence community's budget process.

That attitude has permeated the Central Intelligence Agency with direct and indirect impact on recruitment and training policies and practices. It has also directly impacted on the perceptions of the rest of the intelligence agencies and on the key users of intelligence. Until recent years, CIA policy was that officers from the clandestine service rather than from the analytical portion of that agency were to deal with the State and Defence Departments and the White House. Thus, whatever interaction there may have been with policy levels, it was with the operations directorate not the analytical directorate and there was precious little interaction within the CIA between the analyst and the operators.

Even though some improvements have been made in recent years in this regard, the House Subcommittee staff report on Iran revealed the frustration of a senior CIA analyst over his inability to get the clandestine collection part of the Agency to respond to his plea for collection on such issues as 'whether Iranians were loyal to the concept of a monarchy as distinguished from a particular dynasty, to what extent the Tehran urban masses provided an exploitable tool to support or oppose a new government, etc.'[23]

Correct anticipation of the intentions of foreign decisionmakers will always be one of the most difficult tasks our analysts and our own policymakers face. Particularly difficult is the task of correctly estimating a mistake in judgement on the part of foreign leaders. For example, one of the contributing causes to our failure to anticipate the Japanese attack was our leaders' belief that such an outright attack on the United States would be an error in judgement the Japanese leaders would not make. Our estimators failed to anticipate Khrushchev's decision to emplace strategic missiles in Cuba, a mistake in judgement on his part which turned out to be a factor in costing Khrushchev his job.

From the point of view of surprise, the Cuba Missile Crisis is instructive. Although Khrushchev's intentions were not divined, once the Soviets began *to implement* that decision, United States intelligence collection assets were able to detect evidence which led the analysts to make a correct judgement as to Khrushchev's intentions and to get that intelligence judgement to the President in a timely enough fashion so that he was able to develop and place into operation options to defuse the situation.

In the entire attack warning area, United States intelligence has made vast improvements over the last 15–20 years. Analysts may still have difficulty in correctly anticipating foreign decisions but our ability to detect steps to implement those decisions and to recognise those steps for what they are is markedly, not marginally, better than previously.

That is not to say that even greater improvements are not needed and cannot be made. They can and must be made. Perhaps continued Congressional attention to this area will assist the Executive Branch in making those improvements.

We should not leave this subject without several observations on our intelligence capabilities in operational evaluation and defence planning. As a nation, we seem to have tried to cast the Vietnam War from our memory. Yet, one of the lessons learned by our armed forces in that conflict was the operational, battlefield use of modern intelligence. Second World War and Korean War veterans, by and large, looked with disdain upon their intelligence components, giving little weight to their input into command decisions. That attitude prevailed during the first years of the Vietnam War. It is one of the ironies of warfare that the United States armed forces understanding and use of modern combat support intelligence only began to peak after the political will to continue the war had begun to ebb beyond any reviving. The contrast between the surprise of the Tet 1968 communist offensive and the fully anticipated attack of 1972 gives one measure of the dramatic way operational intelligence improved during the course of that unfortunate war.

All three military services today are making vigorous efforts to improve and to integrate combat support intelligence with the operational commands in a fashion and to a degree never before seen in our armed services and that effort is in no small measure due to the experiences in Vietnam of the new generation of general and flag rank officers in the Army, Navy and Air Force.

Looking beiefly at the intelligence role in defence planning, again the improvements in recent years have been dramatic although they may still fall short of keeping up with the developing threat. Our Government's knowledge of the size and deployment of our major adversary's armed forces is orders of magnitude better than it was twenty years ago. Our Department of Defence planners are not groping in the dark about the magnitude of the military threat we face. Granted, there are still analytical shortfalls, as well as gaps in data in certain areas. But viewed as a trend over the past two decades, our ability has been increasing steadily.

A legitimate question is whether our intelligence estimates of enemy strength are improving as fast as the threat. Here again, greater improvements can and need to be made. But the point is that we have been getting better; we need to get even better faster and the successes of recent years hold promise that needed improvements can be achieved. Here again, major qualitative improvements could be made in analysis if the policy levels would build upon the available intelligence to form net assessments of our military capabilities against Warsaw Pact capabilities. Some effort in this regard has been made in recent years by the Net Assessment office in the Department of Defence but much more could be done by a truly 'national' net assessment.

Congress can and should play a role in insisting that we do our best in attack warning, operational support and intelligence support for defence planning. After all, the Constitution assigns to Congress the power 'to raise and support armies' and 'to provide and maintain a navy' as well as 'to declare war'. Today as never before, intelligence plays a vital role in Congressional action in those areas.

Must we accept the fatalistic conclusion that we develop and accept a 'tolerance for disaster'? Cannot measurable improvements be made in the analytical process? The answer is that we cannot know until the management of the intelligence community, fully supported by the President, makes an all-out effort to accomplish major improvements *and until* those efforts are given enough time to achieve results. Congress can assist this process by monitoring and encouraging such efforts.

LEGISLATION

The fifth area in which Congress has come to exercise control over the intelligence activities of the United States is in the enactment of legislation. Two recent major pieces of legislation have already been noted. One was the 'Foreign Intelligence Surveillance Act of 1978', and the second was the bill authorising appropriation for the fiscal year 1979 intelligence and intelligence-related activities of the United States Government. The latter marked the first time in the history of the United States that such a piece of legislation had ever been enacted into law.

Other significant pieces of legislation have been introduced into both Houses of Congress and have been the subject of hearings. Several pieces of proposed legislation deal with the effort to make it a violation of law to disclose the identity of an intelligence agent to anyone not authorised to receive such information. Other proposed legislation would attempt to regularise in law procedures whereby classified national security information can be used in criminal trials while protecting the disclosure of classified information on the one hand and protecting the right of the accused to a fair trial on the other.

Finally, the Executive Branch, the oversight committees of Congress and interested segments of the American public have been discussing for many months the enormously complex task of drafting an omnibus law that would provide updated charters for the major components of the intelligence community and that would legitimise those activities deemed proper for those agencies and proscribe those activities judged to be inappropriate.

CONCLUSION

As the United States moves into the last two decades of the twentieth century, it is clear that Congress is asserting its newly expanded role in the intelligence activities of the Government. Senate concern over our ability to monitor and verify Soviet compliance with strategic arms limitation treaties will continue to mean increased demands for substantive intelligence support for that body of Congress as well as a keen interest on the part of both Houses in the budget requests by the Executive Branch for systems to maintain and improve that verification capability. Increasingly the committees of Congress have come to rely on intelligence to help them reach decisions on a wide variety of issues involving foreign affairs, military matters, international economic developments and national security matters in general. This newly developed closer relationship between Congress and the intelligence community is here to stay and it can and should be of ultimate benefit for the American people.

NOTES

1. Senate Resolution 21 (21 January 1975), 94th Cong., 1st US Senate.
2. House Resolution 591 (17 July 1975), 94th Cong., 1st Sess., US House of Representatives.
3. 'Recommendations of the Final Report of the House Select Committee on Intelligence', Union Calendar No. 421, House Report No. 94–833, 94th Congress, 2nd Sess. (11 February 1976) and 'Final Report of the Select Committee to Study Governmental Operations with Respect to Intelligence Activities', Report No. 94–755, 94th Cong., 2nd Sess., US Senate (26 April 1976).
4. *The Federalist*, No. 51 – Fairfield, Roy P. (ed.), *The Federalist Papers* (New York, Doubleday & Company, 1961), pp. 158–9.
5. Ibid, p. 160.
6. In Executive Order 11905 (18 February 1976).
7. In Executive Order 12036 (26 January 1978).
8. Public Law 95–511, 95th Cong. (50 USC 1801) (25 October 1978).
9. Senate Resolution 400, Report No. 94–675 and Report No. 94–770, 94th Cong., 2nd Sess. (19 May 1976), US Senate.
10. House Resolution 658, Report No. 95–498, 95th Cong., 1st Sess. (14 July 1977), US House Representatives.

11. House version only. This will be discussed in detail later in the paper.
12. Non-intelligence gathering activities such as planting propaganda in news media, assisting foreign political leaders and parties, paramilitary actions such as the secret war in Laos run by the CIA, coups, etc.
13. (22 USC 2422).
14. Department of Defence Budget Guidance Manual 7110-1-M.
15. House version only. As noted above, the House included the intelligence-related activities of the Department of Defence within the purview of its Select Committee on Intelligence whereas the Senate did not.
16. 'U.S. Intelligence Analysis and the Oil Issue, 1973–1974', Staff Report, Select Committee on Intelligence, Subcommittee on Collection, Production and Quality, 95th Cong., 1st Sess., US Senate (December 1977).
17. 'Annual Report by the Permanent Select Committee on Intelligence', Report No. 95–1795, 95th Cong., 2nd Sess., US House of Representatives (14 October 1978), p. 6.
18. National Security Act of 1947, as amended (50 USC 402).
19. Betts, Richard K., 'Analysis, War and Decision; Why Intelligence Failures Are Inevitable', *World Politics* 31, No. 1 (October 1978), p. 61.
20. Ibid, p. 67.
21. 'Iran: Evaluation of US Intelligence Performance Prior to November 1978', Staff Report, Subcommittee on Evaluation, Permanent Select Committee on Intelligence, US House of Representatives, (Committee Print), US Government Printing Office (Washington, DC, 1979).
22. Press release by Representatives Les Aspin (26 March 1979).
23. Staff Report on Iran, p. 3.

22 The Role of Congress in the Intelligence Evaluation Process

Warren Milberg

Over the years, Congress' interest in the intelligence process has changed dramatically. Less than ten years ago, a few men in Congress were privy to the inner workings of the intelligence community. Vietnam, Watergate, and the sensational investigations and revelations of the Pike and Church Committees just a few short years ago have changed all that. For the first time in our history, we now have two Select Committees of Congress specifically charged with the oversight of United States intelligence activities. Interestingly, Senator Inouye, the first Chairman of the Senate Select Committee on Intelligence, demonstrated that Congressional oversight of intelligence activities need not be done on an adversary basis, but rather on a cooperative basis and with a measure of trust existing between Congress and the intelligence community. That relationship has set the tone for the current Chairman of Senate Select Committee on Intelligence and its companion committee in the House as well. No amount of oversight can really exist without that element of trust. But trust is not developed overnight, and Congress must consider a number of crucial actions in the coming months and years if it is to continue any meaningful form of oversight.

Oversight is more than keeping the intelligence community honest – to prevent the abuses of the past from being repeated in the future. The role of Congress is certainly much more than enacting restrictive legislation and castigating the intelligence community when so-called 'intelligence failures' occur. The first step that I would suggest is the passage of clear, concise, and realistic charters for all agencies, departments, and activities having intelligence responsibilities.

The intelligence community, as we all know, consists of at least twelve distinct agencies, or activities within departments. Considering that the foreign policy of the United States is global in nature, and that intelligence is a service or support activity making an input to that policy process, the analytical tasks assigned to the intelligence community can probably be described as limitless. While President Carter attempted to delineate the specific missions and functions of each component in the intelligence community, he only dealt with national intelligence responsibilities in his January 1978 Executive Order. Anyone who has ever been engaged in the business of intelligence analysis knows that at least two other types, or forms, of intelligence exist: Departmental intelligence to serve the needs of individual departments; and tactical intelligence to meet the needs of military commanders in the field. The importance of the latter cannot be overemphasised in that about 80 per cent of the intelligence budget consists of Department of Defence programmes and activities. If the resources required to satisfy intelligence requirements could somehow be separated into three distinct budgets, with little or no overlap, perhaps problems would disappear. But that is not the case. Put simply, the resources required to satisfy national intelligence programmes do have some capability to satisfy departmental intelligence needs, and, to some extent, tactical intelligence requirements as well. The ensuing internal battles within the intelligence community for these resources are fierce – and most importantly, it is counterproductive. The charters for intelligence agencies must clearly delineate who has responsibility for what so that the whole community can get on with the business of producing the best intelligence analyses that are possible.

At this juncture, I note that Senate Bill 2525, the 'National Intelligence Reform and Reorganisation Act of 1978', has been languishing for nearly two years. While this bill is certainly not the total answer to problems to which I have already alluded, it is a step in the right direction, considering that the views of appropriate Executive Branch components are being given full consideration as this bill nears the time of being reported out. The House Permanent Select Committee is also in the process of developing similar legislation.

If clear and concise charters are the first step that Congress can take to help create an improved atmosphere, the second step must be in the area of legislation to protect intelligence sources and methods from unauthorised disclosure. Intelligence analysis is, of course, dependent on sources and analytical methodology and, without protection of these inputs into the intelligence process, adequate intelligence analysis becomes impossible. I hope I am not guilty of hyperbole by emphasising the direct relationship between the sources of raw intelligence data and finished intelligence products. Without advocating anything similar to the British Official Secrets Act, I think that, as a minimum, the Director of Central Intelligence must be given a meaningful legislative backup if his responsibility to protect sources and methods is to be enhanced. William Colby has proposed that criminal sanctions be imposed on the people who, while having legitimate access to sensitive sources and methods, disclose these secrets to unauthorised individuals or the press. In effect, this would be characterised as a 'Leaker's Law' in that it would only penalise those who leak information. But more than this is required, since leaks have become a way of life in all branches of government. Such a law at this time can be seen as only treating the symptoms of the disease, not the cause. How, for instance, do you deal with the ever-elusive definition of 'in the interests of national security?' Perhaps a point of departure is a harder look, in both the Executive and Legislative Branches of government, at the rules and procedures used to classify or make something secret, in the first place. The inconsistencies and absurdities that now exist are legion: they are as familiar to you as they are to me. Over the years, the classification system has grown into a multiheaded monster, a modern-day Frankenstein. For only when a more realistic, and equitable, system is devised and implemented can there be any meaningful protection of sources and methods. Just as Congress must deal with this responsibility of the Director of Central Intelligence, so must it deal with certain of his other responsibilities.

As we all know, the DCI is a multihatted individual; being the executive head of the CIA, the President's senior adviser on intelligence matters, and the leader of the intelligence community. Each Director of Central Intelligence has, to some extent, held the same responsibilities, which can be seen as both mutually complementary and mutually exclusive, dependent on the issue, or issues, at hand. As the Director of the CIA he is responsible for the full range of Agency activities, which range from the collection and production of national intelligence, to covert operations, to the development of new and improved intelligence systems used to maintain the technological superiority of the United States' intelligence effort. As the President's senior intelligence official, the DCI must provide him, the National Security Council, the Cabinet, and other officials of the government with the best possible intelligence inputs to the policy process. And finally, as the leader of this loose confederation of agencies, departments, and activities known as the intelligence community, the DCI has, to the fullest extent possible in law, 'full and exclusive jurisdiction over the preparation and submission of the National Foreign Intelligence Programme budget'. The pros and cons of this longstanding arrangement have been debated for years – and the arrangement has been continued. One of Frank Church's 88 recommendations when his Select Committee on Intelligence concluded its work in 1976 was, *inter alia*, that the DCI and the DCIA be separated. I note that the House Permanent Select Committee on Intelligence, in their recent report[1] also echoes the same sentiment. Such a change has been resisted in the past and may be resisted in the future. Cogent arguments for the maintenance of the *status quo* can certainly be made, the primary one being that the DCI must have an organisational power base to be effective. Perhaps it is time for Congress to take a realistic look at the varied responsibilities now assigned to the DCI and to recommend alternatives. Certainly, there are a number of 'powerful' individuals in Washington – some exceeding that of the DCI – who virtually have no organisational base for this power. But to the extent that organisational structures contribute to, or inhibit, the production of the best possible intelligence, Congress must also look inward.

With the establishment of permanent Select Committees on Intelligence in both the House and Senate, the number of Committees having some piece of the jurisdictional action over intelligence activities has risen to at least eight. I am referring, of course, to the Committees on Foreign Relations, Appropriations, and Armed Services. Each of these Committees is reluctant to relinquish any or all of the power it now has to review, guide, and oversee intelligence activities. And the result has been that the senior intelligence officials in the government are often reporting to too many masters, each having conflicting views on how the business of intelligence is conducted. This number of committees must be reduced to more manageable proportions; perhaps a single joint committee of the House and Senate would suffice. Reasons, other than political ones, why this could not work better than the existing system, have yet to surface. By way of conclusion, some comment seems necessary on the subject of evaluating the utility of intelligence products.

By choice or by chance, Congress seems to have evolved into the after-the-fact role of evaluating what it believes to be 'intelligence failures'. This may be due to a number of factors; chief among them has been the reluctance of the intelligence community to provide Congress with current intelligence products. Although that situation may still obtain, significant changes have taken place. First and foremost, President Carter has designated the DCI as the intelligence community's principal spokesperson for all facets of intelligence activity, to include 'facilitating the use of national foreign intelligence products by the Congress in a *'secure manner'*. President Carter has also directed the DCI and the heads of departments and agencies of the United States involved in intelligence activities to provide ' . . . any information or document in [their] . . . possession', to the House and Senate Intelligence Committees, 'upon the request of such committee'. So Congress has become a part of the intelligence process and can no longer enjoy the dubious, responsibility-free position of contenting itself with the writing of critical post-mortems in the wake of the next 'intelligence failure'. Just as Congress has asked the intelligence agencies why they may have misinterpreted past, current and perhaps future events in the international arena, so must the public ask why has Congress allowed this to happen when it is Congress that controls intelligence community funds.

Just as the concept of 'plausible denial' (in regard to covert action) has been repudiated by the President, so must the concept of plausible denial (in regard to ongoing intelligence analyses by the intelligence community) be put aside by Congress. Congress must focus its attention on 'pre-mortems' rather than post-mortems – if it is to live up to its own charter to improve the quality of intelligence analysis.

NOTES

1. 'Iran: Evaluation of US Intelligence Performance Prior to November 1978' (January 1979).

Part Nine

Conclusions

23 Intelligence, Deception and Surprise: Implications for United States Policy in the 1980s

Robert L. Pfaltzgraff, Jr

The problems of intelligence examined in this volume are fraught with implications for United States policy in the 1980s – both in its organisational and substantive dimensions. Several themes have been prominent both in the chapters here and in the broader discussions of the intelligence community in light of United States policy needs for the next decade. Such a discussion takes place in the aftermath of the widespread dissatisfaction with the intelligence community in the United States in the early-to-mid-1970s. On the one hand, the community was faulted for its alleged excesses, especially in misguided, or unguided, clandestine operations in support of supposedly dubious policies. On the other hand, our intelligence services were condemned for their deficiencies in providing accurate and timely estimates of the growth of Soviet military power. Hence the criticisms emanated from diverse sources. They reinforced an historic suspicion in the United States of secrecy in government focused especially on intelligence, most of whose operations have not, and cannot be, conducted under full public scrutiny.

The chapters in this volume have contained analyses addressed to the adequacy of existing, and past, organisational structures to cope with the increasing demand for intelligence; the closely related issues of command and control; the problem of warning in its several discrete, but nevertheless linked, aspects: Surprise and deception – strategic–military, political–diplomatic and technological; problems of translating consumers' (that is, policymakers') needs into intelligence collection guidance and establishing coherent priorities for the acquisition and analysis of intelligence data; the issues of SALT verification; and political and psychological–perceptual–cultural factors, both in historic and contemporary context, as they affect intelligence gathering and analysis. The linkages among the topics considered in the various chapters are numerous and, taken together, provide ample scope for reflective comment as we ponder implications and policy options for the United States in the intelligence field in the 1980s.

STRUCTURE AND ORGANISATION

Analysis has been focused on the organisational framework – the structures that have been devised for intelligence gathering and evaluation, and the process by which intelligence is transmitted through a bureaucracy from the data-gathering to the policymaking phases. There has been a proliferation of intelligence issues as organisational units and the issues confronting policymakers have grown both in immensity and in complexity. Problems of control have increased as bureaucratisation has been enlarged to deal with the proliferation of national security and foreign policy problems for which intelligence is needed.

Emphasis has been placed on the implications of policy and intelligence compartmentation, or compartmentalisation. Among other reasons, the failure of the United States to ascertain the impending attack on Pearl Harbour resulted from the fact that the information needed to alert our forces to launch reconnaissance aircraft was scattered among the Army, the Navy, and the Department of State. Other examples were cited, including the failure of the intelligence community to predict the 1973–74 oil embargo and price rise. According to William Colby, the 'intellectual scope' of the intelligence analyst has grown to reflect the numerous factors and disciplines – to examine 'all of the relevant political, strategic, economic, social, psychological, cultural and biographical data'. But there was little, if any, support for the proposition that our intelligence capability, especially in a centralised structure created after the Second World War in order to integrate all of the factors essential to effective intelligence gathering and analysis, had been adequate to recent needs, or would even have given timely warning of Pearl Harbour. In fact, numerous subsequent failures were cited. For example, Thomas Latimer, in his analysis of the role of Congress in intelligence oversight, even suggested that, according to one Congressional study, certain public sources had done as good, or better, a job of analysing the major issues of the 1973–74 energy crisis than had the intelligence community. We have not succeeded in achieving an integrated conception of intelligence, any more than we have devised an integrated approach to national security policy, at whose service the intelligence must always be placed. Here, a distinction must be drawn between organisational centralisation and intelligence integration. The former pertains to the organisational structure for intelligence gathering and analysis. The latter refers to the ability of the intelligence community, and the individual analyst, to think conceptually so as to encompass all of the factors relevant to intelligence. Organisational centralisation represents no panacea for a conceptually integrated approach to intelligence. Centralisation is said to increase the prospect for politicisation by stifling pluralism and diversity – themes examined elsewhere in this volume, and in this chapter. The policymaker needs intelligence that is drawn from a diversity of sources and presented in integrated fashion. The policymaker must have available intelligence in which political, economic, military and other dimensions are linked conceptually. The problem, as noted by John P. Roche, is how to bring together all of the relevant information that has been collected and analysed in time to be useful to the President of the United States, especially when momentous decisions must be taken quickly.

The adequate conceptualisation of intelligence can be illustrated by reference to economic issues. Because economic issues, especially energy and other sources, impinge heavily upon national security, the United States faces the need, as Richard B. Manke suggested, to improve its intelligence in economic matters. He noted three types of economic intelligence that are essential: a factual data base about the domestic economies of other states, systematic information in support of 'plausible projections of future international economic events and trends'; and the development of an 'analytical framework' to enable policymakers to evaluate these two categories of data. In part, it was suggested, the grave deficiencies that have beset the United States are more attitudinal than structural in nature. For the most part, those charged with national security policymaking have not had an adequate appreciation, perhaps by virtue of their training, of the economic dimensions of national security issues. Less than at any time in the past will it be possible to separate economic and military issues. Similarly, the international ramifications of United States domestic economic policies need to be understood, just as the implications of international economic trends for the American economy must be assessed more adequately. From these generalisations emerge a set of conceptual problems and policy priorities that will confront the intelligence community in the 1980s and, specifically, the need to integrate economic factors more extensively into intelligence collection and analysis.

Other chapters, especially that of Thomas Latimer, considered such issues as executive and congressional oversight. The increased role of Congress in the 1970s in intelligence included the need perceived by some for Congress to monitor, to the extent feasible, the intelligence activities of the executive branch, although excessive Congressional oversight, such as imposed by the Hughes–Ryan Amendment, makes difficult, and probably impossible, the conduct of covert operations that may be necessary for American national security. Thus the issue facing the United States in the structuring of its intelligence community for the 1980s, unlike that of the mid-1970s, will be to ensure that the executive has adequate capabilities in the intelligence field while maintaining Congressional and public scrutiny consistent with the values of a democratic society. We have yet to reconcile fully the values of the 'open society' with the exigencies of the intelligence community and its secrecy requirements. Of equal importance, however, is the need for the Congress to have access to intelligence to enable it to perform effectively its Constitutional functions in reviewing the policies set by the executive branch. Examples such as SALT verification, international economic developments, and foreign affairs and national security generally were cited.

Although there was not an extended examination in this volume of the role – past or prospective – of covert activities in the intelligence community, it was suggested that cabinet level scrutiny of such operations in the United States is probably higher now than in the recent past because there are simply fewer covert activities over which to exercise scrutiny at the highest political level because of the restrictions placed by legislation, such as noted below. Undoubtedly, it will be necessary to draw a new balance between, on the one hand, the need for effective oversight and scrutiny and, on the other hand, the conduct of those covert operations that are deemed vital to the United States.

Although there was consideration of organisational structure in several chapters, no one was prepared to advocate such changes as a panacea to the problems facing the American intelligence community, except to warn of the dangers of excessive centralisation of the official intelligence community. It was pointed out that no administration of recent memory has inherited an organisational structure for intelligence with which it has been wholly satisfied. The Nixon, Ford and Carter Administrations have each made changes in the organisation of the official United States intelligence community. They have been what John Roche described as a rearrangement of the paintings in a museum, without altering the contents of the museum itself. Thus the problems that were to have been addressed in such reorganisations, by and large, remain with us. As Richard Betts suggested, most organisational, or structural, problems are never solved because they are inherent in the nature of the intelligence function. Hence, the solution to problems such as those considered in this volume lies beyond organisational 'quick fixes'.

The relationship between command and control and the conduct of operations in a strategic–military conflict and the intelligence community was addressed in more than one chapter. In a future conflict, strategic–military warning time may be measured in minutes rather than hours, and on the NATO–Warsaw Pact Central Front, in hours rather than days. Such changed circumstances enhance the dangers inherent in surprise. They place a premium not only on the collection and evaluation of intelligence to minimise surprise, but also to maintain during any conflict, and especially in its initial phases, an adequate system for rapid information gathering, processing and transmission. It was noted that intelligence is integral to command and control during military operations as much as it is in the period preceding the outbreak of hostilities. For this reason, the survivability of information systems and command and control capabilities has been an object of concern to all administrations for at least a generation – including the Carter Administration. To carry the analysis one step further: the lower the quality of intelligence, the greater the likelihood of strategic surprise; the greater the strategic surprise, the lower the prospects that command and control structures will be adequate in the crucially important first stage of a military confrontation.

In an extended discussion of surprise from the Soviet perspective, John Erickson noted that the Soviet Union seeks, with the use of surprise, to gain the ability to fight a nuclear war 'on a sustained basis'. He maintained that the first tenet in Soviet doctrine is for the Soviet Union not to be surprised itself – as evidenced in the commitment to combat readiness and civil defence programmes, to forces-in-being and to strategic reserves 'on an ever-growing scale', and to the 'sustainability' and 'survivability' of strategic military forces and post-attack recovery capabilities. But the Soviet Union views surprise as an indispensable war-waging asset – of critical importance in effecting the outcome of a military conflict, as related inextricably, as Erickson put it, first to the 'application of "manoeuvre", that is, by repetition of actions until the opposing system is made decreasingly sensitive to the actual possibility of military attack', and, second, to gaining the upper hand in the initial phase of war and thus influencing its subsequent stages and ultimately its outcome on favourable terms.

STRATEGIC–POLITICAL WARNING AND SURPRISE

In light of the foregoing, the question of strategic and political warning becomes indispensable for the United States. In this volume, several chapters focused on the question of how to maximise warning for the United States and its allies, and how to prevent an opponent from making effective use of surprise and deception. Here, ample reference was made both to historical and contemporary examples. In addition to the example of Pearl Harbour noted elsewhere, each of the international crises that have beset the United States in the past half-century has pointed up deficiencies both in command and control and in intelligence gathering and evaluation. These include the outbreak of the Korean conflict, the 1964 Tonkin Gulf crisis, the 1968 seizure of the *Pueblo*; the Soviet decision to build the Berlin Wall in 1961, the Soviet invasion of Czechoslovakia in 1968, the outbreak of the Yom Kippur War of October 1973; and the *Mayaguez* crisis of 1975. Improvements in technology, whose effect is to speed the communications process, have done little to improve the capacity of decisionmakers to reduce surprise, even though there has been a vast growth in the capacity for consultation between and among levels of decisionmakers and in the communication of intelligence up the chain of command.

There was consideration of the nature of surprise as a political and military phenomenon. Surprise as a political phenomenon has both internal and external manifestations. According to Michael Handel, political surprise includes an unanticipated change of government either by means of a revolution or through the electoral process that has an important impact on the international system. At the external level, surprise consists of any unexpected move directly involving more than one state. A series of interesting linkages between the potential for political surprise and the structure of the international system was noted. Such surprise is said to be greater in a classical balance-of-power system than in a hierarchial tight bipolar system; more in a multipolar system than in a bipolar system, and more frequent in a loose bipolar than in a tight bipolar system. Hence, it was inferred, the impact of diplomatic surprise is said to be in inverse relation to its probability. If diplomatic surprise is greater in a heterogeneous than in a homogeneous political system, a similar macrocosmic analysis of the relationships between system structure and propensity for conflict would yield a series of general propositions about strategic–military surprise. But the question of the extent to which bipolar systems are more, or less, prone to military conflict has long preoccupied the attention of international relations theory scholars without producing definitive results. Even if it did yield such conclusions, the task of drawing inferences for specific intelligence situations from macrotheory – or theory at the international systemic level – would be formidable. Yet, because the intended effect of a surprise attack is to attain immediate, short-range military objectives with longer-term consequences, and that of diplomatic surprise to produce changes of dramatic proportions of permanent effect in the international system, the need exists to bring to bear all of the theoretical insights available to estimate accurately the trends about which intelligence should be gathered and evaluated. This argues for better international relations theory, and for a more adequate capability within and outside the official policy community to link theory to practice, to provide the intelligence needed to anticipate, and thus to minimise, surprise.

Thus, strategic warning is the answer to strategic surprise, which may be accompanied by strategic deception. Alternatively, the purpose of strategic surprise, which is likely to take place in conjunction with strategic deception, is to deprive an adversary of strategic warning. According to R. V. Jones, inherent in the concept of good intelligence is the invocation of deception on the part of an ingenious adversary. The prospects for deception are enhanced if the object of the deception is dependent on only one or just a few channels of information, or if the real thing can be hidden among the spurious. This latter proposition has useful implications for our consideration of the policy problems inherent in SALT verification. The proposition noted above – about the prospects for deception lessening as the sources of information increase – holds useful implications for intelligence gathering and analysis: a multiplicity of sources of information and analytical capabilities, *provided they can be brought together for the policymaker*, will be more effective than only one or a few sources – sources that must be adequately protected, although a review of systems of classification should be undertaken. From such propositions we may infer that the need for alternative sources of intelligence runs counter to a form of organisational centralisation that would produce intelligence homogenisation. Similarly, the need for an integrated conceptual approach to intelligence must be reconciled with pluralism in the gathering and analysis of intelligence.

If deception has been central to political–diplomatic surprise, it has been equally important to the practice of warfare from ancient times to the twentieth century. It was suggested that behind every political ploy or military operation there is at least some guile or deception. Guile is common to all societies and cultures, although the quantitative analysis leads one to conclude that some have more than others and that it is more prevalent at some times than at others. Other chapters have dealt with deception and, especially in R. V. Jones' and in Ladislav Bittman's essays, historical examples such as the planting of verbal or written information on spies known to be working for the enemy, the use of double agents, and feints on the battlefield, are set forth. Modern technology has provided both the basis and the need for the practice of deception. According to Ladislav Bittman, the Soviet Union has used disinformation with increasing frequency and the Cold War has ushered in a new historical period in the use of a phenomenon that is probably as old as mankind.

THE TECHNOLOGICAL DIMENSION OF SURPRISE

Much of the analysis contained in this volume deals with the nature of surprise in its technological dimension. It was suggested that technological surprise has increased in importance as a result of the greater salience of strategic–military issues in the 1970s. Controversy about the adequacy of intelligence gathering and analysis – especially analysis – in understanding the range of strategic–military issues confronting the United States has grown dramatically in recent years. When the United States enjoyed demonstrable strategic–military superiority over the Soviet Union, the problem of technological surprise was of less immediate consequence. The greater the R & D effort made by the United States, the less likely we are to confront the spectre of technological surprise in that particular area. The possession of technological superiority by the United States enhanced our capacity to monitor Soviet R & D, since we could assess Soviet programmes in the light of what we had already accomplished. This may be a more difficult task for the United States in an age of asymmetries in technology, some of which are likely to favour the Soviet Union in the 1980s. Here, the problem confronting the intelligence community will be both to assess the areas of potential for Soviet technological surprise – for a 'breakout' in one or more weapons categories – and to minimise the response time that would be needed by the United States.

In his chapter, Patrick Friel dealt with another aspect of the intelligence problem facing the United States; the relationship between Soviet strategic–military doctrine and strategic force level configuration – another critically important aspect of the analysis of Soviet conceptions of surprise undertaken by John Erickson in this volume. Viewed through Soviet strategic–military literature, technological programmes and force levels, the 'technical indicators suggest that the Soviet Union is systematically developing a significant nuclear war-fighting capability'. Precisely how the Soviet Union might use such a capability – the age-old problem of inferring intentions from capabilities – was addressed only in passing. It forms an issue area of immense complexity, for which solutions have usually eluded both the policy practitioners and the more theoretically oriented academic community.

Yet, the theme of another chapter – by Clarence Robinson – emphasised a narrowing technological advantage for the United States. In some areas, notably high energy lasers and charged particle beam weapons, the Soviet Union was said to be at least several, and as much as five to seven years, ahead of the United States. A survey of the range of Soviet R & D programmes reveals that the Soviet Union is seeking a technological breakthrough whose effect would be to provide a 'potential for nuclear blackmail in world politics' and to 'force the other side to back down through the capability of neutralising the ICBM and submarine–launched ballistic missile forces'. Such was said to be the political meaning of technological surprise. Although there was a consensus that the Soviet Union is placing considerable R & D into high energy lasers and charged particle beam weapons development, there has been sharp disagreement in the intelligence–policy communities about the prospects for success in this area, especially in charged particle beam weapons, with the inference to be drawn here that the potential for technological surprise exists in the 1980s.

Other areas holding the possibility of surprise, or at least great Soviet efforts, were considered. These include: improved ICBM accuracy; antisubmarine warfare; an antisatellite system; antiship missiles; and new generation aircraft. Edgar Ulsamer noted the substantial Soviet R & D effort in antisatellite technologies, but also alluded to alternative ASAT options being pursued by the United States, as well as the formidable problems in an ASAT ban verification. The Soviet Union is well advanced in its effort to develop a manned command-and-control spacecraft that can perform along the lines of the US E4B National Emergency Airborne Command Post. Such a capability will have adverse effects upon the United States, especially in the opening phase of a strategic nuclear conflict. The development of such a system accords with the doctrinal emphasis, noted in several contributions to this volume, placed by the Soviet Union on war-waging and war-winning in its strategic–military literature. Thus one key to understanding this important dimension of Soviet policy is to assess the level of correspondence between statements contained in Soviet writings and evolving military technologies and capabilities. The Soviet Union has shown a propensity to surprise the United States, especially since SALT I, by the pace and extent of the introduction of new weapons into its military inventory, from ICBMs to SLBMs, from the strategic–nuclear level to the battlefield.

TRANSLATING POLICYMAKERS' NEEDS INTO INTELLIGENCE COLLECTION GUIDANCE

In this volume there is extended consideration of the problems of translating the needs of the consumer – the policymaker – into collection guidance and establishing coherent topical priorities for the acquisition and analysis of data. It is suggested that intelligence analysis often fails to keep pace with the collection of intelligence data. This problem has been compounded by personnel policies that either have resulted in the hiring of inadequate numbers of intelligence analysts or the excessive dependence on technical collection capabilities to the detriment of personnel for analysis, in addition to the deficiencies, noted especially by Richard Pipes, stemming from biases in the American intelligence and policy communities attributable to logical positivism. The problem of human versus technical means of intelligence gathering and analysis is said to have hampered the official United States intelligence community in recent years and deserves examination in light of the growing intelligence needs of the United States in the 1980s.

The problem of translating intelligence acquisition priorities into the needs of policymakers is rendered more difficult by virtue of the failure of policymakers to define for the intelligence community what their real needs are. Accurate intelligence estimates must always bear some relationship to policy needs. There is a critical need for the intelligence collector to have a continuing understanding of the requirements, priorities, and assumptions of the policymaker. If adequate policies are impossible in the absence of adequate intelligence, it is equally true that intelligence priorities must be drawn from the policy priorities established by those charged with the development of policy. The lack of an integrated conception of policy will result invariably in a similar deficiency in the gathering and analysis of intelligence.

In considering this dimension of the relationship between intelligence and policymaker – between the collection and analysis of data – the issue of the politicisation of intelligence, and the dangers flowing therefrom, was examined in this volume. This problem has confronted the American intelligence community during administrations of both political parties. Political and ideological judgements have diminished greatly the ability of the intelligence community to perform effectively its tasks of information gathering and analysis. The result has been a decline in morale, together with a loss in public confidence in the reliability of the intelligence that is available to our policymakers. If there must always exist a relationship of fundamental importance between consumer needs and intelligence collection, a distinction should be drawn between the legitimate needs of the policymaker to determine collection priorities and the equally great need of the policymaker to allow for the dispassionate, objective analysis of intelligence. One of the reasons for the failure of intelligence to predict such events as the fall of the Shah of Iran, it was suggested, was the politicisation of intelligence – its use to reinforce the preconceptions and the assumptions of policymakers rather than as a source of information leading, where needed, to their timely modification. To such use of intelligence may be attributable at least some of the failures of intelligence in anticipating events such as those that have befallen Iran. In fact, the politicisation of intelligence is a form of self-deception, another theme addressed in this volume.

Here again, the discussion turned to what was perceived to be a need for a multiplicity of channels of intelligence – a kind of 'marketplace of intelligence'. The policymaker who relies upon one source of intelligence may be the object of self-deception as great in its potential consequences as the deception successfully practised by an adversary. As Ithiel de Sola Pool suggested: the problem for gathering and interpreting intelligence arises from the general inclination of those gathering and interpreting it to accept what they want to hear. He concluded that it takes two to disinform, although in fact it may take only one person, the one who is unprepared to search for and to accept where necessary ideas that run counter to his preconceptions. This theme was evident in Roberta Wohlstetter's analysis, drawn from historical and contemporary cases – British views, or misperceptions, of Hitler's armament effort, United States underestimation of Soviet strategic–military programmes, and the apparent self-induced confusion relating to the Indian peaceful or military nuclear programme. She alluded to the tendency toward self-confirming beliefs that has been prevalent in a large segment of our intellectual community – in Britain between the World Wars, and in the United States and elsewhere in more recent times. R. V. Jones quoted the passage from Churchill's history of the First World War, *The World Crisis*, which states: 'The temptation to tell a chief in a great position the things he most likes to hear is the commonest explanation of mistaken policy. Thus the outlook of the leader on whose decisions fateful events depend is usually far more sanguine than the brutal facts admit.' Closely associated is the idea that, with the complexity of issues inherent in decisionmaking in the twentieth century, the prospect looms large that knowledge necessary for an effective decision is not directly proportional to one's rank in an organisation. 'The firmly inculcated doctrine that an Admiral's opinion was more likely to be right than a Captain's, and a Captain's than a Commander's, did not hold good when questions entirely novel in character, requiring keen and bold minds unhampered by long routine, were under debate.' The implications for political leadership are obvious; the need to go far down into the ranks, and outside the usual channels, for information relevant to momentous decisions.

Professor Pipes developed yet another dimension of this problem of self-deception and intelligence and provided a linkage between the collection of intelligence and its analysis. No society has available to it more information or data about other societies, including the Soviet Union and China, than does the United States. Yet our analysis is hampered by the tendency to study other societies through American eyes. According to Uri Ra'anan, we have made ineffective use of the ample military literature published in the Soviet Union because we have often assumed erroneously that such writings were produced principally for propagandistic reasons. Instead, we should evaluate such writings from the perspective of an understanding of their purpose: to convey to the political élites their 'operational directives' sometimes in language that appears to be 'Aesopian and somewhat arcane', but which can be '"deciphered" with relative ease'. The faulty analysis of intelligence about the Soviet Union and other societies, Richard Pipes notes, results in part from the methodological flaws inherent in the logical positivism of the social sciences as practised in the United States, and has diminished greatly our capacity for the analysis of other societies. Because logical positivism is addressed principally to the validation of propositions by rigorous logical and linguistic analysis, its proponents, many of whom have helped shape the social sciences and the public policy community in the United States, reject any statement that does not meet the criteria of linguistic or logical verification. The result, Pipes suggests, is to eliminate from policy analysis, including intelligence, many phenomena that are indispensable to an understanding of strategy, warfare, and foreign policy. These include history, ideology, psychology, values, and irrational behaviour – all of which may shape an adversary's perceptions of the world but which cannot be validated by social science methods acceptable to the logical positivist and therefore excluded from the intelligence and policy process. Uri Ra'anan contended, moreover, that intelligence evaluation consists of the formulation of perceptions about the capabilities and eventual moves of another power. Here, perception plays a central role. Perception may be manipulated or spontaneous, static or dynamic. Perception may lead to analysis that feeds back into the data themselves – changing their meaning. Thus deception may be easy to perpetrate against those willing to be deceived. If so, there is perhaps a grey area in which self-deception and deception induced by others upon an adversary become one and the same.

Closely related to the problem of politicisation, and of intelligence based on preconceived notions reinforced by the analyst's desire to please a superior is the tendency to present intelligence estimates that run few risks of being wrong. Such estimates usually hold the least value for policy guidance. The intelligence analyst, it was suggested, must be prepared to reject conformity in favour of originality, to take the risk of being wrong, and to provide the basis for creative policy in his estimates. The prerequisites for such intelligence did not form the topic for extended consideration in the various chapters in this volume. But it is appropriate to ask what are the bureaucratic and other impediments to such intelligence in the United States government, and in other political systems as well, and how in the case of the United States can intellectual risk-taking in intelligence evaluation be encouraged and the tendency reduced toward homogenised intelligence based on bureaucratic compromise and consensual softening. On the one hand, it was acknowledged, we have had a virtual flood of information as a result of the growth of communications and the speed with which information can be transmitted. On the other hand, technology has contributed decisively to the growth of a large governmental, including intelligence, bureaucracy, or bureaucracies. The expansion of the technology of communications works against conformity by producing a diversity of sources of information. But the growth of bureaucratisation was said to encourage conformity with the emphasis placed on concurrence with an official view.

VERIFICATION

Central to strategic warning is verification as a problem for the intelligence community. Interest in the verification issue in context of SALT stems from the growing problems inherent in the shift in the strategic–military relationship between the United States and the Soviet Union to, at best, a form of strategic parity and, at worst, a marked increase in the vulnerability of the fixed, land-based portion of the United States strategic nuclear force to a surprise Soviet first-strike – that might be designed, according to John Erickson, to 'alter the "correlation of forces" at one blow, though it may not be necessarily decisive in its own right'. Verification in the SALT context was examined as a high-priority strategic–intelligence responsibility.

SALT verification, including what constitutes 'adequate verification', is both a political and a technical issue, as well as an intelligence problem. Specifically, the degree of verifiability is a domestic political issue. It is also related to the terms of the Treaty itself and to a judgement as to whether violations would be significant in their implications for the strategic–military balance. To a certain extent, verification adequacy is subjective in nature. To proponents of the Treaty, verification by national technical means is deemed to be adequate under the assumption that violations in any event could not alter the existing condition of strategic–military stability. To certain of its opponents, the verification issue is important because the Treaty codifies a condition of emerging Soviet strategic superiority, with attendant adverse implications for strategic stability. To other opponents, verification is unimportant because the Treaty supposedly concedes such advantages to the Soviet Union that they could gain only marginally by cheating. The political dimension of SALT verification has been highlighted by the loss of monitoring stations in Iran, and temporarily at least the termination of United States access to such facilities in Turkey with the Turkish arms embargo imposed by the Congress in the mid-1970s and subsequently lifted. Indeed, there is no single political dimension – only a series of political dimensions of the SALT verification problem.

It was acknowledged that the problems of SALT verification are increasing in complexity as a result of changes in weapons technology since the SALT I. These include the development of mobile strategic missile systems, the Soviet silo reload capability, the fractionation of warheads, the availability of new generation systems whose range can be increased to intercontinental level. Major-General Jasper Welch contended that 'the difficult task is to make a net assessment which takes into consideration factors such as the provision in question, the impact of non-compliance with provision, monitor ability, freedom to pursue United States options and United States hedges against non-compliance'. In his view, 'a wholly verifiable bad treaty would still be a bad treaty'. He also pointed out the dangers inherent in omitting provisions governing missile production and storage, even though part of the usual rationale for such omission is the difficulty of verification. But he and other participants expressed concern about the potential that exists for covert activity, including the production, storage, and even deployment of strategic systems in violation of the Treaty. Both Albert Carnesale and Richard Perle emphasised the gaps in information about verifiability that favour the Soviet Union. It is far easier for the Soviet Union to collect intelligence needed for verifying United States compliance with an arms control agreement than it is for the United States to penetrate secrecy of the Soviet Union. But Albert Carnesale suggested that SALT, with its verification provisions, however imperfect, can help reduce the effects of this asymmetry. For the United States, as an open society, to practise deception successfully in verification would be difficult, if not impossible, except perhaps against itself. It was suggested that we are deceiving ourselves, with some Soviet cooperation. As the issues of verification have become more complex, there has been a decline in the standard of verifiability. According to Perle, this standard should be that the other party could not cheat in ways that we could not detect. Albert Carnesale, while expressing cautious support for the SALT II Treaty, pointed to the need to develop an adequate definition of 'adequacy' in judging verification based on the criterion of what is the net benefit of having a constraint contrasted with not having a constraint in the form of an arms control treaty.

Amrom Katz touched on what constitutes a paradox for SALT verification, if not for arms control verification in a broader sense: the inconsistency between criteria of significance and of verifiability. We do not wish to exclude anything that is significant. To apply both criteria to arms control would mean that what was significant would have to be verifiable, and that only what was insignificant would be unverifiable. As Katz noted, significance and verifiability are seldom, if ever, 'coincident properties'. For this reason, arms control agreements seldom, if ever, enhance greatly the security of their signatories. In SALT, for example, the United States can limit the numbers of Soviet fixed ICBM launchers, but it cannot place effective constraints on numbers of missiles – the ammunition of launchers. Since Soviet launchers deployed since SALT I have a retrofire capability, the failure to limit missiles represents a serious deficiency in the SALT II Treaty. But adequate technical means for verifying production levels on missiles do not exist. This is but one example of the gap between verifiability and significance in arms control – a gap that is likely to widen in the 1980s unless the technologies and other means of verification keep pace with innovations in weaponry – which they clearly did not in the 1970s. According to Amrom Katz, the covert deployment by the Soviet Union of a large number of ICBMs could have profoundly adverse effects on the United States. In a crisis, the United States could not threaten credibly to retaliate against a threatened Soviet strategic attack, for the Soviets could deploy demonstrably superior capabilities.

POLICY IMPLICATIONS

The purpose of this volume is not to produce a series of specific policy recommendations for the United States. However, the chapters contain policy implications, some of which are explicitly stated, and others of which are only implicit. The view seemed to be widely held that, as Richard Betts suggested, the dilemmas of collecting, organising, and analysing intelligence are only malleable, not soluble. For a large number of reasons, many of which were the object of discussion in this volume, the solutions to problems of intelligence collection and analysis confronting the United States in the 1980s are likely to be difficult indeed by virtue of the vitally important national security issues that the United States will confront. Nevertheless, several broad policy implications can be drawn from our discussions.

(1) The United States must have a diversity of intelligence sources and analysis capabilities both within the government and outside. Inside the government, it was suggested, separate and effective analytic capabilities should exist in several places: the CIA, the Department of Defence, the Department of State. Although it was acknowledged that organisational solutions are likely to prove inadequate to the problems facing us, the need nevertheless exists to ensure that centralisation of intelligence is not a codeword for politicisation and for ensuring uniformity of analysis. Centralisation is harmful if it leads to politicisation or to homogenisation of intelligence in place of pluralism and diversity.

However, a single joint intelligence oversight Committee in the Congress, in place of numerous such congressional committees that now exist, should receive active consideration.

(2) At least one chapter referred to the potential afforded by groups outside the government – what William Colby termed the 'many centers of private analysis'. An effort should be made to subject the predilections, preconceptions, assumptions, methodologies, and findings of the intelligence community to outside critique – an institutional-isation of the 'Team B' exercise that had provided an opportunity for a group of experts from outside the official intelligence community to examine CIA methodologies data and analyses of the Soviet military buildup. The conclusion that the United States had consistently underestimated the rate of growth of Soviet armaments led the CIA to revise its estimates and its techniques for analysis. The team B idea might be extended to other, and perhaps all other, areas of intelligence: to represent a spectrum including the academic and the governmental; the right and the left. At the very least, more than one office should be charged with the development of National Intelligence Estimates.

(3) Greater priority than in the recent past should be given to intelligence analysis, where major deficiencies exist in the United States. The need to strike a better balance between an emphasis on collection and on analysis is essential not only to the quality of intelligence itself, but also to the need to rebuild morale and to strengthen the official intelligence organization for the challenges of the 1980s. The quality of analysis can be improved by giving the analyst more than one boss, by ensuring that his or her career advancement is not dependent on the approval of only one person. Both in the gathering and analysis of intelligence, the human factor remains indispensable. Technical means of intelligence gathering, however indispensable, cannot replace human judgement. Therefore, a growing need exists to make more extensive and effective use of trained and skilled personnel in our intelligence agencies. The trend toward the substitution of technical means for human expertise should be reversed.

(4) Communications between the analyst and decisionmaker should be improved. This represents a problem whose origins lie deep in the past. It has not proven to be soluble by means of the technologies for modern communication which, to some extent, were examined in this volume. It can perhaps be improved by enhancing the relevance of intelligence to the needs of the policymaker. This, in turn, is a complex set of issues, encompassing criteria of relevance in light of the policymaker's priorities and criteria of objectivity in the gathering and analysis of intelligence.

(5) No one was prepared to suggest, quite prudently, that surprise is no longer possible. Here again, the theme of the need for a diversity of

intelligence sources emerged in the chapters in this volume: it was even suggested that the only protection available to a society against surprise lies in the existence of diverse groups, inside and outside government, producing ideas – the symbiotic relationship between age versus youth; experience versus imagination; official responsibility versus the outside critic. But there was some support for the proposition that strategic surprise is less likely to occur for lack of early warning than for lack of proper appreciation of such warning and its meaning.

(6) Economic factors will continue to impinge on the vital national security interests of the United States and its allies, with numerous linkages between, on the one hand, energy, inflation, trade, commodities cartelisation, international monetary issues, and technology transfer, and, on the other hand, the military dimensions of national security. Therefore, the United States will need to integrate more fully the economic dimensions into its intelligence collection and analysis. We must acquire a more adequate capacity for economic forecasting that is linked to, and integrated with, the political and military factors vital to our national security.

(7) Last but not least, because of the vital importance of intelligence in the policymaking decisional process, the idea of courses in intelligence in schools of international affairs, and especially in professional schools, emerges from the consideration of the needs of the intelligence community set forth in this volume. Such courses would encompass the methodologies of intelligence gathering and analysis, as well as the role of intelligence in the decisionmaking process.

In the final analysis, there seemed to be agreement that among the main linkages between intelligence, surprise and deception was the notion that deception was the key to surprise, and that faulty intelligence could often be traced to deception, and even more to self-deception. But we will probably never evolve an intelligence system adequate to remove the element of surprise. Here, the only surprise would be the absence of surprise. We need not more information, but more adequate analysis – analysis devoid of self-deception. We need to understand the thought processes and the cultures of our adversaries and our allies and friends alike. The failure to do so seemed to be the most prevalent cause of self-deception, and the power of self-deception seemed to outweigh even the capacity of our adversaries to deceive us.

Our ability to remove the element of self-deception from our mind-set remains in doubt, especially because many of us may not even be aware of the need to do so. This should be the cause of great concern, for there was a general recognition that the United States will need an effective intelligence community in the years ahead. The condemnation of the intelligence community that was popular in the United States in the early 1970s has given way to a realisation that the problems facing us in the 1980s will place a greater premium than ever before upon our capacity both to collect and analyse intelligence and to minimise deception and surprise in a decade that may hold many surprises and great dangers for the United States and its allies.

Index